**Books are to be returned on or before
the last date below.**

1 2 MAY 2015

LIBREX —

Foo   ge
Ser

111344

050282

D1418812

Food and Beverage Service seventh edition

Dennis Lillicrap & John Cousins

Hodder Arnold
A MEMBER OF THE HODDER HEADLINE GROUP

Orders: please contact Bookpoint Ltd, 130 Milton Park, Abingdon, Oxon OX14 4SB. Telephone: (44) 01235 827720. Fax: (44) 01235 400454. Lines are open from 9.00 – 5.00, Monday to Saturday, with a 24 hour message answering service. You can also order through our website www.hodderheadline.co.uk.

British Library Cataloguing in Publication Data
A catalogue record for this title is available from the British Library

ISBN-10: 0 340 90524 7
ISBN-13: 978 0 340 90524 1

First Published 2006
Impression number   10 9 8 7 6 5 4 3 2
Year   2012 2011 2010 2009 2008 2007 2006

Copyright © 2006 Dennis Lillicrap and John Cousins

All rights reserved. No part of this publication may be reproduced or transmitted in any form or by any means, electronic or mechanical, including photocopy, recording, or any information storage and retrieval system, without permission in writing from the publisher or under license from the Copyright Licensing Agency Limited. Further details of such licenses (for reprographic reproduction) may be obtained from the Copyright Licensing Agency Limited, 90 Tottenham Court Road, London W1T 4LP.

Cover photo © Peter M Fisher/Corbis.
Original photography by Carl Drury
Typeset by Fakenham Photosetting Ltd, Fakenham, Norfolk
Illustrations by Mike Humphries, Clifton Graphics.
Printed in Great Britain for Hodder & Stoughton Educational, a division of Hodder Headline Plc, 338 Euston Road, London NW1 3BH by CPI Bath.

CONTENTS

INTRODUCTION TO THE SEVENTH EDITION

The aim of the book

Food and Beverage Service has been written to detail the basic knowledge and skills necessary for those studying and/or working at a variety of levels in food and beverage service. The book also provides a framework on which to build further studies and on which to relate further acquired knowledge and experience.

In revising this seventh edition we have taken into account recent developments in examining and awarding body recommendations and specifications, in education and training, as well as in the industry at large. In particular, the revision has taken into account the National Vocational Qualification (NVQ) and Scottish Vocational Qualification (SVQ) Standards for Food and Beverage Service from Levels 1 to 3.

The book has been prepared to support the studies of those wishing to be assessed at NVQ Levels 1 to 3 in Food and Beverage Service, and a range of other qualifications including those of the City and Guilds. In addition, the book is intended to support the broader-based study requirements in food and beverage service for programmes leading to the award of the National Diploma, the General National Vocational Qualification, the Higher National Diploma, Foundation Degree and undergraduate degree programmes, and the programmes of the Hotel and Catering International Management Association (HCIMA).

Foodservice operations

The basis for this text continues to be the recognition that food and beverage service is not an end in itself but part of the business of hospitality operations. Food and beverage (or foodservice) operations in the hospitality industry are concerned with the provision of food and drink ready for immediate consumption (but excluding retailing and food manufacturing).

Foodservice operations are therefore concerned with:

a) The *consumer needs and market potential* in the various sectors of the foodservice industry.

b) The *formulation of policy and business objectives* which will guide the choice of operational methods that will be used.

c) The *interpretation of demand* in order to make decisions on the food and beverages to be provided, as well as other services.

d) The *planning and design of facilities* required for the food and beverage operations and the plant and equipment required.

e) The *organisation of provisioning* for food and beverages and other purchasing to meet the needs of the food production, beverage provision and the service methods being used.

f) *Operational knowledge* of food production, beverage provision and service processes and methods, and decision-making on the appropriateness of the various processes and methods to meet production and service needs.

g) *Control of costs* of materials and other costs associated with the operation of food production, beverage provision and service, and the *control of revenue.*

h) The *monitoring of customer satisfaction.*

This sequence may be referred to as the *Catering Cycle* (see figure). This serves our purposes in that it states succinctly what food and beverage operations are concerned with and illustrates that it is not merely about food production, beverage provision or service.

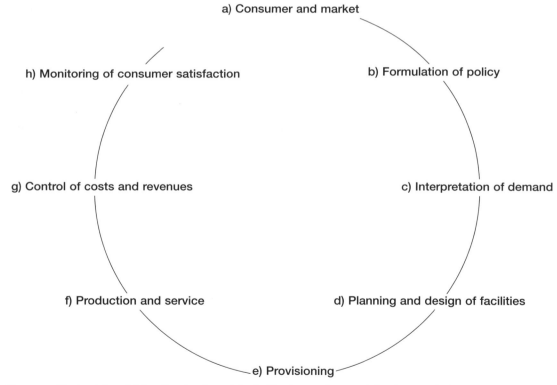

Catering Cycle (after H.L. Cracknell and R.J. Kaufman, *Practical Professional Catering Management,* 2002, Thomson Learning)

Trends in the foodservice industry

Foodservice operations are continuing to enjoy tremendous improvement and development together with considerable advances in quality. The demand for food and beverages away from the home has increased and, with a broader spectrum of the population eating out, customer needs have diversified.

Food and restaurant styles are also diversifying to meet the challenges of the demands being made by increasingly knowledgeable and value conscious customers. Menu and beverage list contents are also continually being influenced by trends, fads and fashions, the relationship between health and eating, special diets, cultural and religious influences, the advance of vegetarianism, and customer acceptance, or otherwise, of irradiation and genetically modified foods.

The development of a diverse range of foodservice operations has necessitated developments in the approaches to food and beverage service. The traditional view of food and beverage service was that it was only a bridge between the food production system, the beverage provision and the customer. It was therefore primarily managed as a delivery process, with the customer being considered as a passive recipient of the service. Only the requirements of the operation itself would determine how the service was designed, planned and controlled. More recently, however, this view has changed significantly. The customer is now seen as being central to the process and also as an active participant within it. Increasing competition has also meant the quality of the service and the perceived value of the experience by customers are the main differentiators between operations who are seeking to attract similar customers. Consequently, understanding the customers' involvement in the process, and identifying the experience they are likely to have, and should expect, have become critical to the business success of foodservice operations.

Expansion of the industry has generally meant greater choice. This together with potential skill shortages and drives for efficiency has seen a streamlining of foodservice operations. There is now less emphasis on sophisticated service techniques, in some sectors, but more emphasis throughout the industry on sound product knowledge, well-developed interpersonal skills, technical competence and the ability to work as part of a team.

However, service, both in level and standards, still varies greatly throughout the whole range of foodservice operations. While there are many examples of operations that are working with the highest levels of competence, there are unfortunately operations that believe that service is something that anyone can do. Where there are well-developed operating systems, and where the members of staff are well trained to work within them, the operation works efficiently and effectively. The enjoyment of the meal by the customer is also greatly enhanced as the members of the service staff have the confidence and the time to be genuinely welcoming.

Any successful foodservice operation requires all elements to work as a whole: service personnel working together with chefs, and the wine and drink lists being in harmony with the food. Recently, however, there has been an over emphasis on chefs with the media reinforcing this position. Articles in the trade press have continuously focused heavily on chefs and food. Perhaps though this is because food and beverage service represents the ultimate paradox: the better it is, the less it is noticed.

Modern foodservice operations are not simply offering food and beverages but holistic experiences. The essential contribution to the creation of these experiences by food and beverage service professionals cannot be underestimated: Michelin Stars or AA Rosettes, for instance, are awarded to restaurants as a whole, not to individuals. Service managers and service staff, and their skills and professionalism, should therefore have the same focus of attention as any other industry professionals.

Good food and beverage service, in any sector, is achieved where customers' needs are being met and where management consistently reinforce and support service staff in the maintenance of clearly identified technical standards and service goals. It is against this background that the revisions for this seventh edition have taken place.

The seventh edition

An explanation of the ways information can be found in the book is given in the section *How to use this book*. This section also contains a *Master Reference Chart*, which summarises the tasks and duties for staff working in food and beverage service. An overview of the foodservice industry is then given in Chapter 1. This Chapter also provides an identification of the sectors, types of operation, service methods and the reasons for eating out. Service staff roles and the attributes needed by service personnel are also identified.

The next three chapters then provide a base of underpinning knowledge about: service areas and equipment (Chapter 2); the menu, its construction, example dishes and accompaniments (Chapter 3), and all types of beverages (Chapter 4).

Chapter 5 details basic skills, both interpersonal and technical, and indicates how these are applied to the service sequence for a variety of service settings.

The application of skills is then further developed for a variety of other service settings: breakfast and afternoon tea (Chapter 6); specialised forms of service (Chapter 7); guéridon service (Chapter 8) and function catering (Chapter 9).

Finally, consideration is given to a number of supervisory aspects (Chapter 10), including legal requirements, control, performance measurement, customer relations, staff organisation and sales promotion. There are also three annexes which cover: foods in season (Annex A); a glossary of cuisine and service terms (Annex B) and a cocktail and mixed drink listing giving recipes and methods (Annex C).

Throughout the book we have endeavoured to avoid sexist terms for job titles and job categories. These have been referred to as, for instance, manager, waiter, floor service staff, room attendants, servers and stewards. In all cases these terms, in line with general trends within the industry, refer to both male and female personnel.

The content of the book, while having its origins in classic cuisine and service (the context and the body of knowledge on which modern foodservice operations are based) is also intended to reflect current practice within the industry. Therefore while the book gives information and describes various aspects of food and beverage service, it should not be seen as a prescriptive book. Clearly the actual operation of the service will be substantially affected by the style and the business needs of the individual operation.

Dennis Lillicrap and John Cousins
March 2006

HOW TO USE THIS BOOK

The information in the book can be accessed in three main ways:

1. Using the contents list at the front of the book.

2. Finding information through the index at the back of the book.

3. Using the Master Reference Chart (pages xii–xiii).

The Master Reference Chart takes account of the various examining and awarding body recommendations and assessment requirements, especially Vocational Qualifications. This chart is set out on the following pages. The chart identifies aspects of food and beverage service and identifies the chapter or section where that information is detailed.

Because of the wide variety of hospitality operations, the chart indicates the broad range of knowledge and skills that will be relevant to a range of food service operations. The chart can be used as a checklist to identify the relevance of a particular aspect to a particular operation, job or qualification requirement, as well as a means of finding information.

To use the chart, first select the aspect you are interested in from the tasks and duties column. Then note the chapter and/or section identified. Next go to the detailed contents listing on pages v to vi to find the page number.

Master reference chart

Task/Duties	Relevant Chapters/Sections
Interpersonal skills	
● Present a positive personal image to the customer	1.1 to 1.6 and 10.5
● Balance the needs of the customer and the organisation	1.7 and 1.8
● Respond to feelings expressed by the customer	5.2 and 10.5
● Adapt methods of communication	
● Deal with:	
– adults	
– children	
– those with mobility difficulties	
– those with communication difficulties	5.2 and 5.6
– customer complaints	
– customer incidents.	
Health, safety and security	
● Maintain personal health and hygiene	1.8
● Maintain a safe environment	
● Maintain a secure environment:	
– report suspicious items	10.1
– report accidents	
● Carry out procedures in the event of a fire	
Service areas equipment and product knowledge	
● Demonstrate and apply knowledge of:	
– service areas and equipment	Chapter 2
– menu, menu knowledge and accompaniments	Chapter 3 and Annexes A and B
– non-alcoholic drinks	
– wine	Chapter 4 and Annex C
– other alcoholic beverages	
Service sequence	
● Establish and maintain working relationships	1.7 and 1.8
● Take bookings	5.3
● Prepare service areas	5.4
● Take orders for food and beverages and determine customer requirements	5.2, 5.5 and 5.6
● Serve food	5.1 and 5.7

- Serve beverages:
  - non-alcoholic beverages
  - wine   } 5.8 and 5.9
  - other alcoholic beverages
- Clear during service   5.10
- Deal with payments   5.11 and 10.2
- Clear service areas after service   5.12

Specialised service skills

- Provide specialised forms of service:
  - breakfast   6.1
  - afternoon teas   6.2
  - room service   7.2
  - lounge service   7.3
  - guéridon service
  - prepare, cook and serve food in a food service area } Chapter 8

Function catering

- Prepare for and serve at functions
- Contribute to function administration   } Chapter 9
- Contribute to function organisation

Supervisory responsibilities

- Supervise operations within licensing (and other) laws   10.1
- Receive, store and return wines and drinks   10.3
- Maintain cellars   4.15
- Maintain practices and procedures for handling payments 5.11 and 10.2
- Contribute to the control of food and beverage operations 10.2, 10.3 and 10.4
- Maintain cleaning programme in own area   10.1
- Maintain vending machine service   2.8
- Supervise the running of a function/event   Chapter 9
- Improve service reliability for customers   10.5
- Contribute to the development of teams and individuals   10.6
- Implement sales development activities   10.7

ACKNOWLEDGEMENTS

The preparation of the seventh edition of this book has drawn upon a variety of experience and literature. The authors would like to express their thanks to all the organisations and individuals who gave the assistance and support in the revision of this text. In particular we would like to thank:

Academy of Culinary Arts, UK; Academy of Food and Wine Service, UK; Mathew Alexander, Lecturer, The Scottish Hotel School, University of Strathclyde, Glasgow; British Airways plc; Burgess Furniture Ltd, London; City and Guilds of London Institute; Copthorne Hotel, Birmingham; Croners Catering, Croners Publications; Anne Dubberley and Julie Bromfield, Petals of Piccadilly, Birmingham; Dunk Ink; Andrew Durkan, author and consultant, formerly of Ealing College, London; Elia International Ltd, Middlesex; Euroservice UK, Welford, Northants; Foodservice Consultants Society International, UK; Professor David Foskett, author, consultant and Associate Dean at the London School of Tourism, Hospitality and Leisure, Ealing; German Wine Information Service, London; Cailein Gillespie, author, consultant and Lecturer in Hospitality Management, The Scottish Hotel School, University of Strathclyde, Glasgow; Simon Girling, Restaurant Manager, The Ritz Hotel, London; The Glasgow Hilton Hotel; Gleneagles Hotel, Auchterarder, Scotland; David Graham, Lecturer, Leeds Metropolitan University; Great Western Trains Company Limited; Hunters and Frankau, cigar importers and distributors; IFS Publications; The International Coffee Organisation; International Standards Organisation; London School of Tourism, Hospitality and Leisure at Thames Valley University, Ealing; Mark Kirby, Rooms Division Manager, Sheraton Park Tower, London; Le Columbier Restaurant, London; Louvet Turner Coombe Marketing; National Checking Co UK; Darren Neilan, Manager, Restaurant One-O-One, Knightsbridge, London; Kevin O'Gorman, Graduate Teaching Assistant, The Scottish Hotel School, University of Strathclyde, Glasgow; Elaine O'Sullivan, Operations Manager, and the operations team at the London School of Tourism, Hospitality and Leisure at Thames Valley University, Ealing; PalmTEQ Limited UK; The Ritz, Hotel, London; The Restaurant Association of Great Britain; Frânkmâ Giña Romerio, Maître d'hotel, The Glasgow Hilton Hotel; Joachim Schafheitle, Senior Lecturer, Bournemouth University; The Sheraton Park Tower Hotel, Knightsbridge, London; Six Continents Hotels, London; Robert Smith, Head of Food and Beverage Service at Birmingham College of Food, Tourism and Creative Studies; Louise Smith, Flowers by Louise, Birmingham; Snap-Drape Europe Limited; Steelite International; The Tea Council; Alistair Telfer, Club Secretary, The Carlton Club, St James's, London; Uniwell Systems (UK) Ltd; Linden Wilkie, Managing Director, The Fine Wine Experience Ltd, London; and John Williams, Executive Chef, The Ritz Hotel, London.

THE FOODSERVICE INDUSTRY

CHAPTER 1

1.1 INTRODUCTION

Today more people than ever are eating outside the home and to meet this demand there is widening diversity in the nature and type of food and beverages on offer. Because of the expansion of the industry, and increasing pressures for improved professionalism in food and beverage service staff, there is even greater need for more people to make their careers in this noble profession, alongside the need for improved confidence and performance through higher standards of knowledge and skills.

Food and beverage service is the essential link between the customers and the menu, beverages and other services on offer in an establishment. The server is the main point of contact between the customers and the establishment and plays an important role in a profession with increasing national and international status. The skills and knowledge of food and beverage service, and therefore careers, are transferable between establishments, sectors and throughout the world.

To be successful in food and beverage service requires:

- sound product knowledge
- well developed interpersonal skills
- a range of technical skills, and
- the ability to work as part of a team.

Working in food and beverage service offers a wealth of opportunity for professional development and advancement – for those committed to the hospitality industry and to working in food and beverage service, a fulfilling, exciting and enjoyable career awaits.

1.2 TYPES OF FOODSERVICE OPERATIONS

The industry provides millions of meals a day in a wide variety of types of foodservice operation.

- *Food* can include a wide range of styles and cuisine types. These can be classified by country, for example, traditional British or Italian; by type of cuisine, for example, oriental; or a particular speciality such as fish, vegetarian or health food.

- *Beverages* include all alcoholic and non-alcoholic drinks. Alcoholic beverages include wines and all other types of alcoholic drink such as cocktails, beers and cider, spirits and liqueurs. Non-alcoholic beverages include bar beverages such as mineral waters, juices, squashes and aerated waters, as well as tea, coffee, chocolate, milk and milk drinks and also proprietary drinks such as Bovril.

Food and beverage (or foodservice) operations include, for example, various types of restaurants (bistros, brasseries, coffee-shops, first class/fine dining, ethnic, themed), cafés, cafeterias, take-aways, canteens, function rooms, tray service operations, lounge service operations, home delivery operations and room service operations for hotel guests. Some examples of the types of operation are given in Table 1.1.

Table 1.1 Examples of types of foodservice operations

Type of operation	Description
Bistro	Often a smaller establishment, with check tablecloths, bentwood chairs, cluttered decor and friendly informal staff. Tends to offer honest, basic and robust cooking.
Brasserie	This is generally a largish, styled room, with a long bar, normally serving one-plate items rather than formal meals (though some offer both). Often it is possible just to have a drink, coffee or just a snack. Service by waiters, often in traditional style of long aprons and black waistcoats.
New wave brasserie (Gastrodome)	Slick modern interior design, coupled with similar approaches to contemporary cuisine and service. Busy and bustling and often large and multileveled.
Coffee shop	Similar to brasserie-style operations, often themed. May be open all day and serve all meal types from breakfast through to supper.
First class restaurant	Tend to be formal fine dining restaurants with classical preparation and presentation of food and offering a high level of table (silver, guéridon and/or plated) service. Often associated with classic/haute cuisine.
Restaurant	Term used to cover a wide variety of operations. Price, level and type of service, décor, styles, cuisines and degree of choice varies enormously across the range of types of operation. Service ranges from full table service to assisted service such as in carvery-style operations.
Ethnic restaurant	Indian, Oriental, Asian, Spanish, Greek, Italian, Creole and Cajun are just some of the many types of ethnic cuisine available, with establishments tending to reflect ethnic origin. Many of the standard dishes are now appearing within a range of other menu types.
Themed restaurant	Often international in orientation, for example, Icelandic hot rock with food prepared and cooked at the table, 'Beni-hana' oriental theme, again with food prepared and cooked at table. Also includes themes such as jungle, rainforest or music/opera, where waiting staff perform as well as serve.
International destination restaurant	Often Michelin-starred fine dining restaurants, offering a distinctive personality, cuisine, ambiance, beverages and service. Usually table service at various levels but mostly personal and attentive. Generally considered as the home of gastronomy. Expensive but value laden.
Health food and vegetarian restaurants	Increasing specialisation of operations into vegetarianism and/or health foods (though vegetarian food is not necessarily healthy), to meet lifestyle needs as well as dietary requirements.

Table 1.1 continued	
Type of operation	**Description**
Cafétéria	Primarily self-service with customer choosing selection from a counter or counters in varying designs and layouts. Originally developed for the industrial feeding market but now seen in a variety of sectors.
Popular catering and fast-food outlets	Developed from table service teashops and cafés through to steakhouses, and now incorporating snack bars, kiosks, diners, takeaways and cafétérias, with modern-day burger, chicken and fish concepts, and with ethnic foods also being incorporated. Meeting the needs of all-day meal taking (grazing) and also the need for 'grab and go' service, especially for the leisure, industrial and travelling markets.
Public houses	Licensed environment primarily for drinking alcoholic beverages. May be simply a serving bar with standing room for customers or may have more plush surroundings incorporating the offer of a variety of foods. These can range from simple plated dishes through to establishments offering full restaurant service (sometimes called gastropubs).
Wine bars	Often a mixture of bar and brasserie-style operation, commonly wine themed, serving a variety of foods.

1.3 SECTORS OF THE FOODSERVICE INDUSTRY

The list of operations given in Table 1.1 identifies types of operations but not necessarily the type of customer demand being met. For example, cafeterias may be found in motorway service stations, in airline terminals, at railway stations, in retail catering, and in industrial or welfare catering. Throughout the industry similar types of operation are therefore found in various types of sector.

To help identify the nature of demand being met within each sector, Table 1.2 provides a list of industry sectors and identifies the prime purpose of the foodservice operations within them. An historical summary is also given together with an identification of both UK and international terminology. This identification of sectors also provides a framework for those studying the food and beverage service industry to which further studies and experience may be related.

In order to be seen in more detail, each sector may be analysed by reference to a set of variables that exist in the different sectors (Table 1.3). These variables represent elements which vary in particular sectors and thus provide a basis for examining the operation of outlets within specific sectors. They enable a comprehensive picture of industrial sectors to be compiled, and also provide for comparison of sectors.

There are a wide variety of sectors such as hotels, independent and chain restaurants, popular catering, pubs and wine bars, fast food, leisure attractions and banqueting. There are also sectors where food and beverages are provided as part of another business. These include transport catering, welfare, clubs, education, industrial feeding and the armed forces.

Table 1.2 Sectors of the foodservice industry

Industry sector – UK terminology	Purpose of the foodservice operation	Historical summary	Industry sector – international terminology
Hotels and other tourist accommodation	Provision of food and drink together with accommodation services	Developed from inns. Supported by developments in transport and increases in business and leisure-related tourism	Hotel, motel and other tourist accommodation Often referred to as the Lodging industry
Restaurants including conventional and specialist operations	Provision of food and drink, generally at a high price with high levels of service	Grew out of hotel restaurants (which were originally highly formal) through chefs wishing to start their own businesses	
Popular catering including cafés, pizza, grills, specialist coffee shops, roadside restaurants and steak houses	Provision of food and drink, generally at low/medium price with limited levels of service and often high customer throughput	Developed from ABC and Lyons concepts. Has gone through various phases. More recently highly influenced by the USA	Separate eating and drinking places Categories usually defined by reference to three criteria: • level of service, e.g. quick service to full service or fine dining • extent of menu, e.g. limited to full • price range, e.g. low to high
Fast food including McDonalds and Burger King	Provision of food and drink in highly specialised environment, characterised by high investment, high labour costs and vast customer throughput	Grew from combination of popular catering and take away, heavily influenced by USA concepts; highly sophisticated meal packaging and marketing	
Take away including ethnic, spuds, KFC, snacks, fish and chips, sandwich bars, kiosks	Fast provision of food and drink	Developed in UK from original fish and chip concepts. Influenced by USA and trends in food tastes	

Table 1.2 continued

Industry sector – UK terminology	Purpose of the foodservice operation	Historical summary	Industry sector – international terminology
Retail stores	Provision of food and drink as an adjunct to retail provision	Developed originally from prestigious stores wishing to provide food and drink as part of the retailing experience	Retail market
Banqueting/ conferencing/ exhibitions	Provision of large scale food and drink alongside services such as conferencing	Originally associated with hotels but has now become major sector in its own right	Leisure and special event market
Leisure attractions such as theme parks, museums, galleries, cinemas and theatres	Provision of food and drink to people engaged in another pursuit	Increases in leisure have made profit from food and drink attractive to leisure and amenity providers	
Motorway service stations	Provision of food and drink together with petrol and other retail services, often in isolated locations	Born in UK in 1960s with the advent of motorway building. Influenced by USA and became specialised because of government regulations on provision of foodservice operations, retail and fuel as well as location	Highway (interstate) market

Table 1.2 continued

Industry sector – UK terminology	Purpose of the foodservice operation	Historical summary	Industry sector – international terminology
Industrial catering, either in-house operations or through catering/foodservice contractors	Provision of food and drink to people at work	Born out of recognition that better-fed workers work better. Boosted in UK by legislation during First and Second World Wars. Further developed by worker unions wanting to preserve conditions and the emergence of professional contract caterers/foodservice operators	Business/industry markets
Welfare catering	Provision of food and drink to people in colleges, universities and the forces and to people through established social need	Regulated and given substantial boost in the UK by the creation of the Welfare State in 1948. Maintained now through public social conscience	Social caterer/foodservice (Student, healthcare, institutional and military)
Licensed trade including public houses, wine bars, licensed clubs and members' clubs	Provision of food and drink in an environment dominated by licensing requirements	Developed in UK from inns: also origin of steakhouses, e.g. 1960s Berni Inns	Separate drinking places But also some units included in Separate Eating and Drinking Places above

Table 1.2 continued

Industry sector – UK terminology	Purpose of the foodservice operation	Historical summary	Industry sector – international terminology
Transport catering including railways, airlines and marine	Provision of food and drink to people on the move	Grew out of the need to meet the demands of travelling public. Originally services were of high levels, reflecting the type of traveller. Eventually changed to meet the needs of a wide range of travellers	Transportation market
Outdoor catering (ODC) (or 'off-premises catering' or 'event catering')	Provision of food and drink away from home base and suppliers usually associated with a major event	Developed through need to provide services at special events. The term ODC is misleading as little of this catering actually takes place outside	Catering market

Two further issues come out of the identification of sectors. First, some sectors are providing food and drink for profit, whereas others are working within the constraints of a given budget, often called cost provision (e.g. welfare and industrial). Second, some sectors provide services to the general public whereas others provide them for restricted groups of people.

Table 1.3 Variables in foodservice sectors

- Historical background
- Reasons for customer demand
- Size of sector:
  - in terms of outlets
  - in terms of turnover
- Policies:
  - financial
  - marketing
  - catering
- Interpretation of demand/catering concept
- Technological development
- Influences
- State of sector development
- Primary/secondary activity
- Types of outlets
- Profit orientation/cost provision
- Public/private ownership

Table 1.4 Summary of sectors in the foodservice industry

PROFIT ORIENTATED (public or private ownership) (catering, main or secondary activity)		COST PROVISION
RESTRICTED MARKET	GENERAL MARKET	RESTRICTED MARKET
Transport catering	Hotels/restaurants	Institutional catering
Clubs	Popular catering	Schools
Industrial (contract)	Fast food/Take away	Universities and colleges
Private welfare	Retail stores	Hospitals
	Banqueting/conferences/exhibitions	The Forces
	Leisure attractions	Prisons
	Motorway service stations	Industrial (own catering)
	Pubs and wine bars	
	ODC (off-premises catering)	

It is useful to define these different types of market as follows:

■ General market

  – *Non-captive*: customers have a full choice.

■ Restricted market

  – *Captive*: customers have no choice, e.g. welfare.

  – *Semi-captive*: customers have a choice before entering, e.g. marine, airline, trains, some hotels and some leisure activities. The customers could have chosen alternatives to these but, once chosen, have little choice of food and drink other than that on offer.

Taking these definitions into account, a general summary of sectors may be drawn up as shown in Table 1.4. Defining the nature of the market in this way helps us to understand why different methods of organisation may be in operation. For example, in captive markets customers might be asked to clear their own tables, whereas in non-captive markets this is unlikely to be successful.

1.4 VARIABLES IN FOODSERVICE OPERATIONS

The list of types of outlets in Table 1.1 indicates by itself very little in terms of methods of organisation adopted and the management of them. In a similar way to the identifying variables for sectors (Table 1.3), variables can also be identified for outlets/operations. These variables have been identified from a variety of published sources as well as from experience. They can be separated into three groups:

1 Organisational

2 Customer experience

3 Performance measures.

These different groups of variables enable the systematic examination and comparison of types of food and beverage operations. Profiles of the differing operations can be drawn, based upon these variables (Table 1.5).

Performance measures are further dealt with in Chapter 10 (Supervision). Customer experience variables are discussed in Section 1.5. The remainder of this book presents further information on a variety of organisational variables.

Table 1.5 Variables in foodservice operations

Organisational variables
- nature of market being met
- legislative controls
- scale of operation
- marketing/merchandising
- style of menu and drinks list
- range of choice
- opening times/service period
- production methods
- type and capability of equipment
- service methods
- dining arrangements
- seating time
- number of covers available
- capacity
- staff working hours
- staff organisation
- staff capability
- number of staff
- specialised service requirements
- provisioning and storage methods
- billing methods
- checking (order taking) methods
- clearing methods
- dishwashing methods
- control method costs/revenue.

Customer experience variables
- food and drink available
- level of service and other services
- price range/value for money
- cleanliness and hygiene
- atmosphere (including decor, lighting, air-conditioning, acoustics, noise, size and shape of room, other customers, attitude of staff).

Performance measure variables
- seat turnover/customer throughput
- customer spend/average check
- revenue per member of staff
- productivity index
- ratio of food and beverage sales to total sales
- sales/profit per sq m (or ft)/per seat
- sales analysis
- departmental profit
- stock turnover
- stock holding
- complaint levels
- level of repeat business.

1.5 THE MEAL EXPERIENCE

There are many different kinds of food and beverage (or foodservice) operation, designed to meet a wide range of demand. These different types of operation are designed for the needs people have at a particular time, rather than for the type of people they are. For example, a person may be a business customer during the week, but a member of a family at the weekend; they may want a quick lunch on one occasion, a snack while travelling on another, and a meal with the family on another occasion. Additionally, the same person may wish to book a wedding or organise some other special occasion.

The main aim of food and beverage operations is to achieve customer satisfaction. In other words, to meet the customers' *needs*. The needs that customers might be seeking to satisfy include:

- *Physiological*: for example, the need to sate one's appetite or quench one's thirst, or the need for special foods such as diabetic or vegetarian.

- *Economic*: for example, the need for good value; rapid, fast service; a convenient location.

- *Social*: for example, going out with friends or business colleagues; attending a function in order to meet others.

- *Psychological*: for example, the need for enhancement of self-esteem; fulfilling life-style needs; the need for variety; as a result of advertising and promotion.

- *Convenience*: for example, as a result of being unable to get home (shoppers, workers) or attending some other event (cinema, theatre); the desire for someone else to do the work; the physical impossibility of catering at home (weddings and other special functions).

Customers may want to satisfy some or all of these needs.

As the reasons for eating out vary, then so do the types of operation that may be appropriate at the time. Differing establishments offer different service, in both the extent of the menu and the price, as well as varying service levels. The choice offered may be restricted or wide.

It is important to recognise that the specific reasons behind a customer's choice will often determine the customer's satisfaction (or dissatisfaction), rather than the food and beverage service by itself. One example is the social need to go out with friends: if one person fails to turn up or behaves in a disagreeable way, then the customer may be dissatisfied with the meal.

The customer who is not able to satisfy his/her needs will be a dissatisfied customer. The customer may, for instance, be dissatisfied with unhelpful staff, cramped conditions or the lack of choice available. These aspects are the responsibility of the food and beverage operation. However, sometimes the reasons for the customer being dissatisfied might be beyond the operation's control, for example, location, the weather, other customers or transport problems.

In *non-captive markets* the customer has a choice of eating out opportunities both in terms of the food and drink to be consumed and the type of operation they may wish to patronise. While it is true that certain types of catering operations might attract certain types of customer, this is by no means true all the time. The same customers may patronise a variety of different operations depending on the needs they have at a given time, for example, a romantic night out, a quick office lunch or a wedding function.

In *semi-captive markets* this availability of choice is also important. Customers may choose, for example, a certain airline or boat or hotel based upon the identification of certain needs they wish to satisfy.

In *captive markets* where the customer does not have a choice of operation, there is still a need for satisfaction. For instance, it is generally recognised that better fed workers work better and that better fed patients recover quicker. 'Better fed' here, though, does not just refer to the food and drink provided but the whole experience of the meal.

From the food and beverage operator's point of view it is important to recognise that the

Table 1.6 Meal experience factors

Factor	Description
The food and beverages on offer	Includes the range of foods and beverages, choice, availability, flexibility for special orders and the quality of the food and beverages.
Level of service	Depending on the needs people have at the time, the level of service sought will be appropriate to these needs. For example, a romantic night out may call for a quiet table in a top-class restaurant, whereas a group of young friends might be seeking more informal service. This factor also takes into account services such as booking and account facilities, acceptance of credit cards and also the reliability of the operation's product.
Level of cleanliness and hygiene	This factor relates to the premises, equipment and staff. Over the last few years this factor has increased in importance in customers' minds. The recent media focus on food production and the risks involved in buying food have heightened awareness of health and hygiene aspects.
Perceived value for money and price	Customers have perceptions of the amount they are prepared to spend and relate this to differing types of establishments and operations. Value is the personal estimate of a product's capacity to satisfy a set of goals and also a perception of the balance between worth and cost. Good value for a food and beverage operation is where the worth (the perception of the desirability of a particular product over another in order to satisfy a set of established goals) is perceived as greater than the total cost. (As well as cash price, total cost includes, for instance, the cost of not going somewhere else, the cost of transport and time, the cost of potential embarrassment, the cost of having to look and behave in a required manner and the cost in terms of effort at work to earn the money to pay the required price.) Poor value is where the costs are perceived as greater than the worth.
Atmosphere of the establishment	This factor takes account of issues such as design, decor, lighting, heating, furnishings, acoustics and noise levels, other customers, the smartness of the staff and the attitude of the staff.

customer's needs may vary and that food and beverage operators should be aware of factors that might affect the customer's meal experience. Much research has been carried out in recent years identifying these factors. They range from location to the acceptance of credit cards, and from attitudes of staff to the behaviour of other customers. These factors are summarised in Table 1.6.

Customer service

In order the meet the customers' expectations and to enhance their meal experience, a foodservice operation will determine the level of customer service that the customer should expect within that operation.

Customer service in foodservice operations can be defined as being a combination of five characteristics. These are:

1 *Service level*: the intensity of or limitations in, the individual personal attention given to customers.

2 *Service availability*: for example, the opening times and variations in the menu and beverage list on offer.

3 *Level of standards*: for example, the food and beverage quality, décor, standard of equipment being used, level of staffing professionalism.

4 *Service reliability*: the extent to which the product is intended to be consistent and its consistency in practice.

5 *Service flexibility*: the extent to which alternatives are available, and to which there can be variations in the standard products that are offered.

A foodservice operation will determine the *customer service specification* of the operation by taking account of these five customer service factors.

Use of resources

Although a foodservice operation is designed to provide customer service, it must also be efficient in its use of resources. The resources used in foodservice operations are:

- *materials*: food, beverages and short use equipment (such as paper napkins)
- *labour*: staffing costs
- *facilities*: premises and plant.

The management team must always take into account the effect that the level of business has on the ability of the operation, in order to maintain the customer service requirements, while at the same time ensuring productivity in all of the resources being used.

Level of customer service

Within foodservice operations the level of service in a specific operation may be defined as follows:

1   *Technical specification*: refers to the food and beverage items on offer, the portion size or measure, the cooking method, the degree of cooking, the method of presentation, the cover, accompaniments, the cleanliness of items etc.

2   *Service specification*: refers to two aspects: first, the procedures for service and second, the way in which the procedures are carried out. Procedures include meeting and greeting, order taking, seeking customer comment, dealing with complaints, payment and the special needs of customers. The method in which the service is carried out includes paying attention to the level of staff attentiveness, their tone of voice, body language etc.

Operations will usually have written statements of both technical and service specification (often called a customer service specification). These may also be detailed in staff manuals that outline expected standards of performance.

Level of service and standards of service

There can be confusion when referring to the levels of service and the standards of service:

■   The *level of service* in foodservice operations can range from being very limited to complex, with high levels of personal attention.

■   The *standards of service* are a measure of the ability of the operation to deliver the service level it is offering.

Thus an operation might be offering low levels of service, such as a fast food operation, but may be doing this at a very high standard. Equally, an operation may be offering a high level of service, such as a full service restaurant, but may be doing so with low standards.

1.6 FOOD AND BEVERAGE SERVICE METHODS

The service of food and beverages may be carried out in many ways depending on the following factors:

■   type of establishment

■   time available for the meal

■   type of menu presented

■   site of the establishment

■   type of customer to be served

■   turnover of custom expected

■   cost of the meal served.

A foodservice operation can be seen as a simple model comprising three operating systems:

1   Food production

2   Beverage provision

3   Food and beverage service

Although food and beverage service was traditionally seen as primarily a delivery system, it actually consists of two separate sub-systems, operating at the same time. These are:

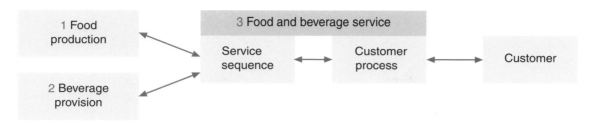

Fig 1.1. Simple model of a foodservice operation

Table 1.7 Food and beverage service sequence

- Preparation for service
- Taking bookings
- Greeting and seating/directing
- Taking food and beverage orders
- Serving of food
- Serving beverages

- Clearing during service
- Billing
- Dealing with payments
- Dishwashing
- Clearing following service

- *The service sequence* – which is primarily concerned with the delivery of the food and beverages to the customer.
- *The customer process* – which is concerned with the experience the customer undertakes to be able to order, be served, consume and have the area cleared.

The service sequence

The service sequence is essentially the bridge between the production system, beverage provision and the 'customer process' (or experience). The service sequence consists of eleven or more stages. This is summarised in Table 1.7.

Each of these stages may be carried out by a variety of methods and these methods are detailed throughout the book. The choice of method for the individual stage depends on the factors listed at the start of this section and the process that the customer is to experience.

The customer process

The customer receiving the food and beverage product is required to undertake or observe certain requirements: this is the customer process. Essentially, a customer enters a food service area, orders or selects his/her choice and then is served (the customer may pay either at this point or later). Food and beverages are then consumed, following which the area is cleared. Using this approach, five basic types of customer process can be identified. These processes are summarised in Table 1.8.

All modern food and beverage service methods can be grouped under the following five customer processes.

Table 1.8 Simple categorisation of the customer processes in food and beverage service

Service method	Service area	Ordering/ selection	Service	Dining/ consumption	Clearing
Table service	Customer enters and is seated	From menu	By staff to customer	At laid cover	By staff
Assisted service	Customer enters and is usually seated	From menu, buffet or passed trays	Combination of both staff and customers	Usually at laid cover	By staff
Self-service	Customer enters	Customer selects items onto a tray	Customer carries	Dining area or take away	By staff or customers
Single point service	Customer enters	Orders at single point	Customer carries	Dining area or take away	By staff or customers
Specialised or in situ service	Where the customer is	From menu or predetermined	Brought to the customer	Where served	By staff or customers

A *Table service*: the customer is served at a laid table. This type of service, which includes plated service or silver service, is found in many types of restaurant, cafés and in banqueting.

B *Self-service*: the customer is required to help him or herself from a buffet or counter. This type of service can be found in cafeterias and canteens.

C *Assisted service*: the customer is served part of the meal at a table and is required to obtain part through self-service from some form of display or buffet. This type of service is found in 'carvery' type operations and is often used for meals such as breakfast in hotels. It may also be used for functions.

D *Single point service*: the customer orders, pays and receives the food and beverages, for instance at a counter, at a bar in licensed premises, in a fast food operation or at a vending machine.

E *Specialised service* (or service in situ): the food and drink is taken to where the customer is. This includes tray service in hospitals and aircraft, trolley service, home delivery, lounge and room service.

In A–D of these customer processes, the customer comes to where the food and beverage service is offered and the service is provided in areas primarily designed for that purpose, such as a restaurant or take away. In customer process E, the service is provided in another location, where the area is not primarily designed for the purpose, for example in a guest room, lounge or hospital ward.

A detailed listing of all the modern food and beverage service methods is given in Table 1.9 (pages 17 to 19). A particular service method, such as waiter service, requires a number of tasks and duties that are undertaken during the actual service of food and beverages. However, there are other tasks and duties that contribute to the service. These may be identified using the service sequence (see Table 1.7). The level of complexity of food and beverage service in terms of staff skills, tasks and duties reduces from Group A (the most complex) to Group D. Group E contains specialised forms of service and these are further considered in Chapter 7.

Note: Apart from for fast food operations, there is no particular link between a specific service method and a specific food production method. It is also possible that the production and service may be separated by distance, time or both, as for example in off-premises catering.

Table 1.9 Food and beverage service methods

Group A: Table service
Service to customers at a laid cover

1 Waiter	a) Silver/English	Presentation and service of food by waiting staff, using a spoon and fork, onto a customer's plate, from food flats or dishes.
	b) Family	Main courses plated (but may be silver served) with vegetables placed in multi-portion dishes on tables for customers to help themselves; sauces offered separately.
	c) Plate/American	Service of pre-plated foods to customers. Now also widely used for banqueting.
	d) Butler/French	Presentation of food individually to customers by food service staff for customers to serve themselves.
	e) Russian	Table laid with food for customers to help themselves (this is a modern interpretation and may also sometimes be used to indicate Guéridon or Butler service).
	f) Guéridon	Food served onto customer's plate at a side table or trolley; may also include carving, jointing and fish filleting, the preparation of foods such as salads and dressings and flambage.
2 Bar counter		Service to customers seated at bar counter (often U-shaped) on stools.

Table 1.9 continued

Group B: Assisted service
Combination of table service and self-service

| 3 Assisted | a) Carvery | Some parts of the meal are served to seated customers; other parts are collected by the customers. Also used for breakfast service and for banqueting. |
| | b) Buffets | Customers select food and drink from displays or passed trays; consumption is either at tables, standing or in lounge area. |

Group C: Self-service
Self-service of customers

4 Cafeteria	a) Counter	Customers queue in line formation past a service counter and choose their menu requirements in stages before loading them on to a tray (may include a 'Carousel' — a revolving stacked counter, saving space)
	b) Free-flow	Selection as in counter (above) but in food service area where customers move at will to random service points; customers usually exit area via a till point.
	c) Echelon	Series of counters at angles to the customer flow within a free-flow area, thus saving space.
	d) Supermarket	Island service points within a free-flow area.

Note: some 'call order' production may be included in cafeterias.

Group D: Single Point Service
Service of customers at single point — consumed on premises or taken away

5 Take-away	a) Take away	Customer orders and is served from single point, at a counter, hatch or snackstand; customer consumes off the premises; some take-away establishments provide dining areas
	b) Drive-thru	Form of take-away where customer drives vehicle past order, payment and collection points
	c) Fast food	Term originally used to describe service at a counter or hatch where customers receive a complete meal or dish in exchange for cash or ticket; commonly used nowadays to describe type of establishment offering limited range menu, fast service with dining area, and take-away facility

Table 1.9 continued

6 Vending	Provision of food service and beverage service by means of automatic retailing
7 Kiosks	Outstation used to provide service for peak demand or in specific location; may be open for customers to order and be served, or used for dispensing to staff only
8 Food court	Series of autonomous counters where customers may either order and eat (as in 2 Bar counter, above) or buy from a number of counters and eat in separate eating area, or take-away
9 Bar	Term used to describe order, service and payment point and consumption area in licensed premises

Group E: Specialised (or in situ)
Service to customers in areas not primarily designed for service

10 Tray	Method of service of whole or part of meal on tray to customer in situ, e.g. at hospital beds; at aircraft seats; at train seats, also used in ODC
11 Trolley	Service of food and beverages from a trolley, away from dining areas, e.g. for office workers at their desks; for customers at aircraft seats, or at train seats
12 Home delivery	Food delivered to customer's home or place of work, e.g. 'meals on wheels', pizza home delivery, or sandwiches to offices
13 Lounge	Service of variety of foods and beverages in lounge area e.g. hotel lounge
14 Room	Service of variety of foods and beverages in guest bedrooms, or in meeting rooms
15 Drive-in	Customers park motor vehicle and are served at their vehicles

(**Note:** banquet/function is a term used to describe catering for specific numbers of people at specific times in a variety of dining layouts. Service methods also vary. In these cases banquet/function 'catering' refers to the organisation of service rather than a specific service method – see Chapter 9.)

1.7 FOOD AND BEVERAGE SERVICE PERSONNEL

Typical organisation charts for small and larger hotels are given in Figures 1.2 and 1.3. Among food and beverage operations that are not set within hotels, the organisation might resemble the food and beverage section of the hotel organisation charts. However, different terminology is used in differing types of establishment. In the section that follows, the various types of personnel in food and beverage operations is set out. Smaller operations may combine a number of these responsibilities.

Food and beverage manager

Depending on the size of the establishment, the food and beverage manager is either responsible for the implementation of agreed policies or for contributing to the setting of catering policies. The larger the organisation the less likely the manager is to be involved in policy setting. In general, managers are responsible for:

- ensuring that the required profit margins are achieved for each food and beverage service area, in each financial period
- updating and compiling new wine lists according to availability of stock, current trends and customer needs
- compiling, in liaison with the kitchen, menus for the various food service areas and for special occasions
- the purchasing of all materials, both food and drink
- ensuring that quality in relation to the price paid is maintained
- determining portion size in relation to selling price
- departmental training and promotions, plus the maintenance of the highest professional standards
- employing and dismissing staff
- holding regular meetings with section heads to ensure all areas are working effectively, efficiently and are well co-ordinated.

Restaurant manager/supervisor

The restaurant manager or supervisor has overall responsibility for the organisation and administration of particular food and beverage service areas. These may include the lounges, room service (in hotels), restaurants and possibly some of the private banqueting suites. It is the restaurant manager who sets the standards for service and is responsible for any staff training that may be required, either on or off the job. He/she may make out duty rotas, holiday lists and hours on and off duty, and contribute to operational duties (depending on the size of the establishment) so that all the service areas run efficiently and smoothly.

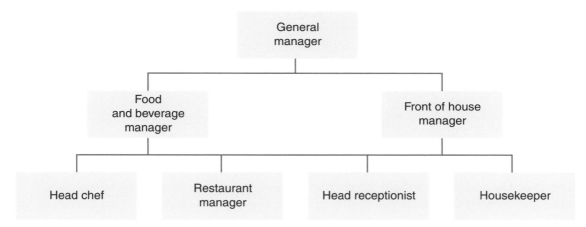

Fig 1.2. Small hotel organisation chart

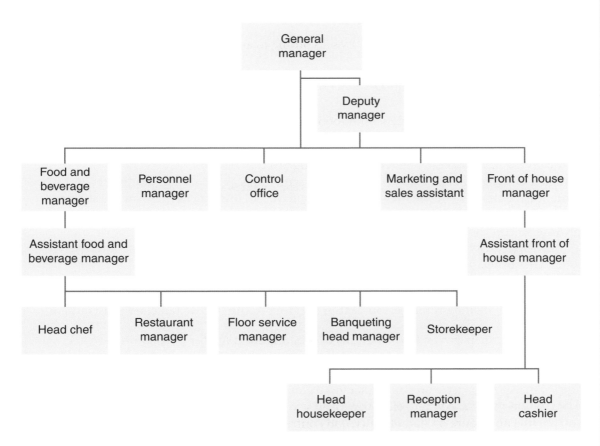

Fig 1.3. Large hotel organisation chart

Reception headwaiter

The reception headwaiter is responsible for accepting any bookings and for keeping the booking diary up to date. He/she will reserve tables and allocate these reservations to particular stations. The reception headwaiter greets guests on arrival and takes them to the table and seats them.

Headwaiter/maître d'hôtel/supervisor

The headwaiter has overall charge of the staff team and is responsible for seeing that all the duties necessary for the pre-preparation for service are efficiently carried out and that nothing is forgotten. The headwaiter will aid the reception headwaiter during the service and will possibly take some orders if the station waiter is busy. He/she helps with the compilation of duty rotas and holiday lists, and may relieve the restaurant manager or reception headwaiter on their days off.

Station headwaiter/section supervisor

The station headwaiter has the overall responsibility for a team of staff serving a number of sets of tables (which may be anything from four to eight in number), from one sideboard. Each set of tables under the station headwaiter's control is called a station.

The station headwaiter must have a good knowledge of food and wine and its correct service, and be able to instruct other members of the staff. He/she will take the order (usually from the host) and carry out all the service at the table with the help of the chef de rang, who is in command of one station.

Station waiter/chef de rang

The chef de rang must be able to carry out the same work as the station headwaiter and relieve him on days off. The chef de rang will normally have had less experience than the station headwaiter. Both the chef de rang and the station headwaiter must work together as a team to provide an efficient and speedy service.

Assistant station waiter/demi-chef de rang

The demi-chef de rang is the person next in seniority to the chef de rang and assists where necessary.

Waiter/server/commis de rang

The commis de rang acts by instruction from the chef de rang. He/she mainly fetches and carries, may do a little service of either vegetables or sauces, offers rolls, places plates upon the table and so on, and helps to clear the tables after each course. During the pre-preparation period some of the cleaning and preparatory tasks will be carried out by the commis de rang.

Trainee commis/debarrasseur/apprentice

The debarrasseur is the 'learner', having just joined the food service staff, and possibly wishing to take up food service as a career. During the service this person will keep the sideboard well filled with equipment and may help to fetch and carry items as required. The debarrasseur would carry out certain of the cleaning tasks during the pre-preparation periods. He/she may be given the responsibility of looking after and serving hors-d'oeuvre, cold sweets or assorted cheeses from the appropriate trolleys.

Carver/trancheur

The carver is responsible for the carving trolley and the carving of joints at the table as required. The carver will plate up each portion with the appropriate accompaniments.

Floor service staff/chef d'étage/floor waiter

The floor service staff are often responsible for a complete floor in an establishment or, depending on the size of the establishment, a number of rooms or suites. Floor service of all meals and beverages throughout the day is normally only offered by a first-class establishment. In smaller establishments floor service may be limited to early morning teas and breakfasts with the provision of in-room mini bars and tea and coffee facilities.

If full floor service is in operation, the staff will consist of a head floor waiter with the appropriate number of floor waiters working for him. This team of staff are then responsible for the service of all meals and beverages (alcoholic and non-alcoholic) in rooms. A thorough knowledge of food and drink, and their correct service, is therefore essential. The importance of good liaison and co-operation with the housekeeping staff cannot be over-emphasised here. The floor service staff would normally work from a floor pantry or from a central kitchen with all food and drink reaching the appropriate floor and the required room by lift and in a heated trolley (see Section 7.2, page 280).

Lounge staff/chef de sale

Lounge staff may deal with lounge service as a specific duty only in a first-class establishment. In a smaller establishment it is usual for members of the food service staff to take over these duties on a rota basis. The lounge staff are responsible for the service of morning coffee, afternoon teas, apéritifs and liqueurs before and after both lunch and dinner, and any coffee required after meals. They would be responsible for setting up the lounge in the morning and maintaining its cleanliness and presentation throughout the day.

Wine butler/wine waiter/sommelier

The sommelier is responsible for the service of all alcoholic drinks during the service of meals. The sommelier must also be a sales person. This employee should have a thorough knowledge of all drink to be served, of the best wines to go with certain foods, and of the licensing laws in respect of the particular establishment and area.

Cocktail bar staff

The person who works on the cocktail bar must be responsible and well versed in the skills of shaking and stirring cocktails. He should have a thorough knowledge of all alcoholic and non-alcoholic drinks, the ingredients necessary for the making of cocktails and of the licensing laws.

Buffet assistant/buffet chef/chef de buffet

The chef de buffet is in charge of the buffet in the room, its presentation, the carving and portioning of food and its service. This staff member would normally be a member of the kitchen team.

Cashier

The cashier is responsible for billing and taking payments, or making ledger account entries for a food and beverage operation. This may include making up bills from food and drink checks or, alternatively, in a cafeteria, for example, charging customers for their selection of items on a tray (see Section 10.2, page 401).

Counter assistants

Counter assistants are found in cafeterias where they would stock the counter and sometimes serve or portion food for customers. Duties may also include some cooking of call order items.

Table clearers

Again, table clearers can be found in seating areas where the service is not waiter service. These people are responsible for clearing tables using trolleys specially designed for the stacking of crockery, glassware, cutlery etc.

Function catering/banqueting staff

In establishments with function catering facilities there would normally be a certain number of permanent staff. These would include the banqueting manager, one or two assistant banqueting managers, one or two banqueting headwaiters, a dispense person and a secretary to the banqueting manager. All other banqueting staff required are normally engaged on a casual basis. In small establishments where there are fewer functions the manager, the assistant manager and the headwaiter would undertake the necessary administrative and organisational work.

Table 1.10 Examples of staffing requirements for different types of foodservice operation

Medium class hotel	Cafeteria
Hotel manager	Catering manager
Assistant manager	Supervisors
Head waiter	Assistant supervisors
Waiters	Counter service hands
Wine waiter	Clearers
Cashier	Cashier

Department store	Industrial foodservice/welfare catering
Catering manager	Catering manager
Assistant catering manager	Assistant catering manager
Supervisor	Supervisors
Assistant supervisors	Assistant supervisors
Cashier	Waiter
Dispense bar staff	Steward/butler
Wine waiting staff	Counter service staff
Waiting staff	Clearers
	Cashiers

	Popular price restaurant
	Restaurant manager/supervisor
	Waiting staff
	Dispense bar assistant

Staffing requirements

The staffing requirements in various establishments will differ for a number of reasons. Table 1.10 gives examples of the food and beverage staffing that might be found in different types of operation.

1.8 ATTRIBUTES OF FOOD AND BEVERAGE SERVICE PERSONNEL

As stated in Section 1.5, the product of any food and beverage operation is not just the food and drink itself. Any member of staff coming into contact with the customer is also part of the product. No matter how good the quality of the food, beverage, decor and equipment, poorly trained, scruffy or unhelpful staff can destroy a customer's potential satisfaction with the product. It is also true that well-trained, smart and helpful staff can sometimes make up for aspects that are lacking elsewhere in the operation.

Below are listed the principal attributes necessary in food and beverage service personnel.

A professional and hygienic appearance

How you look and the first impressions you create are more often than not seen as a reflection of the hygiene standards of your establishment and the quality of service to come.

All staff should be aware of the factors listed below and it is their individual responsibility to ensure that they are put into practice.

- Staff should be clean and should use deodorants (but not strong smelling ones).
- Aftershave and perfumes should not be too strong (as this may have a detrimental effect on the customer's palate).
- Sufficient sleep, an adequate and healthy intake of food and regular exercise is essential for good health and the ability to cope with the pressures and stress of work.
- Particular attention should be paid to the hands. They must always be clean, free of nicotine stains and with clean, well-trimmed nails.
- Men should normally be clean-shaven or with any moustache or beard neatly trimmed.
- Women should only wear light make-up. If nail varnish is worn then it should be clear.
- Earrings should not be worn with the possible exception of studs/sleepers.
- Uniform should be clean, starched as appropriate and neatly pressed. All buttons must be present.
- Hair must be clean and well groomed. Long hair must be tied up or back to avoid hairs falling into foods and drinks, and to avoid repeated handling of the hair.
- Shoes must be comfortable and clean, and of a plain, neat design. Fashion is not as important here as safety and foot comfort.
- Teeth should be brushed immediately before coming on duty.
- Cuts and burns should be covered with waterproof dressings.
- Any colds or other possible infections should be reported immediately.
- Hands should be washed immediately after using the toilet, smoking or dealing with refuse. Hot water and soap must be used.
- Staff should try to avoid any mannerisms they may have, such as running their fingers through their hair, chewing gum, or scratching their face.
- Excessive jewellery should not be worn. The establishment policy should be followed.

Knowledge of food and beverages and technical ability

The staff must have sufficient knowledge of all the items on the menu and wine and drink lists in order to advise and offer suggestions to customers. In addition, they must know how to serve correctly each dish on the menu, what its accompaniments are, the correct cover, and the make-up of the dish and its garnish. For beverage service the staff should know how to serve various types of wine and drink, in the correct containers (e.g. glasses, cups) and at the right temperature.

Punctuality

Punctuality is all-important. If staff are continually late on duty it shows a lack of interest in their work and a lack of respect for the management and customers.

Local knowledge

In the interest of customers the staff should have a certain knowledge of the area in which they work so they may be able to advise the guests on the various forms of entertainment offered, the best means of transport to places of interest and so on.

Personality

Staff must be tactful, courteous, good humoured and of an even temper. They must converse with the customer in a pleasing and well-spoken manner and the ability to smile at the right time pays dividends.

Attitude to customers

The correct approach to the customer is of the utmost importance. The staff must not be servile, but should anticipate the customer's needs and wishes. A careful watch should be kept on customers at all times during the service without staring. Care should always be taken when dealing with difficult customers. (There is really no such thing as a 'difficult' customer – they are normally people whom one is uncertain how to deal with.) Staff should never argue with customers as this will only aggravate the situation – all complaints should be referred to someone in authority in the food service area.

Memory

A good memory is an asset to food and beverage service staff. It may help them in various ways in their work if they know the likes and dislikes of customers, where they like to sit in the food service area, what are their favourite drinks, and so on.

Honesty

This is all-important for the staff in dealings with both the customer and the management. If there is trust and respect in the triangle of staff, customer and management relationships, then there will be an atmosphere of work which encourages efficiency and a good team spirit among the food and beverage service operators.

Loyalty

The staff's obligations and loyalty are firstly to the establishment in which they are employed and its management.

Conduct

Staff conduct should be impeccable at all times, especially in front of customers. The rules and regulations of an establishment must be followed and respect shown to all senior members of staff.

Sales ability

The staff reflect the image of the establishment. They are salespeople and must therefore have a complete knowledge of all forms of food and drink and their correct service, and so be able to contribute to personal selling and merchandising.

Sense of urgency

In order for the establishment to generate the maximum amount of business over the service period, with as high a net profit as possible, staff must develop a sense of urgency.

Customer satisfaction

The food and beverage service staff must see that the guests have all they require and are completely satisfied. The ability to anticipate a customer's needs is of great importance. If a customer is comfortable in their surroundings then this is because of the warm and friendly atmosphere in the food service area, and the team spirit among the waiting staff.

Complaints

Staff should have a pleasant manner and show courtesy and tact, an even temper and good humour. They should never show their displeasure even during a difficult situation. Staff should never argue with a customer and if they are unable to resolve a situation, it should be referred immediately to a senior member of the team who will be able to calm the guest and put right any fault. Remember, loss of time in dealing with complaints only makes the situation worse.

Contribution to the team

Above all, the staff should be able to work as part of a team within and between departments.

FOOD AND BEVERAGE SERVICE AREAS AND EQUIPMENT

CHAPTER 2

2.1 INTRODUCTION

In any establishment a customer's first impressions on entering the service area are of great importance: a customer may be gained or lost on these impressions alone. The creation of atmosphere, by the right choice of décor, furnishings and equipment, is therefore a major factor that contributes to the success of the foodservice operation. A careful selection of items in terms of shape, design and colour enhances the overall décor or theme and contributes towards a feeling of total harmony. The choice of furniture and its layout and the linen, tableware, small equipment and glassware will be determined by considering:

- the type of clientele expected
- the site or location of the establishment
- the layout of the food and beverage service area
- the type of service offered
- the funds available.

The general points to be considered when purchasing equipment for a food and beverage service area are:

- flexibility of use
- type of service being offered
- type of customer
- design
- colour
- durability
- ease of maintenance
- stackability
- cost and funds available
- availability in the future – replacements
- storage
- rate of breakage, i.e. crockery
- shape
- psychological effect on customers
- delivery time.

Depending on the style of operation, there may be many service areas behind the scenes, or what may be termed 'back-of-house'. These are required to be well organised, efficiently run and supervised, and stocked with well-designed equipment. It is necessary for all these factors to work together to contribute to the overall success of the food and beverage operation.

The back-of-house service areas are usually between the kitchen and food and beverage service areas. They are important parts of the design of a foodservice operation, acting as the link between kitchen or food preparation areas and the restaurant or food and beverage service areas. They are also meeting points for staff of various departments as they carry out their duties, and therefore there must be close liaison between these various members of staff and the departments.

The service areas themselves are some of the busiest of a foodservice establishment, especially during the service periods. Because of this, it is important that department heads ensure all staff know exactly what their duties are and how to carry them out efficiently and effectively.

In general, especially in large operations, five main back-of-house service areas can be identified:

- stillroom
- silver or plate room
- wash-up
- hotplate
- spare linen store.

A well-designed layout of these areas is essential to ensure an even flow of work by the various members of staff. However, the layout itself may vary with different establishments, depending on the type of operational needs. Each of the areas is considered in more detail in Sections 2.2 to 2.6 below.

2.2 STILLROOM

The main function of the stillroom is to provide items of food and beverages required for the service of a meal and not catered for by the other major departments in a foodservice operation, such as the kitchen, larder and pastry.

The duties performed in this service area will vary according to the type of meals offered and the size of establishment concerned.

Staff

In a large first-class establishment a stillroom supervisor is in charge of the stillroom. Depending on its size and the duties to be performed, he/she may have a number of staff under his/her control. The person in charge is responsible for the compilation of work rotas for all stillroom staff so that all duties are covered and the area is staffed throughout the whole of the service periods. The stillroom supervisor is also responsible for the ordering of supplies from the main dry goods store and the effective control of these items when issued to the various departments.

When ordering goods from the main dry goods store, all requirements should be written out on a requisition sheet in duplicate. The top copy goes to the store to be retained by the storekeeper after issuing the goods and the duplicate remains in the requisition book as a means of checking the receipt of goods from the store by a member of the stillroom staff. The storekeeper should not issue goods unless the stillroom supervisor or another person in authority has signed the requisition.

Because of the number of hours that the stillroom has to remain open and to ensure it is run efficiently, staff might work on a shift basis.

Equipment

The equipment in all stillrooms is of a similar nature. A wide range of food items is offered and so to ensure their proper storage, preparation and presentation, a considerable amount of equipment is used. The following are examples of items that might be needed:

- Refrigerator for storage of milk, cream, butter, fruit juices and so on.
- Beverage making facilities.
- Large double sink and draining board for washing-up purposes.
- Dishwasher of a size suitable for the stillroom but large enough to ensure efficient turnover of equipment.
- Salamander or toasters.
- Bread slicing machine.
- Worktop and cutting board.
- Necessary storage space for all small equipment such as crockery, glassware and silverware.
- Storage cupboard for all dry goods held in stock and for such miscellaneous items as doilies, kitchen papers, paper napkins etc.
- Coffee grinding machine to ensure the correct 'grind' of coffee for the brewing method to be used.
- Ice maker.

Provisions

As a basic guide, the following food items would normally be dispensed from the stillroom:

- All beverages such as coffee, tea, chocolate, tisanes, Bovril, Horlicks, Ovaltine and other drinks.
- Assorted fruit juices: orange, tomato, pineapple and grapefruit.
- Milk, cream and alternatives.
- Sugars: loose, pre-wrapped portions, brown coffee crystals, Demerara etc. and alternatives.
- Preserves: marmalade, cherry, plum, raspberry, strawberry, apricot and honey. For the purpose of control and to reduce wastage, many establishments now offer pre-portioned jars or pots of jams or preserves at breakfast and for afternoon tea, rather than a preserve dish.
- Butter: either passed through a butter pat machine, curled or pre-wrapped portions and also butter alternatives.
- Sliced and buttered brown, white and malt bread.
- Rolls, brioche and croissants.
- Bread items.
- Dry cracker, digestive and water biscuits for service with cheese; sweet biscuits for service with early morning and afternoon teas and coffees.
- Assorted breakfast cereals: Cornflakes, Weetabix, Shredded Wheat, Rice Crispies, muesli and so on. In many establishments cereals of all types are offered in pre-wrapped, portion-controlled packets.

- Toasted scones and teacakes.
- Pastries, gâteaux and sandwiches: in a large establishment the pastries and gâteaux will come from the Pastry department, and the assorted savoury sandwiches from the Larder. In a smaller establishment the pastries and gâteaux may be bought from an outside firm but issued from the stillroom, and sandwiches would be made and issued from the stillroom.
- Porridge and boiled eggs: often provided by the stillroom in small establishments.

Control

There are two main ways of checking for goods to be issued from the stillroom:

- By issuing items in bulk on receipt of a requisition received from a food service area. Someone in authority must sign the requisition. This would include such food items as butter, preserves, sugar, and so on.
- By issuing tea, coffee or any other beverage required in the necessary portions on receipt of a waiter's check.

2.3 SILVER ROOM OR PLATE ROOM

In larger, more luxurious establishments, the silver room, or plate room as it is sometimes known, is a separate service area. In smaller establishments it is often combined with the pantry wash-up area.

Equipment

The silver room should hold the complete stock of silver required for the service of all meals, together with a slight surplus stock in case of emergency. Silver for banqueting service may be of a different design and kept specifically for that purpose.

The large silver such as flats, salvers, soup tureens, and cloches, will be stored on shelves, with all the flats of one size together, and so on. All shelves should be labelled showing where each different item goes. This makes it easier for control purposes and for stacking. When stacking silver the heavier items should go on the shelves lower down and the smaller and lighter items on the shelves higher up. This helps to prevent accidents. All cutlery and flatware, together with the smaller items of silver such as ashtrays, cruets, butter dishes, special equipment, tables numbers and menu holders, are best stored in drawers lined with green baize. This helps to prevent noise and stops the various items sliding about the drawer when it is opened and closed and so becoming scratched and marked.

Staff

All the service silver should be cleaned on a rota basis. It is the duty of the head plate person to ensure that this is carried out and that all silver is cleaned regularly. Obviously items that are in constant use will require more attention. He/she will also put on one side any articles of silver that are broken or that require buffing up or replating, so that they may be sent to the manufacturer for any faults to be corrected.

The head plate person may have a number of staff under him/her, depending on the size of the establishment. In the smaller medium class establishment, however, where the plate room is possibly combined with the pantry wash-up, it would be the duty of either the washing-up staff or the waiting staff to ensure that all the service silver is kept clean.

Silver cleaning methods

There are various methods of silver cleaning, and the method used generally depends on the size and class of establishment. The larger establishments use a burnishing machine, which would be in constant use all through the day, whereas the smaller establishments may use a manual method. The main methods used are as follows:

Burnishing machine

This is a revolving drum with a safety shield. It may be plumbed into the mains or remain portable with the water being poured in by means of a hose from a tap. Depending on the size of burnishing machine used, it may be divided into compartments to hold specific sizes of silver. It may also be possible to insert a rod through the centre of the drum from one end to the other. This rod is removable and is passed through the handles of teapots, coffee pots, milk jugs, sugar basins etc., to hold them in position while the drum is revolving.

In order for the burnishing machine to run effectively and efficiently it is approximately half-full of ball bearings. To these a certain amount of soap powder is added according to the maker's instructions. The silver is placed inside and then the lid clamped down tightly. The main water supply is then turned on to ensure a constant flow of water. If the machine is not plumbed in, then water should be poured into the drum until the ball bearings are covered, before the lid is clamped down. The machine is then switched on. As the drum revolves the mixture of water and soap powder acts as a lubricant between the silver and the ball bearings. Thus any tarnish is removed but the silver is not scratched. On being removed from the burnishing machine the silver should be rinsed in hot water and dried with a clean tea cloth.

This method of silver cleaning keeps the silver in good condition with minimum effort and gives a lasting polish. The ball bearings must always be kept covered with water otherwise they rust very easily.

Polivit

Polivit is an aluminium metal sheet containing holes, which is best used in an enamel or galvanised iron bowl. The polivit is placed in the bowl together with some soda. The silver to be cleaned is then put into the bowl, ensuring that at least one piece of silver has contact with the polivit. Sufficient boiling water is poured into the bowl to cover the silver being cleaned. A chemical reaction takes place between the polivit, soda, boiling water and silver, which causes the tarnish to be lifted. After three to four minutes the silver should be removed from the bowl and placed into a second bowl of boiling water and rinsed. On removal from the second bowl the silver is allowed to drain and then polished with a clean, dry tea cloth.

A simpler version of this may be used for silver fork tips that have become tarnished. An aluminium saucepan half filled with water and boiling on the stove can be used to put fork tips into for a short time. The forks need to touch each other, and the side of the saucepan at the same time, for the chemical reaction to take place. This easily removes the tarnishing and is less harmful to the silver than using silver dip.

Plate powder

This is a pink powder, which needs mixing with a little methylated spirit to obtain a smooth paste. The reason for using methylated spirit rather than water to mix the powder is that when the paste is rubbed on the article the spirit evaporates much more quickly than water, and the silver is therefore ready for polishing sooner. If, however, methylated spirit is not available, then water may be used, but the cleaning process will take a little longer.

The smooth paste, once prepared, is rubbed onto the article being cleaned with a clean piece of cloth. The paste must be rubbed well in to remove all tarnish. The article is then left until the paste has dried and the paste is then rubbed off with a clean cloth. It is advisable to rinse the article well in very hot water and to give a final polish with a clean dry tea cloth. When silver is cleaned that has a design or engraving on it, a small toothbrush may be used to brush the paste into the design and a clean one used to remove it. This method is both time-consuming and messy, but produces very good results.

Silver dip

This is a pink-coloured liquid, which must be used in a plastic bowl. The silver to be cleaned is placed into a wire basket and dipped into the plastic bowl containing the silver dip. The liquid should cover all the silver articles being cleaned. The silver should be left in the bowl only a very short while and then lifted out and drained. After draining it is placed in warm water, rinsed and then polished with a clean dry tea cloth. This method is very quick and produces good results, but it is harder on the silver than the other methods because of the chemical reaction between the liquid and the silver. However, it is a popular method in medium-sized establishments because it is quicker than other methods.

2.4 WASH-UP

Organisation

The wash-up must be sited so that staff can work speedily and efficiently when passing from the food service areas to the kitchens. Servers should stack trays of dirties correctly within the service area, with all the correct sized plates together, and tableware stacked on one of the plates with the blades of the knives running under the arches of the forks. All glassware should be stacked on separate trays and taken to a separate wash-up point.

The wash-up service area should be the first section in the stillroom when the waiter enters from the service area. Here he/she deposits all the dirty plates, stacking them correctly and placing all the cutlery in a special wire basket or container in readiness for washing. The server must place any debris into the bin or bowl provided. All used paper napkins, doilies or kitchen paper should be placed in a separate bin.

Dishwashing methods

There are five main methods of dishwashing for foodservice operations and a summary of these is shown in Table 2.1.

Manual (tank) method

The dirty crockery is placed into a tank of hot water containing a soap detergent. After washing, the plates are placed into wire racks and dipped into a second sterilising tank containing clean hot water at a temperature of approximately 75°C (179°F). The racks are left for two minutes and then lifted out and the crockery left to drain. If sterilised in water at this temperature the crockery will dry by itself without the use of drying-up cloths. This is more hygienic. After drying, the crockery is stacked into piles of the correct size and placed on shelves until required for further use.

Semi-automatic

Many of the larger establishments have dishwashing machines. These are necessary because of the high usage of crockery. The instructions for use of a dishwashing machine are generally supplied by the manufacturer, together with details of detergent to be used, and in what quantity. These directions should be strictly adhered to.

Debris should be removed from the crockery before it is placed into the wire racks. The racks are then passed through the machine, the crockery being washed, rinsed, and then sterilised in turn. Having passed through the machine the crockery is left to drain for two to

Table 2.1 Summary of dishwashing methods (Based on a chart from Croner's Catering)

Method	Description
Manual	Soiled ware washed by hand or brush machine
Semi-automatic	Soiled ware loaded manually into dishwashing machine by operators
Automatic conveyor	Soiled ware loaded in baskets, mounted on a conveyor, by operators for automatic transportation through a dishwashing machine
Flight conveyor	Soiled ware loaded within pegs mounted on a conveyor, by operators for automatic transportation through a dishwashing machine
Deferred wash	Soiled ware collected together, stripped, sorted and stacked by operators for transportation through a dishwashing machine at a later stage

three minutes and is then stacked and placed on shelves until required for further use. As with the tank method, the plates do not require drying with tea cloths. Developments of this method include the automatic conveyor and the flight conveyor dishwashing methods, as described in Table 2.1.

2.5 HOTPLATE

Organisation

The hotplate (or pass) may be regarded as the meeting point between the service staff and the food preparation staff. Active cooperation and a good relationship between the members of staff of these two areas help to ensure that the customer receives an efficient and quick service of the meal. This cooperation also ensures that all the food dishes are served well and attractively presented.

Aboyeur

The 'aboyeur' (or barker) is in charge, and controls the hotplate (or pass) during the service period. As an aid to the food service staff the aboyeur would control the 'off board', which tells the waiter immediately of any menu item that is not available (off). It should be sited in a prominent position for all to see. The hotplate itself should be stocked with all the crockery necessary for the service of a meal. This may include some or all of the following items: soup plates, fishplates, joint plates, sweet plates, consommé cups, platters and soup cups.

The silver required for service is often placed on the top of the hotplate and used as required. The hotplate is usually gas or electrically operated and should be lit/switched on well in advance of the service to ensure all the necessary crockery and silver is sufficiently heated before the service commences.

The aboyeur who controls the hotplate over the service period will initially receive the food check from the waiter. Any written food orders must be legible to the aboyeur so that there is no delay in calling-up a particular dish. He/she checks that none of the dishes ordered are off the menu. Then the order from the various 'corners' (or 'parties' or 'sections') of the kitchen is called up, as each particular dish is required. If a dish required has to be prepared and cooked to order, then it is important that the aboyeur orders this to be done before the waiter comes to the hotplate to collect it. This ensures there will be no major delay for the waiter who is going to serve the dish, or for the customer who is waiting for the next course to be served. When a food check is finished with it is placed into a control box. This box is often kept locked and can only be opened by a member of staff from the control department who, for control purposes, marries the copy of the food check from the kitchen with the copy the cashier has and the duplicate copy of the bill.

Hotplate language and terminology

To ensure there is no delay in any food dish reaching the hotplate, the aboyeur should call it up allowing time for preparation, cooking and presentation. Various special kitchen terms are used to warn the food preparation staff working in various corners to get ready certain dishes. Examples of these terms are as follows:

■ *Le service va commencer*: general warning to kitchen that the service is about to commence.

■ *Ça marche trois couverts*: indication to the kitchen of the number of covers on the table.

■ *Poissonnier, faites marcher trois soles Véronique*: example of fish corner informed of the order required, in this case three sole Véronique.

■ *Poissonnier, envoyez les trois soles Véronique*: when the order is required at the hotplate by the waiter, the aboyeur calls it up. In this example it is the fish corner being told to bring the order for the three sole Véronique.

■ *Oui*: the reply given by the chef de partie (section chef) to the order called out by the aboyeur.

■ *Bien soigné*: the term called out by the aboyeur before the actual order when an extra special order is required.

■ *Dépêchez-vous*: the words used to hurry up an order.

■ *Arrêtez*: the term used to cancel an order.

■ Foods requiring special degrees of cooking are given the following terms:

  – Omelette baveuse: soft inside.

  – Steak grillé:

    (a) bleu: (rare) surfaces well-browned, inside raw

    (b) saignant: underdone

    (c) à point: medium

    (d) bien cuit: cooked right through, well done.

All food service staff should be familiar with these terms in order to appreciate exactly what is going on at the hotplate and how the particular 'kitchen French' terms help to ensure quick and efficient service. However, many establishments in the UK now use English for these instructions. Again, all members of staff do need to know the system for their own establishment.

Carvery-type operations

In carvery-type operations the customer is served part of the meal at a table and is required to obtain part through self-service from some form of display or buffet. Carvery menus are often restricted and customers are able to help themselves to joints and other dishes but usually with the assistance of a carver or server at the buffet. The most important factor in the profitability of a carvery is the accuracy of estimates related to the:

- average weight of each portion
- type of meat, fish or other dish that customers might choose
- number of customers coming on any particular day.

As a guide the average main course portion with vegetables is in the region of 525 g (1 lb 5 oz), but in estimating costs the average main course is assumed to be 600 g (1 lb 8 oz) – the additional 75 g (3 oz) being wastage. There is weight loss after cooking as well as wastage in carving.

After cooking, the joints are normally put into a hot cupboard (or closet) where they can be held at a temperature somewhere between 78°C and 82°C (170–180°F). If the temperature were higher than this, the joints would start cooking again. Even when holding joints at this temperature prior to carving, it is almost inevitable that joints of lamb commence cooking again. Thus lamb joints should never be fully roasted in the oven. If the temperature of the hot closet is too low there can be bacteriological problems.

On the carvery itself the meat and other dishes are maintained at a temperature of around 74–82°C (160–180°F) by the use of overhead infrared heat lamps. These lamps are generally mounted on telescopic stands so various sized joints may be accommodated and carving may be carried out safely.

The anticipated demand can be calculated through a number of factors:

- figures from the previous week
- figures for the same week the year before
- adjustment of figures according to any local conditions, for example, the location of the establishment, the number of local residents and visitors, and the location of nearby attractions such as exhibitions and theatres.

2.6 SPARE LINEN STORE

Another back-of-house service area that is generally found within establishments is the spare linen cupboard or store. This is normally the responsibility of a senior member of the service staff and is kept locked for control purposes. This spare linen stock is held near the food service area in case of emergency. The linen is changed when necessary, and usually on the basis of one clean item in exchange for one dirty item. See also Section 2.11 Linen, page 52.

2.7 DISPENSE BAR

The term 'dispense bar' refers to any bar situated within a food and beverage service area that dispenses wine or other alcoholic drinks which are to be served to a customer consuming a meal or using a lounge area. However, in many establishments, because of the planning and layout, wine and other alcoholic drinks for consumption with a meal are sometimes dispensed from bars situated outside the food and beverage service area itself – in other words, from one of the public bars. All drinks dispensed must be checked for and controlled in some way (see Section 5.6 Taking customer food and beverage orders, page 225, and Section 10.3 Beverage control, page 411). All alcoholic drinks are usually served by the member of the service team often known as a sommelier or wine butler, unless it is the custom for the food service waiters to serve their own customers with the wine and drinks they require.

Equipment

In order to carry out efficiently the service of all forms of wine and drink requested, the bar should have available all the necessary equipment for making cocktails, decanting wine, serving wine correctly, making fruit cups and so on. The equipment should include the following items.

Main items

■ *Cocktail shaker*: the ideal utensil for mixing ingredients that will not normally blend together well by stirring. A three-part utensil.

■ *Boston shaker*: consists of two cones, one of which overlaps the other to seal in the 'mix'. Made of stainless steel, glass or plated silver. The mix is strained using a Hawthorn strainer.

■ *Mixing glass*: like a glass jug without a handle, but has a lip. Used for mixing clear drinks which do not contain juices or cream.

■ *Strainer*: there are many types, the most popular being the Hawthorn. This is a flat spoon-shaped utensil with a spring coiled round its edge. It is used in conjunction with the cocktail shaker and mixing glass to hold back the ice after the drink is prepared. A special design is available for use with liquidisers and blenders.

■ *Bar spoon*: for use with the mixing glass when stirring cocktails. The flat 'muddler' end is used for crushing sugar and mint in certain drinks.

■ *Bar liquidiser or blender*: used for making drinks that require puréed fruit.

■ *Drink mixer*: used for drinks that do not need liquidising, especially those containing cream or ice cream. If ice is required, use only crushed ice.

Other items

Examples include:

■ assorted glasses
■ ice buckets and stands
■ wine baskets
■ water jugs
■ assorted bitters: peach, orange, Angostura
■ cutting board and knife
■ coasters
■ refrigerator
■ cork extractor

■ soda syphons
■ coloured sugars
■ sink unit
■ glass washing machine
■ optics/spirit measures
■ wine measures
■ cooling trays
■ bottle opener
■ ice crushing machine

- ice pick
- ice making machine
- drinking straws
- cocktail sticks
- carafes
- wine and cocktail lists
- glass cloths, napkins and service cloths
- small ice buckets and tongs

- muslin and funnel
- lemon squeezing machine
- swizzle sticks
- strainer and funnel
- service salvers
- wine knife and cigar cutter
- bin
- hot beverage maker.

Food items

Examples include:

- olives
- Worcestershire sauce
- salt and pepper
- nutmeg
- Angostura bitters
- caster sugar

- Maraschino cherries
- Tabasco sauce
- cinnamon
- cloves
- cube sugar
- Demerara sugar

Fig 2.1. Examples of cocktail bar equipment: (1) cocktail shaker, (2) Boston shaker, (3) mixing glass with bar spoon, (4) Hawthorn strainer, (5) jug strainer insert, (6) mini whisk, (7) straws, (8) ice crusher, (9) juice press, (10) ice bucket and tongs

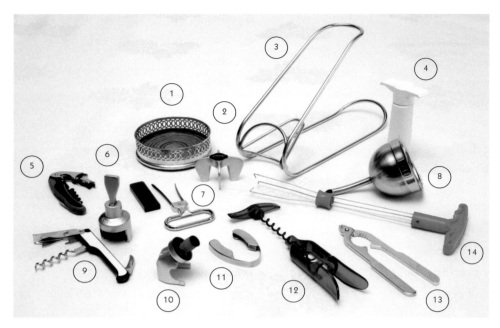

Fig 2.2. Examples of bar equipment: (1) bottle coaster, (2) Champagne star cork grip, (3) wine bottle holder, (4) vacu-pump, (5, 7, 9, 12) wine bottle openers, (6, 10) Champagne bottle stoppers, (8) wine funnel, (11) wine bottle foil cutter, (13) Champagne cork grip, (14) wine cork extractor, (15) appetiser bowls and cocktail stick holder, (16) measures on drip tray, (17) cutting board and knife, (18) cigar cutters, (19, 21) bottle stoppers, (20) bottle pourers, (22) crown cork opener, (23) mini juice press

- eggs
- mint
- orange
- coconut cream

- cream
- cucumber
- lemon
- lime.

Glassware

The choice of the right glass is a vital element if the cocktail is to be invitingly presented. Well-designed glassware combines elegance, strength and stability, and should be fine rimmed and of clear glass. All glassware should be clean and well polished (see Section 2.14 Glassware, page 62).

Planning of the bar

There are certain essentials necessary in the planning of every bar. They are factors that should be given prime consideration when planning for a fixed bar or when setting up a temporary bar for a particular function, as follows:

Siting

A major factor is the siting of the bar. The position should be chosen so that the bar achieves the greatest possible number of sales.

Area

The bar staff must be given sufficient area or space in which to work and move about. There should be a minimum of 1 m (3 ft 3 in) from the back of the bar counter to the storage shelves and display cabinets at the rear of the bar.

Layout

Very careful consideration must be given, in the initial planning, to the layout of the bar. Adequate storage must be provided, in the form of shelves, cupboards and racks, for all the stock required and equipment listed. Everything should be easily to hand so that the bar staff do not have to move about more than necessary to provide a quick and efficient service.

Plumbing and power

It is essential to have hot and cold running water for glass washing. Power is necessary for the cooling trays, refrigerators and ice-making machines.

Safety and hygiene

Great care must be observed to ensure that the materials used in the make-up of the bar are hygienic and safe. Flooring must be non-slip. The bar top should be of a material suited to the general decor that is hard wearing, easily wiped down and has no sharp edges. The bar top should be of average working height – approximately 1 m (3 ft 3 in) and a depth (across the top from the bar to the service side) of about 0.6 m (20 in).

2.8 AUTOMATIC VENDING

In the broadest sense, automatic vending may be defined as selling by automation. It is a form of automatic retailing using one of the following methods of payment:

- coin
- banknote
- moneycard
- token.

The types of service available may be broken into two areas, namely, service and facilities and consumables, for example:

Service and facilities

- TV time
- gas
- water
- electricity
- shoe cleaning
- car parking
- toilets
- baggage store

Consumables

- hot and cold beverages
- meals
- confectionery
- tobacco
- alcoholic drinks.

Within food and beverage operations automatic vending mainly is used for the supply of a wide variety of food and beverages, both hot and cold, through coin/token-operated machines.

Two sectors of the foodservice industry benefit most at the present time from automatic vending, namely industrial and transport catering. Vending machines are found in canteens, factories, offices, industrial concerns, railway stations, garages (including motorway service stations), schools, hospitals, leisure centres and hotels.

Advantages of vending

The machines themselves may be used in conjunction with the conventional kitchen approach to catering. At the same time they relieve some of the pressure of work on the counter hands and cashier by taking some of the customers away from the counter and to the machines. This is especially true where only hot or cold beverages are required together with a limited range of snacks for a certain percentage of those being catered for. This is one of the many advantages of automatic vending. Other advantages are:

- *24-hour service*: automatic vending machines provide a round-the-clock 24-hour service.

- *Low cost*: automatic vending machines are cheaper to operate than conventional methods of service.

- *Increase in productivity*: it is generally recognised that good staff facilities mean an increase in productivity. To this end, the correct siting of the automatic vending machines can give a boost to the employees' morale by providing for their needs 24 hours a day. This should ensure that staff do not have to move any great distance from their place of work or waste time in queuing.

- *Food cost control*: this is a great advantage because automatic vending allows for strict portion control.
- *Economy of labour*: which results in a reduction in the wages bill.
- *Natural tea-break*: with the advent of these machines the fixed tea-break has given way to the natural tea-break, with the result that less working time is lost due to workers slowing down in anticipation of the break and being back a few minutes late from their break. This also means that productivity is increased.
- *Fresh beverages*: while a main meal may be served, if beverages are available by machine then they are fresh, piping hot and taken as and when required. This means the beverage does not then go cold while the main meal is being consumed.
- *Variety*: automatic vending machines offer a wide variety of hot and cold snacks and beverages, all contained within a space considerably smaller than is necessary for conventional forms of large equipment. This is another important consideration and saving, as commercial space is so costly.
- *Hot meals*: automatic vending machines are also being used in conjunction with the microwave oven. Here, all snacks and meals are kept in refrigerated compartments. The customer chooses his meal, takes it from the machine, and then places it in the microwave oven to reheat.
- *Reduced wastage*: as long as the customer demand has been correctly gauged, wastage is reduced to a minimum. However, this is dependent on the 'right machines' providing the 'right items' at the 'right price' and sited in the 'right place'.
- *Ease of maintenance*: a member of the permanent staff can be trained to replenish and clean the vending machines daily.

Disadvantages of vending

There are disadvantages to automatic vending and these have to be considered in relation to the total operation before making a final decision on usage. These may be summarised as follows:

- *Speed of service*: for a beverage this is approximately 10 seconds; a cafeteria operator would be faster. It is also important to bear in mind that conventional systems are more suitable for large-scale operations.
- *Quality*: although quality has improved in both the product and its packaging, customer resistance still exists.
- *Human presence*: there may be very little, if any, 'human presence'. Manufacturers have researched this problem and attempted to overcome it with attractively designed and colourful machines.
- *Electricity*: the machines are subject to power failure and power surges.
- *Maintenance*: automatic vending machines require regular daily servicing and cleaning. Depending upon the style of operation, the machines may require servicing and cleaning twice a day.
- *Vandalism*: most modern machines are robust, but loss of revenue and lack of service result in frustration to all concerned.
- *Breakdown*: can take vital hours to repair.

Types of vending machine

These include:

- *Merchandiser*: customer can view the products on sale, for example, confectionery machines.
- *Beverage vendor*: mixes the ingredients to produce the product.
- *In-cup system*: ingredients are already in individual cups to which water is added.
- *Micro-vend system*: provides a range of hot or cold foods from which the customer may make a selection and heat in an accompanying microwave oven.

Catering services

The catering services provided by vending machines may come in the form of:

- *Hot beverages*: by use of powdered ingredients.
- *Cold beverages*: by use of post-mix syrup and water (carbonated or non-carbonated).
- *Hot meals*: by internal heating or with the use of microwaves and time cards/tokens.
- *Meals and snacks*: by means of refrigeration.

The numbers and types of machines required will depend on their location, the type and numbers of people they are providing a service for, the cost factor and the variety of food and beverage items required.

The machines required may be installed either individually or in small groups, to supplement the conventional catering establishment or to cover a small sales demand that does not warrant the expense of employing the extra labour and plant. The opposite to this would be the installation of a complete vending service where demand is highly volatile, space is limited and the use of staffed operations would be uneconomical.

A further advancement in the development of microwave oven techniques in conjunction with vending is the micro-vend buffet. This is a complete refreshment unit for both hot and cold meals and hot and cold drinks. Here, complete meals are prepared to standard recipes and retained in refrigerated conditions. With each meal the customer receives a small token that enables her to operate a microwave oven incorporated in the automatic vending unit. General factors that should be considered prior to purchasing vending equipment may be summarised as follows:

- *Cup sales*: may be one to two drinks per person per day when charged but could double if offered free.
- *Ingredient capacity*: related to required periods of restocking.
- *Number of selectors (items) available*: this will often relate to the demand (anticipated number of customers).
- *Hygiene*: ease of cleaning.
- *Extraction efficiency*: for heat/steam systems.
- *Restocking*: ease of filling.

- *Maintenance*: regular servicing contract.
- *Physical dimension/acceptability*: whether the machine will fit into the environment and blend in with the décor.
- *Siting*: as close as is feasible to those using the machine, that is, either on the work floor or in a food service area so as to maximise use.
- *Weight (floor loading)*: ease of moving for cleaning and siting purposes.
- *Availability of services*: power and plumbing.
- *Capital available*: whether the machine should be leased or purchased.
- *Training*: whether staff can be trained easily to replenish, clean and maintain machines.
- *Policy*: there must be clear guidelines linked to failure of a machine and insurance cover.

Cleaning of vending machines

Automatic vending machines are neither self-cleaning nor self-maintained and human help is needed here. Therefore, regular service contract maintenance is required and should be guaranteed if all is to run smoothly and without the problems of mechanical breakdown. The type of vending machine and the service demand upon it will help to determine the regularity of the service contract.

Regular daily cleaning and replenishment is nearly always required although demand may necessitate two or even three daily visits for cleaning and replenishment.

Staff should be trained in the techniques of cleaning and replenishing vending machines. The checklist below stresses the key factors to be considered.

- Clean at times when demand is at its lowest to avoid unnecessary loss of sales.
- To avoid electrical accidents, use the minimum amount of water while cleaning or disconnect from the mains where possible.
- Read the supplier's recommendations carefully and use only nominated cleaning agents.
- Ensure the temperature controls are functioning correctly.
- Always wipe down the complete outside of the vending machine to project an image of good hygiene.
- Ensure all sales items are clearly visible and operating instructions are easy to follow.
- When replenishing the machine, check the sell-by dates and put older items to the front.
- Ensure all packaging and labelling is correct.
- Check slow moving sales items very carefully for the correct use by dates and any deterioration in the commodity.
- Refill appropriate containers with the relevant powders for the products being sold.
- Ensure as appropriate that cups, plates and napkins are available in the machines.

Note: At all times extreme care must be taken concerning the various aspects of hygiene and safety when foods and beverages are being served in this way.

2.9 LIGHTING AND COLOUR

Lighting

Modern designs tend towards a versatile system of lighting by which a food and beverage service area may have bright lighting at lunchtime and a more diffused form of lighting in the evening. It is also an advantage to be able to change the colour of the lights for special functions, cabarets etc. The foodservice operator must find a colour and lighting scheme that will attract and please as many people as possible. Basically restaurants may select from two main kinds of interior illumination: incandescent and fluorescent lighting.

Incandescent lighting is warmer in colour but less efficient to operate than fluorescent bulbs of the same wattage. It can be easily directed to specific spots such as a particular table or pointing. However, its warmth appeal can cause a colour problem. It may make surroundings cheerful and inviting, but the yellowish hue of its bulbs, especially when dimmed, makes meats and lettuce appear muddy in colour. Warmer bulbs such as pink light make red meats look natural but salads unappetising.

The main virtue of fluorescent lighting is its lower operating cost, but it is often criticised for giving a dull and lifeless illumination. Food may be made to look appealing by using blue-white light from fluorescent fixtures, but the blue-white glow may also detract from a warm romantic atmosphere.

A balance is usually needed for both warmth and good food appearance. Many experts recommend a lighting system made up of 70 per cent cool or blue-white fluorescent bulbs and 30 per cent incandescent. This will give mood and a pleasant and natural appearance for food.

The foodservice area needs more than proper décor lighting. Functional lighting is a must, giving proper illumination for chefs to prepare food, staff to serve it and customers to order and eat it. Functional lighting may amount to as much as 75 per cent of a restaurant's total lighting system. In the dining room two basic areas require functional lighting: the table and the room as a whole. The aim therefore is to mix the right blend of décor and functional lighting at the lowest possible cost.

Table lighting is most flattering to customers when it shines down from the ceiling. Incandescent ceiling lights serve the purpose well here. Care must be taken, however, to ensure that the bulbs used do not give off too bright a light as this will create too much contrast between dark and light spots. Clean and well-polished silver, glassware and crockery on a dining table, or a well-polished reflective tabletop in the lounge, will bounce light gently upwards, acting as a softener to overhead lights. Table top lighting can serve a similar purpose and includes, for example, candles, gaslights and electric lighting.

Functional lighting in the dining room must serve a number of purposes.

- Fixtures directing light onto ceilings and walls should indicate to customers the dimensions of the room, together with any special attractions, such as pictures and old oak beams. Low wattage incandescent bulbs are best suited for this purpose.

- The lighting should project a subdued atmosphere, with contrasts between bright and dark areas and tabletops capturing much of the light, while ceilings and upper walls remain dark.

- It may be necessary to feature special areas of a dining room, such as a buffet or self-service salad bar.

The food and beverage service area needs to have a good mix of décor and functional lighting. It is only the fast food areas that may successfully eliminate décor or mood lighting altogether. Brighter lights appear to subconsciously tell customers to eat more quickly and leave and is therefore the recommended way to illuminate for quick turnover and high volume throughput.

Colour scheme

There is a definite association between colour and food that must be considered. The following colour schemes are generally regarded as most acceptable: pink, peach, pale yellow, clear green, beige, blue and turquoise. These colours reflect the natural colours found in good and well-presented foodstuffs. The colour scheme should help to reflect the character of the restaurant. A well-designed colour scheme can easily be spoilt by a badly planned lighting system and therefore the two aspects should be considered together at the design stage.

The restaurant surroundings can contribute a great deal towards the price-quality relationship in the minds of potential customers. What may be suitable for a fast food operation would be entirely unsuitable for a restaurant operation catering for an executive market. Bright illumination may be found in bars with light colours on the walls, but food service areas are better with dimmer illumination and warmly coloured walls, as these give a more relaxed and welcoming atmosphere. Colour should also contribute to a feeling of cleanliness.

Just as colour and light play an important role, so table accessories need careful choice: slip cloths, serviettes and place mats all help to make the environment more attractive.

2.10 FURNITURE

Certain principles need to be borne in mind when planning food and beverage service areas to maximise the seating area. For example, when planning a cafeteria operation care should be taken to ensure that customers waiting for a meal from the various service points do not interrupt the flow of customers around the tables, or those going out through the main entrance. The seating arrangements will therefore depend on:

- the size and shape of the food service area
- the design of tables and chairs used
- the allowance made for gangways and clearing trolleys
- the type of establishment.

Furniture must be chosen according to the needs of the establishment. Examples of various dining arrangements are shown in Table 2.2.

Materials and finishes

By using different materials, designs and finishes of furniture and by their careful arrangement, often the atmosphere and appearance of the service area can be changed to suit different occasions.

Table 2.2 Dining arrangements (Based on a chart from Croner's Catering)

Type	Description of furniture
Loose random	Freestanding furniture positioned in no discernable pattern within a given service area
Loose module	Freestanding furniture positioned within a given service area to a pre-determined pattern, with or without the use of dividers to create smaller areas within the main area
Booth	Fixed seating (banquette), usually high backed, used to create secluded seating
High density	Furniture with minimum dimensions and usually fixed, positioned within a given service area to create maximum seating capacity
Module	Seating incorporates tables and chairs constructed as one and may be fixed to the floor
In situ	Customers served in areas not designed for service, e.g. aircraft and hospital beds
Bar and lounge areas	Customers served in areas not primarily designed for food and beverage service

Various types of wood and wood grain finishes are available, each suitable to blend with a particular décor. Wood is strong and rigid and resists wear and stains. It is the principal material used for chairs and tables in all food and beverage service areas with the exception of canteens, some staff dining rooms and cafeterias.

Although wood predominates, more metals (mainly aluminium and aluminium-plated steel or brass) are gradually being introduced into dining furniture. Aluminium is lightweight, hardwearing, has a variety of finishes, is easily cleaned and the costs are reasonable. Nowadays a wooden-topped table with a metal base may be found together with chairs with lightweight metal frames and plastic finishes for the seat and back.

Formica or plastic-coated tabletops may be found in many cafeterias or staff dining rooms. These are easily cleaned, hardwearing and eliminate the use of linen. The tabletops come in a variety of colours and designs suitable for all situations. Place mats may take the place of linen.

Plastics and fibreglass are now being used extensively to produce dining-room chairs. These materials are easily moulded into a single-piece seat and back to fit the body contours, the legs usually being made of metal. The advantages are that these are durable, easily cleaned, lightweight, may be stacked, are available in a large range of colours and designs and are relatively inexpensive. They are more frequently found in bars, lounges and staff dining rooms than in the first-class hotel or restaurant.

Chairs

Chairs come in an enormous range of designs, materials and colours to suit all situations and occasions. Because of the wide range of styles available, chairs vary in height and width, but as a guide, a chair seat is 46 cm (18 in) from the ground, the height from the ground to the top of the back is 1 m (39 in) and the depth from the front edge of the seat to the back of the chair is 46 cm (18 in).

General points to note when purchasing equipment are given in Section 2.1 (page 30). When purchasing chairs the main considerations should be size, height, shape and even the variety of seating required, for example, banquette (fixed bench seating), armchairs, straight-backed and padded chairs, to give the customer a choice. A leather or wool fabric is much better to sit on than PVC which tends to become uncomfortable around the back and seat.

Tables

Tables come in three main shapes: round, square and rectangular. An establishment may have a mixture of shapes to give variety, or tables of all one shape depending on the shape of the room and the style of service being offered. Square or rectangular tables will seat two or four people and two tables may be pushed together to seat larger parties, or extensions may be provided in order to cope with special parties, luncheons, dinners, weddings etc. By using these extensions correctly a variety of shapes may be obtained, allowing full use of the room and enabling the maximum number of covers in the minimum space. The tabletop may have a plastic foam back or green baize covering which is heat resistant and non-slip so the tablecloth will not slide about as it would on a polished wooden top table. This type of covering also deadens the sound of crockery and tableware being laid. As a guide tables may be approximately the following sizes:

Square

- 76 cm (2 ft 6 in) square to seat two people.
- 1 m (3 ft) square to seat four people.

Round

- 1 m (3 ft) in diameter to seat four people.
- 1.52 m (5 ft) in diameter to seat eight people.

Rectangular

- 137 cm × 76 cm (4 ft 6 in × 2 ft 6 in) to seat four people, extensions being added for larger parties.

Sideboards

The style and design of a sideboard (or workstation) varies from establishment to establishment and is dependent upon:

- the style of service and the food and beverages on offer
- the number of service staff working from one sideboard
- the number of tables to be served from one sideboard
- the amount of equipment it is expected to hold.

It is essential that the sideboard is of minimum size and portable so that it may be easily moved if necessary. If the sideboard is too large for its purpose it is taking up space which could be used to seat more customers. Some establishments use smaller fixed sideboards and also use 'tray jacks' (movable folding tray stands, see Figure 2.3) when serving and clearing.

The material used in the make-up of the sideboard should blend with the rest of the décor. The top of a sideboard should be of a heat resistant material that can be easily washed down. After service the sideboard is either completely emptied out or restocked for the next service. In some establishments the waiters are responsible for their own equipment on their station. After service they restock their sideboard and it is then locked. Where this system is carried out the sideboard also carries its own stock of linen. Thus, in this example a sideboard has everything necessary to equip a particular waiter's station or set of tables.

The actual lay-up of a sideboard depends firstly on its construction – the number of shelves and drawers for tableware etc. – and, secondly, on the type of menu and service offered. Therefore the lay-up in every establishment will vary, each being suited to its own needs and style of service and presentation. It is suggested, however, that in each particular establishment the sideboards be laid up in the same way. If this is done the staff get used to looking for a certain item in a certain place and this facilitates speedy service. Examples of the items that may be found in a sideboard are given on pages 194–5. These would be required if the service was a full silver service from a large table d'hôte menu running in conjunction with a limited à la carte menu. The items required would be adjusted according to the style of service.

2.11 LINEN

There are many qualities of linen in present day use, from the finest Irish linen and cotton to synthetic materials such as nylon and viscose. The type of linen used will depend on the class of establishment, type of clientele and cost involved, and the style of menu and service to be offered. The main items of linen normally to be found are shown below:

Tablecloths

- 137 cm × 137 cm (54 in × 54 in) to fit a table 76 cm (2 ft 6 in) square or a round table 1 m (3 ft) in diameter.

Fig 2.3. Example of a tray jack

Fig 2.4. Examples of sideboards (courtesy of Euroservice UK)

- 183 cm × 183 cm (72 in × 72 in) to fit a table 1 m (3 ft) square.
- 183 cm × 244 cm (72 in × 96 in) to fit rectangular shaped tables.
- 183 cm × 137 cm (72 in × 54 in) to fit rectangular shaped tables.

Slip cloths

- 1 m × 1 m (3 ft × 3 ft) used to cover a slightly soiled tablecloth.

Napkins (serviettes)

- 46–50 cm (18–20 in) square if linen.
- 36–42 cm (14–17 in) square if paper.

Buffet cloths

- 2 m × 4 m (6 ft × 12 ft) – this is the minimum size; longer cloths will be used for longer tables.

Waiters' cloths or service cloths

- Servers use these as protection against heat and to help to keep uniforms clean.

Tea and glass cloths

- These are used for drying items after washing; tea cloths should be used for crockery and glass cloths for glassware. The best are made of linen or cotton and are lint free.

Use and control of linen

Linen should be used only for its intended purpose in the restaurant and not for cleaning purposes, as this often results in permanent soiling which will render the item unusable in the future.

Linen should be stored on paper-lined shelves, the correct sizes together, and with the inverted fold facing outward, which facilitates counting and control. If the linen is not stored in a cupboard it should be covered to avoid dust settling on it.

The original stock of clean linen is issued upon receipt of a requisition form written in duplicate and signed by a responsible person from the service department. The top copy of the requisition form goes to the housekeeping department or linen room and the duplicate copy remains in the requisition book held in the food and beverage service area. A surplus linen stock is usually held in the food service area in case of emergency.

At the end of each service the dirty linen should be noted and sent to the housekeeping department to be exchanged for clean. Because of the high cost of laundering such linen, where a tablecloth is perhaps only a little grubby, a slip cloth would be placed over it for the succeeding service. This is not as expensive to re-launder as a tablecloth.

A range of disposable linen, including napkins, place mats and tablecloths, are available in varying colours and qualities. There are also now reversible tablecloths with a thin polythene sheet running through the centre that prevent any spillages from penetrating from one side to the other. Although the expense of such items may seem high, there are many advantages and comparable laundry charges may well be higher. For more information on disposables, see Section 2.15 Disposables, page 66.

2.12 CROCKERY

The crockery must blend in with the general décor of the establishment and also with the rest of the items on the table. An establishment generally uses one design and pattern of crockery, but when an establishment has a number of different service areas it is easier, from the control point of view, to have a different design in each service area. Nowadays manufacturers produce a range of patterns and styles and will guarantee a supply for a period of ten years in order to be able to replace breakages etc.

When purchasing crockery the general points previously identified in Section 2.1 (page 30) should be borne in mind. Other factors to consider here are as follows:

■ Every item of earthenware should have a complete cover of glaze to ensure a reasonable length of life.

■ Crockery should have a rolled edge to give added reinforcement at the edge. (One word of caution here is that hygiene is most important – chipped crockery can harbour germs.)

■ The pattern should be under rather than on top of the glaze. However, this demands additional glaze and firing. Patterns on top of the glaze will wear and discolour very quickly. Crockery with the pattern under the glaze is more expensive but its life will be longer.

■ Crockery must be dishwasher-proof.

Some manufacturers stamp the date, month and year on the base of the item. From this, the life of the crockery can be determined with some accuracy. Crockery that is produced as being suitable for the foodservice industry is often referred to as 'hotelware'. Manufacturers also tend to give trade names to their hotelware to indicate strength or durability. Some examples of these names are:

- Vitreous
- Vitresso
- Vitrock
- Ironstone

- Vitrex
- Vitrified
- Steelite.

Foodservice crockery

There are various classifications of foodservice crockery. Although referred to as crockery here (and throughout the book), all glazed tableware was traditionally referred to as china. Items include:

- flatware, for example, plates and saucers and serving flats
- cups and bowls, for example, tea and coffee cups, soup and sweet bowls and serving dishes
- hollow-ware, for example, pots and vases.

Types of crockery

Bone china

This very fine, hard china is expensive. Decorations are only found under the glaze. It can be made to thicker specifications, if requested, for hotel use. The price of bone china puts it out of reach of the majority of everyday caterers, and only a few of the top-class hotels and restaurants use it. Metalised bone china has been developed specially for the hospitality industry. It contains added metallic oxides to make it much stronger than bone china.

Hotel earthenware

Vitrified (or vitreous) earthenware is produced in the United Kingdom in vast quantities. It is the cheapest but least durable hotelware although it is much stronger than regular domestic earthenware. There is a standard range of designs and patterns in varying colours.

Domestic weight earthenware is lighter and thinner than hotel earthenware (or vitrified hotelware). Because of its short life, lack of strength and possible high breakage rate it is not regarded as suitable for commercial use.

Stoneware

This is a natural ceramic material traditionally made in the United Kingdom and fired at a very high temperature, about 120°C (284°F). It is shaped by traditional handcrafting techniques so there are a wide variety of shapes and finishes available, from matt to a high-gloss glaze. It is non-porous and extremely durable with high thermal and shock resistance. The price is slightly higher than earthenware due to its long-life guarantee.

Porcelain

This is of a different composition with a semi-translucent body, normally cream/grey, and has a high resistance to chipping.

Storage

Crockery should be stored on shelves in piles of approximately two dozen. Any higher may result in their toppling down or damage to plates at the bottom of the stack because of the weight bearing down on them. Crockery should be stored at a convenient height for placing on and removing from the shelves without fear of accidents occurring. If possible crockery should be kept covered to prevent dust and germs settling on it.

Crockery sizes

A wide range of crockery items are available and their exact sizes will vary according to the manufacturer and the design produced. As a guide, the sizes are as follows:

- side plate: 15 cm (6 in) diameter
- sweet plate: 18 cm (7 in) diameter
- fish plate: 20 cm (8 in) diameter
- soup plate: 20 cm (8 in) diameter
- joint plate: 25 cm (10 in) diameter
- sweet plate: 13 cm (5 in) diameter
- breakfast cup and saucer: 23–28 cl (8–10 fl oz)
- teacup and saucer: 18.93 cl (6⅔ fl oz)
- coffee cup and saucer (demi-tasse):   9.47 cl (3½ fl oz)
- teapot: 28.4 cl (½ pint)
                                                   56.8 cl (1 pint)
                                                   85.2 cl (1½ pint)
                                                   113.6 cl (2 pint)

Other items of crockery required include:

- consommé cup and saucer
- soup bowl/cup
- platter (oval plate)
- salad crescent
- egg cup
- butter dish
- ashtray

- hot water jug
- coffee pot
- milk jug
- cream jug
- hot milk jug
- sugar basin.

Although crockery has been the traditional medium for presenting and serving food, there is now an increasing trend to use contemporary styles of glassware instead. Figure 2.5 gives examples of both traditional crockery and also contemporary styled glassware that can be used as alternatives to crockery.

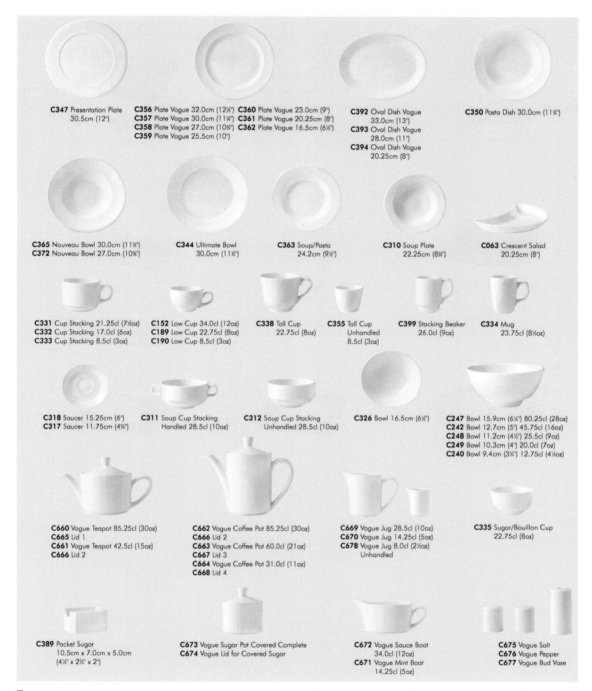

C347 Presentation Plate 30.5cm (12")

C356 Plate Vogue 32.0cm (12½")
C357 Plate Vogue 30.0cm (11¾")
C358 Plate Vogue 27.0cm (10⅝")
C359 Plate Vogue 25.5cm (10")

C360 Plate Vogue 23.0cm (9")
C361 Plate Vogue 20.25cm (8")
C362 Plate Vogue 16.5cm (6½")

C392 Oval Dish Vogue 33.0cm (13")
C393 Oval Dish Vogue 28.0cm (11")
C394 Oval Dish Vogue 20.25cm (8")

C350 Pasta Dish 30.0cm (11¾")

C365 Nouveau Bowl 30.0cm (11¾")
C372 Nouveau Bowl 27.0cm (10⅝")

C344 Ultimate Bowl 30.0cm (11¾")

C363 Soup/Pasta 24.2cm (9½")

C310 Soup Plate 22.25cm (8¾")

C063 Crescent Salad 20.25cm (8")

C331 Cup Stacking 21.25cl (7½oz)
C332 Cup Stacking 17.0cl (6oz)
C333 Cup Stacking 8.5cl (3oz)

C152 Low Cup 34.0cl (12oz)
C189 Low Cup 22.75cl (8oz)
C190 Low Cup 8.5cl (3oz)

C338 Tall Cup 22.75cl (8oz)

C355 Tall Cup Unhandled 8.5cl (3oz)

C399 Stacking Beaker 26.0cl (9oz)

C334 Mug 23.75cl (8½oz)

C318 Saucer 15.25cm (6")
C317 Saucer 11.75cm (4⅝")

C311 Soup Cup Stacking Handled 28.5cl (10oz)

C312 Soup Cup Stacking Unhandled 28.5cl (10oz)

C326 Bowl 16.5cm (6½")

C247 Bowl 15.9cm (6¼") 80.25cl (28oz)
C242 Bowl 12.7cm (5") 45.75cl (16oz)
C248 Bowl 11.2cm (4½") 25.5cl (9oz)
C249 Bowl 10.3cm (4") 20.0cl (7oz)
C240 Bowl 9.4cm (3¾") 12.75cl (4½oz)

C660 Vogue Teapot 85.25cl (30oz)
C665 Lid 1
C661 Vogue Teapot 42.5cl (15oz)
C666 Lid 2

C662 Vogue Coffee Pot 85.25cl (30oz)
C666 Lid 2
C663 Vogue Coffee Pot 60.0cl (21oz)
C667 Lid 3
C664 Vogue Coffee Pot 31.0cl (11oz)
C668 Lid 4

C669 Vogue Jug 28.5cl (10oz)
C670 Vogue Jug 14.25cl (5oz)
C678 Vogue Jug 8.0cl (2½oz) Unhandled

C335 Sugar/Bouillon Cup 22.75cl (8oz)

C389 Packet Sugar 10.5cm x 7.0cm x 5.0cm (4⅛" x 2¾" x 2")

C673 Vogue Sugar Pot Covered Complete
C674 Vogue Lid for Covered Sugar

C672 Vogue Sauce Boat 34.0cl (12oz)
C671 Vogue Mint Boat 14.25cl (5oz)

C675 Vogue Salt
C676 Vogue Pepper
C677 Vogue Bud Vase

Fig 2.5a. Selection of crockery – traditional style (Image courtesy of Steelite International)

6527B809
Cubol Dimple Large 505318
29.0cm x 29.0cm (11½" x 11½")

6527B810
Cubol Dish Dimple Large 505328
29.0cm x 29.0cm (11½" x 11½")

6527B750
Riven Blue Large 514102
29.0cm x 29.0cm (11½" x 11½")

6527B749
Riven Red Large 514101
29.0cm x 29.0cm (11½" x 11½")

6527B829
Riven White Large 514114
29.0cm x 29.0cm (11½" x 11½")

6527B752
Riven White Small 514014
15.0cm x 15.0cm (6" x 6")

6527B785
Bubbles Blue Large 518033
30.0cm x 20.0cm (12" x 8")

6527B787
Bubbles Blue Small 518133
23.0cm x 20.0cm (9" x 8")

6527B795
Bubbles Blue Round 520303
31.0cm (12½")

6527B601
Red Border Plate 507125R
25.0cm x 25.0cm (10" x 10")

6527B602
Blue Border Plate 507325B
25.0cm x 25.0cm (10" x 10")

6527B603
Rectangle Deep 512001
31.0cm x 13.0cm (12½" x 5")

6527B612
Double Square 512012
31.0cm x 31.0cm (12½" x 12½")

6527B574
Flower Candle Clear 610181

6527B585
Flower Candle Frosted 611181

Fig 2.5b. Selection of glassware as alternative to crockery – contemporary style (Image courtesy of Steelite International)

2.13 TABLEWARE (FLATWARE, CUTLERY AND HOLLOW-WARE)

'Tableware' is a term recognised as embracing all items of flatware, cutlery and hollow-ware and may be classified as follows:

- flatware in the catering trade denotes all forms of spoon and fork, as well as serving flats
- cutlery refers to knives and other cutting implements
- hollow-ware consists of any other item, apart from flatware and cutlery, for example, teapots, milk jugs, sugar basins, serving dishes.

Manufacturers produce varied patterns of flatware, hollow-ware and cutlery in a range of prices to suit all demands. There are also patterns of flatware and cutlery that are scaled down to three-quarters the normal size specifically for tray service.

Although traditionally the term 'flatware' included spoons and forks, and 'cutlery' referred to knives, the modern usage of these terms has changed. All spoons, forks and knives used as eating implements are now referred to as cutlery. The term 'cutlery' is therefore used throughout the rest of the book.

The majority of food service areas use either plated silverware or stainless steel. Once again, the points mentioned previously concerning purchasing should be borne in mind. In addition, when purchasing tableware it is important to consider:

- the type of menu and service offered
- the maximum and average seating capacity
- the peak demand period turnover
- the washing-up facilities and their turnover.

Fig 2.6. Examples of cutlery (left to right): side knife, fish fork, joint fork, sweet fork, sweet spoon, joint knife, fish knife, soup spoon, tea spoon, coffee spoon, serving (table) spoon

Silver

Manufacturers will often quote 20-, 25- or 30-year plate. This denotes the length of life a manufacturer may claim for their plate subject to fair or normal usage. The length of life of silver also depends upon the weight of silver deposited. There are three standard grades of silver plate – full standard plate, triple plate and quadruple plate.

Caterers in doubt about the quality of silver plated tableware and stainless steel should refer to British Standard 5577. The aim of the Standard is to ensure that details of component materials are provided and was first introduced in 1978.

In silver-plated tableware two grades have been specified:

1 Standard for general use.

2 Restaurant thicker grade for restaurant use and marked with an 'R'.

The minimum thickness of silver plating quoted should give a life of at least 20 years, depending on usage.

The hallmark on silver tells two things. The two symbols represent the standard of silver used and the Assay office responsible. The two letters are the maker's mark and the date letter.

Plain cutlery is more popular than patterned for the simple reason that it is cheaper and easier to keep clean. The best investment is knives with handles of hard soldered silver plate, nickel or good stainless steel. Handles are an important factor in cutlery. Plastic materials, however, are much cheaper and usually satisfactory.

Stainless steel

Stainless steel tableware is available in a variety of grades. The higher priced designs usually incorporate alloys of chromium (which makes the metal stainless) and nickel (which gives a fine grain and lustre). Good British flatware and cutlery is made of 18/8 stainless steel. This is 18 per cent chromium and 8 per cent nickel.

Stainless steel is finished by different degrees of polishing:

■ high polish finish

■ dull polish-finish

■ a light grey matt, non-reflective finish.

Stainless steel resists scratching far more than other metals and may therefore be said to be more hygienic. Although it does not tarnish it can stain. There are special cleaning products for stainless steel such as a commercial powder that is applied with a wet sponge or cloth and rubbed on the surface before being rinsed off. Such products can be used to keep stainless steel looking clean and polished.

Table 2.3 Items of specialist equipment and their use

Equipment	Use
1 Asparagus holder	Used to hold asparagus spears when eating
2 Sugar tongs	Required for cube sugar
3 Pastry slice	Sweet trolley – serving portions of gâteau
4 Oyster fork	Shellfish cocktail/oysters
5 Pastry fork	Afternoon tea
6 Corn-on-the-cob holders	One to pierce each end of the cob
7 Lobster pick	To extract the flesh from the claw
8 Butter knife	To serve butter portion
9 Sauce ladle	Service from sauce boat
10 Fruit knife and fork	Dessert – cover
11 Nutcrackers	Dessert – fruit basket
12 Grape scissors	To cut and hold a portion of grapes
13 Grapefruit spoon	Grapefruit halves
14 Ice-cream spoon	For all ice-cream dishes served in coupes
15 Sundae spoon	Ice-cream sweet in a tall glass
16 Snail tongs	Used to hold the snail shell
17 Snail dish	Dish is round with two ears, having six indentations to hold a portion (6) of snails
18 Snail fork	Used to extract the snail from its shell
19 Cheese knife	Cheese board
20 Stilton scoop	Service of Stilton cheese
21 Caviar knife	Part of the cover for caviar
22 Gourmet spoon	Sauce spoon for cover
23 Preserve spoon	Used with preserve/jam dish

Storage

Careful storage of cutlery is most important. Ideally, there should be boxes or drawers for each specific item, each box or drawer being lined with baize to prevent the items concerned sliding about and becoming scratched and marked. Other items of hollow-ware and flatware should be stored on shelves that are labelled to show where the different items go. They must be stored at a convenient height for placing on and removing from the shelves.

Theoretically all flatware, cutlery and hollow-ware should be stored in a room or cupboard that can be locked, since they constitute a large part of the capital of the restaurant. Cutlery may be stored in cutlery trolleys or trays, of which there are a number on the market to suit all purposes.

Fig 2.7. Specialised equipment as listed in Table 2.3

Specialist equipment

There is an almost unlimited range of flatware, cutlery and hollow-ware in use in the catering industry today. These items are those necessary to give efficient service of any form of meal at any time of the day. Everyone is familiar with the knife, fork, spoon, flats, vegetable dishes and lids, entrée dishes and lids, soup tureens, teapots, hot water jugs, sugar basins and so on that we see in every day use. Over and above these, however, there are a number of specialist items of equipment provided for use with specific dishes. Some of these more common items of specialist equipment are shown in Table 2.3, together with a brief note of the dishes that they may be used for.

2.14 GLASSWARE

Glassware contributes to the appearance of the table and the overall attraction of the service area. There are many standard patterns available to the caterer. Most manufacturers now supply hotel glassware in standard sizes for convenience of ordering, availability and quick delivery.

A good wine glass should be plain and clear so that the colour and brilliance of a wine can be clearly seen; it should have a stem for holding the wine glass so that the heat of one's hand does not affect the wine on tasting; there should be a slight incurving lip to help hold the

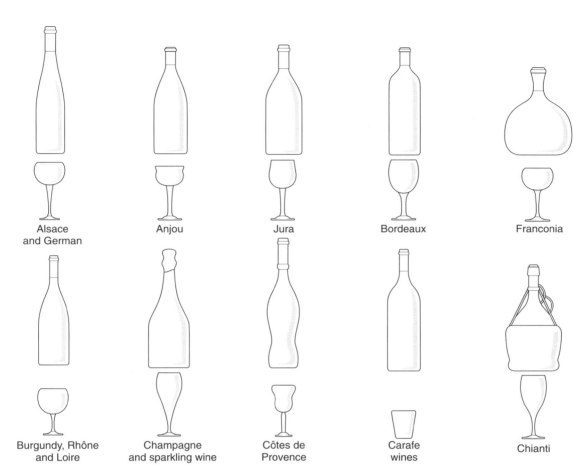

Fig 2.8. Glasses for wine

aroma and it should be large enough to hold the particular wine being tasted. Although standard goblets can be used for a range of wines there are various glass shapes that are traditionally associated with certain wines. Examples of these are shown in Figure 2.8.

Modern drinking glasses take many new forms and shapes, although all are primarily designed to meet the needs of the range of modern drinks being offered. Examples of drinking glasses and their use are shown in Figure 2.9.

Type and sizes of glassware

Glass is produced from sand (silicon dioxide), which is combined with other substances to produce particular characteristic properties. The mixture is heated to a very high temperature which forms a molten mass. This glass is either blown or moulded to different shapes and then allowed to cool and solidify. Examples of sizes for drinking glasses are shown in Table 2.4. The various types of glass used in the hospitality industry are outlined below.

Cocktail glasses: for cocktails generally and smaller: for Pink Lady and White Lady

The saucer: for Champagne cocktails and Daisies. Not really used much now

The tulip: all Champagne and sparkling wines and also for Buck's Fizz and the Grasshopper

The flute: for sparkling wines generally and also for Brandy Alexander and Kir Royale

Paris goblet: in various sizes and used for wines, waters and beers. Also used for Cobblers, Pina Colada and Green Blazer

Worthington: for bottled beers, soft drinks and for Pimms, Coolers and long drinks such as Fruit Cups

Rocks/Old Fashioned glass: also known as whisky glass, often used for any spirits and mixers. Also used for drinks such as Old Fashioned and Negroni

Highball/Collins glass: used for spirits and mixers and for Highballs, John Collins, Tom Collins, Mint Julep, Tequila Sunrise and Spritzers

Brandy balloon: small for brandies and for B & B and brandy and liqueur-based cocktails, for frappés and for liqueurs. Larger for long drinks such as Pimms

Sour glass: for spirits and mixers and for sours and as an alternative to rocks glass

Martini Cocktail glass: for Dry, Medium and Sweet Martinis and Manhattans but also used for other cocktails

Slim Jim: for spirits and mixers and for sours and as an alternative to highball glass

Copita (sherry): mainly for sherry but also used for sweet wines

Elgin: traditional glass used for sherry in single and double measure (Schooner) sizes. Also in smaller version used for liqueurs

Port or sherry (dock) glass: used for both ports and sherries and also for sweet wines

Lager/pilsner: different sizes used for bottled and draft lager beers

Beer (straight): traditional beer glass in different sizes for half and full measures of any beers and also beer based mixed drinks

Beer (dimple): traditional beer glass in different sizes for half and full measures of any beers and also beer based mixed drinks, including Black Velvet and also Pimms

Fig 2.9. Examples of drinking glasses and their uses

Soda lime glass

This glass contains sand, soda ash and limestone as the principal ingredients. It is used for day-to-day, relatively inexpensive glassware.

Lead crystal

This form of glass includes sand, red lead and potash, which produces a slightly softer glass of high brilliance. The surface can be left plain or can be cut to produce prismatic effects and sparkle.

Borosilicate glass

This is glass made with the addition of borax, which increases its hardness and heat resistance. This type of glass is used for flame ware.

Tempered and toughened glass

This glass has additional treatments to make it more resistant to the effects of heat. It is mostly used as ovenware glass, but the treatment is also used to produce glassware that needs to withstand heavy usage.

Glassware decoration

The surface of glassware may be decorated by:

- cutting to produce patterns or badging
- sand-blasting to texture the surface
- acid-etching to make patterns or to add badging
- engraving using grinding wheels to add patterns
- surface-printing with patterns from transfers.

As well as being used for drinking glasses, jugs, vases etc., contemporary glassware is now used as an alternative to crockery for the presentation and service of food (see Section 2.12 Crockery, page 54).

Storage and cleaning

Drinking glasses are normally stored in a glass pantry and should be placed in single rows on paper-lined shelves, upside down to prevent dust settling in them. Alternatively, thin plastic grid matting may be used as this allows for space between the glasses and the shelf top. Plastic coated wire racks made specifically for the purpose of stacking and storing glasses are yet another alternative. Such racks are also a convenient method of transporting glassware from one point to another, which cuts down on breakages. Tumblers and other straight-sided glassware should not be stacked inside one another as this may result in breakages and can cause accidents to staff.

Most day-to-day glassware used in the industry can be washed using dishwashers. However, for certain glassware this is not recommended. This includes lead crystal and other forms of

Table 2.4 Examples of sizes for glassware

Glass	Size
Wine goblets	14.20, 18.93, 22.72, 28 cl (5, 6⅔, 8, 10 fl oz)
Flûte/tulip	18–23 cl (6–8 fl oz)
Saucer champagne	18–23 cl (6–8 fl oz)
Cocktail glasses	4–7 cl (2–3 fl oz)
Sherry, Port	5 cl (1.75 fl oz)
Highball	23–28 cl (9–10 fl oz)
Lowball	18–23 cl (6–8 fl oz)
Worthington	28–34 cl (10–12 fl oz)
Lager glass	28–34 cl (10–12 fl oz)
Brandy balloon	23–28 cl (8–10 fl oz)
Liqueur glass	2.5 cl (0.88 fl oz)
Tumbler/Slim Jim	28.40 cl (½ pint)
Beer	25–50 cl (½–1 pint)

fine glassware, which should be hand washed. Over time most glassware will become milky in appearance, and the glassware will then need to be replaced. Finer glassware will become like this very quickly, unless hand washed.

Glass decanters should also be hand washed. They can also be cleaned using the proprietary denture cleaner Steredent. An alternative product contains small ball bearings that are put into the decanter with warm water and a small amount of detergent. The decanter is then moved so that the ball bearings move around inside it. Afterwards the decanter is emptied though a filter so as to reclaim the ball bearings for use another time. The decanter is then thoroughly rinsed in hot water. After cleaning and rinsing, decanters should be stood upside-down on special stands made for the purpose, or on wooden dowels set into a wooden base (to prevent the decanters falling over). This ensures that the decanters drain and dry fully, and that no lime scale deposits build up inside.

2.15 DISPOSABLES

There has been considerable growth in the use of disposables or 'throw-aways' as they are sometimes called and this is due to a number of factors:

- the need to reduce costs
- the difficulty of obtaining labour for washing up
- to reduce the high cost of laundering
- improved standards of hygiene
- breakage cost minimisation

- reduction in storage space required
- changes in cooking and storage technology, for example, cook/chill and cook/freeze
- the needs of transport caterers on trains, boats and planes
- the development of fast-food and take away operations
- increased customer acceptability.

Although many establishments use disposables to cut costs, the disposables must be attractive, presentable and acceptable to the client and also help to attract customers. The choice of which disposables to use may be determined by:

- necessity because of operational needs for:
  - outdoor catering
  - automatic vending
  - fast food
  - take aways
- cost considerations such as:
  - traditional forms of service equipment
  - cost of laundry
  - wash-up costs.

Types of disposables

The main varieties of disposables available are generally used as follows:

- storage and cooking purposes
- service of food and beverages, for example, plates, knives, forks, cups
- décor – napkins, tablecloths, slip cloths, banquet roll, place mats
- hygiene – wipes
- clothing, such as aprons, chef hats, gloves
- packaging – for marketing and presentation purposes.

The types of disposables that may be used to replace the normal restaurant linen would be serviettes, place mats, tray cloths, tablecloths, coasters etc. Today, most forms of disposables can be of various colours, patterned or have the house-style motto or crest reproduced on them. The vast range of colours available also allows for changes in a service area with different colours being used for each meal.

   Throwaway packs of knives, forks and spoons are more convenient and hygienic where the turnover of custom is very high over very short periods of time. This might apply in industrial canteens and transport catering. Throwaway packs eliminate delays at service points where the speed of washing-up is inadequate.

   A considerable advance in the range of disposables available has been the introduction of disposables whose approximation to crockery and tableware is very close. For instance, they may have a high quality, overall finish and a smooth, hard, white surface. The plates themselves are strong and rigid with no tendency to bend or buckle, and a plasticising ingredient ensures that they are greaseproof and moisture-proof, even against hot fat and gravy. Oval meal plates, snack trays and compartmentalised plates are all available to the caterer.

Hygiene

Using a conventional glass cloth for drying up increases the likelihood of cross infection. This risk is eliminated when disposables are used. A great variety of disposables are used in hospitals, where any form of cross infection must be avoided.

Advantages of disposables

- *Equipment and labour*: disposables reduce the need for washing-up equipment, staff and materials.
- *Hygiene*: usage improves the standard of hygiene in an establishment.
- *Time*: disposables may speed up service, for example, for fast food.
- *Properties*: disposables have good heat retention and insulation properties.
- *Marketing*: disposables can be used as a promotional aid.
- *Capital*: usage reduces the amount of capital investment.
- *Carriage*: they are easily transported.
- *Cost*: disposables may be cheaper than hiring conventional equipment.

Disadvantages of disposables

- *Acceptability*: customer acceptability may be poor.
- *Cost*: disposables can be more expensive than some conventional equipment.
- *Storage*: back-up quantities are required.
- *Supply*: there is heavy reliance on supply and delivery time.

Multiple food outlets at the Trafford Centre, Manchester (courtesy of FCSI, UK)

THE MENU, MENU KNOWLEDGE AND ACCOMPANIMENTS

CHAPTER 3

3.1 ORIGIN OF THE MENU

The menu is primarily a selling aid. Originally the bill of fare (English) or menu (French) was not presented at the table. Banquets generally consisted of two courses, each made up of a variety of dishes, anything from 10 to 40 in number. The first set of dishes were placed on the table before the diners entered – hence the word 'entrée' – and, when consumed, these dishes were removed or relieved by another set of dishes – hence the words 'relevés' or 'removes'.

The word 'menu' dates back to the eighteenth century, although the custom of making a list of the courses for a meal is much older. The bill of fare was originally very large and was placed at the end of the table for everyone to read. As time progressed the menu became smaller in size and a number of copies were made which allowed individuals to read their own copy. Modern menus first appeared duing the early nineteenth century, in the Parisian restaurants of the Palais-Royal.

3.2 CLASSIC MENU SEQUENCE

Over the last 100 or so years the sequence of the European menu has taken on a classical format or order of dishes. This format is used to lay out menus as well as to indicate the order of the various courses. Although the actual number of courses on a menu, and dishes within each course, will depend on the size and class of the establishment, most follow the classic sequence. This sequence is as follows:

1   *Hors-d'œuvres*

Traditionally this course consisted of a variety of compound salads (see page 94) but now includes items such as pâtés, mousses, fruit, charcuterie and smoked fish.

2   *Soups (potages)*

Includes all soups, both hot and cold.

3   *Egg dishes (oeufs)*

There are a great number of egg dishes beyond the usual omelettes, but these have not retained their popularity on modern menus.

4   *Pasta and rice (farineux)*

Includes all pasta and rice dishes. Can be referred to as farinaceous dishes.

5   *Fish (poisson)*

This course consists of fish dishes, both hot and cold. Fish dishes such as smoked salmon or seafood cocktails are mainly considered to be hors-d'œuvres dishes and therefore would be served earlier in a meal.

6   *Entrée*

Entrées are generally small, well garnished dishes which come from the kitchen ready for service. They are usually accompanied by a rich sauce or gravy. Potatoes and vegetables are not usually served with this course if it is to be followed by a main course. If this is the main course then it is usual for potatoes and vegetables to also be offered. Examples of this type of dish are tournedos, noisettes, sweetbreads, garnished cutlets or filled vol-au-vent cases.

7   *Sorbet*

Traditionally sorbets (sometimes now called granites) were served to give a pause within a meal, allowing the palate to be refreshed. They are lightly frozen water ices, often based on un-sweetened fruit juice, and may be served with a spirit, liqueur or even Champagne poured over. Russian cigarettes also used to be offered at this stage of a meal.

8 *Relevé*

This refers to main roasts or other larger joints of meat, which would be served together with potatoes and vegetables.

9 *Roast (rôti)*

This term traditionally refers to roasted game or poultry dishes.

10 *Vegetables (légumes)*

Apart from vegetables served with the Relevé or Roast courses, certain vegetables (e.g. asparagus and artichokes) may be served as a separate course, although these types of dishes are now more commonly served as starters.

11 *Salad (salade)*

Often refers to a small plate of salad that is taken after a main course (or courses) and is quite often simply a green salad and dressing.

12 *Cold Buffet (buffet froid)*

This course includes a variety of cold meats and fish, cheese and egg items together with a range of salads and dressings.

13 *Cheese (fromage)*

Includes the range of cheeses and various accompaniments, including biscuits, breads, celery, grapes and apples. This course can also refer to cheese-based dishes such as soufflés.

14 *Sweets (entremets)*

Refers to both hot and cold puddings.

15 *Savoury (savoureux)*

Sometimes simple savouries, such as Welsh Rarebit or other items on toast, or in pastry, or savoury soufflés, may be served at this stage.

16 *Fruit (dessert)*

Fresh fruit, nuts and sometimes candied fruits.

17 *Beverages*

Traditionally this referred to coffee but nowadays includes a much wider range of beverages being generally available, including tea, tisanes, chocolate and proprietary beverages. Although listed here to indicate the sequence for meals, beverages are not counted as a course as such and therefore should not be included when the number of courses of a meal are stated. Thus if a meal is stated as having four courses, this means that there are four food courses and that the beverages are in addition to these.

The classic menu sequence outlined above is based on a logical process of taste sensations. This classic sequence also provides the guide for the compilation of both à la carte and table d'hôte menus (see below for definitions), as is evident in many examples of modern European menus. However, a number of courses are often now grouped together. At its most simple this might comprise:

■ starters – courses 1 to 4

■ main courses – courses 5, 6 and 8 to 12

■ afters – courses 13 to 16

■ beverages.

This sequence is also used as a guide for the compilation and determination of the order of courses for function and special party menus.

Although this sequence shows the cheese course after the main course and before the sweet course, it was common in Britain for the sweet to be offered before the cheese course: in the UK either sequence may still be found.

Note: The modern European classic menu sequence outlined here is derived from traditional European (mainly Franco-Russian, Swiss and English) cuisine and service influences. The menu structure and menu sequence can change considerably within the various world cuisines. Menu terms also vary, for instance in the USA a main course is commonly called an entrée and sweets are commonly called dessert. The term dessert is also now becoming more commonly used to denote sweets generally.

3.3 CLASSES OF MENU

Menus may be divided into two classes, traditionally called à la carte (from the card) and table d'hôte (table of the host). The key difference between these two is that the à la carte menu has dishes separately priced, whereas the table d'hôte menu has an inclusive price either for the whole meal or for a specified number of courses, for example any two or any four courses. There are, however, usually choices within each course.

Sometimes the term 'menu du jour' is used instead of the term 'table d'hôte menu'. Another menu term used is 'carte du jour' (literally 'card of the day'), or 'menu of the day', which is usually a fixed meal with one or more courses for a set price. A 'prix fixe' (fixed price) menu is similar. A 'tasting menu' ('menu degustation') is a set meal with a range of courses (often between 6 and 10). These tasting menus are offered in restaurants where the chef provides a sample of the range of dishes available on the main menu. These tasting menus can also be offered with a flight (selection) of wines (sometimes this can be a different wine for each course). For all classes of menu the price of the meal may also include wine or other drinks.

The table d'hôte menu

The key characteristics of the table d'hôte menu are:

- the menu has a fixed number of courses
- there is a limited choice within each course
- the selling price is fixed
- the food is usually available at a set time.

Restaurant area with banquette seating on right (courtesy of Dunk Ink)

Winter Menu

To reflect upon the history of The Ritz, John Williams, Executive Chef is pleased to present his Winter Menu.

Drawing inspiration from classic and traditional dishes of the last century here in our Restaurant and developing his own light, fresh, "Palace style cooking".

The menu changes seasonally and is composed of the "Best of British".

Our philosophy is to retain the natural aroma and taste of the best ingredients available.

Thursday 6ᵗʰ October 2005

£35

Tomato gazpacho with marinated prawns and avocado cream

Artichoke mousse with vegetable bouillon and white radish

Cannelloni of scallop with ginger veloute

Roast monkfish with foie gras and red wine jus

Poached Bresse chicken with a blanquette of root vegetables and morels

Confit of duck with foie gras veloute and braised cabbage

Fondant of strawberry with Lychee sorbet

Almond Dacquoise and honey roasted figs with Liquorice ice cream

Citrus chilled parfait with mixed berry sorbet

Coffee and Friandises

Fig 3.1. Example of a table d'hôte menu (courtesy of The Ritz Hotel, London)

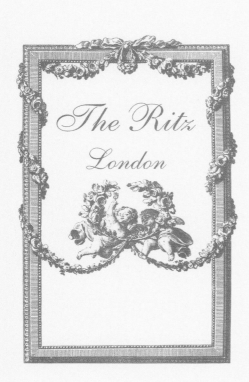

First Courses

Mosaique of game with redcurrant preserve
and soused vegetables
£19

Ballotine of foie gras en gelee
with pickled girolles and cured duck
£28

V Ravioli of spinach with quail egg,
truffle cream, and sage scented jus
£16

V Cappuccino of Jerusalem artichoke
with stilton and celery tortellini
£12

Saute of sea scallops with confit potatoes and chorizo salad
£24

Roasted cep tart with artichoke bavarois,
preserved lemon dressing
£18

Confit of salmon with crab, avocado mousse
and chilled tomato consomme
£21

Saute of dublin bay prawns with braised pork belly
and comice pear puree
£24

Stuffed pigs trotter Marie Antoinette
£19

Warm salad of lobster with sweet pepper
and olive oil emulsion
£24

Half a dozen native oysters
£23

V Denotes Vegetarian Dish
Prices include Value Added Tax and Service

Fig 3.2. Example of an à la carte menu (courtesy of The Ritz Hotel, London)

Main Courses

Red wine poached fillet of turbot with cod brandade
and horseradish jus
£41

Roasted seabass with caramelised endive
and stuffed baby squid, olive oil emulsion
£35

Butter poached lobster
with parsnip paillette and braised oxtail
£49

Braised fillets of sole with lobster jus, red wine and clam vinaigrette
£38

Civet of rabbit shoulder with black olives,
roasted loin with mustard veloute
£34

Roasted stuffed quail with root vegetables,
ginger and lime sauce
£28

Roast loin of lamb with a fricasse of sweetbread and rosemary jus
£35

Rotisserie of mallard duck with red cabbage,
foie gras and peach pastilla, sauce bigarade
£32

Fillet of beef with parsley cream, Alsace bacon
and snails with hermitage jus
£35

Roasted partridge with chestnuts and grapes,
cep and lemon verbena jus
£34

V Fricasse of autumn vegetables, mousseline of celeriac
and herb gnocchi
£23

 Menu items in **bold print** indicate Organic and are
certified to Soil Association standards for
organic food and farming

Prices include Value Added Tax and Service

Dishes Always Available

Beluga caviar £185

Oak smoked Scottish organic salmon **£23**

Cesar Ritz Salad £17

Fillet of Aberdeen Angus £33

Grilled organic sirloin steak **£35**

Roast rack of organic Welsh lamb **£36**

Grilled whole Dover sole or meuniere £39

Grilled turbot £43

Ritz mixed grill £45

Fillet of beef Wellington £78 (2 persons)

Menu Sonata

*A Tasting selection of the Ritz specialities consisting of five courses
for the whole table, incorporating dishes that are delicately flavoured
with herbs and spices*
£75

Desserts and Savouries

*A separate menu will be presented.
Please place your order at the beginning of the meal for Souffles and Crepes Suzettes.*

Fig 3.2. Example of an à la carte menu, continued

Starters

Asparagus Soup with a Chive Crème Fraiche	£5.25
Gravadlax, Cured Scottish Smoked Salmon served with a Sweet Mustard Dressing	£7.50
Cajun style Calamari accompanied with a Garlic & Lemon Mayonnaise	£6.25
King Prawn and Avocado Salad	£7.50
Sweet Galia Melon, Prosciutto Ham and Balsamic Figs	£6.50
Wild Mushroom Bruschetta topped With a Camembert Fondu	£6.50
Honey & Mustard Baked Back Ribs Served with a Watercress Salad	£5.95
Classic Caesar Salad	£6.25
Smoked Haddock & Crab Risotto Flavoured with Lemon and Dill	£6.95

Fish Dishes

Traditional Cod in a Crispy Brown Ale Batter	£11.50
Served with Homemade Chips and Garden Peas Monkfish & Salmon Kebab served with Braised Lemon rice	£12.50
Warm Salad of Red Snapper, Chorizo Sausage and Sauté Potatoes	£13.95
Whole Baked Sardines served with a Fennel, Shallot and Oregano Dressing	£10.95
Loch Fyne Mussels cooked with Shallots, Garlic, Parsley & White Wine served into a Large Bowl With Fries and Mayonnaise on the side	£11.50

Sweets

Sticky Toffee Pudding in a Caramel Sauce	£6.25
White Chocolate & Champagne Torte	£6.25
Iced Strawberry Parfait	£6.25
Vanilla Crème Brulee	£6.25
Chilled Lemon Cheesecake	£6.25
Chef's Cheese Plate, Biscuits, Grapes & Celery	£6.25

Mains

10Oz Aberdeen Angus Rump or 8Oz Sirloin Steak Cooked to your liking served with Béarnaise or Peppercorn Sauce & Chunky Chips	£16.50
Pan Fried Chicken Breast Served on top of a Corn Mash With a Smoked Bacon and Parmesan Crust	£12.50
Warm Duck Breast Salad Covered in Plum Jus set on a bed of Oriental Salad	£14.95
Goldie's Mixed Grill 5Oz Rump Steak, Lamb Cutlet, Toulouse Sausage, Black Pudding and hand cut Fries	£16.95
Honey Glazed Pork Fillet Served with a Scallion and Parsley Mash	£12.95
Spaghetti Arabbiata Topped with a Herb Ricotta Cheese	£10.50
Baked Aubergine, Cherry Tomato & Mozzarella Tart served with a Balsamic and Basil Reduction	£10.95

Sides

Fries with Garlic Mayonnaise (optional)
Panache of Seasonal Vegetables
Buttered Baby New Potatoes
Mixed House Salad
Garlic Ciabatta
Wilted Spinach
Caesar Salad   All £2.75

For those with special dietary requirements or allergies who may wish to know the ingredients within any dish, please consult your server.

Coffees

Cappuccino	£2.35
Americano	£2.35
Caffe Latte	£2.35
Espresso	£2.25
Mocha	£2.35
Regular & Speciality Teas	£2.25

COPTHORNE
HOTEL
BIRMINGHAM

Fig 3.3. Example of a brasserie style menu (Courtesy of the Copthorne Hotel, Birmingham)

The à la carte menu

The key characteristics of the à la carte menu are:

- the choice is generally more extensive
- each dish is priced separately
- there may be longer waiting times as some dishes are cooked or finished to order.

Brasserie, coffee shop and popular catering menus

These menus may be regarded as limited forms of à la carte menus, with all of the dishes listed and priced separately. This allows customers to have a snack with a beverage, a full meal or just a beverage.

3.4 INFLUENCES ON THE MENU

Modern day menus are the result of a combination of a number of factors. Menu content, traditionally based on classic cuisine, is continually being influenced by food trends, fads and fashions. In the main, customer demand is being affected by a greater understanding of:

- the relationship between health and eating
- special diets
- cultural and religious influences
- vegetarianism.

Because of these influences there is now a greater emphasis on offering alternatives such as low fat milks (for example, skimmed or semi-skimmed), non-dairy creamers for beverages, alternatives to sugar such as sweeteners, sorbets alongside ice creams and polyunsaturated fat and non-animal fats as alternatives to butter. These influences have also affected cooking ingredients and methods, with the development of lower fat dishes, lighter cuisine, and attractive and decent alternatives for non-meat eaters with greater use of animal protein substitutes such as Quorn and tofu.

Health and eating

The key issue in the relationship between health and eating is eating a healthy diet. This means eating a balanced diet rather than viewing individual foods as more or less healthy. Customers are increasingly looking for the availability of choices that will enable them to achieve a balanced diet. Customers are also requiring more specific information on methods of cooking used, for example, low fat or low salt methods. General consensus suggests that the regular diet should be made up of at least one third based on a range of bread, cereals, rice and potatoes, one third based on a variety of fruit and vegetables, and the remainder based on dairy foods, including low fat milk, low fat meats and fish and small amounts of fatty and sugary food.

Special diets

There are a variety of medical conditions, including allergies, which are more common than was previously understood. Customers may therefore require a special diet for medical reasons (including the prevention of allergic reactions). Such customers will need to know about the ingredients used in a dish as eating certain things may make them very ill and at worst could be fatal. Although such customers will usually know what they can and can't eat, it is important that when asked, a server is able to accurately describe the dishes so that the customer can make the appropriate choice. The server should *never* guess and if in doubt, should seek further information.

Special diets include:

Allergies	Food items that are known to cause allergies include the gluten in wheat, rye and barley (known as coeliac), peanuts and their derivatives, sesame seeds and other nuts such as cashew, pecan, brazil and walnuts as well as milk, fish, shellfish and eggs.
Diabetic	This refers to the inability of the body to control the level of insulin within the blood. An appropriate diet may include foods listed in the low cholesterol section below and the avoidance of dishes with a high sugar content.
Low cholesterol	Diets will include polyunsaturated fats and may include limited quantities of animal fats. Other items eaten may include lean poached or grilled meats and fish, fruit and vegetables and low fat milk, cheese and yoghurt.
Low sodium/salt	This requires a reduction of sodium or salt consumed. Diets will include low sodium/salt foods and cooking with very limited or no salt.

Cultural and religious dietary influences

Various faiths have differing requirements with regard to the dishes/ingredients that may be consumed, and these requirements often also cover preparation methods, cooking procedures and the equipment used. A summary is given below:

Hindus	Do not eat beef and rarely pork. In addition, some Hindus will not eat any other meats, fish or eggs. Diets may include cheese, milk and vegetarian dishes.
Jews	Only 'clean' (kosher) animals may be consumed. Jews do not eat pork or pork products, shellfish or animal fats and gelatine from beasts considered to be unclean or not slaughtered according to the prescribed manner. There are restrictions placed on methods of preparation and cookery. The preparation and eating of meat and dairy products at the same meal is not allowed.
Muslims	Will not eat meat, offal or animal fat unless it is halal (i.e. lawful, as required under Islamic Dietary Law) meat. Will not consume alcohol, even when used in cooking.
Sikhs	Do not eat beef or pork. Some will keep to a vegetarian diet. Others may eat fish, mutton, cheese and eggs. Sikhs will not eat halal meat.
Rastafarians	Will not eat any processed foods, pork or fish without fins (e.g. eels). Will not consume tea, coffee or alcohol.
Roman Catholics	Few restrictions on diet. Usually will not eat meats on Ash Wednesday or Good Friday. Some keep with the past requirement for no meat to be eaten on Fridays. Fish and dairy products may be eaten instead.

Vegetarianism

Vegetarianism may derive from cultural, religious, moral or physiological considerations. It is therefore important that food descriptions are accurate. The various forms of vegetarianism may be summarised as:

Vegetarians: semi	Will not eat red meats, or all meats other than poultry, or all meats. Diets will include fish and may include dairy produce and other animal products.
Vegetarians: lacto-ovo	Will not eat meat, fish or poultry but may eat milk, milk products and eggs.
Vegetarians: lacto	Will not eat meat, fish, poultry and eggs but may eat milk and milk products.
Vegans	Will not eat any foods of animal origin. Diets will mainly consist of vegetables, vegetable oils, cereals, nuts, fruits and seeds.
Fruitarians	This is a more restricted form of vegetarianism. Excluded are all foods of animal origin together with pulses and cereals. Diets may include mainly raw and dried fruit, nuts, honey and olive oil.

3.5 MENU AND SERVICE KNOWLEDGE

Knowledge about the product is at the core of successful food and beverage service. This knowledge enables the server to advise the customer of the content of dishes, the methods used in making the dishes and also ensures that the customer is provided with an appropriate service lay-up and the correct accompaniments. This section provides information on a variety of individual food items used in food service and this is followed in Sections 3.6 to 3.17 by information on the lay-ups and accompaniments for a selection of menu items by course. Additional information is contained in Annex A: Foods in Season (page 439) and Annex B: Glossary of Cuisine and Service Terms (page 444).

There are a number of dishes where traditional accompaniments are normally served. Additionally there are also traditions indicating the appropriate lay-up or cover for certain dishes. The sections that follow contain guides to these lay-ups and accompaniments. However, these guides are not intended to be prescriptive, as changes are constantly taking place and new accompaniments being tried. Also, the desire for healthier eating has led to a number of changes, for example, alternatives to butter such as Flora are often provided and frequently bread is not buttered in advance, thereby allowing the customer to choose his or her requirements. In addition the availability of lower fat milks, non-dairy creamers and non-sugar sweeteners is now standard.

For the lay-up the most important consideration is to aid eating. The use of fish knives and forks, for instance, is becoming less fashionable (the original reason for these Victorian items was as much to do with people wanting to show that their silver was new rather than inherited as it was to do with keeping these items separate from other items). Small (demi-tasse) coffee cups are now seen less often in restaurants (although these cups are now used for espresso coffee).

Using underplates (or liners)

The use of underplates varies. Underplates (liners) are used for four main purposes:

- to improve presentation on the table
- to make carrying of soup plates, bowls and other bowl-shaped dishes easier
- to isolate the hand from hot dishes
- to allow cutlery to be carried along with the item.

The use of doilies, dish papers or napkins on underplates can also improve presentation, reduce noise and help to prevent the dish being carried slipping on the underplate. As a general guide it is worth considering the use of underplates wherever a food item is being served in a cup or bowl-shaped dish. This also applies to vegetable and entrée dishes.

A note on sauces

Although there appear to be a wide variety of sauces, they are almost always variations on the same base sauces. These are:

Fond brun	Basic brown meat sauce.
Velouté	White sauce using fish, meat or vegetable stock.
Allemande	A velouté thickened with cream and egg yolks.
Béchamel	Savoury white sauce made with milk.
Tomato sauce	Made with fresh, tinned or puréed tomatoes.
Mayonnaise	Cold sauce made from egg yolks, oil, vinegar, salt, pepper and mustard.
Hollandaise	Hot sauce made from melted butter, egg yolks, shallots and vinegar.
Vinaigrette	Cold sauce made from mixing oil, vinegar and a selection of seasonings.

These sauces provide the base for other sauces. By adding a variety of different ingredients, for example adding cheese to a béchamel sauce to create a Mornay sauce, a wide range of sauces can be created.

Food items used as accompaniments

Accompaniments that are offered with certain dishes are mainly to assist in improving the flavour or to counteract richness. Depending on the nature, style and the extent of the menu on offer, there will be a variety of food items available which support the service of a range of dishes. Some of these items have specific use for particular dishes and others are used generally across a number of dishes. Examples of a variety of these items and their use is given in Table 3.1 below.

Table 3.1 Examples of food items used in food service

Item	Description	Use
Aïoli/ailloli	Garlic mayonnaise	Cold fish dishes and as a salad dip, e.g. for crudities
Apple sauce	Purée of cooking apples, slightly sweetened, served hot but more usually cold	Roast pork, roast duck and roast goose
Balsamic vinegar	Aromatic vinegar, acid product made from sweet grape wine, aged in oak	Dressings
Cayenne	Hot, red pepper (actually a species of powdered capsicum)	Oysters, smoked salmon
Chilli sauce	Hot sauce, mostly Chinese made	With Chinese-style foods
Chilli vinegar	Vinegar flavoured with chillies	Oysters
Chives	Herb (fresh chopped)	Salad garnish and for the surface of chilled soups, e.g. Vichyssoise
Chutney	Generic name for Indian sauces. Common varieties are sweet mango or hot mango, also Piccalilli and others such as the proprietary Branston Pickle	Indian chutneys for Tandoori and other Indian dishes. Other chutneys for cold meats, with cheeses and Ploughman's Lunch
Cider vinegar	Acid product made from cider	Can be used in salad dressings. Seen by some as a product for the health conscious
Cocktail sauces	Manufactured sauces of mayonnaise with added flavourings, e.g. tomato	Seafood cocktails
Cocktail gherkins	Small gherkins	Appetisers or garnish for charcuterie
Cocktail onions	Small, pearl onions	Appetisers or garnish for charcuterie
Corn oil	Light-flavoured oil made from corn	Dressings
Cranberry sauce	Sauce made from cranberries, usually available as a proprietary sauce. Can be served hot or cold	Roast turkey
Croûtons	Small cubes of fried or toasted bread	Garnish for soups and also used in some salad dishes, e.g. Caesar salad

Table 3.1 continued

Item	Description	Use
Cucumbers, pickled	Pickled cucumbers	For meats, salad dishes, charcuterie and cheese
Cumberland sauce	Sweet-and-sour sauce including, orange and lemon juice and zest, redcurrant jelly and port. Can be kitchen made or proprietary bottled	Game dishes and for charcuterie
Dill pickle	Pickled gherkins or cucumbers flavoured with dill	Meats, salads dishes, charcuterie and cheese
French dressing	Dressing made from oil and usually wine vinegar or lemon juice, with seasoning. Mustards and herbs may be added	Salads
Gherkins	Small pickled cucumbers	Charcuterie
Ginger	Spicy root used in many forms. Ground ginger is most common in restaurants	Melon
Gros sel	Literally 'fat salt', not finely ground. Also called rock salt	Boiled beef but also widely used in table grinders
Groundnut oil	Bland oil made from groundnuts	Dressings
Horseradish sauce	Hot-tasting sauce made from horseradish root, usually available as proprietary sauce, often needs creaming down	Roast beef and Chicken Maryland and also for cold smoked fish dishes when creamed down
HP Sauce	Brown proprietary, spicy, vinegar-based sauce	Cold meats and other dishes
Indian pickles	Unsweetened hot pickles, featuring limes, mango, brinjals etc.	Accompaniment for Indian (and other) savoury dishes
Kasundi	Hot Indian pickle featuring chopped mango	Accompaniment for Indian (and other) savoury dishes
Ketchup, mushroom	Old-style English proprietary sauce now seldom seen. Chinese mushroom sauce is substituted	Flavouring in lamp cookery and for other dishes
Ketchup, tomato	Sauce of tomato pulp, vinegar and sweetening. Usually available as a proprietary sauce	Grills, fish, burgers

Table 3.1 continued

Item	Description	Use
Lemon	Citrus fruit (slices, segments or halves)	Infinite variety of uses, especially smoked fish, fried fish and a range of drinks including tea
Lime	Citrus fruit (slices, segments or halves)	Similar to lemon above
Mayonnaise	Made from combination of oil and egg yolks, flavoured with vinegar, herbs and seasoning	Dressing for poached fish and sauce for salads
Malt vinegar	Acid product of brewed malted barley	Dressings and traditionally (in UK) for chips
Mint sauce	Vinegar-based sauce with chopped mint and sweetening. Proprietary versions usually used	Roast lamb
Mint jelly	Sweetish jelly made with mint. Proprietary versions often used	Roast lamb, as an alternative to mint sauce. Also offered with roast mutton
Mixed pickles	Assortment of vegetables pickled in vinegar	Cold meats, charcuterie
Mustard, English	Generally the hottest. Available as powder for making up or as proprietary bottled, sometimes with other ingredients such as whole seeds	Roast beef, boiled beef, grills, cold meats, pâtés and as ingredient in dressings, e.g. vinaigrette
Mustard, other	Wide variety including French, au poivre, vert, Bordeaux, Meaux, Dijon, Douce, German (senf)	Cold meats, grills, dressings
Mustard sauce	Warm sauce, generally kitchen made, but also available as proprietary sauce	Traditionally grilled herring but is used for other meat and fish dishes
Olive oil	Oil made from olive pressings (cholesterol free)	Dressings
Olives	Black or green fruit lightly pickled in brine	Appetisers but also garnish for food and drinks, or chopped as flavouring
Oil (general)	Many varieties, usually low in unsaturated fats	Dressings and increasingly for cooking

Table 3.1 continued

Item	Description	Use
Onions – pickled	Small onions pickled in malt vinegar (brown) or white vinegar (silverskin)	Cold meats, Ploughman's Lunch
Oriental vinegars	Several varieties	Give character to dressings and food dishes
Paprika	Powdered, mild, red capsicum	Garnish on and in seafood cocktails
Parsley	Chopped or sprig	Garnish on wide variety of dishes. Sometimes deep fried with fried fish
Parmesan	Italian hard cheese (grated or shredded)	Used in soups, e.g. minestrone and for pasta dishes
Pepper	Ground white pepper	Traditional form of pepper in table shaker
Peppercorns	Green are usually pickled in brine and soft	In food dishes
	White and black	Black used for the table in pepper mills but sometimes mixed
Piccalilli	Mixed pickle in thickened, spiced sauce (predominantly turmeric and sugar)	Cold meats, Ploughman's Lunch, buffet, snacks
Piri-piri	Hot chilli sauce of Portuguese/African origin	Prawns, crayfish, chicken
Redcurrant jelly	Proprietary sauce	Traditionally offered with hare. Also traditionally offered with roast mutton but now also commonly offered with roast lamb
Rouille	Provençale sauce made from pounded chillies, garlic and breadcrumbs (or cooked potatoes) blended with olive oil and fish stock	Used as accompaniment to boiled fish and fish soups such as bouillabaisse. If served with chicken bouillabaisse then chicken stock is used
Salt, refined	Ground table salt	Traditionally used as salt in table cellar or shakers
Sea salt	Salt derived from evaporated sea water	Seasoning, especially with boiled beef and used in table grinders

Table 3.1 continued

Item	Description	Use
Soy sauce	Clear, dark brown sauce, usually Chinese, made from soy beans	Chinese and sometimes other dishes
Soya oil	Oil made from crushed soya bean	Dressings
Sunflower oil	Light textured and flavoured oil from sunflower seeds	Dressings
Tabasco sauce	Hot, spicy, pepper proprietary sauce	Oysters, clams, other seafood and in other dishes
Tartare sauce	Mayonnaise-based sauce with addition of chopped gherkins, capers and lemon juice	All deep fried fish
Vinaigrette	Combination of oil and vinegar or lemon juice with seasoning. May also include mustards and herbs	Dressings
Walnuts, pickled	Whole pickled walnuts	Cold meats and some savouries
Wine vinegar	Acid product of wine, red or white	Dressings
Worcestershire sauce	Maceration of blend of spices and fruit in vinegar. Often known by the maker's brand name 'Lea and Perrins'	Tomato juice, Irish stew, Scotch broth, seafood cocktails and in dressings. Also used as a flavouring in a variety of other dishes

3.6 HORS-D'OEUVRE AND OTHER APPETISERS

Hors-d'oeuvre

Traditionally hors-d'oeuvres were a selection of salads, fish and meats. The selection was served onto a cold fish plate and the cover was a fish knife and fork. The cover nowadays is more likely to be dictated by the type of food being served and its presentation. Oil and vinegar were also traditionally offered but this has become less common because such foods are usually already well dressed. Buttered brown bread is also offered less often, thereby allowing the customer a choice of breads and also butter or alternatives.

Service can be a pre-plated selection or offered as a selection from individual ravier dishes, from a tray, guéridon or from the traditional hors-d'oeuvre trolley, although this trolley is seldom seen now.

Common hors-d'oeuvre items include:

Salads	Plain or compound. Examples of plain salads include fish and meat salads, cucumber salad, tomato salad, potato salad, beetroot salad, red cabbage and cauliflower. Compound salads include, for example, Russian (mixed vegetables in mayonnaise); Andalouse (celery, onions, peppers, tomatoes, rice and vinaigrette); Italienne (vegetable salad, cubes of salami, anchovy fillets and mayonnaise), and Parisienne (slices of crayfish, truffles, Russian salad and bound with mayonnaise and aspic).
Fish	May include items such as anchovies, herring (fresh or marinated), lobster, mackerel (marinated, smoked or fresh), smoked eel (filleted or sliced) and prawns (plain, in cocktail sauce or in a mousse).
Meats	Includes items such as pâtés, ham (raw, boiled or smoked) and salamis of all varieties.
Canapés	These are slices of bread with the crusts removed, cut into a variety of shapes, then toasted or fried in oil or butter and garnished. Garnishes can include smoked salmon, foie gras, prawns, cheese, asparagus tips, tomato, egg, capers, gherkins, salami and other various meats.
Eggs	These can be poached, presented in aspic or mayonnaise, or hard-boiled, cut in two and garnished or stuffed with various fillings, which include the yolk.

Other appetisers

Other appetisers include:

Asparagus (Asperges)	Fresh asparagus can be eaten hot with, for example, melted butter or Hollandaise sauce or cold with vinaigrette or mayonnaise. It is useful to place an upturned fork under the right hand side of the plate to tip the plate so that the sauce will form in a well at the bottom of the plate towards the left hand side. Eating can be with a side knife and fork, with an asparagus holder or with the fingers. If with the fingers, then a finger bowl and a spare napkin should be offered.
Avocado	Generally served in halves with a salad garnish on a fish plate. Can be served with vinaigrette (now more likely to be made with a wine vinegar), which is served separately, or with prawns in a cocktail sauce. There are also special dishes to hold half an avocado. Brown bread and butter is less common now. Alternative methods of presentation are also found, for example, where the avocado is sliced and fanned out. A side knife and sweet fork are then laid.
Caesar salad	Salad of cos (or Romaine) lettuce, dressed with vinaigrette or other similar dressing (originally containing near-raw egg), garlic, croûtons and grated (or shaved) parmesan cheese. There are a number of variations to these ingredients. Side knife and sweet fork are laid. Sometimes this salad is served in a bowl.
Caviar	Served with a caviar knife (broad blade knife) or side knife, on the right hand side of the cover. Served onto a cold fish plate and accompaniments include blinis (buck wheat pancakes) or hot breakfast toast, butter, segments of lemon, chopped shallots and chopped egg yolk and egg white. Portion size is usually up to about 30 g (1 oz).

Charcuterie	This can include a selection of a range of meat (mainly pork) items including Bayonne ham, salamis, smoked ham, Parma ham and also pâtés and terrines. Cover is a side knife and sweet fork, or a joint knife and fork if taken as a main course. Accompaniments are peppermill and cayenne pepper, gherkins and sometimes onions. Occasionally a small portion of potato salad is offered. Bread is usually offered but brown bread and butter is now less common.
Corn on the cob	These are usually served with special holders which are like small swords or forks. Three wooden cocktail sticks in each end can be used, but avoid trying to use two sweet forks as it is possible to painfully catch teeth on the prongs. There are special dishes available, but a soup plate will do to provide a reservoir for the melted butter or Hollandaise sauce. A finger bowl and spare napkin might be advisable. A peppermill is offered.
Fresh fruit	Either served on a plate or in a bowl. Eaten with a side knife and sweet fork if served on a plate and sweet spoon and fork if served in a bowl. Usually no accompaniment is offered although some people might like caster sugar. Both caster sugar and ground ginger are offered with melon if it is served by itself. (For guéridon preparation of fruit see page 360.)
Fruit cocktails	Usually served in a glass or some form of bowl. These are eaten with a teaspoon and caster sugar is offered, especially if grapefruit is included in the cocktail.
Fruit juices	Usually served in a glass. Sometimes caster sugar is offered in which case a teaspoon should be given to stir in the sugar. For tomato juice, salt and Worcestershire sauce are offered, and again a teaspoon should also be given to aid mixing in these accompaniments.
Globe artichokes	This vegetable is usually served whole as a starter. The edible portion of the leaves is 'sucked off' between the teeth after being dipped in a dressing (for example, vinaigrette if served cold or melted butter or Hollandaise sauce if served hot). The leaves are held with the fingers. The heart is finally eaten with a side knife and sweet fork. A finger bowl and spare napkin are essential. There are special dishes for this vegetable, but a fish plate with a small bowl for the dressing will also suffice. In this case a spare plate for the discarded leaves will be needed. Alternatively a joint plate may be used.
Gravlax (Gravadlax)	Salmon pickled with salt, sugar and dill. Usually eaten with a fish knife and fork or a side knife and sweet fork. Traditional accompaniments are a slightly sweetened sauce of mustard and dill and often half a lemon (which may be wrapped in muslin to prevent the juice squirting onto the customer when the lemon is squeezed). A variety of unbuttered breads are often offered, with butter and alternatives served separately.
Mousses and pâtés	Normally these are eaten using a side knife and sweet fork. Hot, unbuttered breakfast toast or another bread is offered. Butter may be offered and other accompaniments appropriate to the dish itself, for example, lemon segments with fish mousses, although lemon is often offered with meat based pâtés.
Niçoise salad	There are a number of versions of this salad. Generally it includes boiled potatoes, whole French beans, tomatoes, hard-boiled eggs (quartered or sliced), stoned black olives, flakes of tuna fish and anchovy fillets. This salad is usually made up and plated. Vinaigrette is often offered.

Other salads	Salads can be made up and served plated or constituted at the guéridon. Dressings vary. Cover is usually related to the main ingredient, i.e. fish knife and fork for fish-based salads but a side knife and fork can be used for all. For guéridon service of salads see Chapter 8 (page 318).
Oysters (huîtres)	Cold oysters are usually served in one half of the shell on a bed of crushed ice in a soup plate. An oyster fork is usually offered but a small sweet fork can also be used. Oysters are usually eaten by holding the shell in one hand and the fork in the other, therefore a finger bowl and an extra napkin could be offered. Accompaniments include half a lemon and the oyster cruet (cayenne pepper, pepper mill, chilli vinegar and Tabasco sauce). Traditionally brown bread and butter was also offered.
Potted shrimps	A fish knife and fork or a side knife and sweet fork should be laid. Accompaniments include hot, unbuttered, breakfast toast (there is plenty of butter already in this dish), cayenne pepper, a peppermill and segments of lemon.
Seafood cocktails	These are usually made up and served in glasses or bowls. A teaspoon and small fork are often laid for eating. Sometimes the cutlery is placed on the underplate and placed on the table with the dish. Accompaniments are lemon segment, peppermill, sometimes cayenne pepper and traditionally brown bread and butter, although this is less common now.
Smoked salmon (saumon fumé)	Usually eaten with a fish knife and fork or a side knife and sweet fork. Traditional accompaniments are half a lemon (which may be wrapped in muslin to prevent the juice squirting onto the customer when the lemon is squeezed), cayenne pepper, peppermill and brown bread and butter. Often nowadays a variety of unbuttered bread is offered with butter and alternatives served separately. Oil is sometimes offered and also chopped onions and capers.
Other smoked fish	As well as the accompaniments offered with smoked salmon, creamed horseradish has become a standard offering with all other smoked fish including trout, eel, mackerel, cod, halibut and tuna.
Snails (escargots)	Snail tongs are placed on the left and a snail fork on the right. The snails are served in an escargot dish, which has six or twelve indentations. French bread is offered for mopping up the sauce. Half a lemon may be given and a finger bowl and an extra napkin may also be offered.

3.7 SOUPS

Soups are divided into a number of categories. These include consommés, veloutés, crèmes, purées, potages, bisques (shell fish soups) broths and various national soups.

Consommé	Clarified soup made from poultry, beef, game or vegetable bouillon. Usually served in consommé cups with a sweet spoon. These soups were once drunk from the cup using the handles and the spoon was provided to help in eating the garnish. The tradition continues of the use of the cup but this is now presented at the table. The handles on some styles of cups have become merely representative ears. Warmed Sherry or sometimes Madeira might be added to the consommé in the restaurant just before serving. Although consommé is usually served hot it can also be served cold or jellied (en gelée).

Veloutés, crèmes and purées	These soups are usually eaten from a soup plate with a soup spoon. It is however common now to see soup bowls of varying designs. Traditionally croûtons were only offered with purées and Cream of Tomato soup, but they are now commonly offered with a range of soups.
Potages, broths and bisques	These are usually served in soup plates and eaten with a soup spoon but again bowls of varying designs are also used.

National soups

These soups usually have special treatments. Some examples include:

Batwinia (Russian)	Purée of spinach, sorrel, beetroot and white wine, with small ice cubes served separately. Served very cold.
Bortsch (Polish)	Duck flavoured consommé garnished with duck, diced beef and turned vegetables. The accompaniments are sour cream, beetroot juice and bouchées filled with duck pâté. A soup plate is often used, as there is a large amount of accompaniments.
Bouillabaisse (French)	This is really a form of fish stew. Although a soup plate and soup spoon are used, it is common for a knife and fork to also be given. Thin slices of French bread, dipped in oil and grilled (sippets), are offered as well as rouille (see page 84).
Cherry (German)	Bouillon consisting of cherry purée, cherry juice and red wine, served with stoned cherries and sponge finger biscuits.
Cock-a-leekie (Scottish)	Veal and chicken consommé garnished with shredded leeks and chicken. Served with prunes: these may have been put into the soup plate at the service point.
Kroupnich (Russian)	Barley and sections of poultry offal garnished with small vol-au-vents stuffed with poultry meat.
Mille fanti (Italian)	Consommé with a covering of breadcrumbs, Parmesan cheese and beaten eggs.
Minestrone (Italian)	Vegetable paysanne soup with pasta. Traditional accompaniments are grated Parmesan cheese and grilled flutes.
Petit Marmite (French)	Beef and chicken flavoured soup garnished with turned root vegetables and dice of beef and chicken. Served in a special marmite pot, which resembles a small casserole. A sweet spoon is used to eat this soup, as it is easier to get this spoon into the small pot. Accompaniments are grilled flutes, poached bone marrow and Parmesan cheese. Sometimes the bread and cheese are done as a croûte on top of the soup before serving at the table.
Potage Germiny (French)	Consommé thickened before service with egg yolks and cream. Cheese straws are offered.
Shchi (Russian)	Bortsch consommé, garnished with sauerkraut. Beetroot juice and sour cream are offered separately.
Soupe à l'oignon (French)	French onion soup, often served in a consommé cup or soup bowl. Can be served with grilled flutes and Parmesan cheese but is often topped with a slice of French bread gratinated with cheese.

3.8 EGG DISHES

Egg dishes as separate courses have become less common in recent years. Omelettes have retained their popularity while dishes such as eggs en cocotte occasionally feature on menus.

The following egg dishes have specific service requirements:

Oeuf sur la plat	The egg is cooked in the oven in the oeuf sur la plat dish and is then served to the customer in this dish on an underplate. A sweet spoon and fork are used but a side knife may be given, depending on the garnishes. A sur la plat dish is a small, round, white earthenware or metal dish with two ears.
Oeuf en cocotte	The egg is cooked in the cocotte dish and served in this dish with various garnishes. The dish is placed on an underplate and a teaspoon is used to eat the dish. A cocotte dish is a small round earthenware dish with straight sides about the size of a small teacup.
Omelettes	As an egg course an omelette is eaten with a joint fork and is served onto a hot fish plate. The joint fork is placed on the right hand side of the cover. Omelettes are often plated but may be served from a flat using two forks or two fish knives. The ends may also be trimmed as part of this service.

3.9 PASTA AND RICE DISHES

These dishes, which are also referred to as farinaceous dishes, include all pastas such as spaghetti, macaroni, nouilles and ravioli, and also rice dishes such as pilaff or risotto. It also includes dishes such as Gnocchi Piedamontaise (potato), Parisienne (choux paste) and Romaine (semolina).

Most pasta and rice dishes are served plated these days. For spaghetti, a joint fork should be laid in the right hand side of the cover and a sweet spoon on the left. For all other dishes a sweet spoon and fork are used, with the sweet spoon on the right and the fork on the left. Grated Parmesan cheese is normally offered with all these dishes. Sometimes the Parmesan cheese is shaved from the piece rather than grated.

3.10 FISH DISHES

Traditionally, fish dishes were eaten with a fish knife and fork but this practice is declining. For a fish course the usual lay-up is a fish plate and side knife and fork. If fish is to be served as a main course, a joint plate with fish knife and fork or a joint knife and fork should be used.

The general accompaniments for fish dishes are:

Hot fish dishes with a sauce	Usually no accompaniments.
Hot fish dishes without a sauce	These often have Hollandaise or another hot butter-based sauce offered. Lemon segments may also be offered.

Fried fish which has been bread crumbed (à l'Anglaise)	These dishes often have tartare sauce or another mayonnaise-based sauce offered, together with segments of lemon.
Fried or grilled fish dishes not bread crumbed	These dishes are usually offered with lemon. Sometimes sauces such as Hollandaise or tartare are offered.
Deep fried fish which has been dipped in batter (à l'Orly)	A (kitchen-made) tomato sauce is sometimes offered together with segments of lemon. Proprietary sauces can also be offered, as can vinegar if chips are being served.
Cold poached fish dishes	Usually mayonnaise or another mayonnaise-based sauce such as Sauce Vert is offered, together with segments of lemon.

Fish dishes with special service requirements include:

Grilled herring (hareng grillé)	Usually served with a mustard sauce.
Whitebait (blanchailles)	Served on a hot fish plate and traditionally eaten with a fish knife and fork. Accompaniments are cayenne pepper, peppermill, segments of lemon and brown bread and butter.
Mussels (moules marinière)	Usually served in a soup plate or bowl on an underplate with brown bread and butter, or more commonly now a variety of breads. Cayenne pepper may be offered. A fish knife and fork and sweet spoon are often laid for eating. A plate for the debris is usually placed on the table together with a finger bowl and a spare napkin.
Cold lobster (homard froid)	Cover is a fish knife and fork and a lobster pick together with a spare debris plate and a finger bowl with a spare napkin. Lemon and sauce mayonnaise are the usual accompaniments.

3.11 MEATS, POULTRY AND GAME

Roast meats

In all cases roast gravy is offered. For dishes where the roast is plain (not roasted with herbs, for instance) then the following are usually offered:

Roast beef (boeuf rôti)	Horseradish sauce, mustards and Yorkshire pudding.
Roast lamb (agneau rôti)	Traditionally mint sauce, although redcurrant jelly is sometimes also offered.
Roast mutton (mouton rôti)	Traditionally redcurrant jelly, although mint sauce is sometimes also offered. An alternative traditional accompaniment is a white onion sauce.
Roast pork (porc rôti)	Apple sauce and sage and onion stuffing.

Boiled meats

Boiled mutton (mouton bouilli)	Caper sauce is traditionally served.
Salt beef (silverside)	Turned root vegetables, dumplings and the natural cooking liquor.
Boiled fresh beef (beouf bouilli)	Turned root vegetables, natural cooking liquor, rock salt and gherkins.
Boiled ham (jambon bouilli)	Parsley sauce or white onion sauce.

Other meat dishes

Irish stew	This stew is often served in a soup plate and a sweet spoon is offered together with the joint knife and fork. Accompaniments are Worcestershire sauce and pickled red cabbage.
Curry (kari)	General accompaniments are poppadums (crisp, highly seasoned pancakes), Bombay Duck (dried fillet of fish from the Indian Ocean) and mango chutney. Also offered is a Curry Tray, which will have items such as diced apple, sultanas, sliced bananas, yoghurt and desiccated coconut.
Mixed grill and other grills	These dishes may be garnished with cress, tomato and fried potatoes. Various mustards and sometimes proprietary sauces (tomato ketchup and brown sauce) are offered as accompaniments.
Steaks	As for mixed grill. Sauce Béarnaise is offered with Chateaubriand (double fillet) and sometimes with other steaks.

Poultry

Roast chicken (poulet rôti)	The accompaniments are bread sauce, roast gravy and parsley and thyme stuffing. Sage and onion stuffing is also used.
Roast duck (caneton rôti)	Sage and onion stuffing, apple sauce and roast gravy are served.
Wild duck (caneton sauvage)	Roast gravy and traditionally an orange salad with an acidulated cream dressing is offered as a side dish.
Roast goose (oie rôti)	Sage and onion stuffing, apple sauce and roast gravy.
Roast turkey (dinde rôti)	Cranberry sauce, chestnut stuffing, chipolata sausages, game chips, watercress and roast gravy are the usual accompaniments.

Furred game

Jugged hare	Heart-shaped croûtons, forcemeat balls and redcurrant jelly.
Venison (venaison)	Cumberland sauce and redcurrant jelly.

Feathered game

When roasted, the accompaniments for all feathered game such as partridge (perdreau), grouse (lagopède) and pheasant (faisan) are fried breadcrumbs, hot liver pâté spread on a croûte on which the meat sits, bread sauce, game chips, watercress and roast gravy.

3.12 POTATOES, VEGETABLES AND SALADS

A wide variety of potatoes and vegetables, including salads, may be served with various main dishes and courses. These can be either:

■ silver served onto the main plate alongside the main dish

■ pre-plated onto the main plate alongside the main dish

■ silver served onto a crescent or side plate, separate from the main plate, and placed at the left hand side of the main plate. A separate sweet fork or spoon may be placed for the potatoes and vegetables

■ pre-plated onto a crescent or side plate, separate from the main plate, and then placed at the left hand side of the main plate. A separate sweet fork or spoon may be placed for the potatoes and vegetables

■ placed on the table in multi-portion serving dishes from which customers can serve themselves, using service spoons and forks (family service).

A baked potato (pomme au four) is often served separately on a hot side plate, with a sweet fork on the plate to aid eating. Accompaniments are cayenne pepper, peppermill and butter (or substitutes). Butter is not now automatically put on the top of the potato, but is offered separately, together with alternatives.

For further information on the service of potatoes and vegetables see Section 5.7 Service of food, page 233.

Salads

There are two main types of salad:

■ *Plain salads*, which consists of two main types. These may be either green salads made up of green leaf ingredients or vegetable salads made up of one main vegetable ingredient which will dominate the overall flavour of the dish. Plain salad may often be served with a main course or as a separate dish after the main course.

- *Compound salads*, which may be a plain salad plus other ingredients, such as meat, fish and mushrooms, or a combination of a number of ingredients, mixed together using specific dressings and sauces. A fruit (orange) salad is generally offered as an accompaniment with roast duck.

Examples of salads are:

- *Française*: lettuce hearts, sections of skinned tomato, hard boiled egg, vinaigrette separate.
- *verte*: lettuce hearts, vinaigrette separate.
- *Saison*: lettuce hearts plus salad vegetables in season, vinaigrette separate.
- *d'orange*: lettuce hearts, in sections, filleted orange, freshly made acidulated cream dressing.
- *Mimosa*: lettuce hearts, filleted orange, grapes skinned and stoned, sliced banana, sprinkle with egg yolk, acidulated cream, dressing separate.
- *Japonaise*: lettuce, bananas, apple, tomatoes all in dice, shelled walnuts, fresh cream separate.
- *Lorette*: corn salad, julienne of beetroot, raw celery heart, vinaigrette separate.
- *Russian*: vegetable salad decorated with tomatoes, eggs, anchovies, lobster, ham, tongue, mayonnaise sauce.
- *Niçoise*: French beans, tomato quarters, sliced potatoes, anchovies, capers, olives, sauce vinaigrette.
- *Endive*: hearts of lettuce, endive, sauce vinaigrette.

The cover for a salad when offered separately with a main course should be a salad crescent (quarter moon shaped dish) or a small round wooden bowl, with a sweet fork, or sometimes a small wooden spoon and fork. The prongs of the small or sweet fork should be pointing downwards when placed over the rim of the salad crescent as part of the cover. This is to avoid tarnishing the silver with the acid in the dressing.

When a salad is served separately after the main course the cover would be:

- a cold fish plate or bowl such as a soup plate
- a small (side) knife and fork.

A selection of salads may often be offered as hors d'oeuvre (see page 85) and these are served in the same way.

For the preparation and service of salads on the guéridon see page 318.

All salads should be served chilled, crisp and attractive. Remember a salad is not complete without a well-made salad dressing or sauce, such as vinaigrette or mayonnaise. For examples of salad dressings see pages 319 to 320.

3.13 CHEESE

Cheeses are distinguished by flavour and categorised according to their texture. They differ from each other for a number of reasons, mainly arising through variations in the making process. Differences occur in the rind and how it is formed, in the paste and in the cooking process (relating here to both time and temperature). Cheeses also vary because the milk used comes from such different animals as cows, sheep and goat.

Dependent upon use, cheeses may be purchased either whole or pre-portioned. Cheese should be stored in a cool, dark place, with good air circulation or in a refrigerator. If it is not covered in its original wrapping, it should be wrapped in either greaseproof paper or aluminium foil to prevent any drying out taking place. It should also be stored away from food items that absorb flavours/odours, such as dairy produce.

The texture of a cheese depends largely on the period of maturation. The recognised categories are:

- fresh
- soft
- semi-hard
- hard
- blue.

Some examples of cheeses commonly available are given below.

Fresh cheese

Cottage	Unripened low-fat, skimmed milk cheese with a granular curd. Originated in the USA and now has many variations.
Cream	Similar to cottage cheese but is made with full fat milk. There are a number of different varieties available, some made from non-cow milks.
Mozzarella	Italian cheese made from buffalo milk but may now also be made from cow's milk.
Ricotta	Italian cheese made from the whey of cow's milk. A number of other Italian varieties are available, made from sheep's milk.

Soft cheese

Bel Paese	This light and creamy Italian cheese has a name that means 'beautiful country' and was first produced in 1929.
Brie	Famous French cheese made since the eighth century. Other countries now make this style of cheese, distinguishing it from the original French brie by the addition of the country's name, e.g. German brie.
Camembert	Famous French cheese which is stronger and often more pungent than Brie.
Carré de l'est	A soft cheese produced in France that is made from pasteurised cow's milk, and packed in square boxes. Like Camembert, it softens on ripening and is darker in colour than Brie. When ripe it has a mild flavour.
Epoisses de Bourgogne	Small, sticky, pale orange, soft-washed rind, double cream cow's milk cheese, washed in Marc de Bourgogne, which has a creamy, runny pungent centre. Originally invented at the beginning of the sixteenth century by Cistercian monks. Production started again in 1956 by a M. Berthaut from the village Epoisses in Burgundy.

Feta	Greek cheese made from both goat and sheep's milk.
Liptauer	Hungarian cheese spread made from sheep and cow's milk. Often found with various additions, such as onions, mustard or spices.
Mont d'Or, Vacherin du Haut-Doubs	Soft, slightly acidic, full-flavoured, herby, washed-rind cheese made from cow's milk. Vacherin Mont d'Or (Swiss) and Vacherin du Haut-Doubs/Le Mont d'or (French) come from the Swiss/French border region. Only produced between 15th August and 31st March and therefore exclusive to the autumn and winter months. Sold in characteristic round pine or spruce wood boxes and traditionally served from the box, but may also be enjoyed directly from the box with a spoon.
Munster	French Vosges cheese similar to Camembert in shape but with an orange-red rind. American, German and Swiss versions are also available.
Stracchino	Italian cheese originally from Lombardy. A soft, delicate cheese which now has a number of varieties.

Semi-hard cheese

Appenzeller	Typical example of Swiss cheese textures. The name is from the Latin for 'abbot's cell'.
Caerphilly	Buttermilk-flavoured cheese with a soft paste. Some people will find it almost soapy. Originally a Welsh cheese but now manufactured all over Britain.
Cantal	French cheese from the Auvergne, similar to Cheddar.
Cheddar	Classic British cheese now made all over the world and referred to as, for example, Scottish cheddar, Canadian cheddar.
Cheshire	Crumbly, slightly salty cheese, available as either white or red. It was originally made during the twelfth century in Cheshire but is now made all over Britain.
Chèvre d'Argental	The name means 'goat', which denotes the origin of the milk from which this cheese is made. Full-flavoured, densely textured, creamy cheese from the Rhône-Alps, with a bloomy rind.
Derby	English Derbyshire cheese now more often known by the sage-flavoured variety, Sage Derby.
Edam	A Dutch cheese that is similar to, but harder than, Gouda. It has a fairly bland, buttery taste and a yellow or red wax coated rind. It is sometimes flavoured with cumin.
Emmenthal	The name of this Swiss cheese refers to the Emme Valley. It is similar to Gruyère, although it is softer and slightly less tasty.

Esrom	Similar to the French Port Salut, this Danish cheese has a red rather than yellow rind.
Gloucester/ **Double Gloucester**	Full-cream, classic English cheeses originally made only from the milk of Gloucestershire cows.
Gouda	Buttery textured, soft and mild flavoured well-known Dutch cheese with a yellow or red rind.
Gruyère	Mainly known as a Swiss cheese, but both the French and Swiss varieties can legally be called by this name. It has small pea-size holes and a smooth, relatively hard texture. The French varieties may have larger holes.
Jarlsberg	Similar to Emmenthal, this Norwegian cheese was first produced in the late 1950s. It has a yellow wax coating.
Lancashire	Another classic English cheese similar to Cheshire (white Cheshire is sometimes sold as Lancashire).
Leicester	Mild flavoured and orange-coloured English cheese.
Limberger	Often quite pungent, this cheese originated in Belgium but is now also available from Germany.
Manchego	Relatively hard cheese, which may have holes, and has either a white or sometimes yellow paste. Made in Spain from sheep's milk.
Monterey	Creamy, soft American cheese with many holes. A harder version known as Monterey Jack is suitable for grating.
Pont l'Evêque	Similar to Camembert, but square in shape, this French cheese originates from Normandy.
Port Salut	Mild flavoured cheese with a name meaning 'Port of Salvation', referring to the abbey where exiled Trappist monks returned after the French Revolution.
Reblochon	Creamy, mild flavoured cheese from the Haute-Savoie region of France. The name comes from the illegal 'second milking' from which the cheese was originally made.
Tilsit	Strong flavoured cheese from the East German town of the same name where it was first produced by Dutch living there. Now available from other parts of Germany.
Wensleydale	Yorkshire cheese originally made from sheep or goat's milk but now made from cow's milk. This cheese is the traditional accompaniment to apple pie.

Hard cheese

Caciocavallo	Originating from ancient Roman times, the name means 'cheese on horseback' because its shape is said to resemble saddlebags.
Kefalotyri	Literally Greek for 'hard cheese', this is a tasty cheese from Greece which is suitable for grating.
Parmesan	Classic Italian hard cheese, more correctly called Parmigiano Reggiano. It is also known as the grated cheese used in and for sprinkling over Italian dishes, especially pasta.
Pecorino	Hard, sheep's milk, grating or table cheese from southern Italy. Also available with added peppercorns as Pecorino Pepato from Sicily.
Provolone	Smoked cheese made in America, Australia and Italy. Now made from cow's milk but originally from buffalo milk. Younger versions are softer and milder than the longer kept varieties.

Blue cheese

Bleu d'Auvergne	Strong, spicy, full-flavoured cow's milk blue cheese from the Auvergne, with a lingering finish and a salty tang. Has a natural rind and the cheese is creamy and moist with a sharp aroma. Invented in 1845 by farmer, Antoine Roussel, who used a needle to make holes in the cheese to allow air inside, facilitating mould veins to develop in the cheese.
Blue de Bresse	Fairly soft and mild flavoured French cheese from the area between Soane-et-Loire and the Jura.
Blue Cheshire	One of the finest of the blue cheeses which only becomes blue accidentally, although the makers endeavour to assist this process by pricking the cheese and maturing it in a favourable atmosphere.
Danish Blue	One of the most well-known of the blue cheeses. Softish and mild flavoured, it was one of the first European blue cheeses to gain popularity in Britain.
Dolcelatte	Factory-made version of Gorgonzola. The name is Italian for 'sweet milk' and the cheese is fairly soft with a creamy texture and greenish veining.
Dorset Blue	A strong, hard-pressed cheese, being close textured and made from skimmed milk. It is straw-coloured with deep blue veins, rather crumbly and has a rough rind.
Fourme D'Ambert	Rich, un-pressed cylindrical blue cow's milk cheese from the Auvergne, with a natural yellowish-grey rind and creamy open texture. Good depth of flavour, with a slight sharpness on the palate. Matured in caves for around eight weeks. It is the tangiest of the French variety of blue mould cheeses. The name is derived from the Latin forma meaning form.

Gorgonzola	Softish, sharp flavoured, classic Italian cheese with greenish veining, which is developed with the addition of mould culture.
Roquefort	Classic, sheep's milk cheese from the southern Massif Central in France. The maturing takes place in caves which provide a unique humid environment which contributes to the development of the veining.
Stilton	Famous and classic English cheese made from cow's milk; so called because it was noted as being sold in the Bell Inn at Stilton by travellers stopping there. According to legend it was first made by a Mrs Paulet of Melton Mowbray. Traditionally served by the spoonful but nowadays usually (and perhaps preferably) portioned. The pouring of port on to the top of a whole Stilton, once the top rind had been removed, was also popular but this practice has declined. The White Stilton has also become popular and is slightly less flavoursome than the blue variety.

Cover, accompaniments and service for cheese

Cover

The cover for cheese is:

- side plate
- side knife
- sometimes a small fork (sweet).

Accompaniments

Accompaniments set on the table may include:

- cruet (salt, pepper, and mustard)
- butter or alternative
- celery served in a celery glass part filled with crushed ice, on an underplate
- radishes (when in season) placed in a glass bowl on an underplate with teaspoon
- caster sugar for cream cheeses
- assorted cheese biscuits (cream crackers, Ryvita, sweet digestive, water biscuits etc.) or various breads.

Service

If not plated, the cheese board or trolley will be presented to the customer containing a varied selection of cheeses in ripe condition together with sufficient cheese knives for cutting and portioning the different cheeses (see Figure 3.4 for examples of the methods for presenting and cutting and portioning). If cheese is wrapped in foil this must be removed by the waiter before serving. The waiter should remove the cheese rind if it is not palatable (edible). This is not necessary in the case of Camembert and Brie as the rind of these two French cheeses is palatable.

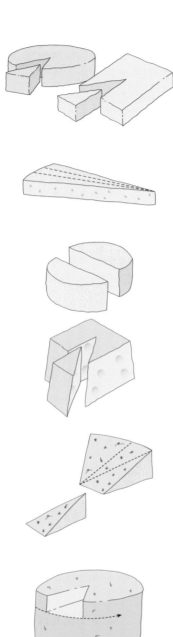

Round and square cheeses can be presented whole and then portioned by being cut into triangular pieces. Note that with square or oblong cheeses one of the cuts is at an angle.

Brie or similar type cheeses may be either presented whole or cut into triangular slices and then portioned by being sliced (much like a cake) as required.

Small soft cheeses such as goat's cheeses may be presented whole and then portioned by being cut in half or quarter as the customer requests.

Flattened or pyramid shaped cheeses may be presented whole and then portioned by being cut into small triangles by keeping one side of each cut at an angle.

Largish wedges of blue cheeses can be cut from a cylinder or half cylinder of cheese for presentation, and these wedges are then cut into smaller wedges for service. Other cheeses bought in cylinders or half cylinders can be cut and presented for service and then portioned in the same way.

A cylinder (truckle) or half cylinder of cheese may also be presented whole and then portioned by individual wedges being cut from it. In order to do this the cheese is first cut around at about 25 to 30 cm. This is also an alternative to the tradition of Stilton being portioned by scooping the cheese out from the top of the cylinder after removing the top rind.

Fig 3.4. Examples of methods for cutting cheeses

3.14 SWEETS

Most sweets are generally served onto sweet plates or are pre-plated. Puddings and various hot dishes can be pre-plated onto or served into various bowls. The lay-up is usually the sweet spoon and fork. Often the customer may require a sugar sifter. Various items may require different lay ups, for instance a sundae spoon, ice cream spoon or teaspoon. The main consideration is always to aid eating.

The range of possible sweets is very extensive and varied. Sweets dishes include:

- Bavarois, mousses, syllabubs.
- Charlottes (moulds lined with sponge and filled with bavarois in various flavours and sometimes with fruits).
- Coupes and sundaes (usually ice cream and various fruit combinations, served in coupe dishes or sundae dishes).
- Creams such as Chantilly (sweetened whipped cream flavoured with vanilla), custard (Sauce Anglaise) and dishes such as Egg Custard or Crème Brûlée.
- Fritters (beignets).
- Fruit dishes such as fruit salads, poached fruits (Compôte) and baked apples.
- Gâteaux.
- Ices (ice cream, frozen yoghurt) and sorbets (water ices) presented in various forms, including bombs (ice cream preparations made into bomb shapes using moulds).
- Omelettes with a variety of fillings and flavourings, for example, rum, jam or apple.
- Pancakes with a variety of fillings, for example, cherries or other fruits.
- Pies, flans and other pastries.
- Puddings including Bread and Butter, Cabinet, Diplomate and various fruit puddings.
- Soufflés, hot or cold.

There are no particular accompaniments to sweets and the choice of whether to serve on a plate or in a bowl is often dependent on the texture of the sweet dish, i.e. fruit salad in a bowl and gâteau portions on a sweet plate.

With service-portioned items such as gâteau portions, flans or pies, then the cut face, or point of the cut item, is placed facing the customer.

The serving of sauces such as custard and whipped cream can be from sauce boats (ladled or spooned not poured), or there may be individual portion jugs. Alternatively, the sauceboats may be left (on an underplate) on the table for the customers to help themselves. If sauces are served then it is usual not to serve these over the item but around it – unless the customer specifically requests it.

3.15 SAVOURIES

On the lunch and dinner menu a savoury may generally be served as an alternative to a sweet. In a banquet it may be a separate course served in addition to either a sweet or cheese course.

Savouries may be as follows:

On toast	Usually shaped pieces of toast with various toppings such as anchovies, sardines, mushrooms, smoked haddock and the classic Welsh rarebit (toasted seasoned cheese, egg and béchamel sauce mixture), or Buck rarebit (Welsh rarebit with a poached egg on the top).
Canapés or croûtes	Shaped pieces of bread about 6 mm (1/4" inch) thick, brushed with melted butter and grilled, or may be shaped shallow fried bread. Examples include: ● Scotch woodcock (scrambled egg, topped with a trellis of anchovies and studded with capers) ● Croûte Diane (chicken livers wrapped in streaky bacon) ● Croûte Derby (ham purée garnished with a pickled walnut) ● Devils on horseback (prunes wrapped in bacon) ● Angels on horseback (poached oysters wrapped in bacon) ● Canapé Charlemagne (shrimps in a curry sauce) ● Canapé Quo Vadis (grilled roes garnished with small mushrooms).
Tartlettes	Round pastry cases with various fillings such as mushrooms, or cheese soufflé mixtures with various garnishes, or prawns or other fish in various sauces.
Barquettes	Filled boat-shaped pastry cases, similar to tartlettes.
Bouchées	Filled small puff pastry (vol-au-vent) cases.
Omelettes	Two- and three-egg omelettes with various flavours/fillings such as parsley, anchovy, cheese or fines herbes (mixed herbs).
Soufflés	Made in a soufflé dish with various flavours such as mushroom, spinach, sardine, anchovy, smoked haddock or cheese.
Flans	Either single or portioned savoury flans such as Quiche Lorraine.

Cover, accompaniments and service

Savouries are usually pre-portioned by the kitchen and served onto a hot fish plate. The main cover for a savoury is usually a side knife and a sweet fork. The accompaniments are:

■ salt and pepper

■ cayenne pepper

■ pepper mill

■ Worcestershire sauce (usually only with meat savouries).

The savoury is served to the customer plated, after the cover has been laid and the accompaniments placed on the table. Where a savoury is being served as an alternative to sweets or cheese, with other customers in the party taking these, then the convention of serving all cold dishes before hot dishes (irrespective of the host) usually applies.

3.16 DESSERT (FRESH FRUIT AND NUTS)

Dessert may include all types of fresh fruits and nuts according to season, although the majority of the more popular items are now available all the year round. Some of the more popular items are dessert apples, pears, bananas, oranges, mandarins, tangerines, black and white grapes, pineapple and assorted nuts such as brazils. Sometimes a box of dates may appear on the fruit basket.

The dessert is usually dressed up in a fruit basket by the larder section and may be used as a central piece on a cold buffet until required.

Cover, accompaniments and service

Cover

The cover to be laid for dessert is:

- fruit plate
- fruit knife and fork: traditionally interlocked on the fruit plate
- spare napkin
- one finger bowl: on a sideplate and containing lukewarm water and a slice of lemon. It will be placed at the top right-hand corner of the cover and may be used by the customer for rinsing his/her fingers
- one finger bowl: on a sideplate and containing cold water for rinsing the grapes. It will be placed on the top left-hand corner of the cover
- nut crackers and grape scissors: to be placed on the fruit basket
- spare sideplate for shells and peel.

Accompaniments

The accompaniments should be set on the table. These are:

- caster sugar holder on a sideplate
- salt for nuts.

Service

The fruit basket is presented to the customer who makes his/her choice of a portion of fresh fruit or nuts. If the customer chooses nuts, then the nutcrackers would be removed from the fruit basket, placed on a side plate and left on the table at the head of the cover. If grapes are chosen then the waiter rests the fruit basket on the table, supporting it with one hand and cuts off the selected portion of grapes with the aid of the grape scissors. These are so made that they will grip the stem once the portion has been cut and removed from the main bunch, and thus by holding the portion with the grape scissors they may be rinsed in the finger bowl at the top left-hand corner of the cover and placed on the fruit plate. If guéridon service is being used, the procedure will be the same but takes place from the guéridon or trolley. The guéridon preparation of fruit is described in Chapter 8, page 351.

3.17 BEVERAGES

Traditionally the term beverages on a menu referred to coffee but it has become more common now for it to encompass tea, tisanes, milk drinks (hot or cold) and proprietary drinks such as Bovril or Horlicks.

Fairly rigid guidelines used to exist for the service of tea and coffee:

■ Morning coffee was traditionally served in teacups, with hot milk and white sugar only.

■ In the evening the demi-tasse (half cups) were used for coffee and cream might have been offered. Brown sugar was usually the only sugar available.

■ Similarly with tea, breakfast cups were used in the morning and the standard teacup used in the afternoon and in the evening – if you were lucky enough to be offered tea!

■ Lemon was offered only with China tea and milk with other teas.

Fortunately there is now more choice available. Tea, coffee (in both standard and de-caffeinated versions) and a range of other beverages are commonly available throughout the day, with a choice of milks, creams (including non-dairy creamers) and sugars (including non-sugar sweeteners). The use of the small coffee cups (demi-tasse) has declined for conventional coffee service (although they are still used in function catering), however these cups are now being used for espresso coffee.

For more information on tea and coffee see Chapter 4, pages 106 to 120, and Chapter 5, pages 252 to 255, for the table service of tea and coffee.

An informal restaurant: Dormy House (by Mike Caldwell, courtesy of Gleneagles Hotel, Scotland)

A formal restaurant: Strathern Restaurant (by Mike Caldwell, courtesy of Gleneagles Hotel, Scotland)

BEVERAGES
NON-ALCOHOLIC AND ALCOHOLIC

CHAPTER 4

4.1 TEA

Tea was discovered by accident over 5000 years ago, when leaves from a tea bush accidentally dropped into some boiling water and delicately flavoured the liquid. Tea was originally drunk for its medicinal benefits and it was not until the 1700s that it began to be consumed as the delicious beverage that we know today.

Tea is prepared from the leaf bud and top leaves of a tropical evergreen bush called Camellia sinensis. It produces what is regarded as a healthy beverage, containing approximately only half the caffeine of coffee and at the same time it aids muscle relaxation and stimulates the central nervous system. The leaf particle size is referred to as grades. These are Pekoe (pecko) – the delicate top leaves, Orange Pekoe – a rolled leaf with a slim appearance and Pekoe Dust – the smallest particle of leaf size. In between these grades there are a set of grades known as fannings. In tea terminology, 'flush' refers to a picking, which can take place at different times of the year.

All teas are fermented (oxidised) during the process of manufacture, which gives them their black colour. The one exception is the China green tea.

Tea producing countries

Tea is grown in more than 25 countries around the world. The crop benefits from acidic soil, a warm climate and where there is at least 130 cm of rain a year. It is an annual crop and its flavour, quality and character is affected by the location, altitude, type of soil and the climate. The main tea producing countries are:

China

This is the oldest tea growing country and is known for speciality blends such as Keemun, Lapsang Souchong, Oolongs and green tea.

East Africa (Kenya, Malawi, Tanzania and Zimbabwe)

This area produces good quality teas, which are bright and colourful and used extensively for blending purposes. Kenya produces teas which are easily discernible and have a reddish or coppery tint, and a brisk flavour.

India

India is the largest producer of tea, producing about 30 per cent of the world's tea. Best known are the teas from Assam (strong and full bodied), Darjeeling (delicate and mellow) and also Nilgiri, which is second only to Assam and produces teas similar to those of Sri Lanka.

Indonesia

Teas produced here are light and fragrant with bright colouring when made and are used mainly for blending purposes.

Sri Lanka (formerly Ceylon)

Teas here are inclined to have a delicate, light lemon flavour. They are generally regarded as excellent afternoon teas and also lend themselves to being iced.

Purchasing tea

Most teas used are blended teas sold under proprietary brands or names. Other teas, sometimes called speciality or premium teas, are sold by the name of the specific tea (see Service of Tea below). The word 'blend' indicates that a named tea may be composed of a variety of different teas to produce one marketable tea, which is acceptable to the average consumer taste. For instance, what is sometimes termed a standard tea may contain somewhere in the region of 15 different teas, some of which would almost certainly include Indian tea for strength, African tea for colour and China tea for flavour and delicacy.

Tea may be purchased in a variety of forms depending on requirements such as volume of production, type of establishment and clientele, the occasion, method of service, storage facilities available and cost.

The different means of purchasing are:

- *Bulk*: this is leaf tea (also called loose tea), which allows the traditional method of serving.
- *Tea bags*: these are heat-sealed and contain either standard or speciality teas. They come in one-cup, two-cup, pot-for-one or bulk brew sizes up to several litres.
- *String and tag*: this comes as a one-cup teabag with string attached and a tag that remains outside the cup or teapot for easy and quick identification of the tea by the customer.
- *Envelopes*: this is again a string and tag teabag but in an envelope for hygienic handling. These are used for trays for in-room tea and coffee-making facilities.
- *Instant*: instant tea granules, soluble in boiling water.
- *Pods*: these are specially designed individual portions of tea that are used in proprietary tea and coffee makers. Each pod makes one portion of tea and the pod is then disposed of.

Storage

Tea should be kept:

- in a dry, clean and covered container
- in a well ventilated area
- away from excess moisture
- away from any strong smelling foods as it very quickly absorbs strong odours.

Making of tea

The type of tea used will, of course, depend on the customer's choice, but most establishments carry a varied stock of Indian, Ceylon, China and speciality teas, together with a variety of tisanes available upon request.

The quantities of dry tea used per pot or per gallon may vary slightly with the type of tea used, but as an approximate guide the following may be used:

- 42.5–56.7 g (1½–2 oz) dry tea per 4.546 litres (1 gallon).
- ½ litre (1 pint) of milk will be sufficient for 20–24 cups.
- ½ kilogram (1 lb) sugar for approximately 80 cups.

When brewing smaller amounts in the stillroom, such as a pot for one or two, it is often advisable to install a measure for the loose tea. This ensures standardisation of the brew and control on the amount of loose tea being used. Alternative methods of pre-portioning tea may also be used, such as tea bags.

When making tea in bulk and calculating quantities of tea required for a party, allow approximately ⅙ litre (⅓ pint) per cup or 24 cups per 4.546 litres (1 gallon). If breakfast cups are used, capacity approximately ¼ litre (½ pint), then allow only 16 cups to 4.546 litres (1 gallon).

Because tea is an infusion the flavour is obtained by allowing the tea to brew. To achieve good results, a few simple rules can be applied:

1 Heat the pot before putting in the dry tea so that the maximum heat can be obtained from the boiling water.

2 Measure the dry tea exactly.

3 Use freshly boiled water.

4 Make sure the water is boiling on entering the pot.

5 Allow the tea to brew for 3–6 minutes (depending on the tea) to obtain maximum strength from the brew.

6 Remove the tea leaves at the end of the brewing period if required, but especially if making the tea in multi-pot insulated urns.

7 Ensure all the equipment used is scrupulously clean.

Service of tea

Afternoon tea	Usually a blend of delicate Darjeeling tea and high-grown Ceylon tea to produce a refreshing and light tea. As the name of the blend suggests this tea is suitable for afternoon tea but may also be taken at any time. Served with milk or lemon and sugar offered separately.
Assam	Rich full and malty flavoured tea, suitable for service at breakfast, usually with milk. Sugar would be offered separately.

China	Tea made from a special blend of tea that is more delicate in flavour and perfumed than any other tea. Less dry tea is required than for making Indian or Ceylon tea. Traditionally China tea is rarely served with milk. It is made in the normal way and is best made in a china pot. China tea is normally drunk on its own, but may be improved, according to taste, by the addition of a slice of lemon. Slices of lemon would be offered on a sideplate with a sweet fork. Sugar may be offered separately.
Darjeeling	Delicate tea with a light grape flavour and known as the 'Champagne of Teas'. Usually served as an afternoon or evening tea with either lemon or a little milk if preferred. Sugar may be offered separately.
Earl Grey	Blend of Darjeeling and China tea, flavoured with oil of Bergamot. Usually served with lemon or milk. Sugar would be offered separately.
English Breakfast	Often a blend of Assam and Kenya teas to make a bright, flavoursome and refreshing tea. Usually served as a breakfast tea but may also be offered at any time. Usually served with milk but can also be taken with lemon. Sugar is offered separately.
Iced tea	This is strong tea that is made, strained and well chilled. The tea is then stored chilled until required. It is traditionally served in a glass, such as a tumbler. A slice of lemon may be placed in the glass and some additional lemon slices served separately as for Russian tea. Sugar may be offered.
Indian or Ceylon Blend	Indian or Ceylon Blend tea may be made in either china or metal teapots. These teas are usually offered with milk. Sugar is offered separately.
Jasmine	Green (unoxidised) tea that is dried with Jasmine Blossom and produces a tea with a fragrant and scented flavour.
Kenya	Consistent and refreshing tea usually served with milk. Sugar would be offered separately.
Lapsang Souchong	Smoky, pungent and perfumed tea, delicate to the palate and may be said to be an acquired taste. Usually served with lemon. Sugar would be offered separately.
Multi-pot	There are many occasions when tea has to be produced in bulk. Such occasions might be a reception tea, tea breaks in an industrial catering concern, or for functions catering for large numbers. In these instances tea may be made in multi-pots/urns, which may be described as teapots or urns, varying in capacity from one to 25 litres (1 to 5 gallons). These containers have infusers, which hold the required quantity of tealeaves for the size of pot/urn being used. The infuser would be placed in the pot/urn and freshly boiled water added. The mix would then be allowed to brew for a number of minutes – a maximum of 10 minutes for a 25-litre urn – and the infuser is then removed to ensure a good quality product is served. The quantity of tea made should always relate to the number to be served – this will ensure minimum delay in the service and minimum wastage.
Russian or lemon tea	Tea that is brewed from a special blend similar to China tea, but is also often made from either Indian or Ceylon tea. It is made in the normal way and is usually served with a slice of lemon. The tea is served in quarter litre (half pint) glasses, which stand in a silver holder with a handle, and on a sideplate with a teaspoon. A slice of lemon may be placed in the glass and a few slices of lemon served separately. Sugar would be served separately.

Sri Lanka	Makes a pale golden tea with a good flavour. Ceylon Blend is still used as a trade name. Served with lemon or milk. Sugar would be offered separately.
Tisanes	These are fruit flavoured teas and herbal infusions which are often used for medicinal purposes and are gaining in popularity with trends towards more healthy eating and drinking. Often these do not contain caffeine. Examples are:

Herbal teas
- camomile
- peppermint
- rosehip
- mint

Fruit teas
- cherry
- lemon
- blackcurrant
- mandarin orange

These teas are usually made in china pots or can be made by the cup or glass. Sometimes served with sugar.

4.2 COFFEE

There is evidence to suggest that coffee trees were cultivated about 1000 years ago in the Yemen. The first commercial cultivation of coffee is thought to have been in the Yemen district of Arabia in the fifteenth century. By the middle of the sixteenth century coffee drinking had spread to Sudan, Egypt, Syria and Turkey. Venetian traders first brought coffee to Europe in 1615 and the first coffee house in England was opened in Oxford in 1650. The drinking of coffee spread from Britain to America, but after the Boston Tea Party, in 1773, the North American palate changed from drinking tea as a beverage to coffee.

The trees that produce coffee are of the genus *Coffea*, which belongs to the *Rubiaceae* family. There are somewhere in the region of 50 different species, although only two of these are commercially significant. These are known as *Coffea arabica* and *Coffea camephora*, which is usually referred to as *Robusta*. Arabica accounts for some 75 per cent of world production.

The coffee tree is an evergreen shrub, which reaches a height of two to three metres when cultivated. The fruit of the coffee tree is known as the 'cherry' and these are about 1.5 cm in length and have an oblong shape. The cherry usually contains two coffee seeds. The coffee tree will not begin to produce fruit until it is 3–5-years-old and it will then usually yield good crops for up to 15 years.

Coffee producing countries

Coffee is a natural product grown in many countries of the tropical and sub-tropical belt in South and Central America, Africa and Asia. It is grown at different altitudes in different basic climates and in different soils and is looked upon as an international drink consumed throughout the world. Brazil is the world's largest grower of coffee, Columbia is second, the Ivory Coast third and Indonesia fourth.

Purchasing coffee

The different means of purchasing coffee are:

- *Bulk*: (either as beans or in vacuum packs of pre-ground beans) allowing for the traditional methods of making and serving.
- *Coffee bags*: these are heat-sealed and come in one-cup, two-cup, pot-for-one or bulk brew sizes up to several litres.
- *Instant*: instant coffee granules, available in sizes from one cup to pot size.
- *Individual filters*: vacuum packed and containing one portion.
- *Pods*: these are specially designed individual portions of pre-ground coffee that are used in proprietary coffee and tea makers. Each pod makes one portion of coffee and the pod is then disposed of.

Companies who sell coffee have their own blending experts whose task it is to ensure that the quality and taste of their particular coffee brand is consistent, despite the fact that the imported beans will vary from shipment to shipment.

Samples of green coffee beans are taken from bags in the producing countries and the port of arrival. The samples are sent to prospective buyers whose experts roast, brew and taste samples to test their quality before deciding on the type of blend for which the particular coffee is suitable.

Most brands of coffee sold in shops are, in fact, a blend of two or more batches of beans. Because they have no smell or taste, green beans have to be roasted in order to release the coffee aroma and flavour. The roasting process should give a uniform colour. The outputs from different roastings are used to form different blends.

The common degrees of roasting are:

- *Light or pale roastings*: suitable for mild beans to preserve their delicate aroma.
- *Medium roastings*: give a stronger flavour and are often favoured for coffees with well defined character.
- *Full roastings*: popular in many Latin countries, they have a bitter flavour
- *High roasted coffee*: accentuates the strong bitter aspects of coffee, although much of the original flavour is lost.

Commercial coffee roasters can either convert the beans into instant (soluble) coffee or prepare them for sale as roasted or ground beans. The higher the roast, the less acidity and the more bitterness there is in the coffee.

Certain coffees also have flavourings added, either in the blend or during the process of making. Examples of these include:

- Turkish coffee – vanilla
- French coffee – chicory
- Viennese coffee – fig.

The grind

Roasted coffee must be ground before it can be used to make the brew. Coffee is ground to different grades of fineness to suit the many different methods of brewing. The most suitable grinds for some common methods of brewing coffee are:

Method	Grinding grade
Cafetière	Medium
Espresso	Very fine
Filter/Drip	Fine to medium
Jug	Coarse
Percolator	Medium
Turkish	Pulverised
Vacuum infusion	Medium fine to fine

Storage

Some tips for storing coffee:

- Store in a well ventilated storeroom.
- Use an air-tight container for ground coffee to ensure that the oils do not evaporate, causing loss of flavour and strength.
- Keep coffee away from excess moisture.
- Do not store near any strong smelling foods or other substances, as coffee will absorb their odours.

Making coffee

Methods of brewing can vary, ranging from instant coffee brewed by the cup, through to 1½–3 litre (3–6 pints) units and up to machines that may produce large quantities for functions. Coffee beans may be purchased and then ground according to requirements. The beans should not be ground until immediately before they are required as this will ensure the maximum flavour and strength from the oils within the coffee bean. If ground coffee is purchased it normally comes in vacuum-packed packets in order to maintain its qualities until use. These packets contain set quantities to make 4.5 litres (1 gallon) and 9 litres (2 gallons) and so on.

When making coffee in bulk 283.5–340 g (10–12 oz) of ground coffee is sufficient to make 4.5 litres (1 gallon) of black coffee. Assuming that cups with a capacity of 20 cl (½ pint) will be used then 283.5–340 g (10–12 oz) of ground coffee is sufficient to provide 22 cups of black coffee or 44 cups if serving half coffee and half milk. When breakfast cups are used then 16 cups of black coffee or 32 cups of half coffee and half milk will be available. Capacity, at a dinner where demi-tasse 10 cl (⅙ pint) cups are used, is 44 cups of black coffee or 88 cups half black coffee and half milk.

The rules to be observed when making coffee in bulk are as follows:

- Use freshly roasted and ground coffee.
- Buy the correct grind for the type of machine in use.
- Ensure all equipment is clean before use.
- Use a set measure of coffee to water: 283.5–340 g per 4.5 litres (10–12 oz per gallon).
- Add boiling water to the coffee and allow to infuse.
- The infusion time must be controlled according to the type of coffee being used and the method of making.
- Control the temperature since to boil coffee is to spoil coffee (it will develop a bitter taste).
- Strain and serve.
- Offer milk (hot or cold) or cream separately and sugar and alternatives.
- The best serving temperatures are 82°C (180°F) for coffee and 68°C (155°F) for milk.

Characteristics of good coffee

Coffee should have:

- good flavour
- good aroma
- good colour when milk or cream are added – not grey
- good body.

Reasons for bad coffee

Weak coffee:

- Water has not reached boiling point.
- Insufficient coffee used
- Infusion time too short

- Stale or old coffee used.
- Incorrect grind of coffee used for equipment in operation.

Flat coffee:

- All points for weak coffee listed above.
- Coffee kept too long before use, or kept at wrong temperature.

- Dirty equipment.
- Water not fresh.
- Coffee reheated.

Bitter coffee:

- Too much coffee used.
- Infusion time too long.
- Coffee not roasted correctly.
- Sediment remaining in storage or serving compartment.

- Infusion at too high a temperature.
- Coffee may have been left too long before use.

Coffee making methods

Coffee may be made in many ways and the service depends on the method used. A description of the various methods is given below. Figure 4.1 illustrates ways in which coffee may be made. Examples of modern coffee service styles are given in Table 4.1 on page 119.

Instant

This may be made in individual coffee or teacups, or in large quantities. It involves the mixing of soluble coffee solids with boiling water. When making instant coffee in bulk, approximately 71 g (2½ oz) to each 4.5 litres (one gallon) of water should be allowed. This form of coffee may be made very quickly, immediately before it is required, by pouring freshly boiled water onto a measured quantity of coffee powder. Stir well.

Saucepan or jug method

This is an American method of making coffee, more often used in the home than in a catering establishment. A set measure of ground coffee is placed in a saucepan or jug and the required quantity of freshly boiled water is poured onto the coffee grounds. This should then be allowed to stand for a few minutes to extract the full flavour and strength from the ground coffee. It is then strained and served.

Fig 4.1. Coffee brewing methods (clockwise from top): pour through filter machine, single filter, Turkish/Greek/Arabic coffee, jug and plunger/cafetière

La cafetière (coffee or tea maker)

La cafetière, or plunger method, makes coffee simply and quickly by the infusion method and to order. This ensures that the flavour and aroma of the coffee are preserved. La cafetière comes in the form of a glass container with a lip held in a black, gold or chrome finished holder and sealed with a lid which also holds the plunger unit in position.

The method of making is completed simply by adding boiling water to the ground coffee, stirring and then placing the plunger unit and lid in position. It has a visual attraction and involves the client in completing the process by ensuring the plunger unit is pushed to the base of the glass container before serving.

A guideline to the quantity of coffee to be used might be:

■ 2 level sweet spoonfuls for the 3 cup size

■ 6 level sweet spoonfuls for the 8 cup size

■ 9 level sweet spoonfuls for the 12 cup size

Infusion time is from 3 to 5 minutes. During this time the coffee grains will rise to the top of the liquid. After this if the plunger is slightly moved the coffee grains will fall to the bottom of the glass container. This action makes the pushing of the plunger down easier.

Percolator method

This method was used more in the home than commercially. A set quantity of coffee grounds is placed in the percolator, which is then filled with freshly drawn water. The water, upon reaching boiling point, rises up through a tube and percolates the coffee grounds, extracting the full flavour, colour and strength. Hot or cold milk, cream and sugar may be added to taste.

The length of infusion time is determined by the strength of coffee required, which in turn is controlled by a thermostat. When this infusion time has been completed the coffee liquid no longer continues to infuse with the coffee grounds but is held in the main body of the percolator at the correct serving temperature of 82°C (180°F). The use of this method of making coffee is declining.

Vacuum infusion ('Cona')

This traditional method of making coffee had considerable visual appeal in the restaurant, and had the advantage that the coffee served was always fresh as only limited quantities were made at one time. It also avoids making too much coffee and therefore prevents wasting or serving old, flat, bitter coffee during another food service period.

The filters in this vacuum-type equipment are sometimes glass, but more often than not are made of plastic or metal. The bowls are either glass or metal.

In this method of making coffee the lower bowl is filled with cold water or, to speed up the operation, freshly heated but not boiled water, up to the water level. The upper bowl is then set in the lower bowl, making sure it is securely in place. The filter is placed in the upper bowl, ensuring it is securely fitted, and the required quantity of ground coffee is then added according to the amount of water being used. The water is then heated.

As the water reaches boiling point it rises up the tube into the upper bowl, mixing with the ground coffee. As it rises in the upper bowl, it is often best to stir the mixture gently to ensure that all coffee grounds infuse with the liquid, as sometimes the grounds are inclined to form a cap on top of the liquid and therefore do not fully infuse. At the same time, care must be taken that the filter is not knocked as this may cause grains to pass into the lower bowl.

On reducing the heat, the coffee liquid passes back into the lower bowl leaving the grounds in the upper bowl. The upper bowl and filter are then removed and washed ready for re-use. The coffee in the lower bowl is ready for use and should be served at a temperature of approximately 82°C (180°F).

Filter (café filtre)

This is a method originating from and traditionally used in France and may be made individually in the cup or in bulk. The filter method produces excellent coffee. Fresh boiled water is poured into a container with a very finely meshed bottom, which stands on a cup or pot. Within the container is the required amount of ground coffee. The infusion takes place and the coffee liquid falls into the cup/pot below. Filter papers may be used to avoid the grounds passing into the lower cup, but this will depend on how fine or coarse is the ground coffee being used. There are now many electronic units available of differing capacities. Cold water is poured into a reservoir and is brought to boiling point and then dripped onto the ground coffee.

Pour through filter method

This is an excellent method of making filter coffee, which has increased in popularity over the past few years. Many of these pour through filter machines are available for purchase, or on loan from a number of the main coffee suppliers.

The principle behind this method is that when the measured quantity of freshly drawn water is poured into the top of the pour through filter machine this water displaces the hot water already in the machine. This hot water infuses with the ground coffee and runs into the serving container as a coffee liquid ready for immediate use. It takes approximately 3–4 minutes to make one brew.

It is seen as a very good method of coffee making for the bar top/back bar in a public house, where coffee may be served in conjunction with hot or cold snacks or where it may be offered at the end of a meal.

When coffee is made by this method, ensure that:

■ the machine is plugged in and switched on at the mains

■ the brew indicator light is on. This tells the operator that the water already held in the machine is at the correct temperature for use

■ the correct quantity of fresh ground coffee, which will usually come in the form of a vacuum-sealed pack, is used. A fresh pack should be used for each new brew of filter coffee being made

■ a new clean filter paper is used for each fresh brew.

Individual filter

This is an alternative way of making filter coffee. It is a plastic, disposable, individual filter, bought with the required amount of coffee already sealed in the base of the filter. Each individual filter is sufficient for one cup and after use the whole filter is thrown away. The advantage of this method is that every cup may be made to order. It also appeals to customers as they see that they are receiving entirely fresh coffee as well as it having a certain novelty value.

When making a cup of coffee by this method, the individual filter is placed onto a cup. Freshly boiled water is then poured into the individual filter to the required level. The liquid then infuses with the ground coffee within the individual filter and drips into the cup. A lid should be placed over the water in the filter to help retain the temperature. Time of making is approximately 3–4 minutes.

Espresso

This method is Italian in origin. The machines used in making this form of coffee can provide cups of coffee individually in a matter of seconds, some machines being capable of making 300–400 cups of coffee per hour.

The method involves passing steam through the finely ground coffee and infusing under pressure. The advantage is that each cup is made freshly for the customer. Served black, the coffee is known as Espresso and is served in a small cup. If milk is required, it is heated for each cup by a high-pressure steam injector and transforms a cup of black coffee into Cappuccino. As an approximate guide, from 12

Fig 4.2. Espresso machine

kg (1 lb) of coffee used, 80 cups of good strength coffee may be produced. The general rules for making coffee apply here but, with this special and delicate type of equipment, extra care should be taken in following any instructions.

Still-set

This method normally consists of a small central container into which the correct sized filter paper is placed. A second, fine-meshed metal filter with a handle is then placed on the filter paper and the ground coffee placed on top of this. There is an urn on either side of varying capacities according to requirements. The urns may be 4½, 9, 13 or 18 litres (1, 2, 3 or 4 gallons) in size.

These still-sets are easy to operate, but must be kept very clean at all times and regularly serviced. The urns should be rinsed before and after each brew until the water runs clear. This removes the thin layer of cold coffee that clings to the side of the urn that, if left, will spoil the flavour and aroma of the next brew.

Fig 4.3. Modern still set

Boiling water is passed through the grounds and the coffee passes into the urn at the side. Infusion should be complete in 6–8 minutes for 4½ litres (1 gallon) of coffee, using medium ground coffee. The milk is heated in a steam jacket container. It should be held at a constant temperature of 68°C because if held at too high a temperature or boiled or heated too soon, on coming into contact with the coffee it will destroy its flavour and taste. At the same time, the milk itself becomes discoloured. The coffee and milk should be held separately, at their correct temperatures ready for serving.

Decaffeinated

Coffee contains caffeine, which is a stimulant. Decaffeinated coffee is made from beans after the caffeine has been extracted. The coffee is made in the normal way.

Fig 4.4. Examples of insulated jugs and dispensers for coffee and tea service (courtesy of Elia®)

Iced coffee

Strong black coffee should be made in the normal way. It is then strained and chilled well until required. It may be served mixed with an equal quantity of cold milk for a smooth beverage, or with cream. It is served in a tall glass, with ice cubes added and with straws. Cream or milk is often served separately and sugar offered.

Turkish or Egyptian coffees

This is made from darkly roasted Mocha beans, which are ground to a fine powder. The coffee is made in special copper pots, which are placed on top of a stove or lamp, and the water is then allowed to boil. The sugar should be put in at this stage to sweeten the coffee, as it is never stirred once poured out. The finely ground coffee may be stirred in or the boiling water poured onto the grounds. The amount of coffee used is approximately one heaped teaspoonful per person. Once the coffee has been stirred in, the copper pot is taken off the direct heat and the cooling causes the grounds to settle. It is brought to the boil and allowed to settle twice more and is then sprinkled with a little cold water to settle any remaining grains. The coffee is served in small cups. While making the coffee it may be further flavoured with vanilla pods but this is optional.

Irish and speciality coffees

An 18.93 cl (6⅔ fl oz) Paris goblet (or other suitable glass) should be pre-warmed and sugar added as required by the customer. (A certain amount of sugar is always required when serving this form of coffee as it is an aid to floating the double cream on the surface of the hot coffee; the waiter must ensure the customer realises this.) A teaspoon is then placed in the goblet to conduct the heat and avoid cracking the goblet as the piping hot, strong black coffee is poured in. The coffee should be stirred well to dissolve the sugar and then one measure of Irish whiskey added. At this stage, it is important to ensure that everything is thoroughly blended. The liquid should now be within 2½ cm (1 in) of the top of the goblet. Double cream should

Table 4.1 Examples of modern coffee service styles

Filter (filtre)	Traditional method of making coffee. Often served with hot or cold milk or cream
Cafetière	Popular method of making and serving fresh coffee in individual or multi-portion jugs. Often served with hot or cold milk or cream
Espresso	Traditional short strong black coffee
Espresso Doppio	Double espresso served in larger cup
Café Crème	Regular coffee prepared from fresh beans, ground fresh for each cup, resulting in a thick cream coloured, moussy head
Espresso Ristretto	Intense form of espresso, often served with a glass of cold water in continental Europe
Americano	Espresso with added hot water to create regular black coffee. May also be regular black coffee made using filter method
Espresso Macchiato	Espresso spotted with a spoonful of hot or cold milk or hot milk foam
Espresso Con Panna	Espresso with a spoonful of whipped cream on top
Cappuccino	Espresso coffee topped with steamed frothed milk, often finished with a sprinkling of chocolate (powdered or grated)
Caffè (or Café) Latté	Shot of espresso plus hot milk, with or without foam
Latte Macchiato	Steamed milk spotted with a drop of espresso
Caffè Mocha (or Mochaccino)	Chocolate compound (syrup or powder) followed by a shot of espresso. The cup or glass is then filled with freshly steamed milk topped with whipped cream and cocoa powder
Iced coffee	Chilled regular coffee, sometimes served with milk or simply single espresso topped up with ice cold milk
Turkish/Egyptian	Intense form of coffee made in special jugs with finely ground coffee
Decaffeinated	Coffee with caffeine removed. Can be used as an alternative to prepare the service styles listed above
Instant coffee	Coffee made from processed powder (often freeze dried). Regular and decaffeinated styles are available

then be poured slowly over the back of a teaspoon onto the surface of the coffee until it is approximately 1.9 cm (¾ in) thick. The coffee must not be stirred: the best flavour is obtained by drinking the whiskey-flavoured coffee through the cream.

This method of making coffee may be carried out at the table and has visual appeal. As the fat content of cream is much higher than that of milk, less may be used and it should not be heated.

When the Irish coffee has been prepared, the goblet should be put on a doily on a side plate and placed in front of the customer. If brandy is used instead of whiskey, the coffee is known as Café Royale.

Irish coffee is often completed and served at the table. The following equipment is required:

Fig 4.5. Tray laid for the service of Irish coffee

- service salver
- tray cloth or napkin
- 18.93 cl (6⅔ fl oz) stemmed glass on an underplate
- teaspoon
- jug of double cream

- 25 ml measure
- coffee pot
- sugar basin of coffee sugar with a teaspoon
- bottle of Irish whiskey.

Order of ingredients in the glass:

1 sugar
2 black coffee
3 spirit or liqueur
4 double cream.

Other forms of speciality, or connoisseur, coffees are:

Monk's coffee:	Bénédictine	*Calypso coffee*:	Tia-Maria
Russian coffee:	Vodka	*Highland coffee*:	Scotch Whisky
Jamaican coffee:	Rum	*Seville coffee*:	Cointreau

Different establishments may give a different name to a speciality coffee containing the same liqueur or spirit. For example:

Café Royale:	Brandy	*Caribbean*:	Rum
Café Parisienne:	Brandy	*Jamaican*:	Rum

4.3 OTHER STILLROOM BEVERAGES

Other beverages may be offered for service and are often made in the stillroom. These include drinks such as cocoa, drinking chocolate, Horlicks, Ovaltine and Bovril. They should be prepared and served according to the maker's instructions.

If milk shakes are requested, then the following basic ingredients are required:

- chilled milk
- syrups (flavouring) see page 125
- ice-cream.

Milk shakes are often served with a straw in a tall glass after making in a mixer or blender.

4.4 NON-ALCOHOLIC DISPENSE BAR BEVERAGES

Non-alcoholic dispense bar beverages may be classified into five main groups:

- aerated waters
- natural spring/mineral waters
- squashes
- juices
- syrups.

Aerated waters

These beverages are charged (or aerated) with carbonic gas. Artificial aerated waters are by far the most common. The flavourings found in different aerated waters are obtained from various essences.

Examples of these aerated waters are:

- *Soda water*: colourless and tasteless.
- *Tonic water*: colourless and quinine flavoured.
- *Dry ginger*: golden straw-coloured with a ginger flavour.
- *Bitter lemon*: pale, cloudy yellow-coloured with a sharp lemon flavour.

Other flavoured waters, which come under this heading, are:

- 'Fizzy' lemonades
- Orange
- Ginger beer
- Coca-cola etc.

Aerated waters are available in bottles and cans and many are also available as post-mix. The term post-mix indicates that the drink mix of syrup and the carbonated (filtered) water is mixed after (post) leaving the syrup container, rather than being pre-mixed (or ready mixed) as in canned or bottled soft drinks. The post-mix drinks are served from hand-held dispensing guns at the bar. These have buttons on the dispensing gun to select the specific drink. The key advantage of the post-mix system is the saving on storage space, especially for a high turnover operation. Dispensing systems need regular cleaning and maintenance to ensure that they are hygienic and working properly. Also, the proportions of the mix need to be checked regularly: too little syrup and the drinks will lack taste; too much syrup and the flavours become too strong.

Natural spring waters/mineral waters

The EU has divided bottled water into two main types: mineral water and spring water. Mineral water has a mineral content (which is strictly controlled), while spring water has fewer regulations, apart from those concerning hygiene. Water can be still, naturally sparkling or carbonated during bottling.

Bottle sizes for mineral and spring waters vary considerably from, for example, 1.5 l to 200 ml. Some brand names sell in both plastic and glass bottles, while other brands prefer either plastic or glass bottles depending on the market and the size of container preferred by that market.

Table 4.2 Examples of varieties of mineral water

Name	Type	Country
Appollinaris	Naturally sparkling	Germany
Badoit	Slightly sparkling	France
Buxton	Still or carbonated	England
Contrex	Still	France
Evian	Still	France
Highland Spring	Still or carbonated	Scotland
Perrier	Sparkling and also fruit flavoured	France
San Pellegrino	Carbonated	Italy
Spa	Still or sparkling	Belgium
Vichy	Naturally sparkling	France
Vittel	Naturally sparkling	France
Volvic	Still	France

Table 4.3 Examples of varieties of spring water

Name	Type	Country
Ashbourne	Still or carbonated	England
Ballygowen	Still or sparkling	Ireland
Llanllyr	Still or sparkling	Wales
Strathmore	Still or sparkling	Scotland

Mineral waters are obtained from natural springs in the ground. They are impregnated with the natural minerals found in the soil and sometimes naturally charged with an aerating gas.

Where mineral waters are found, there is usually what is termed a spa, where the waters may be drunk or bathed in according to the cures they are supposed to effect. Many of the best-known mineral waters are bottled at the source.

Mineral waters can also be classified according to their chemical properties, which are as follows:

Alkaline waters

These are the most numerous of all the mineral waters. It is said they help treatment of gout and rheumatism. Some examples are:

- Aix-la-chapelle
- Aix-les-bains
- Evian
- Malvern
- Perrier
- Saint-Galmier
- Selters
- Vichy.

Aperient waters

So named because of their saline constituents, these being in the main sulphate of magnesia or sulphate of soda. Some examples are:

- Cheltenham
- Leamington-Spa
- Montmirail
- Seidlitz.

Chalybeate waters

These mineral waters are of two kinds, being either carbonated or sulphated. It is recognised that they act as a stimulant and a tonic. Some examples are:

- Forges
- Passy
- Saint Nectaire
- Vittel.

Lithiated waters

These are rich in Lithia salts. Some examples are:

- Baden-Baden
- Carlsbad
- Saint Marco
- Salvator.

Sulphurous waters

These waters are impregnated with hydrogen. Some examples are:

- Challes
- Harrogate
- St. Boes.

Service of spring and mineral waters

Waters should be chilled and are not generally served with ice made of tap water. They may be taken between meals or at mealtimes, either alone or mixed with light wine or spirits.

Squashes

A squash may be served on its own diluted by water, soda water or lemonade. Squashes are also used as mixers for spirits and in cocktails, or used as the base for such drinks as fruit cups. Examples are:

- orange squash
- lemon squash
- grapefruit squash
- lime juice.

Juices

The main types of juices held in stock in the dispense bar are:

Bottled or canned

- orange juice
- pineapple juice
- grapefruit juice
- tomato juice.

Fresh

- orange juice
- grapefruit juice
- lemon juice.

Apart from being served chilled on their own, these fresh juices may also be used in cocktails and for mixing with spirits.

Syrups

The main uses of these concentrated, sweet, fruit flavourings are as a base for cocktails, fruit cups or mixed with soda water as a long drink. The main ones used are:

- *Cassis* (blackcurrant)
- *Cerise* (cherry)
- *Citronelle* (lemon)
- *Framboise* (raspberry)
- *Gomme* (white sugar syrup)
- *Grenadine* (pomegranate)
- *Orgeat* (almond).

Syrups are also available as 'flavouring agents' for cold milk drinks such as milk shakes.

Information on the service of non-alcoholic bar beverages may be found in Section 5.9, page 252.

4.5 WINE AND DRINK LISTS

The function of the wine and drink list is similar to that of the menu and is to be a selling aid. Careful thought is needed in its planning, design, layout, colour and overall appearance to ensure it complements the style of the establishment.

The service staff should have a good knowledge of all the wines and drinks available and of their main characteristics. They should also have an extensive knowledge of which wines are most suitable to offer with certain foods (see Section 4.10, page 156).

Types of wine and drinks lists

Bar and cocktail lists

These may range from a basic standard list offering the common everyday apéritifs such as sherries, vermouths, bitters, a selection of spirits with mixers, beers and soft drinks, together with a limited range of cocktails, to a very comprehensive list offering a good choice in all areas. The actual format and content will be determined by the style of operation and clientele that the establishment wishes to attract. Depending on this, the emphasis may be in certain areas, such as:

- cocktails: traditional or fashionable
- malt whiskies
- beers
- New World wines
- non-alcoholic drinks.

A listing of cocktails, and their recipes and service notes, are given in Annex C pages 470 to 482.

Restaurant wine lists

These may take various formats such as:

- A full and very comprehensive list of wines from all countries, with emphasis on the classic areas such as Bordeaux/Burgundy plus a fine wine/prestige selection.
- A middle-of-the-road, traditional selection, for example, some French, German and Italian wines, together with some New World wines.
- A small selection of well-known or branded wines – a prestige list.
- Predominantly wines of one particular country.

After meal drinks lists (digestifs)

These lists are often combined with the wine list – although occasionally they are presented as a separate liqueur list. The list should offer a full range of liqueurs, together with possibly a specialist range of brandies and/or a specialist range of malt whiskies. Vintage and Late Bottled Vintage (LBV) port may also be offered here. In addition a range of speciality liqueur/spirit coffees might also be included (see Section 4.2, page 120).

Banqueting wine lists

The length of the list will generally depend on the size and style of operation. In most instances there is a selection of popular wine names/styles on offer. There would be a range of prices from house wines to some fine wines to suit all customer preferences. In some instances the banqueting wine list is the same as the restaurant wine list.

Room service drinks lists

There may be a mini-bar in the room, or the room service menu may offer a choice from a standard bar list. The range of wines offered is usually limited and prices will vary according to the type of establishment.

Contents of wine and drink lists

The contents of wine and drink lists are commonly listed in the order in which they may be consumed:

- Apéritifs – which alongside sparkling and still wines (page 142) can include a range of aromatised wines (page 145), fortified wines (page 145) and natural spring and mineral waters (page 122).
- Cocktails (page 132).
- Spirits (page 159) and associated mixers (aerated waters page 121).
- Wines – sparkling and still (page 142).
- Beers (page 165), cider (page 169) aerated waters (page 121) and squashes (page 124).
- Digestifs – which as well as liqueurs (page 163) may also include brandies (page 160), malt whiskies (page 162), ports, other fortified wines, sweet table wines, and vin doux naturels (page 145).
- Speciality coffees (page 120) and cigars (page 249) may also be included in lists.

Listing of wines

Wines are usually listed in three main ways:

1 Listing wines by place of origin (geography).
2 Listing wines by type.
3 Listing wines by grape.

Geographical listing for wines

The traditional approach is to list wines by geographical area. Within this approach the wines are presented by country or region, such as for instance France, or Australasia (which includes Australia and New Zealand), and then within that area by area. It is also usual to have the wines presented under each country, region or area with the white wines first, followed by the rosé wines and then the red wines. Using this approach the listing of wines within a wine list might be:

1	Champagne and sparkling	4	Italy
2	France	5	Spain
3	Germany	6	Portugal

7. England	11	Australasia
8 Other European wines	12	South Africa
9 Australia	13	Other world wines
10 The Americas (USA and South America)	14.	House wines

To help the customer choose a wine and to enable staff to make recommendations, it can be useful for each of the groups of wines to be listed from the lighter wines to more full wines.

Listing wines by type

A modern approach is to have wines listed by type:

- sparkling wines
- white wines
- rosé wines
- red wines
- dessert (sweet) wines.

The wines can then be listed under each type of wine in three main ways:

1 Country by country.

2 Region by region (similar to the geographical listing described above).

3 By the style of the wine.

If the wines are to be listed by type and by style, then the wines could be presented under, for instance, the headings:

- Sparkling wines
- Rosé wines
- White wines
  - grapy whites
  - grassy-fruity whites
  - richer whites
- Red wines
  - fruity reds
  - claret style reds
  - herby-spicy reds.

To help the customer choose a wine and to enable staff to make recommendations, it is useful for each of the groups of wines to be listed in order from the lighter wines to the more full wines. The chart given in Table 4.4 gives examples of wines by type, by style, and from light to full.

Listing wines by grape

If the wines are to be listed by grapes then one approach could be to list the grapes in alphabetical order.

Under each heading the wines made with that grape are listed, as well as the principal blends that are made with that grape as the predominant grape. When the wines are listed under the headings 'Other white grapes' or 'Other red grapes', then the grape(s) of the wine should also be listed next to the name of the wine.

White grapes	Red grapes

White grapes
- Chardonnay
- Chenin blanc
- Gewürztraminer
- Pinot Blanc
- Pinot Gris/Pinot Grigio
- Riesling
- Sauvignon Blanc
- Sémillon
- Other white grapes

Red grapes
- Cabernet Sauvignon
- Gamay
- Merlot
- Pinot Noir
- Sangiovese
- Shiraz/Syrah
- Tempranillo
- Zinfandel
- Other red grapes

Again, to help the customer choose a wine and to aid staff in making recommendations, it is useful for each of the groups of wines to be listed in order from the lighter wines to the more full wines.

General information required

It is usual to give information on wine and drink lists that help the customer in making decisions and also the staff in making recommendations. This information is shown below.

Wines

- Bin number.
- Name of wine.
- Country and area of origin.
- Quality indication (e.g. AOC, Qmp etc.).
- Shipper.
- Château/estate bottled.
- Varietal (grape type(s)).
- Vintage.
- Alcoholic strength.
- ½ bottle, bottle, magnum.
- Price.
- Supplier.
- Descriptive notes as appropriate.

Other drinks

- Type of drink, for example, juices, whisky, gin, sherry.
- Brand name if appropriate, for example, Martini.
- Style (sweet, dry etc.).
- Description, for example, for cocktails.
- Alcoholic strength as appropriate.
- Descriptive notes as appropriate.

TABLE 4.4 Examples of wines by type, by style, and from light to full

light

full

Sparkling White	White wines Grapy whites	Grassy-fruity whites	Richer whites
Dry Champagne Saumur Vouvray Touraine	Yugoslav Riesling Tafelwein Liebfraumilch Grüner Veltliner	Frascati Soave Muscadet	Bordeaux and Loire Sauvignon
Clairette de Die Frizzante	Alsace, Bulgarian and Hungarian Riesling Mosel Kabinett German Trocken	Orvieto Muscadet sur lie Van de Pays de Gascogne	Sancerre Pouilly Blanc Fumé New Zealand Sauvignon
Cuve Close Deutsche Sekt	Australian Dry Muscat Alsace Muscat Alsace Pinot Blanc	Pinot Blanco Italian Chardonnay Pinot Grigio	Lighter Californian and New Zealand Chardonnay St Veran
Crémant d'Alsace Cava Blanquette de Limoux	English wines Rhine Kabinett Mosel Spätlese	Chenin Blanc (South Africa and France) Mâcon Blanc Chablis Penedès White	Pouilly Fussé St Aubin Top class dry white Bordeaux
Crémant de Bourgogne Champagne Blanc de Blancs	Australian, Californian, Alsace and New Zealand Riesling Alsace and New Zealand Gewürztraminer	Rioja (new style) Mâcon Villages (Lugny etc.)	Grand Cru Chablis Puligny and Chassagne Montrachet Mersault Californian Fumé Gavi Saumur demi-sec
Cava semi-secco demi-sec Champagne	Rhine Spätlese and Auslese Alsace Verdange Tardive	Vouvray (medium) Vinho Verde	White Rhône Dão White Rioja (old style) Retsina
Vintage Champagne Australian and Californian sparkling	Trockenbeerenauslese Eiswein Muscat de Beaumes-de-Venise	Californian medium white French medium white	Corton Charlemagne Australian Sémillon Le Montrachet
Rich Champagne Mocasto Asti Spumanti	Tokay Setúbal Australian Muscats	Barsac Sauternes Australian late picked Sémillon	Australian Chardonnay Richer Californian Chardonnay

Rosé	Red wines		
	Fruity reds	*Claret-style reds*	*Herby-spicy reds*
Anjou Rosé Cabernet d'Anjou	Beaujolais Nouveau Côtes du Rhône Nouveau Vino Novello	Red Loire (Cabernet Franc) Grave de Friuli Yugoslav Cabernet	Valpolicella Bardolino Chianti
Spanish Rosé Rosé de Provence Chiaretto di Bardolino	Beaujolais Beaujolais Villages Mâcon Rouge	Southern French Cabernet Sauvignon Côtes du Duras Côtes de Buzet Bergerac	Côtes du Rhône Vins de Pays Syrah de l'Ardeche
Chilean Rosé Rosé de la Loire Bordeaux Rosé Bourgogne Rouge	Bourgogne Passe tout grains Cru Beaujolais	Bordeaux Rouge Bulgarian Cabernet Sauvignon	Gigondas Dolcetto Brunello de Montalcino Chianti Classico
Alsace Pinot Noir Sancerre Rosé Jura Rosé	Sancerre Rouge Côtes de Beaune Beaune Villages Rioja	Médoc New Zealand Cabernet Côtes du Bourg	Dão Barbera Barberesco Bairrada
Portuguese Rosé	Beaune Côtes de Nuits Villages Navarra	Bordeaux Crus Classés Spanish, Italian and the lighter Californian Cabernet Sauvignon	Châteauneuf-du- Pape Australian Cabernet Sauvignon Cabernet Shiraz Zinfandel Cahors Barolo
Rosé Champagne Rosé Saumur Rosé Cava	Volnay Reserva Rioja Gran Reserva Rioja	Californian and Bulgarian Merlot Saint-Emilion Pomerol	Traditional East European, Greek and North African wines
Blanc de Noirs Californian Blush	Pomard Aloxe Corton Nuits St Georges	Chilean, South African and Lebanese Cabernet Sauvignon	Côte Rôtie Nebbiolo d'Alba
Tavel Lirac Californian Rosé	Gevery Chambertin Californian and Australian Pinot Noir	Australian and fuller Californian Cabernet Sauvignon	Hermitage Australian Shiraz Amarone della Valpolicella

light

full

Legal requirements

See Chapter 10, page 391.

Alcoholic strength

The main scale of measurement of alcoholic strength may be summarised as:

1   OIML Scale (European): range 0% to 100% alcohol by volume.

2   Sikes Scale (United Kingdom old scale): range 0° to 175°. 'Proof' was the point 100°; 70° is equal to 40% alcohol by volume.

3   American Scale (USA): range 0° to 200°. Similar to Sikes but has scale of 200° rather than 175°.

The Organisation Internationale Métrologie Légale (OIML) Scale, previously called Gay Lussac Scale, is directly equal to the percentage of alcohol by volume in the drink at 20°C. It is the universally accepted scale for the measurement of alcohol. The by volume measurement indicates the amount of pure alcohol in a liquid. Thus, a liquid measured as 40% alcohol by volume will have 40% of the contents as pure alcohol. The alcoholic content of drinks, by volume, is now almost always shown on the label.

Approximate alcoholic strengths of drinks (OIML scale) are:

0%	non-alcoholic
not more that 0.05%	alcohol free
0.05–0.5%	de-alcoholised
0.5–1.2%	low alcohol
1.2–5.5%	reduced alcohol
3–6%	beer, cider, FABs* and 'alcopops'** with any of these being up to 10%
8–15%	wines, usually around 10–13%
14–22%	fortified wines (liqueur wines) such as sherry and port, aromatised wines such as vermouth, vin doux naturels (such as Muscat de Beaumes-de-Venise) and Sake***
37.5–45%	spirits, usually at 40%
17–55%	liqueurs, very wide range

* FABs is a term used to describe flavoured alcoholic beverages, for example, Bacardi Breezer (5.4%).

** 'Alcopops' is a term used to describe manufactured flavoured drinks (generally sweet and fruity) which have had alcohol, such as gin, added to them. They are also known as alcoholic soft drinks or alcoholic lemonade. Usually 3.5 to 5% but can be up to 10%.

*** Sake is a strong (18%), slightly sweet, form of beer made from rice.

4.6 COCKTAILS AND MIXED DRINKS

England, Mexico, America and France all claim to have originated the cocktail and while there are many stories, no one knows their authenticity. However, it was in the United States that cocktails first gained in popularity. At this stage, the cocktail was as much a pre-mixed stimulant mixture for taking on sporting occasions as it was a bar drink.

The term cocktail is now recognised to mean all mixed drinks. A cocktail is normally a short drink of up to about 10 cl (3½–4 oz) – anything larger being called a 'mixed drink' or 'long drink'.

Fig 4.6. Cocktails (courtesy of Six Continents Hotels)

Types of cocktails

The following drinks are also included under the heading cocktails.

Blended drinks:	Made using a liquidiser.
Champagne cocktails:	For example, Bucks Fizz, which has the addition of orange juice.
Cobblers:	Wine and spirit based, served with straws and decorated with fruit.
Collins:	Hot weather drinks, spirit-based, served with plenty of ice.
Coolers:	Almost identical to the Collins but usually containing the peel of the fruit cut into a spiral; spirit or wine-based.
Crustas:	May be made with any spirit, the most popular being brandy; edge of glass decorated with powdered sugar and crushed ice placed in glass.
Cups:	Hot weather, wine-based drinks.
Daisies:	Made with any spirit; usually served in tankards or wine glasses filled with crushed ice.
Egg nogs:	Traditional Christmas drink; rum or brandy and milk-based; served in tumblers.
Fixes:	Short drink made by pouring any spirit over crushed ice; decorated with fruit and served with short straws.
Fizzes:	Similar to a Collins; always shaken and then topped with soda; must be drunk immediately.
Flips:	Similar to Egg Nogs, containing egg yolk but never milk; spirit, wine or sherry-based.
Frappés:	Served on crushed ice.
Highball:	American; a simple drink that is quickly prepared with spirit and a mixer.
Juleps:	American; containing mint with claret, Madeira or bourbon whiskey base.
Pick-Me-Ups:	To aid digestion.
Pousse-Café:	Layered mix of liqueurs and/or spirits using differences in the specific densities of drinks to create layers – heaviest at the bottom, lightest at the top.

Smashes:	Smaller version of a julep.
Sours:	Always made with fresh juices to sharpen the flavour of the drink.
Swizzles:	Take their name from the stick used to stir the drink; 'swizzling' creates a frost on the outside of glass.
Toddies:	Refreshers that may be served hot or cold; contain lemon, cinnamon and nutmeg.

Making cocktails

A true cocktail is made by one of two methods: shaking or stirring. The art of making a good cocktail is to blend all the ingredients together by shaking or stirring so that upon tasting no one ingredient is predominant.

A rule of thumb to determine whether a cocktail should be shaken or stirred is that if it contains a fruit juice as one of the ingredients, then it should be shaken, and if the ingredients are wine based and clear, then it should be stirred.

The key equipment required when making a cocktail depends on the method being used:

Shaken

- Cocktail shaker or Boston shaker with Hawthorn strainer.
- Blender (for mixes).

Stirred

- Bar mixing glass.
- Bar spoon with muddler.
- Hawthorn strainer.

Points to note in making cocktails

- Ice should always be clear and clean.
- Do not overfill the cocktail shaker.
- Effervescent drinks should never be shaken.
- To avoid spillage, do not fill glasses to brim.
- When egg white or yolk is an ingredient, first break the egg into separate containers.
- Serve cocktails in chilled glasses.
- To shake, use short and snappy actions.
- Always place ice in the shaker or mixing glass first, followed by non-alcoholic and then alcoholic beverages.
- To stir, stir briskly until blend is cold.

- As a general rule the mixing glass is used for those cocktails based on liqueurs or wines (clear liquids).

- Shakers are used for cocktails which might include fruit juices, cream, sugar and similar ingredients.

- When egg white or yolk is an ingredient then the Boston shaker should always be used.

- Always add the garnish after the cocktail has been made and add it to the glass.

- Always measure out ingredients; inaccurate amounts spoil the balance of the blend and taste.

- Never use the same ice twice.

A comprehensive listing of cocktail and mixed drink ingredients and methods is given in Annex C, pages 470 to 482. Examples of glasses for the service of cocktails are shown in Figure 2.9, page 64.

4.7 BITTERS

Bitters are used either as apéritifs or for flavouring mixed drinks and cocktails. The most popular varieties are as follows:

Amer Picon:	A very black and bitter French apéritif. Grenadine or Cassis is often added to make the flavour more acceptable. Traditionalists add water in a proportion 2:1.
Angostura bitters:	Takes its name from a town in Bolivia. However, it is no longer produced there but in Trinidad. Brownish red in colour, it is used in the preparation of pink gin and the occasional cocktail and may be regarded as mainly a flavouring agent.
Byrrh:	(Pronounced beer.) This is a style of bitters made in France near the Spanish border. It has a base of red wine and is flavoured with quinine and herbs and fortified with brandy.
Campari:	A pink, bittersweet Italian apéritif that has a slight flavour of orange peel and quinine. Serve in an 18.93 cl (6⅔ fl oz) Paris goblet or Highball glass. Use one measure on ice and garnish with a slice of lemon. Top up according to the customer's requirements with soda or water (iced).
Fernet Branca:	The Italian version of Amer Picon. Best served diluted with water or soda. Good for hangovers!
Underberg:	A German bitter which looks like and almost tastes like iodine. It may be taken as a pick-me-up with soda.
Other bitters:	Orange and peach bitters are used principally as cocktail ingredients. Other well-known bitters are Amora Montenegro, Radis, Unicum, Abbots, Peychaud, Boonekamp and Welling. Many are used to cure that 'morning after the night before' feeling. Cassis or Grenadine is sometimes added to make the drink more palatable.

4.8 WINE

Wine is the alcoholic beverage obtained from the fermentation of the juice of freshly gathered grapes. The fermentation takes place in the district of origin, according to local tradition and practice.

Only a relatively small area of the world is wine producing. This is because the grape will only provide juice of the quality necessary for conversion into a drinkable wine where two climatic conditions prevail:

- sufficient sun to ripen the grape
- winters that are moderate yet sufficiently cool to give the vine a chance to rest and restore its strength for the growing and fruiting season.

These climatic conditions are found in two main wine producing zones, which lie between the latitudes 30° and 50° north and south of the equator.

Three-quarters of the world's wine is produced in Europe and just over half in the EU. France and Italy produce the most wine, with Italy being the largest producer. Next in order come Spain, USA, Australia, Argentina, Germany, Portugal, Chile and South Africa.

Vinification

The process central to vinification (wine making) is fermentation – the conversion of sugar by yeast to alcohol and carbon dioxide. This process is also necessary to the making of all alcoholic beverages – not only for still, sparkling and fortified wines, but also to spirits, liqueurs and beers (although some variations and further processes will be applied for different types of beverages).

Vine species

The vine species that produces grapes suitable for wine production, and which stocks most of the vineyards of the world, is named *Vitis vinifera*. Most varieties now planted in Europe and elsewhere have evolved from this species through cross-breeding, to suit local soils and climates. The same grape in different regions may be given a different name, for example, Grenache in the Rhône region is also known as Garnacha, which produces fine Spanish wines. There are a number of grapes which have become known as having distinctive characteristics. Examples of these principal grapes of the world, and their general characteristics, are given in Table 4.5, pages 137 to 140.

Table 4.5 Principal white and red grapes

White grapes	Where grown	General characteristics of the wine
Chardonnay	Worldwide	The white grape of Burgundy, Champagne and the New World. Aromas associated with chardonnay include ripe melon and fresh pineapple. The fruity, oaky New World wines tend to be buttery and syrupy, with tropical fruits and richness. In Burgundy the wines are succulent but bone-dry, with a nutty intensity. Chablis, from the cooler northern Burgundy, gives wines that have a sharp, steely acidity that may also be countered by the richness of oak. Also one of the three grapes for Champagne.
Chenin blanc	Loire, California and South Africa (known as Steen)	Variety of styles: bone-dry, medium-sweet, intensely sweet or sparkling wines, all with fairly high acidity making the wines very refreshing. Aroma association tends to be apples.
Gewürztraminer	Alsace, Germany, New Zealand, USA, Chile	One of the most pungent grapes, making wines that are distinctively spicy, with aromas like rose petals, grapefruit and tropical fruits such as lychees. Wines are aromatic and perfumed and are occasionally off-dry.
Muscat	Worldwide	Dry and mainly sweet, perfumed wines, smelling and tasting of grapes and raisins and made in styles from pale, light and floral to golden, sweet and orangey, or brown, rich and treacly. Often fortified (as in the French *vins doux naturels*, e.g. Muscat des Beaumes-de-Venise). Also principal grape for sparkling Asti.
Pinot Blanc/ Weissburgunder	Alsace, northern Italy, Germany, USA	Dry, neutral, fresh and fruity wines with the best having appley and soft spicy and honeyed aromas.
Pinot Gris/Pinot Grigio/Ruländer / Tokay-Pinot Gris	Alsace, Italy, USA, Canada, New Zealand	Generally full-bodied spicy white wines, often high in alcohol and low in acidity. Wines are crisp and neutral in Italy and aromatic and spicy in Alsace and elsewhere, with a hint of honey. Also used to make golden sweet wines, especially from Alsace.

Table 4.5 continued

White grapes	Where grown	General characteristics of the wine
Riesling	Alsace, Germany, Australia, New Zealand, South Africa	Range of wines from the steely to the voluptuous, always well perfumed, with good ageing potential. Aromas tend towards apricots and peaches. Germany makes the greatest Riesling in all styles. Piercing acidity and flavours ranging from green apple and lime to honeyed peaches, to stony and slate-like. Styles can range from bright and tangy to intensely sweet.
Sauvignon Blanc	Worldwide	Common aroma association with gooseberries, the wines are green, tangy, fresh and pungent. When made with oak, it can be a different wine: tropical fruits in the Californian examples, while the Bordeaux classic wines, often blended with Sémillon, begin with nectarine hints and then become more nutty and creamy with age. May be called Blanc Fumé.
Sémillon	Mainly Bordeaux and Australia, but also worldwide	Lemony, waxy dry whites; when oaked they can gain flavours of custard, nuts and honey. Luscious golden sweet wines when grapes are affected by *Botrytis Cinera* (Noble Rot), e.g. Sauternes
Viognier	Rhône Valley, southern France, USA, Australia	Rhône wines, e.g. Condrieu, are aromatic, with hints of apricots and spring flowers; wines from other areas tend to be less perfumed.

Red grapes	Where grown	General characteristics of the wine
Cabernet Sauvignon	Worldwide	Principal grape of Bordeaux, especially in the Médoc. New World wines deliver big wines with upfront blackcurrant fruit; Bordeaux wines need time to mature. Generally benefits from being blended, e.g. with Merlot, Cabernet Franc, Syrah, Tempranillo, Sangiovese. Also used to make aromatic rosé wines.
Gamay	Beaujolais, Loire, Savoie, Switzerland and USA	The grape of Beaujolais, making light and juicy wines. Characteristic pear drop aroma association indicating wine made using macération carbonique method. Makes lighter wine in the Loire Valley in central France and in Switzerland and Savoie. Known as 'Napa Gamay' in California.

Table 4.5 continued

Red grapes	Where grown	General characteristics of the wine
Grenache/ Garnacha	Southern France and Rhône, Spain, Australia, USA	Makes strong, fruity but pale wines and fruity rosé wines. Important as part of blends, e.g. in Châteauneuf-du-Pape in the Rhône and in Rioja in Spain. Characteristics of ripe strawberries, raspberries and hints of spice.
Merlot	Worldwide	Principal grape of Saint-Emilion and Pomerol in France. Aromas tend towards plums and damsons. The wines are low in harsh tannins and can be light and juicy, smooth and plummy or intensely blackcurrant.
Nebbiolo	Italy	One of Italy's best red grapes, used in Barolo and Barbaresco. Fruity and perfumed wines with a mixture of tastes and flavours of black cherry and sloes, tar and roses. Aroma association tends towards prunes. Traditionally tough and tannic when young, with good plummy flavours as they develop.
Pinot Noir/ Spätburgunder Pinot Nero	Worldwide	Principal grape of Burgundy's Côte d'Or. Aromas can be of strawberries, cherries and plums (depending on where grown). Silky and strawberry-like; simple wines have juicy fruit; the best mature wines, such as the great red wines of Burgundy, are well perfumed. Loire and German wines are lighter. Also one of the three grapes of Champagne and used elsewhere (e.g. California and Australia) for making white, sparkling or red and very pale pink wines.
Sangiovese	Italy, Argentina, USA	Principal grape of Chianti. Also known as Brunello and Moreluno. Mouth-watering, sweet-sour red fruit in young wines, reminiscent of juicy cherries, which intensifies in older wines.
Shiraz/Syrah	Worldwide	Warm, spicy, peppery wines with aromas of raspberries; French Syrah tends to be smoky, herby and packed with red fruits (raspberries, blackberries or blackcurrants); Australian Shiraz has sweeter black cherry fruit and often black chocolate or liquorice aromas. Very fruity rosé wines are also made.
Tempranillo	Spain, Portugal, Argentina	Early ripening, aromatic Rioja grape (Ull de Liebre in Catalonia, Cencibel in La Mancha, Tinto Fino in Ribera del Duero, Tinta Roriz in Douro and Aragonez in southern Portugal). Wines are light and juicy with hints of strawberries and plums, silky and spicy with hints of prunes, tobacco and cocoa. Wines in cooler climates are more elegant and are more beefy in warmer climates.

Table 4.5 continued

Red grapes	Where grown	General characteristics of the wine
Zinfandel (Pimitivo in Italy)	California, Italy	Aromas of blackberries, bramble and spice. In California wines have blackberry flavours, which are sometimes slightly metallic. Can be structured and lush and also used to make pale pink 'blush' white wine. Known as Primitivo in Southern Italy, where it makes big, rustic wines.

The grape

The grape consists of a number of elements:

- skin – which provide tannins and colour
- stalk – which provides tannins
- pips – provides bitter oils
- pulp – contains sugar, fruit acids, water and pectins.

The yeast required for the fermentation process is found on the outside of the grape skin in the form of a whitish bloom.

The colour in wine comes mainly from the skin of the grape, being extracted during the fermentation process. Red wine can only be made from red grapes. However white wine can be made from white or red grapes, provided that, in the case of red grapes, the grape skins are removed before fermentation begins.

Factors that influence the quality and final taste of wine

The same vine variety, grown in different regions and processed in different ways, will produce wines of differing characteristics. The factors that affect the quality and final taste of wines include:

1 Climate and microclimate.
2 Nature of the soil and subsoil.
3 Vine family and grape species.
4 Method of cultivation – viticulture.
5 Composition of the grape(s).
6 Yeast and fermentation.
7 Method of wine making – vinification.
8 Luck of the year – vintage.
9 Ageing and maturing process.
10 Method of shipping or transportation.
11 Storage temperature.

Pests and diseases

The vine is subject to pests and diseases in the form of birds, insects, fungi, viruses and weeds. Some examples are given below.

Phylloxera vastatrix

A louse-like, almost invisible aphid, which attacks the roots of the vine. Phylloxera arrived in Europe in the mid 1800s almost by accident, transported on American vines imported into various European countries from the eastern states of North America. It ravaged many of the vineyards of Europe at this time. The cure was to graft the European vine onto resistant American rootstocks. This practice has become standard throughout the world wherever *Vitis vinifera* is grown.

Grey rot or Pourriture gris

This fungus attacks the leaves and fruit of the vine during warm damp weather. It is recognised by a grey mould. The fungus imparts an unpleasant flavour to the wine.

Noble rot or Pourriture noble (*Botrytis cinerea*)

This is the same fungus in its beneficent form, which may occur when humid conditions are followed by hot weather. The fungus punctures the grape skin, the water content evaporates and the grape shrivels, thus concentrating the sugar inside. This process gives the luscious flavours characteristic of Sauternes, German Trockenbeerenauslese and Hungarian Tokay Aszu.

Faults in wine

Faults occasionally develop in wine as it matures in bottles. Nowadays, through improved techniques and attention to detail regarding bottling and storage, faulty wine is a rarity. Some of the more common causes of faulty wine are given below.

Corked wines

These are wines affected by a diseased cork caused through bacterial action or excessive bottle age. TCA (trichloroanisole) causes the wine to taste and smell foul. This is not to be confused with cork residue in wine, which is harmless.

Maderisation or oxidation

This is caused by bad storage leading to too much exposure to air, often because the cork has dried out. The colour of the wine browns or darkens and the taste very slightly resembles Madeira, hence the name. The wine tastes 'spoilt'.

Acetification

This is caused when the wine is over exposed to air. The vinegar microbe develops a film on the surface of the wine and acetic acid is produced, making the wine taste sour, resembling wine vinegar (vin vinaigre).

Tartare flake

This is the crystallisation of potassium bitartrate. These crystal-like flakes, sometimes seen in white wine, may cause anxiety to some customers as they spoil the appearance of the wine, which is otherwise perfect to drink. If the wine is stabilised before bottling, this condition should not occur.

Excess sulphur dioxide (SO$_2$)

Sulphur dioxide is added to wine to preserve it and keep it healthy. Once the bottle is opened, the smell will disappear and, after a few minutes, the wine is perfectly drinkable.

Secondary fermentation

This happens when traces of sugar and yeast are left in the wine in the bottle. It leaves the wine with an unpleasant, prickly taste that should not be confused with the pétillant or spritzig characteristics associated with other styles of healthy and refreshing wines.

Foreign contamination

Examples include splintered or powdered glass caused by faulty bottling machinery or re-used bottles which previously held some kind of disinfectant.

Hydrogen sulphide (H$_2$S)

The wine smells and tastes of rotten eggs and should be thrown away.

Sediment, lees, crust or dregs

This is organic matter discarded by the wine as it matures in the cask or bottle. It can be removed by racking, fining or, in the case of bottled wine, by decanting.

Cloudiness

This is caused by suspended matter in the wine, which disguises its true colour. It may also be caused by extremes in storage temperatures.

Classification of wine types

Still (or light) wine

This is the largest category. The alcoholic strength may be between 8% and 15% by volume. The wines may be:

- *Red*: produced by being fermented in contact with grape skins (from which the wine gets its colour). Normally dry wines.
- *White*: usually produced from white grapes, but the grape juice (must) is usually fermented away from the skins. Normally dry to very sweet.
- *Rosé*: can be made in three ways – from black grapes fermented on the skins for up to 48 hours; by mixing red and white wines together; or by pressing grapes so that some colour is extracted. Rosé wine may be dry or semi-sweet. Rosé wines are called 'blush' wines in the USA when made wholly from red grapes.

Table 4.6 Key differences in methods of production of sparkling wines

Method	Fermentation and maturation	Removal of sediment
Méthode traditionelle	In bottle	By the processes of remuage and dégorgement (moving the sediment to the neck of the bottle and then opening the bottle to remove it), topping up the bottle and then resealing.
Méthode transvasement or transfer method	In bottle	By transfer under pressure to a vat and then filtering before rebottling.
Charmat or méthode cuve close	In tank	By filtration process.
Méthode gazifié or carbonation method	Sometimes termed 'impregnation', where carbon dioxide is injected into a vat of still wine that has been chilled and which is then bottled under pressure. Least expensive method.	

Sparkling wines

Sparkling wines are available from France, Spain (Cava), Italy (Prosecco), Germany (Sekt) and many other countries.

The most famous sparkling wine is Champagne. This is made by the méthode champenoise (secondary fermentation in the bottle) in an area of northeastern France.

Effervescent wines made outside this area are called vins mousseux or sparkling wines. A summary of the four methods for making sparkling wines is given in Table 4.6.

Sweetness in sparkling wine

The dryness or sweetness of the wine is indicated on the label:

- *Extra brut* – very dry
- *Brut* – dry
- *Sec* – medium dry
- *Demi-sec* – medium sweet
- *Demi doux* – sweeter
- *Doux* – luscious

Other sparkling wine terms

French

- *Vin mousseux*: sparkling wine other than Champagne.
- *Méthode traditionelle*: sparkling, made by the traditional method.
- *Pétillant/perlant*: slightly sparkling.
- *Crémant*: less sparkling than mousseux.

German

- *Spritzig*: slightly sparkling.
- *Flaschengarung nach dem traditionellen Verfahren*: sparkling wine made by the traditional method.
- *Sekt*: sparkling (also used to mean the wine itself).
- *Schaumwein*: sparkling of lesser quality than Sekt.
- *Perlwein*: slightly sparkling.

Italian

- *Prosecco*: used as the generic name for Italian sparkling wines.
- *Frizzante*: semi-sparkling.
- *Spumante*: sparkling.
- *Metodo classico/tradizionale*: sparkling wine made by the traditional method.

Portuguese

- *Espumante*: sparkling.
- *Vinho verde*: meaning 'green wine', slightly sparkling.

Spanish

- *Espumosos*: sparkling.
- *Metodo tradicional*: sparkling, made by the traditional method.
- *Cava*: generic name for Spanish sparkling wines made by the traditional method.

Organic wines

These wines, also known as 'green' or 'environmentally friendly' wines, are made from grapes grown without the aid of artificial insecticides, pesticides or fertilisers. The wine itself will not be adulterated in any way, save for minimal amounts of the traditional preservative, sulphur dioxide, which is controlled at source.

Alcohol-free, de-alcoholised and low alcohol wines

These wines are made in the normal way and the alcohol is removed either by hot treatment – distillation – which unfortunately removes most of the flavour as well, or, more satisfactorily, by a cold filtration process, also known as reverse osmosis. This removes the alcohol by mechanically separating or filtering out the molecules of alcohol through membranes made of cellulose or acetate. At a later stage, water and a little must are added, thus attempting to preserve much of the flavour of the original wine.

The definitions for these wines are:

- Alcohol free: maximum 0.05% alcohol
- De-alcoholised: maximum 0.50% alcohol
- Low alcohol: maximum 1.2% alcohol

Vins doux naturels

These are sweet wines that have had their fermentation muted by the addition of alcohol in order to retain their natural sweetness. Muting takes place when the alcohol level reaches between 5% and 8% by volume. They have a final alcoholic strength of about 17% by volume. One of the best known is Muscat de Beaumes-de-Venise, named after a village in the Côtes du Rhône where it is made. The wine is fortified with spirit before fermentation is complete so that some of the natural sugar remains in the wine. It is usually drunk young.

Fortified (liqueur) wines

Fortified wines such as sherry, port and Madeira have been strengthened by the addition of alcohol, usually a grape spirit. These are now known within the EU as liqueur wines or vins de liqueur. Their alcoholic strength may be between 15% and 22% by volume. Examples are:

- *Sherry* (from Spain) 15–18% – Fino (dry), Amontillado (medium), Oloroso (sweet).
- *Port* (from Portugal) 18–22% – ruby, tawny, vintage character, late bottled vintage, vintage.
- *Madeira* (made on the Portuguese island of Madeira) 18% – Sercial (dry), Verdelho (medium), Bual (sweet), Malmsey (very sweet).
- *Marsala* (dark sweet wine from Marsala in Sicily) 18%.
- *Málaga* (from Málaga, Andalusia, Spain) 18–20%.

Aromatised wines

These are flavoured and fortified wines.

Vermouths

The four main types of vermouth are:

- *Dry vermouth*: often called French vermouth or simply French (as in Gin and French). It is made from dry white wine that is flavoured and fortified.
- *Sweet vermouth/bianco*: made from dry white wine, flavoured, fortified and sweetened with sugar or mistelle.
- *Rosé vermouth*: made in a similar way to Bianco, but it is less sweet and is coloured with caramel.
- *Red vermouth*: often called Italian vermouth, Italian or more often 'It' (as in Gin and It). It is made from white wine and is flavoured, sweetened and coloured with a generous addition of caramel.

Popular brands of vermouth

Cinzano red		
Cinzano bianco		
Martini bianco	} sweet	
Martini rosé		
Martini rosso		
Noilly Prat red		

Martini		
Cinzano	} dry	
Chambery		
Noilly Prat		

Other aromatised wines

- *Chamberyzette*: Made in the Savoy Alps of France. It is flavoured with the juice of wild strawberries.

- *Punt-e-mes*: From Carpano of Turin. This is heavily flavoured with quinine and has wild contrasts of bitterness and sweetness.

- *Dubonnet*: Made in France and is available in two varieties: blonde (white) and rouge (red) and is flavoured with quinine and herbs.

- *St Raphael*: Red or white, bittersweet drink from France flavoured with herbs and quinine.

- *Lillet*: Popular French apéritif made from white Bordeaux wine and flavoured with herbs, fruit peel and fortified with Armagnac brandy. It is aged in oak casks.

- *Pineau des Charentes*: Although not strictly an aromatised or fortified wine, Pineau des Charentes has gained popularity as an alternative apéritif or digestif. It is available in white, rosé or red and is made with grape must from the Cognac region and fortified with young Cognac to about 17% alcohol by volume.

Quality control for wines

The majority of the world's wine-makers must ensure that their products conform to strict quality regulations covering such aspects as the location of the vineyards, what variety of grape is used, how the wine is made and how long it is matured.

Many countries now give the name of grape varieties on the wine label. Within the EU, if a grape variety is named on the label then the wine must contain at least 85 per cent of that variety. For EU wines, any number of grapes may be listed as part of descriptive text, but only a maximum of two may appear on the main label. For most countries outside of the EU, the wine must contain 100 per cent of the named variety, although there are exceptions. These include Australia and New Zealand who are permitted 85 per cent and the USA who are permitted 75 per cent. Australia allows up to five varieties, provided each is at least 5 per cent of the blend.

European Union

European Union directives lay down general rules for table wines, for table wines with geographical description, and for quality wines produced in specified regions (QWPSR). For example:

France

- *Vin de table*: this is ordinary table wine in the cheapest price range.

- *Vin de pays*: the lowest official category recognised. Wines of medium quality and price, made from certain grapes grown within a defined area. The area must be printed on the label. A minimum alcohol content is specified.

- *Vin delimité de qualité supérieure (VDQS)*: a quality wine just below appellation controlled standard. Area of production, grape varieties, minimum alcohol content, cultivation (viticulture) and wine making (vinification) methods are specified.

- *Appellation d'origine contrôlée (AC or AOC)*: quality wine from approved areas. Grape varieties and proportions, pruning and cultivation method, maximum yield per hectare, vinification and minimum alcohol content are specified.

Germany

- *Deutscher Tafelwein*: wine made from one of the four wine regions designated for table wine (Rhein-Mosel, Bayern, Neckar and Oberrhein). It is often blended. A minimum alcohol content is specified.

- *Deutscher Landwein*: quality wine from one of 19 designated districts. It can be *trocken* (dry) or *halbtrocken* (medium dry). A minimum alcohol content is specified.

- *Qualitätswein bestimmter Anbaugebiete (QbA)*: quality wine in medium price range (includes Liebfraumilch) from one of the 13 designated regions (*Anbaugebieten*). It must carry an *Amtliche Prüfungsnummer* (control number).

- *Qualitätswein mit Prädikat (QmP)*: quality wines of distinction and special characteristics. They have no added sugar. The *Prädikat* (distinction) indicates how ripe the grape was when it was harvested – generally the riper the grape, the richer the wine. There are six categories:

  1 *Kabinett*: made from grapes harvested at the normal time, usually October, but in a perfect state of ripeness.

  2 *Spätlese*: made from late harvested grapes.

  3 *Auslese*: made from selected bunches of ripe grapes.

  4 *Beerenauslese*: made from selected ripe grapes affected by noble rot.

  5 *Eiswein*: made from ripe grapes left on the vine to be picked and pressed when frozen.

  6 *Trockenbeerenauslese*: made from selected single grapes heavily affected by noble rot.

Italy

- *Vino da tavola*: ordinary table wine, unclassified.

- *Vino da tavola con indicazione geografica typica (IGT)*: wine from a defined area.

- *Denominazione di origine contrallata (DOC)*: quality wine from an approved area. Grape varieties, cultivation and vinification methods and maximum yields are specified.

- *Denominazione di origine controllata e garantia (DOCG)*: guaranteed quality wines from approved areas. Grape variety and proportions, maximum yield, vinification methods, pruning and cultivation and minimum alcohol content are specified.

Spain

- *Vino de mesa*: ordinary table wine.

- *Vino de tierra*: wines from specified regions.

- *Denominación de origen (DO)*: quality wines from specified regions.

- *Denominación de origen calificada (DOCa)*: highest quality grade with strict controls on production and geography.

Portugal

- *Vinho de mesa*: ordinary table wine from no particular region and may be a blend from several regions.

- *Vinho regional*: quality wine from a particular place within a named region.

- *Denominação de origem controlada (DO)*: quality wines from specified regions; the quality and authenticity of the wine is guaranteed.

Estate bottled

The following terms indicate that the wine was bottled on the estate.

- *Mise en bouteille au domaine* or *Mise du domaine* (France).

- *Erzeugerabfullung* or *Aus eigenem Lesegut* (Germany).

- *Imbottligliato all'origine* or *Imbottigliato al'origine nelle cantine della fatoria dei*: bottled at source in the cellars of the estate of (Italy).

- *Embottelado* or *Engarrafado de origen* (Spain).

- *Engarrafado na origem* (Portugal).

Other terms used in France:

- *Mise en bouteille au château*: means the wine was bottled at the château (literally means castle) printed on the label. It is seen mostly on wines from Bordeaux.

- *Mise en bouteille dans nos caves*: means the wine was bottled in the cellars of the company or person (négociant) whose name usually appears on the label.

- *Mise en bouteille par*: indicates that the wine was bottled by the company or individual whose name appears after these words.

Countries other than the EU

Developments in the international wine business, especially in the New World, have led to a more marketing led approach to wines. Simpler information is given on the labels, and also on detailed back labels, including the identification of grape varieties (or the use of the Californian term 'varietals') and straightforward advice on storage, drinking and matching the wine with food.

Although most countries have a category for wines that is similar to EU Table Wine, this is mainly sold locally. On the international markets the wines are classified as Wine with Geographical Description. Each country has it own system for dividing its vineyard areas into regions, zones, districts and so on, and controlling the use of regional names. Where regions, vintages and varieties are named on the label, these wines may also have a small proportion of wine from other regions, vintages and varieties blended with them. All countries have their own legislation covering production techniques and use of label terms to prevent consumers from being misinformed. Examples are:

Argentina

Argentina has a system of DOCs (Controlled Denominations of Origin) but it is common for wines to be labelled by region.

Australia

The Label Integrity Scheme controls regional, varietal and vintage labelling. The Authentication of Origin scheme denotes that if a wine region is mentioned then at least 80 per cent of the wine must come from that source. In addition, a system of regional appellations is being established which is designed to lead to greater geographical descriptions.

Chile

Chile has a system of regional DOs (denominations of origin) in which regions are divided into sub-regions.

New Zealand

New Zealand does not have a hierarchical structure of regional terms, although some regional names, for example, Wairau Valley or Gimblett Gravels, are more specific than others such as Marlborough or Hawkes Bay.

South Africa

The Wine of Origin (WO) scheme in South Africa controls regional labelling of wines, as well as varietal and vintage details on wine bottles. Estates are also included in the WO scheme and estate wines must only include grapes grown by the named estate.

USA

The American Viticulture Areas (AVAs) is a guarantee of source – at least 85 per cent must come from within that area – but not of quality or method of production. Regional terms can range from naming a state or a single vineyard. One increasingly popular term used in California is 'coastal', which allows for blending across almost all the Californian vineyards lying up to 100 km inland of the Pacific.

Reading a wine label

The EU has strict regulations that govern what is printed on a wine bottle label. These regulations also apply to wine entering the EU. In addition, standard sized bottles of light (or still) wines bottled after 1988, when EU regulations on content came into force, must contain 75 cl, although bottles from previous years, containing 70 cl for example, will still be on sale for some years to come. In addition to the quality terms, indicated on pages 144 to 150 and the sparkling wine terms given on pages 143 to 144, examples of taste and colour terms that appear on wine labels are given in Table 4.7.

The label on a bottle of wine can give a lot of useful information about that wine. The language used will normally be that of the country of origin. The information always includes:

- the name of the wine
- the country where the wine was made
- alcoholic strength in percentage by volume (% vol)
- contents in litres, cl or ml
- the name and address or trademark of the supplier.

It may also include:

- the varietal(s) (name of the grape(s) used to make the wine)
- the year the grapes were harvested, called the vintage, if the wine is sold as a vintage wine
- the region where the wine was made
- the property where the wine was made
- the quality category of the wine
- details of the bottler and distributor.

An example of the kind of information that is given on a wine label is shown in Figure 4.7. This example shows a guide to a German wine label.

4.9 TASTING OF WINE

The wine waiter, or sommelier, as well as having an extensive knowledge of the contents of the wine list, should have a good knowledge of the characteristics of the different wines offered. To develop these skills and knowledge he/she must adopt a professional approach to tasting wine.

Table 4.7 Examples of other wine label terms

Term	France	Germany	Italy	Spain	Portugal
Wine	vin	wein	vino	vine	vinho
Dry	sec	trocken	secco	seco	seco
Medium	demi-sec	halbtrocken	abboccato	abocado	semi-seco
Sweet	doux/moelieaux	süß	dolce	dulce	doce
White	blanc	weißwein	bianco	blanco	branco
Red	rouge	rotwein	rosso	tinto	tinto
Rosé	rosé	rosé	rosato	rosado	rosado

1. Specified growing region: one of the 13 designated regions in Germany
2. Year in which the grapes were harvested (vintage)
3. Town and vineyard from which the grapes come
4. Grape variety — here is Riesling
5. Indication of taste or style of the wine — in this case it is *halbtrocken* (medium dry). If it were *trocken*, it would be dry
6. Quality level of the wine
7. The official testing number: proof that the wine has passed chemical and sensory testing which is required for all German quality wines
8. Alcohol content
9. Bottle size
10. Wines bottled and produced by the grower or a cooperative of growers may be labelled *Erzeugerabfüllung*. Estates and growers can use *Gutsabfüllung* as an alternative. Other wineries and bottlers are identified as *Abfüller*

Fig 4.7. Guide to the German wine label (Source: The German Wine Information Service)

Professional tasting

The tasting, or evaluation, of wine is carried out to:

■ develop learning from experience

■ help in the assessment of the quality of a wine in terms of value (the balance between price and worth) when making purchasing decisions

■ monitor the progress of a wine which is being stored, to determine the optimum selling time and as part of protecting the investment

■ assist in the description of a wine when explaining its qualities or deficiencies to customers

■ provide a personal record of wines tasted, which helps to reinforce the experience and the learning.

To appreciate the tasting of wine to the full it should be carried out in an environment that supports the wine evaluation process. That is with:

■ no noise to distract the taster

■ good ventilation to eliminate odours

- sufficient light (daylight rather than artificial if possible), preferably north facing in the northern hemisphere (south facing in the southern hemisphere), as the light is more neutral

- a white background for tables so as not to affect the perception of the colour of the wine

- a room temperature of about 20°C (68°F).

The tool of the taster is the glass, which must be the correct shape. A wine glass with a stem and of sufficient capacity should be chosen (see Figure 4.8). The glass should be fairly wide but narrowing at the top. This allows the elements making up the bouquet to become concentrated and thus better assessed. The wine tasting glass should never be filled to more than one-third capacity. This allows the taster to swirl the wine round the glass more easily. It goes without saying that the tasting glass should be spotlessly clean.

Fig 4.8. Wine taster's glass (International Standards Organisation)

Professional approach

The purpose of the wine tasting is to attempt to identify characteristics that describe the wine, which are then used to assess its quality. When undertaking professional tasting it is important to be logical in the approach and to always follow the same sequence. The professional tasting, or evaluation, of wines includes three key stages:

1 Recording the details of each individual wine.

2 Looking at, smelling and tasting the wine.

3 Recording the findings.

Approaching the process in this way ensures the development of confidence and the ability to make sound judgements.

Recording wine details

To ensure a complete record of the tasting of each wine, it is important to record the following details:

- name of wine
- country and area of origin
- quality indication (e.g. AOC, Qmp etc.)
- shipper
- château/estate bottled
- varietal(s) (grapes)

- vintage
- alcohol level
- ½ bottle, bottle, magnum
- price
- supplier.

Looking at, smelling and tasting the wine

When tasting the wines there are two sets of factors being considered. The first are to do with assessing and evaluating the characteristics of the wine and making a judgement about its quality. The second are to do with identifying taste and aroma associations.

Professional wine tasting is really an analysis and evaluation of qualities of the wine by the senses. This includes:

- looking at the wine to assess its clarity, colour and intensity, and the nature of the colour by identifying the specific shade of white, rosé or red
- smelling, or nosing, the wine to assess the condition of the wine, the intensity of aroma, or bouquet, and to identify other aroma characteristics. Taste is 80 per cent smell!
- tasting the wine to assess the sweetness/dryness, acidity, tannin, body, length and other taste characteristics
- touch, to feel the weight of the wine in the mouth, the temperature etc.
- hearing, to create associations with the occasion
- drawing conclusions about the evaluation (summing up) and making a judgement of the quality of the wine (poor, acceptable, good, outstanding).

Examples of the terms that might be used as part of the evaluation of the wine are given in Table 4.8.

Tasting technique

After assessing the clarity, colour and the smell, take a small amount of the wine in the mouth together with a little air and roll it around so that it reaches the different parts of the tongue. Now lean forward so that the wine is nearest the teeth and suck air in through the teeth. Doing this helps to highlight and intensify the flavour. (Fortified wines, spirits and liqueurs are often assessed by sight and smell without tasting.)

When tasting the following should be considered:

- The taste-character of the wine is detected in different parts of the mouth but especially by the tongue: sweetness at the tip and the centre of the tongue, acidity on the upper edges, saltiness on the tip and at the sides, sour at the sides and bitterness at the back.
- Sweetness and dryness will be immediately obvious.
- Acidity will be recognised by its gum-drying sensation, but in correct quantities acidity provides crispness and liveliness to a drink.
- Astringency or tannin content, usually associated with red wines, will give a dry coating or furring effect, especially on the teeth and gums.
- Body, which is the feel of the wine in your mouth, and flavour, the essence of the wine as a drink, will be the final arbiters as to whether or not you like it.
- Aftertaste is the finish the wine leaves on your palate.
- Overall balance is the evaluation of all the above elements taken together.

Table 4.8 Examples of wine evaluation terms

Sight	*Clarity:* clear, bright, brilliant, gleaming, sumptuous, dull, hazy, cloudy.
	Colour intensity: pale, subdued, faded, deep, intense.
	White wine: water clear, pale yellow, yellow with green tinges, straw, gold, deep yellow, brown, Maderised.
	Rosé wine: pale pink, orange-pink, onion-skin, blue-pink, copper.
	Red wine: purple, garnet, ruby, tawny, brick-red, mahogany.
Smell (nose, aroma, bouquet)	*Condition:* clean – unclean.
	Intensity: weak – pronounced.
	Other aroma descriptors: fruity, perfumed, full, deep, spicy, vegetal, fine, rich, pleasant, weak, nondescript, flat, corky.
Taste	*Sweetness/dryness:* bone dry, dry, medium dry, sweet, medium sweet, sweet, luscious.
	Acidity: low – high.
	Tannin: low – high.
	Body: thin, light, medium, full-bodied.
	Length: short – long.
	Other taste descriptors: fruity, bitter, spicy, hard, soft, silky, floral, vegetal, smooth, tart, piquant, spritzig/ petillant (slightly sparkling).
Conclusion	*Summing up:* well-balanced, fine, delicate, rich, robust, vigorous, fat, flabby, thick, velvety, harsh, weak, unbalanced, insipid, for laying down, just right, over the hill.
	Overall quality/value: poor – acceptable – good – outstanding.

Note: It is important that you make up your own mind about the wines you taste. Do not be too easily influenced by the observations of others.

General grape and wine characteristics

There are a number of grapes that have distinctive characteristics. Examples of these grapes are listed in Table 4.5, pages 137 to 140, and information on their general characteristics is also given. The type and style of various specific wines is identified, and listed from light to full, in Table 4.4 on pages 130 and 131.

Table 4.9 Some common aroma and taste associations

White grapes		Red grapes	
Chardonnay	ripe melon, fresh pineapple, tropical fruits, nutty	Cabernet Sauvignon	blackcurrants
Chenin Blanc	apples	Nebbiolo	roses, prunes, black cherry, sloes
Gewürztraminer	rose petals, grapefruit, tropical fruits, e.g. lychees	Merlot	plum, damson, blackcurrants
Muscat	grapes/raisins	Pinot Noir	strawberries, cherries, plums (depending on where grown)
Riesling	apricots, peaches, lime, peaches, stony	Syrah/Shiraz	raspberries, blackberries, blackcurrants
Sauvignon Blanc	gooseberries, tropical fruits (when sweet — grapes, custard, nuts, honey)	Zinfandel	blackberries, bramble, spice

Other aroma and taste associations can include: pine trees, resin, vanilla, coffee, tea, herbs, smoke, toast, leather, cloves, cinnamon, nutmeg, ginger, mint, truffles, oak, figs, lilac and jasmine.

As well as describing and assessing the quality of the wine, many people also find it useful to apply a range of aroma and taste associations. Some examples of common aroma and taste associations are given in Table 4.9.

Recording the findings

Whenever wine is being evaluated a written record should be kept. These notes should be made at each stage of the process, otherwise it is possible to become muddled and confused. The process of writing down the findings helps to reinforce the discipline of the approach and leads, over time, to the development of greater confidence and skill, and also provides a record of wine tastings over time.

4.10 MATCHING FOOD AND WINE/DRINKS

Food and its accompanying wine/drinks should harmonise well together, with each enhancing the other's performance. However, the combinations that prove most successful are those that please the individual.

When considering possible food and wine partnerships there are no guidelines to which there are not exceptions. For example, although fish is usually served with white wine, some dishes, such as heavily sauced salmon, red mullet or a fish such as lamprey (which is traditionally cooked in red wine) can be successfully accompanied by a slightly chilled red Saint-Emilion, Pomerol or Mercury. The key issue in not having red wine with fish comes from the reaction of oily fish, such as mackerel, with red wine to produce a metal taste in the mouth.

The general guidelines on matching wine and food are summarised in Table 4.10.

Additionally, when making recommendations it is also useful to identify the type and style of the wine required and also the extent to which the wine should be light or full (see Table 4.4, pages 130 and 131).

Some general guidelines when selecting and serving wines are given below.

- Dry wines should be served before sweeter wines.

- White wines should be served before red wines.

Table 4.10 General guidelines for matching wine and food

Characteristic	Food considerations
Acidity	Can be used to match, or to contrast, acidity in foods, for example, crisp wines to match lemon or tomato, or to cut through creamy flavours.
Age/maturity	As wine ages and develops it can become delicate with complex and intricate flavours. More simple foods, such as grills or roasts, work better with older wines, than stronger tasting foods, which can overpower the wines.
Oak	The more oaked the wine then the more robust and flavoursome the foods need to be. Heavily oaked wines can overpower more delicate foods.
Sweetness	Generally the wine should be sweeter than the foods or it will taste flat or thin. Sweet dishes need contrast for them to match well with sweeter wines, for example, acids in sweeter foods can harmonise with the sweetness in the wines. Savoury foods with sweetness (e.g. carrots or onions) can match well with ripe fruity wines. Blue cheeses can go well with sweet wines. Also sweeter wines can go well with salty foods.
Tannin	Tannic wines match well with red meats and semi-hard cheeses (e.g. cheddar). Tannic wines are not good with egg dishes and wines with high tannin content do not work well with salty foods.
Weight	Big, rich wines go well with robust (flavoursome) meat dishes, but can overpower lighter flavoured foods.

- Lighter wines should be served before heavier wines.
- Good wines should be served before great wines.
- Wines should be at their correct temperature before serving.
- Wine should always be served to customers before their food.

Making recommendations to customers

A few general pointers are set out below that may be followed when advising the customer on which beverage to choose to accompany a meal. However, it must be stressed that customers should at all times be given complete freedom in their selection of wines or other drinks.

- Apéritifs are alcoholic beverages that are drunk before the meal. If wine will be consumed with the meal, then the apéritif selected should be a 'grape' (wine-based) rather than a 'grain' (spirit-based) apéritif, since the latter can spoil or dull the palate.
- The apéritif is usually a wine-based beverage. It is meant to stimulate the appetite and therefore should not be sweet. Dry and medium dry sherries, dry vermouths and Sercial or Verdelho Madeira are all good examples of apéritifs.
- Starter courses are often best accompanied by a dry white or dry rosé wine.
- National dishes should be complemented by the national wines of that country, for example, Italian red wine with pasta dishes.
- Fish and shellfish dishes are often most suited to well chilled dry white wines.
- Red meats such as beef and lamb blend and harmonise well with red wine.
- White meats such as veal and pork are acceptable with medium white wines.
- Game dishes require the heavier and more robust red wines to complement the full flavour of these dishes.
- Sweets and desserts are served at the end of the meal and here it is acceptable to offer well-chilled sweet white wines that may come from the Loire, Sauternes, Barsac or Hungary. These wines harmonise best with dishes containing fruit.
- The majority of cheeses blend well with port and other dry robust red wines. Port is the traditional wine harmonising best with Stilton cheese.
- The grain- and fruit-based spirits and liqueurs all harmonise well with coffee.

Beers and food

Recently there has been an increasing trend to offer beers with food, either alongside or as an alternative to wines. As with wines it is a question of trial and error to achieve harmony between particular beers and foods. Generally the considerations for the pairing of beers and foods are similar to those for matching wines with foods, as shown in Table 4.10, and in particular, taking account of acidity, sweetness/dryness, bitterness, tannin, weight and the complexity of the taste. Examples of possible beer and food combinations, together with possible wines, are shown below:

Hors-d'oeuvre	Sometimes combinations can be difficult because of overpowering dressings on salad items. However, fino or manzanilla sherry, Sancerre, Pinot Grigio, Sauvignon Blanc or Gewürztraminer can be tried. Sometimes, depending on the dishes, the lighter reds may make a good combination with the foods. Beers that might be considered include smoked beers and Japanese beers.
Soups	These do not really require a liquid accompaniment but sherry or dry port or Madeira could be tried, as can traditional English ales. Consommés and lobster or crab bisque can be enhanced by adding a glass of heated sherry or Madeira before serving.
Terrines, pâtés and foie gras	Beaujolais or a light, young red wine, white wines from Pinot Gris or Sauvignon Blanc grapes and also some sweet white wines, especially Sauternes or demi-sec Champagne for foie gras. Fruit beers and English porters might also be tried.
Omelettes and quiches	Difficult for wine but an Alsatian Riesling or Sylvaner could be tried, as could white (wheat) beers.
Farinaceous dishes (pasta and rice)	Classically Italian red wines such as Valpolicella, Chianti, Barolo, Santa Maddalena or Lago di Caldaro. Also most lagers or IPA (India Pale Ale).

Fish

Oysters and shellfish	Dry white wines: Champagne, Chablis, Muscadet, Soave and Frascati; also white beers, Guinness or other stouts.
Smoked fish	White Rioja, Hock, white Graves, Verdicchio, smoked beers and Japanese beers.
Fish dishes with sauces	Fuller white wines such as Vouvray, Montrachet or Yugoslav Riesling; white beers.
Shallow fried or grilled fish	Vinho Verde, Moselle, Californian Chardonnay, Australian Sémillon or Chardonnay; most lagers or IPA and English porter, especially with scallops.

White meats

The type of wine/drink to serve is dependent on whether the white meat (chicken, turkey, rabbit, veal or pork) is served hot or cold.

Served hot with a sauce or savoury stuffing	Either a rosé such as Anjou, or light reds like Beaujolais, New Zealand Pinot Noir, Californian Zinfandel, Saint-Julien, Bourg and Burgundy (e.g. Passe-tout-grains) and Corbières; white beers.
Served cold	Fuller white wines such as Hocks, Gran Viña Sol, Sancerre and the rosés of Provence and Tavel; white beers.

Other meats

Duck and goose	Big red wines that will cut through the fat, Châteauneuf-du-Pape, Hermitage, Barolo and the Australian Cabernet Shiraz; most beers.
Roast and grilled lamb	Medoc, Saint-Emilion, Pomerol and any of the Cabernet Sauvignons; most beers.

Roast beef and grilled steaks	Big red Burgundies, Rioja, Barolo, Dão and wines made from the Pinot Noir grape; most beers and especially flavoured beers (e.g. heather or honeydew).
Meat stews	Lighter reds, Zinfandel, Côtes du Rhône, Clos du Bois, Bull's Blood, Vino Nobile di Montepulciano; Belgian Abbey-style and Trappist beers, flavoured beers (e.g. heather or honeydew), darker beers.
Hare, venison and game	Reds with distinctive flavour, Côte Rôtie, Bourgeuil, Rioja, Chianti, Australian Shiraz, Californian Cabernet Sauvignon, Chilean Cabernet Sauvignon, and also fine red Burgundies and Bordeaux reds; Belgian Abbey-style and Trappist beers.
Oriental foods, Peking duck, mild curry, tandoori chicken, shish kebab	Gewürztraminer, Lutomer Riesling, Vinho Verde, Mateus Rosé or Anjou Rosé. Also most lagers and IPA.

Cheese

The wine from the main course is often followed through to the cheese course, although it is also worth considering the type of cheese being served.

Light, cream cheeses	Full bodied whites, rosés and light reds; beers generally.
Strong, pungent (even smelly) and blue-veined varieties	Big reds of Bordeaux and Burgundy, or tawny, vintage or vintage-style ports and also the luscious sweet white wines; beers generally, especially fruit beers.
Sweets and puddings	Champagne works well with sweets and puddings. Others to try are the luscious Muscats (de Beaumes-de-Venise, de Setúbal, de Frontignan, Samos), Sainte-Croix-du-Mont, Sauternes, Banyuls, Monbazillac, Tokay, wines made from late-gathered individual grapes in Germany, and also the Orange Muscats and speciality drinks such as Vin de Frais (fermentation of fresh strawberries) both of which can go well with chocolate. Fruit beers (which can also be especially good with chocolate), porters, and Belgian-style strong golden ales can all pair well with various sweets and puddings.
Dessert (fresh fruit and nuts)	Sweet fortified wines, sherry, port, Madeira, Málaga, Marsala, Commandaria; white beers.
Coffee	Cognac and other brandies such as Armagnac, Asbach, Marc, Metaxa, Grappa, Oude Meester, Fundador; good aged malt whiskies; Calvados, sundry liqueurs and ports; Champagne; white beers.

4.11 SPIRITS

Production

All spirits are produced by the distillation of alcoholic beverages. The history of distillation goes back over 2,000 years when it is said that stills were used in China to make perfumes and by the Arabs to make spirit-based drinks.

Table 4.11 Bases for spirits

Spirit	Base
Whisky, gin and vodka	Barley, maize or rye (i.e. beer)
Brandy	Wine
Calvados	Cider
Rum	Molasses
Tequila	Pulque

The principle of distillation is that ethyl alcohol vaporises (boils) at a lower temperature (78°C) than water (100°C). Thus, where a liquid containing alcohol is heated in an enclosed environment the alcohol will form steam first and can be taken off, leaving water and other ingredients behind. This process raises the alcoholic strength of the resulting liquid.

There are two main methods of producing spirits: the pot still method, which is used for full, heavy flavoured spirits such as brandy, and the patent still (Coffey) method, which produces the lighter spirits such as vodka.

Bases for spirits

The bases used in the most common spirits are listed in Table 4.11. In each case the base is a fermented liquid (alcoholic wash).

Types of spirit

Aquavit

Made in Scandinavia from potatoes or grain and flavoured with herbs, mainly caraway seeds. To be appreciated fully, Aquavit must be served chilled.

Arrack

Made from the sap of palm trees. The main countries of production are Java, India, Ceylon and Jamaica.

Brandy

Brandy may be defined as a spirit distilled from wine. The word brandy is more usually linked with the names Cognac and Armagnac, but brandy is also made in almost all wine producing areas.

Eau de vie

Eau de vie (water of life) is the fermented and distilled juice of fruit. The best eau de vie comes from the Alsace area of France, Germany, Switzerland and Yugoslavia. Examples are:

- *Himbergeist* from wild raspberries (Germany).
- *Kirschwasser* (Kirsch) from cherries (Germany).
- *Mirabelle* from plums (France).
- *Quetsch* from plums (Alsace and Germany).
- *Poire William* from pears (Switzerland and Alsace).
- *Slivovitz* from plums (Yugoslavia).
- *Fraise* from strawberries (France, especially Alsace).
- *Framboise* from raspberries (France, especially Alsace).

Eau de vie, especially the alcohol blanc variety, should be water-clear in appearance.

Gin

The term 'gin' is taken from the first part of the word Genièvre, which is the French term for juniper. Juniper is the *principal botanica* (flavouring agent) used in the production of gin. The word 'Geneva' is the Dutch translation of the botanical, juniper. Maize is the cereal used in gin production in the United Kingdom. However, rye is the main cereal generally used in the production of Geneva gin and other Dutch gins.

Malted barley is an accepted alternative to the cereals mentioned above. The two key ingredients (botanicals) recognised for flavouring purposes are juniper berries and coriander seeds.

Types of gin are:

- *Fruit gins*: as the term implies, these are fruit flavoured gins that may be produced from any fruit. The most popular are sloe, orange and lemon.
- *Geneva gin*: this is made in Holland by the pot still method alone and is generally known as 'Hollands' gin.
- *London Dry Gin*: this is the most well known and popular of all the gins. It is unsweetened.
- *Old Tom*: this is a sweet gin made in Scotland. The sweetening agent is sugar syrup. As the name implies, it was traditionally used in a Tom Collins cocktail.
- *Plymouth Gin*: this has a stronger flavour than London Dry and is manufactured by Coates in Devon. It is most well known for its use in the cocktail Pink Gin, together with the addition of Angostura Bitters.

Grappa

An Italian style brandy produced from the pressings of grapes after the required must – unfermented grape juice – has been removed for wine production. It is similar in style to the French marc brandy.

Marc

Local French brandy made where wine is made. Usually takes the name of the region, for example, Marc de Borgogne.

Mirabelle

A colourless spirit made from plums. The main country of origin is France.

Pastis

Pastis is the name given to spirits flavoured with anis and/or liquorice, such as Pernod. The spirit is made in many Mediterranean countries and is popular almost everywhere. It has taken over from absinthe, once known as the 'Green Goddess'.

Quetsch

A colourless spirit with plums being the main ingredient. The key countries of production are the Balkans, France and Germany. It has a brandy base.

Rum

This is a spirit made from the fermented by-products of sugar cane. It is available in dark and light varieties and is produced in countries where sugar cane grows naturally, for example, Jamaica, Cuba, Trinidad, Barbados, Guyana and the Bahamas.

Schnapps

A spirit distilled from a fermented potato base and flavoured with caraway seed. The main countries of production are Germany and Holland.

Tequila

A Mexican spirit distilled from the fermented juice (pulque) of the agave plant. It is traditionally drunk after a lick of salt and a squeeze of lime or lemon.

Vodka

A highly rectified (very pure) patent still spirit. It is purified by being passed through activated charcoal, which removes virtually all aroma and flavour. It is described as a colourless and flavourless spirit.

Whisk(e)y

Whisky or whiskey is a spirit made from cereals: Scotch whisky from malted barley, Irish whiskey usually from barley, North American whiskey and Bourbon from maize and rye. The spelling *whisky* usually refers to the Scotch or Canadian drink and *whiskey* to the Irish or American.

Scotch whisky is primarily made from barley, malted (hence the term malt whisky) then heated over a peat fire. Grain whiskies are made from other grains and are usually blended with malt whisky.

Irish whiskey differs from Scotch in that hot air rather than a peat fire is used during malting, thus Irish whiskey does not gain the smoky quality of Scotch. It is also distilled three times (rather than two as in the making of Scotch) and is matured longer.

Canadian whisky is usually a blend of flavoured and neutral whiskies made from grains such as rye, wheat and barley.

American whiskey is made from various mixtures of barley, maize and rye. Bourbon is made from maize.

Japanese whisky is made by the Scotch process and is blended.

4.12 LIQUEURS

Liqueurs are defined as sweetened and flavoured spirits. They should not be confused with liqueur spirits, which may be whiskies or brandies of great age and quality. For instance, a brandy liqueur is a liqueur with brandy as a basic ingredient, while a liqueur brandy may be defined as a brandy of great age and excellence.

Production

Liqueurs are made by two basic methods:

1   Heat or infusion method: best when herbs, peels, roots etc., are being used, as heat can extract their oils, flavours and aromas.

2   Cold or maceration method: best when soft fruits are used to provide the flavours and aromas.

The heat method uses a pot still for distillation purposes while the cold method allows the soft fruit to soak in brandy in oak casks over a long period of time.

For all liqueurs a spirit base is necessary and this may be brandy, rum or a neutral spirit. Many flavouring ingredients are used to make liqueurs, and these include:

- aniseed
- apricots
- blackcurrants
- caraway seeds
- cherries
- cinnamon
- coriander
- kernels of almonds
- nutmeg
- rind of citrus fruit
- rose petals
- wormwood.

Types of liqueurs

Table 4.12 lists some of the more popular liqueurs. The service of liqueurs is discussed in Section 5.8, page 248.

Table 4.12 Popular liqueurs

Liqueur	Colour	Flavour/spirit base	Country of origin
Abricotine	Red	Apricot/brandy	France
Avocaat	Yellow	Egg, sugar/brandy	Holland
Anisette	Clear	Aniseed/neutral spirit	France, Spain, Italy, Holland
Amaretto	Golden	Almonds	Italy
Archers	Clear	Peaches/Schnapps	UK
Arrack	Clear	Herbs, sap of palm trees	Java, India, Sri Lanka, Jamaica
Bailey's Irish Cream	Coffee	Honey, chocolate, cream, whiskey	Ireland
Benedictine Dom	Yellow/green	Herbs/brandy	France
Calvados	Amber	Apple/brandy	France
Chartreuse	Green (45% abv)/Yellow (55% abv)	Herbs, plants/brandy	France
Cherry Brandy	Deep red	Cherry/brandy	Denmark
Cointreau	Clear	Orange/brandy	France
Crème de cacao	Dark brown	Chocolate, vanilla/rum	France
Drambuie	Golden	Heather, honey, herbs/whisky	Scotland
Galliano	Golden	Herbs/berries/flowers/roots	Italy
Grand Marnier	Amber	Orange/brandy	France
Glayva	Golden	Herbs, spice/whisky	Scotland
Kirsch	Clear	Cherry/neutral spirit	Alsace
Kahlúa	Pale chocolate	Coffee/rum	Mexico
Kümmel	Clear	Caraway seed/neutral spirit	East European countries

Table 4.12 continued

Liqueur	Colour	Flavour/spirit base	Country of origin
Malibu	Clear	Coconut/white rum	Caribbean
Maraschino	Clear	Maraschino cherry	Italy
Parfait amour	Violet	Violets, lemon peel, spices	France/Holland
Sambuca	Clear	Liquorice/neutral spirit	Italy
Slivovitz	Clear	Plum/brandy	East Europe
Southern Comfort	Golden	Peaches/oranges/whiskey	United States
Strega (The Witch)	Yellow	Herbs/bark/fruit	Italy
Tia Maria	Brown	Coffee/rum	Jamaica
Van der hum	Amber	Tangerine/brandy	South Africa

4.13 BEER

Beer in one form or another is an alcoholic beverage found in all bars and areas dispensing alcoholic beverages. They are fermented drinks, deriving their alcoholic content from the conversion of malt sugars into alcohol by brewers yeast. The alcoholic content of beer varies according to type and is usually between 3.5–10% alcohol by volume.

Types of beer

Bitter

Pale, amber-coloured beer served on draught. May be sold as light bitter, ordinary bitter or best bitter. When bottled it is know as pale ale or light ale depending on alcoholic strength.

IPA (India Pale Ale)

Heavily hopped strong pale ale, originally brewed in the UK for shipping to British colonies. The modern style is a light-coloured, hoppy, ale.

Abbey-style

Ale brewed in the monastic tradition of the Low Countries but by secular brewers, often under licence from a religious establishment.

White beer

Traditional beers made with a high proportion of wheat, sometimes know as wheat beers.

Mild

Can be light or dark depending on the colour of the malt used in the brewing process. Generally sold on draught and has a sweeter and more complex flavour than bitter.

Burton

Strong, dark, draught beer. This beer is also popular in winter when it is mulled or spiced and offered as a winter warmer.

Old ale

Brown, sweet and strong. Can also be mulled or spiced.

Strong ale

Colour varies between pale and brown and taste between dry and sweet. Alcoholic content also varies.

Barley wine

Traditionally an all-malt ale. This beer is sweet and strong and sold in small bottles or nips (originally ⅓ of a pint, now 190 ml).

Stout

Made from scorched, very dark malt and generously flavoured with hops. Has a smooth malty flavour and creamy consistency. Sold on draught or in bottles and was traditionally not chilled (although today it often is). Guinness is one example.

Porter

Brewed from charred malt, highly flavoured and aromatic. Its name comes from its popularity with market porters working in Dublin and London.

Lager

The name comes from the German *lagern* (to store). Fermentation takes place at the bottom of the vessel and the beer is stored at low temperatures for up to six months and sometimes longer. Sold on draught, in a bottle or can.

Trappist beer

Beer brewed in Trappist monasteries, usually under the supervision of monks. Six Belgian breweries produce this beer, which is strong, complex and un-pasteurised, and often includes candy sugar in the recipe.

Pilsner

Clear, pale lagers (originally from Pilsen, hence the name). Modern styles are characterised by a zesty hop taste and bubbly body.

Smoked beers

Beers made with grains that have been smoked as part of the malting process. Various woods are used, including alder, cherry, apple, beech, or oak. Sometimes the process uses peat smoke.

Fruit beers and flavoured beers

Variety of beers with additional flavourings such as heather or honeydew, or fruit beers, which have fresh fruits such as raspberry or strawberry introduced during the making process to add flavour.

Reduced alcohol beer

There are two categories of beer with reduced alcohol levels:

- Non-alcoholic beers (NABs) which, by definition, must contain less than 0.5% alcohol by volume.
- Low alcohol beers (LABs) which, by definition, must contain less than 1.2% alcohol by volume.

The beer is made in the traditional way and then the alcohol is removed.

Conditioning

Cask-conditioned ale is ale that has its final fermentation in the cask (or barrel) from which it is dispensed.

Bottle-conditioned beers

Also known as sediment beers, bottle-conditioned beers tend to throw a sediment in the bottle while fermenting and conditioning takes place. These beers need careful storage, handling and pouring. Available in bottles only.

Draught beer in cans

These draught-flow beers have an internal patented system that produces a pub-style, smooth creamy head when poured from the can. A range of beers are available in this format.

Faults in beer

Although thunder has been known to cause a secondary fermentation in beer, thereby affecting its clarity, faults can usually be attributed to poor cellar management. The common faults are given below.

Cloudy beer

This may be due to too low a temperature in the cellar or, more often, may result from the beer pipes not having been cleaned properly.

Flat beer

Flat beer may result when a wrong spile has been used – a hard spile builds up pressure, a soft spile releases pressure. When the cellar temperature is too low, beer often becomes dull and lifeless. Dirty glasses, and those that have been refilled for a customer who has been eating food, will also cause beer to go flat.

Sour beer

This may be due to a lack of business resulting in the beer being left on ullage for too long. Sourness may also be caused by adding stale beer to a new cask, or by beer coming in contact with old deposits of yeast that have become lodged in the pipeline from the cellar.

Foreign bodies

Foreign bodies or extraneous matter may be the result of production or operational slip-ups.

Beer measures

- Nips   ⅓ pint (about 18.75 cl)
- Half pint   10 fl oz (about 28.40 cl)
- Pint   20 fl oz (about 56.80 cl)
- Litre
- Half litre

Draught beer containers

- Pin   20.457 litres (4½ gallons)
- Firkin   40.914 litres (9 gallons)
- Kilderkin   81.828 litres (18 gallons)
- Barrel   163.656 litres (36 gallons)
- Hogshead   245.484 litres (54 gallons)
- 2½ barrel tanks   205 litres (45 gallons)
- 5 barrel tanks   410 litres (90 gallons)

Mixed beer drinks

A selection of beverages based on beer is given below:

- mild and bitter
- stout and mild
- brown and mild
- light and mild
- shandy: draught bitter or lager and lemonade or ginger beer

- black velvet: Guinness and champagne
- black and tan: half stout and half bitter
- lager and lime
- lager and blackcurrant.

4.14 CIDER AND PERRY

Cider is an alcoholic beverage obtained through the fermentation of apple juice, or a mixture of apple juice and up to 25 per cent pear juice. Perry is similarly obtained from pear juice and up to 25 per cent apple juice.

Cider and perry are produced primarily in England and Normandy, but may also be made in Italy, Spain, Germany, Switzerland, Canada, the USA, Australia and New Zealand. The English areas of production are the counties of Devon, Somerset, Gloucester, Hereford, Kent and Norfolk where the best cider orchards are found.

Cider

The characteristics of the apples that are required for making cider are:

- the sweetness of dessert apples
- the acidity of culinary apples
- the bitterness of tannin to balance the flavour and help preserve the apple.

Main types of cider

Draught

This is unfiltered. Its appearance, while not cloudy, is also not 'star-bright'. It may have sugar and yeast added to give it condition. Draught cider may be completely dry (known as 'scrumpy') or sweetened with sugar. It is marketed in oak casks or plastic containers.

Keg/bottled

This cider is pasteurised or sterile filtered to render it star-bright. During this stage, one or more of the following treatments may be carried out:

- it may be blended
- it may undergo a second fermentation, usually in a tank, to make it sparkling

- it may be sweetened
- its strength may be adjusted
- it will usually be carbonated by the injection of carbon dioxide gas.

The characteristics of keg and bottled ciders are:

- *Medium sweet* (carbonated): 4% alcohol by volume (ABV)
- *Medium dry* (carbonated): 6% ABV
- *Special* (some carbonated): 8.3% ABV – some special ciders undergo a second fermentation to make them sparkling.

Perry

Perry is usually made sparkling and comes into the special range. It may be carbonated or the sparkle may come from a second fermentation in sealed tanks. In the production of perry the processes of filtering, blending and sweetening are all carried out under pressure.

Perries were traditionally drunk on their own, chilled and in saucer-shaped sparkling wine glasses. Today the tulip-shaped sparkling wine glass is more commonly used.

4.15 STORAGE

Beer

The factors that determine good beer cellar management are:

- good ventilation
- cleanliness
- even temperatures of 13–15°C (55–58°F)
- avoidance of strong draughts and wide ranges of temperatures
- on delivery, all casks should be placed immediately upon the stillions
- casks remaining on the floor should be bung uppermost to better withstand the pressure
- spiling should take place to reduce any excess pressure in the cask
- tappings should be carried out 24 hours before a cask is required
- pipes and engines should be cleaned at regular intervals
- all beer lines should be cleaned weekly with a diluted pipe-cleaning fluid and the cellar floor washed down weekly with a weak solution of chloride and lime (mild bleach)
- beer left in pipes after closing time should be drawn off
- returned beer should be filtered back into the cask from which it came
- care should be taken that the cellar is not overstocked
- all spiles removed during service should be replaced after closing time

- all cellar equipment should be kept scrupulously clean
- any ullage should be returned to the brewery as soon as possible
- re-ordering should be carried out on one set day every week after checking the bottle stocks of beers, wines, minerals etc. Strict rotation of stock must be exercised, with new crates placed at the rear and old stock pulled to the front for first issue.

Beer storage and equipment

Beer engines	These are pumps pulled by hand using a handle in the bar. They must be cleaned weekly when the pipelines are cleaned and must be stripped down and inspected on a monthly basis as new washers may be needed etc. Some engines work by carbon dioxide top pressure, which applies force downwards on to the beer in the cask and drives a measured amount up into the bar when a button is pressed.
Dipsticks	These are used to determine how much beer is left in the cask. The dipstick is placed into the cask through the shive.
Electrical impelled pumps	Electrical impelled pumps are situated in the cellar and dispense an accurate amount of beer into the glass in the bar when the bartender presses the button.
Filters	Filters must only be used in the cellar to return sound beer to the cask – for instance, beer that has been drawn out of the pipes before pipe-cleaning started. Filters must be kept clean and used with clean filter papers. To filter beer is not in itself illegal, but to return to cask any over-spill or 'slops' is an offence. To mix or dilute beer in the cask, or to adulterate any produce for sale, is also an offence.
Pipe cleaning bottles	These are used to clean pressurised container pipelines. With the gas turned off, the assembly head should be taken from the keg and locked onto the two-gallon cleaning bottle containing cleaning fluid. The CO_2 should be turned on and the pipes filled with the fluid. After about one hour the process should be repeated using clean water. Automatic beer-line cleaning equipment is also now popular.
Scotches	These are triangular blocks of wood that are used to prevent a beer cask from rolling from side to side.
Shives and spiles	Shives are round pieces of hard wood that are placed in the bunghole of the beer cask just before it is sent out from the brewery after filling. The shive has a small hole in the centre that does not go completely through the wood. When the cask is vented, the hole is completed by punching out the thin centre section with a wooden mallet. The hole will permit gas to escape from the cask. Spiles are used in the hole to allow or prevent the CO_2 gas from escaping. They are small pegs made of two different types of wood. The hardwood spile, when placed in the shive, does not allow any gas to escape. Instead, pressure builds up in the cask and the beer regains its condition (frothy head). The softer porous spile is made from bamboo and when placed in the shive, it allows the gas to escape and so prevents the beer from being too gassy and difficult to serve.
Stillions	Casks in use (on ullage) will be supported on stillions (or thrawls). A stillion is the wooden rack or brick platform upon which the casks are placed for service. Keg pressurised beer containers are usually situated together in one area of the cellar along with the necessary CO_2 gas cylinders strapped or bracketed to the wall.

Wine

Wines should ideally be stored in a subterranean cellar which has a northerly aspect and is free from vibrations, excessive dampness, draughts and unwanted odours. The cellar should be absolutely clean, well ventilated, with only subdued lighting and a constant cool temperature of about 12.5°C (55°F) to help the wine develop gradually.

Wines should be stored on their sides in bins so that the wine remains in contact with the cork. This keeps the cork expanded and prevents air from entering the wine – a process that quickly turns wine to vinegar. The wines are also stored on their sides with the labels uppermost. This ensures that the wines can be easily identified, the protection of the label (away from the base surface of the bin) and ensures that any sediment is always located on the side of the bottle away from the label. This approach is also used for wines with alternative stoppers such as screw tops. White, sparkling and rosé wines are kept in the coolest part of the cellar and in bins nearest the ground (because warm air rises). Red wines are best stored in the upper bins. Commercial establishments usually have special refrigerators or cooling cabinets for keeping their sparkling, white and rosé wines at serving temperature.

Other drinks

Spirits, liqueurs, squashes, juices and mineral waters are stored upright in their containers, as are fortified wines. The exceptions are port-style wines, which are destined for laying down, and these are treated as for wines above. See also Section 10.3 Beverage control, page 411.

Members' bar and seating area at the Scottish Parliament (courtesy of FCSI, UK)

THE FOOD AND BEVERAGE SERVICE SEQUENCE

CHAPTER 5

5.1 BASIC TECHNICAL SKILLS

There are six basic technical food and beverage service skills. These are identified below, together with examples of their application.

Technical skill	Examples of application
Holding and using a service spoon and fork, and other service equipment	For the service of food at a customer's table, especially for silver service, and for serving at a buffet.
Carrying plates	When placing and clearing plates from a customer's table.
Using a service salver (round tray)	For carrying glasses, carrying tea and coffee services, as an under liner for entrée dishes and for potato and vegetable dishes.
Using a service plate	For carrying items to and from a table, including clean cutlery, clearing side plates and knives, crumbing down, clearing accompaniments.
Carrying glasses	Carrying clean glasses by hand or on a salver and for clearing dirty glasses from a service area.
Carrying and using large trays	For bringing equipment or food and beverage items to the service area and for clearing used equipment from the service area.

These basic technical skills are used specifically for table service and assisted service. However, these skills are also used when providing other forms of service, for example, when carrying trays for room service or using a service salver for bar service. More detailed descriptions are given below.

Holding and using a service spoon and fork

Expertise in this technique can only be achieved with practice. The purpose of the service spoon and fork is to enable the waiter to serve food from a flat or dish on to the customer's plate quickly and to present the food on the plate well.

- The service fork should be positioned above, or on top of, the service spoon.
- The key to developing this skill is the locking of the ends of the service spoon and fork with the small finger and the third finger, as illustrated in Figure 5.1a.
- The spoon and fork are manoeuvred with the thumb and the index and second fingers (see Figure 5.1b). Using this method food items may be picked up from the serving dish in between the service spoon and service fork.
- Alternatively, the service fork may be turned to mould with the shape of the items being served, for example, when serving bread rolls (see Figure 5.1c).

There are occasions where two service forks may be used, for example when serving fillets of fish, as this makes the service of this food item easier.

When using a serving spoon and fork for serving at a sweet or cheese trolley, or at a buffet or guéridon, the spoon and fork are held one in each hand.

a   b   c

Fig 5.1. Hand positions for holding a service spoon and fork

Other service equipment that may be used includes serving tongs, fish slices, gateaux slices, serving spoons, scoops, small sauce ladles and larger soup ladles.

Carrying plates

Clean plates can be carried in a stack, using both hands, or using a tray. When carrying clean plates which are to be placed on the customer's table, a single hand is used to hold the plates (usually the left hand) and the right hand is used to place the plates at each cover on the customer's table. If the plates are hot then the plates are held with a service cloth placed on the palm of the left hand. A separate service cloth is then used in the right hand to hold the hot plates when placing them in front of the customer.

When carrying plates of pre-plated foods and when clearing plates from a customer's table, a single hand is used to hold the plates (usually the left hand) and the right hand is used to place and remove plates from the customer's table. Special hand positions are used as follows:

- Figure 5.2a illustrates the initial hand position for the first plate. Care must be taken to ensure that the first plate is held firmly as succeeding plates are built up from here. The second plate will rest firmly on the forearm and the third and fourth fingers.

- Figure 5.2b shows the second plate positioned on the left (holding) hand.

To be able to clear properly ensures efficiency, avoids the possibility of accidents and creates the minimum of inconvenience to customers. Well-developed clearing techniques enable more to be cleared, in less time and in fewer journeys between sideboard or workstation and the customer's table. In addition, clearing properly allows for the stacking of dirties neatly and safely at the sideboard or workstation.

a First plate cleared

b Second plate cleared

Fig 5.2. Hand positions when clearing plates

Using a service salver

A service salver is a round, normally silver or stainless steel tray (but now also sometimes of wood or plastic). A napkin (folded flat) is placed on the tray to help prevent items slipping on the tray as they are being carried. There are also special non-slip mats that are now used instead of napkins. The service salver may be used to:

- carry clean glasses to, and remove dirty glasses from, a customer's table
- carry clean cutlery to and from a customer's table
- place clean cutlery on the table
- place clean cups and saucers on the table
- provide an underflat when silver serving vegetables.

Carrying glasses

When carrying clean glasses on the service salver they should be placed the right way up to reduce the risk of them toppling over. When being placed on the table, the waiter should hold the salver in the left hand behind the customer and then place the glass at the top right-hand corner of the cover and the right way up. The waiter should only hold glasses by the stem to ensure that the bowl of the wine glass is not touched, otherwise finger marks will be left on the glass bowl.

Carrying clean cutlery

When placing clean cutlery on a table, or removing it, the items can be carried on a service salver. This is more efficient, hygienic and safer, and generally more professional, than carrying these items in bunches in the hands. The blades of the knives should be placed under the arch in the middle of the forks, and if carrying sweet spoons and forks, the prongs of the fork should go under the arch in the middle of the spoon. The reason for this is to help hold the items steady on the service salver. Bearing in mind that the handles of the cutlery are generally the heaviest parts, this method prevents them sliding about too much.

Carrying cups and saucers

Tea and coffee cups are carried using a service salver, by stacking the saucers, cups and teaspoons separately. Then before placing the cup, saucer and teaspoon on the table, the cup is put onto a saucer, together with a teaspoon, and then the whole service is placed in front of the customer. This is a speedier and safer method (especially when larger numbers are involved) than carrying individual cups, saucers and teaspoons to the table one by one. Cups and saucers are placed on the table at the right hand side of the customer. The reason for this is that the beverage will most likely be served from the right. This avoids stretching across the front of the customer when laying the beverage service or when serving the beverage.

Silver serving vegetables

When silver serving vegetables and potatoes at the table, an underflat should be used to hold either one large vegetable dish or a number of smaller ones, depending on the customer's orders (see page 235). The purpose of the underflat is to:

- add to the presentation of the food being served
- give the waiter more control when using the service spoon and fork to serve the vegetables from the vegetable dish on to the customer's plate
- provide greater protection in case of spillage, therefore not detracting from the presentation of the food on the plate or the overall table presentation
- give the waiter added protection against heat and possible spillage on the uniform.

Using a service plate

A service plate is a joint plate with a napkin upon it. It has a number of uses during the meal service:

- For placing or removing clean cutlery from the table.
- For clearing side plates and side knives.
- For crumbing down after the main course, or any other stage of the meal if necessary.
- For clearing accompaniments from the table as and when necessary.

Carrying clean cutlery

When placing on, or removing, clean cutlery from a table, the items can be carried on a service plate. The reasons for this are the same as given under using a service salver above.

Clearing side plates and knives

When clearing dirty side plates and side knives from the customer's table, the use of a service plate means that the waiter has a larger area on which to stack the side knives and any debris. Using the hand positions (see Figure 5.2, page 176), the side plates may be stacked above the service plate and all the debris in a separate pile, together with the side knives laid flat upon the service plate. This is a much safer and speedier method, especially when larger numbers are involved.

Crumbing down

To freshen up the appearance of a table after the main course had been consumed and all the dirty items of equipment cleared from the table, a procedure known as 'crumbing down' is used. The waiter brushes any crumbs and other debris lying on the tablecloth onto the service plate, with the aid of either the folded service cloth or a small brush designed for the purpose. There are also metal crumbers that can be used.

Clearing accompaniments

The service plate is also used to clear such items as the cruet, cayenne pepper, pepper mill or other accompaniments, which may not already be set on an underplate.

Fig 5.3. Crumbing down: note the neatly folded service cloth

Carrying glasses

There are two basic methods of carrying glasses in the food and beverage service areas: by hand or on a service salver.

Carrying by hand

Wine goblets should be positioned between alternate fingers as far as is possible. The wine goblets should only be carried in one hand, allowing the other hand to remain free to steady oneself in case of emergencies.

Figure 5.4 provides a close up of the wine goblets held in one hand and shows how the base of each glass overlaps the next, allowing the maximum number of glasses to be held in one hand. This method allows wine goblets that are

Fig 5.4. Carrying clean wine glasses by hand

Fig 5.5. Carrying clean glasses on a service salver

Fig 5.6. Carrying dirty glasses on a service salver

already polished to be handled. They can be carried about the room and set in their correct position on the table without the bowl of the glass being touched.

Carrying glasses on a service salver

The method of carrying clean wine goblets about the restaurant using the service salver is illustrated in Figure 5.5.

A service cloth can be placed underneath the salver on the palm of the hand to allow the service salver to be rotated more easily in order to remove each wine goblet in turn by the base and to set it on the table

Figure 5.6 indicates the use of the service salver for clearing dirty wine goblets from the table.

The first dirty wine goblet cleared should be placed on the service salver nearest to the server. As the dirties are cleared, they should be placed on the service salver to ensure a better and more even distribution of weight, to lessen the likelihood of accidents occurring.

Glass racks are often used to carry glasses during the setting up of functions. These racks enable the transportation of glasses in bulk once they have been washed and polished at a central point.

Carrying trays

Trays are used for:

- carrying food from the kitchen to the restaurant sideboard
- service in rooms and lounges
- clearing from sideboards
- clearing from tables (when the customer is not seated at the table)
- carrying equipment.

Fig 5.7. Carrying a loaded oblong tray

The correct method of holding and carrying an oblong tray is to position the tray lengthways onto the forearm and to support it by holding the tray with the other hand.

Figure 5.7 shows how to carry an oblong tray. Note the tray is organised so that the heaviest items are nearest the carrier. This helps to balance the tray. Also note that one hand is placed underneath the tray and the other at the side.

5.2 INTERPERSONAL SKILLS

Interpersonal skills in food and beverage service centre on the interactions between the customer and the food and beverage service staff. All other interactions are secondary to, and the result of, the prime interaction of customers and staff. This has implications for the way customers are treated. Conversations between customers and staff override conversations between staff. When in conversation with customers, staff should not:

- talk to other members of staff without first excusing themselves from the customer
- interrupt interactions between customers and staff, but should wait until there is a suitable moment to catch the attention of the other member of staff so that they may excuse themselves from the customer first
- serve customers while carrying on a conversation between themselves
- talk across a room, either to each other or to customers.

Customers should always be made to feel that they are being cared for and not that they are an intrusion into the operation.

Interpersonal skills related to specific points of service

The list below shows the interpersonal skills needed at particular points during the service.

- *Showing customers to their table*: always lead and walk with them at their pace.
- *Seating customers*: ladies first, descending in age unless the host is a lady.

- *Handling coats/wraps*: handle with obvious care (see Section 10.1, page 395)

- *Handing menus/wine lists to customers*: offer the list the right way round for the customer and wait for the customer to take it.

- *Opening and placing a napkin*: open carefully, do not shake it like a duster, place it on the customer's lap after saying excuse me to the customer.

- *Offering water or rolls*: say, for example, 'Excuse me Sir/Madam, may I offer you a bread roll?'

- *Offering accompaniments*: only offer them if you have them at the table. Offering them when they are not at the table usually means 'I will get them if you really want them!'

- *Serving and clearing*: always say 'Excuse me' before serving or clearing and 'Thank you' after you have finished with each customer.

- *Explaining food and beverage items*: use terms the customer understands, not technical terms such as turned vegetable or panée. Use terms that make the item sound attractive such as casserole not stew, creamed or purée potatoes not mashed. Do not use abbreviations, for example, 'veg'.

- *Talking to customers*: only talk when standing next to them and looking at them.

Other procedures that contribute to good interpersonal skills are highlighted throughout the rest of this chapter. Also see Section 10.5 Customer relations, page 422.

Addressing customers

'Sir' or 'Madam' should be used when the customer's name is not known. If the name is known, then the customer should be referred to as 'Mr Smith' or 'Miss Jones' etc. First names should only be used in less formal operations and where the customer has explicitly indicated that this is acceptable. If the customer has a title, then appropriate use should be made of the correct form of address (for further information on forms of address, see page 375).

Greetings such as 'Good morning' and 'Good evening' should be used upon receiving customers, or when the member of staff first comes into contact with the customer, for example, when lounge service staff attend people already seated in the lounge.

Dealing with incidents

When an unforeseen incident arises it must be coped with promptly and efficiently without causing any more disturbance than is necessary to any of the other customers. Quick action will very often soothe the irate customer and ensure a return visit to your establishment. It is worth remembering at this stage that complaints, of whatever nature, should be referred immediately to the supervisor. Delay will only cause confusion and very often the situation may be wrongly interpreted if it is not dealt with straight away. In the case of accidents, a report of the incident must be kept and signed by those involved.

Listed below are a few of the incidents that might occur and the suggested steps that might be taken in order to put right any fault.

Spillages

If during the service of a course a few drops of sauce or roast gravy have fallen on the tablecloth, the following steps might be taken:

1 Check immediately that none has fallen on the customer being served. Apologise to the customer.

2 If some has fallen on the customer's clothing, allow the customer to rub over the dirtied area with a clean damp cloth. This will remove the worst of the spillage.

3 If it is necessary for the customer to retire to the cloakroom to remove the spillage then his/her meal should be placed on the hotplate until he returns.

4 Depending on the nature of the spillage the establishment may offer to have the garment concerned cleaned.

5 If the spillage has gone on the tablecloth, the waiter should first of all remove any items of equipment that may be dirtied or be in their way.

6 He/she should then mop or scrape up the spillage with either a clean damp cloth or a knife.

7 An old menu card should then be placed on top of the table but under the tablecloth beneath the spillage area.

8 A second menu should be placed on the tablecloth over the spillage area.

9 A clean rolled napkin should then be brought to the table and rolled completely over the spillage area. The menu will prevent any damp from soaking into the clean napkin.

10 Any items of equipment removed should be returned to their correct position on the tabletop.

11 Any meals taken to the hotplate should be returned and fresh covers put down where necessary (see accident check, page 228).

12 Again, apologies should be made to the customer for any inconvenience caused.

If a customer knocks over a glass of water accidentally, then the following steps might be taken:

1 Ensure none has gone on the customer.

2 If some of the water has fallen on the customer's clothing then follow steps 2 and 3 above.

3 Where possible, as this form of accident usually involves changing the tablecloth, the party of customers should be seated at another table and allowed to continue their meal without delay.

4 If they cannot be moved to another table then they should be seated slightly back from the table so that the waiter can carry out the necessary procedures to rectify the fault speedily and efficiently.

5 The customers' meals should be placed on the hotplate to keep warm.

6 All dirty items should be removed on a tray to the waiter's sideboard ready to go to the wash-up area.

7 All clean items should be removed and kept on the waiter's sideboard for relaying.

8 The tablecloth should be mopped with a clean absorbent cloth to remove as much of the liquid as possible.

9 A number of old menus should be placed on the tabletop but underneath the spillage area of tablecloth.

10 A clean tablecloth of the correct size should be brought to the table. It should be opened out and held in the correct manner as if one were laying a tablecloth during the pre-service preparation period. The table should then be clothed up in the usual manner except that when the clean cloth is being drawn across the table towards the waiter he/she is at the same time taking off the soiled tablecloth. The soiled tablecloth should be removed at the same time that the clean tablecloth is being laid so that the customers cannot see the bare tabletop at any time. The old menus will prevent any dampness penetrating to the clean tablecloth.

11 When the table has its clean tablecloth on it should be relaid as quickly as possible.

12 The customers should then be re-seated at the table and the meals returned to them from the hotplate.

Returned food

If, for example, a customer suggests that their chicken dish is not cooked, then the following steps might be taken:

1 Apologise to the customer.

2 The dish should be removed to the sideboard to be returned to the aboyeur at the hotplate.

3 The customer should be offered the menu and asked if they would like another portion of the same dish or prefer to choose something else as an alternative.

4 A special check for the new order should be written out: this shows the dish being returned and what the customer is having in its place.

5 A fresh cover should be laid.

6 The new dish should be collected as soon as possible from the hotplate and served to the customer.

7 Apologies should be made for any inconvenience caused.

8 The waiter must ensure that the aboyeur receives the dish being returned and checks it immediately, because it may mean that the particular dish concerned has to be taken off the menu to prevent the risk of food poisoning to other customers.

9 The policy of the establishment will dictate whether or not the customer is to be charged for the alternative dish.

Fig 5.8. Example of a returned food check

Lost property

If, for example, a waiter finds a wallet under a chair that has recently been vacated by a customer, the steps listed below might be taken:

1 A check should be made immediately as to whether or not the customer has left the service area. If he is still in the area, the wallet may be returned to him.

2 If the customer has left the service area, the waiter should hand the wallet to the headwaiter or supervisor in charge.

3 The supervisor or headwaiter should check with reception and the hall porter to see if the customer has left the building.

4 If the customer concerned is a resident, then reception may ring their room, stating the wallet has been found and can be collected at a convenient time.

5 If the customer is a regular customer, it is possible that the head waiter or receptionist may know where to contact them to arrange for them to collect the wallet.

6 If the customer is a regular customer but cannot be contacted, the wallet should be kept in the lost property office until the customer's next visit.

7 If the owner has not been found or contacted immediately, the headwaiter or supervisor should list the items contained in the wallet with the waiter who found the wallet. The list should be signed by both the headwaiter or supervisor and the finder (the waiter). The list must be dated and also indicate where the article was found and at what time.

8 A copy of this list should go with the wallet to the lost property office where the contents of the wallet must be checked against the list before it is accepted. The details of the find are then entered in a lost property register.

9 Another copy of the list should go to the hall porter in case any enquiries are received concerning a wallet. Anyone claiming lost property should be passed on to the lost property office.

10 Before the lost property office hands over any lost property, a description of the article concerned and its contents should be asked for to ensure as far as possible that it is being returned to the genuine owner. The office should also see proof of identity of the person claiming ownership.

11 In the case of all lost property, the steps mentioned above should be carried out as quickly as possible as this is in the best interests of the establishment and causes the customer minimum inconvenience. On receipt of lost property, the customer should be asked to sign for the article concerned, also giving their address and telephone number.

12 Any lost property unclaimed after three months may become the property of the finder who should claim it through the headwaiter or supervisor.

Illness

If a customer falls ill in your establishment then the steps below might be taken:

1 As soon as it is noticed that a customer is feeling unwell while in the dining room or restaurant a person in authority should be immediately called.

2 If the customer falling ill is a woman then a female member of staff should attend her.

3 The person in authority must enquire if the customer needs assistance. At the same time he/she must try to judge whether the illness is of a serious nature or not. If in any doubt it is always better to call for medical assistance.

4 It is often advisable to offer to take the customer to another room to see if they are able to recover in a few minutes. It this happens their meal should be placed on the hotplate until their return.

5 If the illness appears to be of a serious nature, a doctor, nurse or someone qualified in first aid should be called for immediately.

6 The customer should not be moved until a doctor has examined him.

7 If necessary the area should be screened off.

8 Although this is a difficult situation to deal with in front of the general public, the minimum fuss should be made and service to the rest of the customers should carry on as normal.

9 The medical person will advise whether an ambulance should be called.

10 The customer may have had a sudden stomach upset and wish to leave without finishing the meal. Assistance should be offered in helping the customer leave the restaurant.

11 Payment for the part of the meal consumed and any ensuing travel costs would be according to the policy of the establishment.

12 It is most important that for all accidents, minor or serious, all details are recorded in an accident book (see below). This is in case of a claim against the establishment at a later date.

13 If after a short period of time the customer returns and continues with the meal, a fresh cover should be laid and the meal returned from the hotplate or a new meal served.

Alcohol over-consumption

If a customer is suspected of having too much to drink the following steps might be taken:

1 If a prospective customer asks for a table and the staff believe the client is under the influence of drink, they may refuse them a table, even though there may be one available. It is not always possible, however, to recognise a customer who may prove objectionable later on.

2 If difficulty is found in handling this type of person then assistance in removing the person from the eating area may come from other members of staff (depending on establishment policy physical contact should be avoided).

3 If a customer is suspected of being drunk this must first of all be ascertained by the headwaiter or supervisor.

4 The customer should then be asked to leave rather than be allowed to become objectionable to other customers.

5 If the customer has already consumed part of the meal but is not being objectionable then the remainder of the meal should be served in the normal fashion, but the headwaiter or supervisor must ensure no more alcoholic beverage is offered.

6   On finishing, the customer should be watched until they have left the premises.

7   It is always advisable to make out a report of all such incidents. They should also be brought to the immediate attention of the restaurant manager in case of any claim at a later date concerning a particular incident.

Unsatisfactory appearance

If a customer's appearance is not satisfactory according to the policy of the establishment, the following steps might be taken:

1   If a customer's appearance does not meet the dress code policy of the establishment or is likely to give offence to others, then the customer should be asked to correct their dress to the approved fashion required by the establishment.

2   If the customer will not comply with the request, they should be asked to leave.

3   If they have partly consumed a meal then whether they will be charged or not depends on the policy of the house and the discretion of the head waiter or supervisor.

4   A report of this incident must be made and signed by the staff concerned.

Recording incidents

It is advisable that when any incident occurs a report is made out immediately. The basic information that should be found in the report is as follows:

- Place.
- Date.
- Time.
- Nature of incident.

- Individual, signed reports from those concerned.
- Action taken.
- Name, address and phone number of the customer involved, and also of the staff involved.

All reports should be kept in case similar incidents occur at a later date, and for future reference should the need arise.

Dealing with children

If children are among the customers arriving in the foodservice area then take the lead in how to care for them from the parents, guardian or accompanying adults. Where applicable, the following factors should be determined.

- Are high chairs/seat cushions required?
- Restrictions on the service of alcohol to minors (see Section 10.1 Legal considerations, page 390).
- Are children's meal menus required?
- The portion size required if items are ordered from the standard menu.

- The provision of children's 'give aways', such as crayons, colouring books etc.
- For the safety of both children and others, the staff should be aware of children's movements.
- Should the children be older, then they should be addressed as either 'Sir' or 'Madam'.

Lost children

Should a child be reported lost, the steps listed below should be taken.

1 A complete description of the lost child should be obtained:
   - male/female
   - name
   - age
   - where last seen
   - clothing worn
   - any predominant features
   - colour of hair
   - whether any accessories were being carried, e.g. a doll.
2 Immediately inform the supervisor/security.
3 Put a constant watch on all entrances/exits.
4 Check all cloakroom/rest areas and the immediate vicinity where the child has been reported missing.
5 Should nothing result from taking the above actions, immediately inform the police.

Customers with special needs

Customer mobility

Extra awareness is needed to meet the requirements of customers who may have special needs, such as mobility difficulties. The following considerations should be given on these occasions.

- Offer wheelchair users places at tables where there is adequate space for manoeuvrability.
- Offer wheelchair users a place out of the main thoroughfare of customer/staff movement.
- Offer wheelchair users a place with easy access to cloakrooms, exits and fire exits.
- Always ensure that menus, wine lists and the like are immediately available to any wheelchair user.
- Never move the wheelchair without asking the customer first.
- Crutches/walking sticks should be placed in a safe but accessible and readily available position.
- Customers with dexterity difficulties may be assisted by first asking the customer how best they can be helped. Assistance may include for example ensuring that all items served or

placed on to the table are near to the customer, offering to fillet/bone fish and meat items and offering to cut up potato and vegetable items.

Blind and partially sighted customers

Awareness is also required to meet the needs of those customers who may be blind or partially sighted. The following considerations should be taken into account:

- Talk to and treat the customer with special needs as you would any other customer.
- Remember it is 'by touch' that blind people see and are made aware that they are involved in what is happening around them.
- If in doubt ask the person directly how they may best be helped.
- Do not talk to their companions as if the person was not there.
- Offer to read menus or wine and drink lists.
- Immediately prior to taking the customer's order, a gentle touch on the hand or arm will attracts their attention to you.
- Offer to fillet/bone fish and meat items.
- Offer to cut up potato and vegetable items should it be necessary.
- Never overfill cups, glasses or soup bowls.
- Should you feel it appropriate, use bowls instead of plates for specific food items, but always ask the customer first.
- Ask if you should describe where the food items are on the plate. Use the clock method to explain the location of food on a plate, for example, 6 o'clock for meat, 10 to 10 for vegetables, 10 past 2 for potatoes.

Customers with communication difficulties

Be aware of communication difficulties that may arise when, for example, customers are deaf or hard of hearing or have little understanding of the English language. In such cases the steps shown below may be helpful.

- Speak directly to the customer.
- Stand in such a position that the customer is able to see your face clearly.
- Speak normally but more distinctly.
- Describe food/drink items in simple, precise and plain language.
- Seat customers away from possible excessive noise, as this is most uncomfortable for customers wearing hearing aids.
- Always read back the food or drink order received to confirm all requests.
- Listen attentively to what is being said to you to ensure you understand the customer's requirements.

5.3 TAKING BOOKINGS

Bookings may be taken by post, by email, via the internet, by telephone and in person. Booking a table is often the first contact that a potential customer has with the establishment and it is therefore important to give the right impression.

The booking sheet

Most establishments use some form of booking sheet, either manual or electronic. An example of the information that might be required on a booking sheet is given in Figure 5.9. This form gives the maximum number of covers to be booked for a service period and enables a running total of pre-booked covers to be kept. The form also has space for the customer's telephone number. Depending on the policy of the establishment, written confirmation of bookings may be required or credit card numbers taken. Other information that might be sought includes whether the occasion of the meal is for a special event, or customer preferences about the size, shape and location of a table.

If party bookings require special menus, the booking should be referred to the supervisor. Procedures similar to function catering booking will then be adopted (see Section 9.2 Function administration, page 360).

Procedure for taking bookings

When taking a booking by telephone the procedure shown below might be used.

- When the telephone rings, lift the receiver and say: 'Good morning (state the name of the establishment), may I help you?'

- If the customer is making the booking in person then say 'Good morning Sir/Madam, how may I help you?'

Restaurant.................................. Day......... Date......... Maximum covers....................

Name	Tel. No.	Covers	Arrival time	Running total	Special requirements	Signature

Fig 5.9. Example of a booking sheet

- When taking a booking the essential information required is as follows:
  - the customer's name and telephone number
  - the day and date the booking is required
  - the number of covers
  - the time the booking is required
  - any special requests.
- When you have received this information from the prospective customer it is advisable to repeat all of the details back to the customer as a means of confirmation.
- If a cancellation is being received then again confirm the cancellation with the customer by repeating his/her request over the telephone and then ask if you can take a booking for any other occasion in place of the cancellation.
- At the end of a telephone call for a booking one should say: 'Thank you for your booking, we shall look forward to seeing you.'

The procedures for taking a booking in person are similar to those for taking a booking via the telephone. When taking bookings by mail the information that is required is the same as that identified above. Confirmation is normally sent back to the customer by the same method as the booking was received, for example, by email or post. See also Section 9.2 Function administration, page 360.

5.4 PREPARATION FOR SERVICE

The term 'mise-en-place' (literally 'put in place' but also meaning 'preparation for service') is the traditional term used for all the duties that must be carried out in order to ready the room for service. A duty rota showing the tasks and duties to be completed before service and the member of staff responsible is drawn up (see Section 10.6 Staff organisation and training, page 425).

Order of working

The duties should proceed in a certain order so that they may be carried out effectively and efficiently. For example, dusting should be done before the tables are laid and vacuuming should be completed before the tables and chairs are put in place. A suggested order of work might be as follows:

1 Dusting
2 Stacking chairs on tables
3 Vacuuming
4 Polishing
5 Arrange tables and chairs according to the table plan
6 Linen

7 Accompaniments
8 Hotplate
9 Stillroom
10 Sideboards
11 Silver cleaning
12 Other duties such as preparing trolleys

Some of these jobs will be carried out at the same time and the headwaiter must ensure they are completed efficiently. As the necessary preparatory work is completed the staff should report back to the headwaiter, who should check that the work has been carried out in a satisfactory manner and then re-allocate the member of staff to other work involving the laying-up of the room.

Using white gloves

In some establishments members of staff wear white cotton gloves when carrying out some preparation tasks, such as:

- handling linen and paper
- clothing up tables
- making napkin folds
- handling clean crockery, cutlery and glassware
- laying tables.

The gloves help to prevent the soiling of clean service items and finger marks on cleaned and polished service equipment.

Preparation duties

The duties to be carried out before the service commences are many and varied according to the particular food and beverage service area concerned. A list of the possible tasks and duties is shown below, but not all of these are applicable to every situation and there may be some jobs not listed which are peculiar to a particular establishment.

Supervisor

- Check the booking diary for reservations.
- Make out the seating plan for the day and allocate customers accordingly.
- Make out a plan of the various stations and show where the staff will be working.
- Go over the menu with staff immediately before service is due to commence.
- Check that all duties on the duty rota are covered and that a full team of staff is present.

Housekeeping duties

Housekeeping duties include the reception area and may involve the following:

- Every day, vacuum the carpet and brush surrounds.
- Clean and polish doors and glass.
- Empty waste bins and ashtrays.
- Perform one of the following daily tasks, as appropriate:

- *Monday*: brush and dust tables and chairs.
- *Tuesday*: polish all sideboards, window ledges and cash desk.
- *Wednesday*: polish all brasses.
- *Thursday*: clean and polish the reception area.
- *Friday*: commence again as Monday.

■ Each day, on completion of all duties, line up tables and chairs for laying up.

Linen/paper

This applies not only to table, buffet and slip cloths and glass and waiter cloths, but also to paper slip cloths and napkins plus dish papers and doilies. Duties might include:

■ Collecting the clean linen from the housekeeping department, checking items against list, distributing them to the various service points, laying tablecloths and folding napkins. Spare linen should be folded neatly into the linen basket.

■ Ensuring that stocks are sufficient to meet needs.

■ Ensuring that glass cloths and waiters' cloths are available.

■ Providing dish papers and doilies as required.

■ The preparation of the linen basket for return to the linen room.

Hotplate

Duties might include:

■ Switching on the hotplate.

■ Ensuring all doors are closed.

■ Placing items in the hotplate according to the menu offered, for example:
  - soup plates
  - consommé cups
  - fish plates
  - joint plates
  - sweet plates.

■ Stocking up the hotplate after each service with clean and polished crockery in readiness for the next meal service.

Cutlery, flatware and hollow-ware

Duties might include:

■ Collection of cutlery, flatware and hollow-ware from the storage area (sometimes called a silver room).

■ Polishing and sorting on to trays the following items in quantities agreed with the supervisor:

- – service spoons
- – joint/service forks
- – soup spoons
- – fish knives
- – fish forks
- – joint knives
- – side knives
- – sweet spoons
- – sweet forks
- – tea/coffee spoons
- – specialist service equipment as required for the menu.
- ■ Daily cleaning of the:
  - – spirit and electric heaters
  - – flare lamps, spirit and gas
  - – carving trolley.
- ■ Additional cleaning of silver cutlery, flatware and hollow-ware as per a daily rota, for example:
  - – *Monday*: all round flats, all knives, large coffee pots and milk jugs.
  - – *Tuesday*: all oval flats, all forks, small coffee pots and milk jugs.
  - – *Wednesday*: round vegetable dishes and lids, all spoons, large coffee pots and milk jugs.
  - – *Thursday*: oval vegetable dishes and lids, small items of special equipment, individual soup tureens.
  - – *Friday*: any other items that it may be necessary to clean on a regular rota basis in order to ensure that everything is cleaned at regular intervals. This method ensures that anything broken or in need of replacing can be noted and put on one side for repair.

Crockery

Duties might include:

- ■ The checking and polishing of side plates ready for lay-up.
- ■ The checking and polishing of crockery for the hotplate according to menu and service requirements.
- ■ Preparation of service plates for sideboards/workstations.
- ■ Preparation of stocks of crockery for sideboards/workstations, such as
  - – fishplates
  - – side plates
  - – coffee and tea saucers.

Cruets, table numbers and butter dishes

Duties might include:

- The collection of cruets, table numbers and butter dishes from the silver room.

- Checking, filling and polishing the cruets.

- The laying on tables of cruets, ashtrays, table numbers and butter dishes with knives, according to the headwaiter's instructions.

- Restoring the items following service.

Stillroom

Duties might include:

- The ordering of stores requirements (including bar and accompaniment requirements).

- The preparation of:
  - beverage service items
  - butter scrolls/butter pats and alternatives
  - bread items.

- The clearing of the stillroom area following service.

- Polishing and refilling oil and vinegar stands, sugar basins and dredgers, peppermills and cayenne pepper pots.

- Preparing all accompaniments such as tomato ketchup, French and English mustard, ground ginger, horseradish sauce, mint sauce, Worcestershire sauce, Parmesan cheese.

- Distributing the cruets to the tables and the accompaniments to the sideboards.

- Checking with the headwaiter the number of accompaniments and sets of cruets to prepare and the number of sideboards and tables that will be in use during the service period.

Sideboards/workstations

After ensuring that the sideboard/workstation is clean and polished, it can be stocked. Figure 5.10 gives an example of a sideboard lay-up including:

1	water jug	11	service spoons and forks
2	butter dish	12	bread basket
3	check pad on service plate	13	service salver/plate
4	assorted condiments	14	underflats
5	hotplate	15	coffee saucers
6	side knives	16	side plates
7	joint knives	17	sweet/fish plates
8	fish knives and forks	18	joint plates
9	soup spoons, teaspoons and coffee spoons	19	trays.
10	sweet spoons and forks		

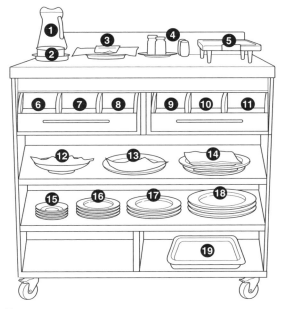

Fig 5.10. Example of a sideboard lay-up

Fig 5.11. Laid sideboard

Other items required might include:

■ specialist cutlery according to the menu, e.g. soup and sauce ladles

■ various crockery according to the menu, e.g. saucers for consommé cups.

Guéridons may also have to be laid up in conjunction with the sideboards, according to the type of service offered.

Dispense bar

Mise-en-place may involve the duties shown below.

1 Open the bar.

2 Bar silver requiring cleaning to be taken to the silver person.

3 Clear any debris left from the previous day.

4 Wipe down bar tops.

5 Clean shelves and swab the bar floor.

6 Check optics.

7 Restock the bar with beverage items as required.

8 Prepare ice buckets, wine coolers, service trays and water jugs.

9 Check pads and wine lists; line up, clean and polish apéritif glasses.

10 Prepare and check the liqueur trolley for glasses, stock and bottle presentation.

11 Prepare the bar service top according to the standards of the establishment which may include:

- cutting board
- fruit knife
- fruit: lemons, oranges, apples
- cucumber
- fresh eggs (for cocktails)
- mixing glass and spoons
- Hawthorn strainer
- wine funnel
- olives, cocktail cherries
- cocktail shaker strainer
- nuts and crisps
- coloured sugar

- Angostura bitters
- peach bitters
- Worcestershire sauce
- cocktail sticks
- cherries in glass
- straws in sherry glass
- tea strainer
- wine coasters
- spirit measures
- soda syphon
- ice bucket and tongs.

Display buffet

Duties may include:

- The preparation of the buffet table to the supervisor's instructions.
- The display of:
  - butter dishes and knives
  - accompaniments
  - food items
  - special cutlery and tableware as required (e.g. grapefruit spoons)
  - underplates for large butter dishes
  - service spoons and forks
  - side plates with doilies or dish papers if necessary
  - water jugs and joint knives for pâtés or mousses
  - cold plates
  - carving knife.

Trolleys

Carving trolley:

- Check the trolley for cleanliness.
- Check and refill burners.
- Fill the water reservoir with boiling water from the still.
- Ensure the sauce and gravy reservoirs are in place under cover. They should be sited beside the plate platform.

- Lay up for the bottom shelf service plate, to include:
  - service spoons and forks
  - sauce ladles
  - service plate with carving knife, fork and steel.

See Section 8.3 Introduction to carving and jointing, page 309, for a photograph of a carving trolley.

Sweet trolley:

- Check trolley for cleanliness and ensure it is polished.
- Place doilies or cloths on top tiers.
- Place the following items on the bottom shelf on a folded slip cloth:
  - sweet plates/bowls
  - gâteau slice, pastry tongs (in the drawer or on a service plate)
  - service spoons and forks
  - joint knives
  - sauce ladles (in a folded napkin)
  - joint plate for dirty service items.

Cheese trolley:

- Check the trolley for cleanliness.
- The top and bottom shelves may be laid up as follows:

  Top shelf:
  - various cheeses on a cheese board
  - knives and forks for cheese service
  - salt and pepper
  - caster sugar
  - flat or dish with assorted biscuits or breads
  - celery glass on underplate.

  Bottom shelf:
  - side plates
  - side knives.

See Section 5.7 Service of food, page 236, for an example of a sweet/cheese trolley.

Clothing-up

Nothing is more attractive in the room than tables clothed-up with clean, crisp and well-starched linen tablecloths and napkins. The tablecloth and napkins should be handled as little as possible, which will be ensured by laying the tablecloth quickly and properly first time.

Laying the tablecloth

Before laying the tablecloth the table and chairs should be in their correct position. The tabletop should be clean and the table level, with care being taken to ensure that it does not wobble. If the table wobbles slightly, a disc sliced from a cork will correct the problem.

Next, the correct size of tablecloth should be collected. Most tablecloths are folded in what is known as a screen fold.

The waiter should stand between the legs of the table while the tablecloth is being laid, to ensure that the corners of the cloth cover the legs of the table once the clothing up has been completed.

The screen fold should be opened out across the table in front of the waiter with the inverted and two single folds facing him, ensuring that the inverted fold is on top.

The cloth should then be laid in the following manner:

1   Place the thumb on top of the inverted fold with the index and third fingers either side of the middle fold.

2   Spread out your arms as close to the width of the table as is possible and lift the cloth so that the bottom fold falls free.

3   This should be positioned over the edge of the opposite side of the table from where you are standing.

4   Now let go of the middle fold and open the cloth out, drawing it towards you until the table is covered with the cloth.

5   Check that the fall of the cloth is even on all sides.

6   Any adjustments should be made from the edge of the cloth.

If the tablecloth is laid correctly the following should be apparent:

■   the corners of the tablecloth should cover the legs of the table

■   the overlap should be even all round the table: 30–45 cm (12–18 in)

■   the creases of the tablecloth should all run the same way in the room.

If two tablecloths are necessary to cover a table for a larger party, then the overlap of the two tablecloths should face away from the entrance to the room. This is for presentation purposes of both the room and the table.

Napkin folds

There are many forms of napkin (or serviette) fold to be found in use in the food and beverage service area. Some are intricate in their detail while others are simpler. The simpler folds are used in everyday service and some of the more complex and difficult folds may only be used on special occasions, such as luncheons, dinners and weddings.

There are three main reasons why the simple folds are better than the more complex ones.

1   The napkin, if folded correctly, can look good and add to the general appearance of the room, whether it is a simple or complex fold.

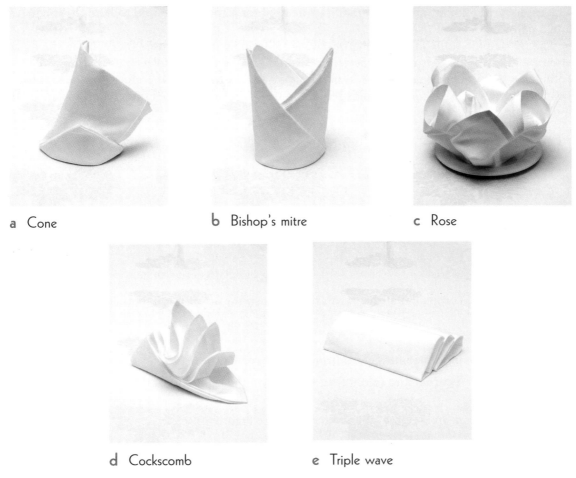

a Cone b Bishop's mitre c Rose

d Cockscomb e Triple wave

Fig 5.12. Napkin folds

2 A simpler fold is perhaps more hygienic as the more complex fold involves greater handling to complete. In addition, its appearance, when unfolded to spread over the customer's lap, is poor as it often has many creases.

3 The complex fold takes much more time to complete properly than a very simple fold.

The majority of napkin folds have special names, for example:

■ Cone
■ Bishop's mitre
■ Rose
■ Cockscomb
■ Triple wave.

The rose fold of a napkin is one in which rolls or Melba toast may be presented at the table.

The triple wave is an attractive fold that may be used for a special function to hold the menu and a name card.

The five napkin folds shown in Figure 5.12 are, in the main, those used every day in the food and beverage service area and for special occasions. These are the simpler folds that may be completed more quickly, requiring less handling by the operator and therefore may be said to be more hygienic. More complex folds require longer to complete, need more handling and can look rather crushed when unfolded.

Napkin folding

Shown below are five basic but decorative napkin folds. These are:

1 Cone

2 Bishop's mitre

3 Rose

4 Cockscomb

5 Triple wave

Once you become competent at these, you should learn the art of folding others to extend your repertoire.

Cone

1 Open the napkin out lengthways in front of you (see Figure 5.13a).

2 Take the top left corner and fold it diagonally on to the right end of the centre line (see Figure 5.13b).

3 Fold the bottom square on to the top triangle (see Figure 5.13c).

4 Take the two points at the top right corner, by placing your hand inside the napkin, and fold them back towards you as far as possible (see Figure 5.13d).

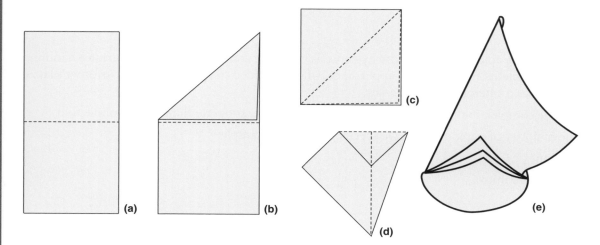

Fig 5.13. Cone

5   Pull the base out so that it is circular and place it in the centre of the cover (see Figure 5.13(e)).

Bishop's mitre

1   Lay the napkin out flat in front of you (see Figure 5.14a).

2   Fold it in half, straight side to straight side (see Figure 5.14b).

3   Take the top right corner and fold it down to the centre of the bottom line (see Figure 5.14c).

4   Take the bottom left corner and fold it up to meet the centre of the top line (see Figure 5.14d).

5   Turn the napkin over so that the folds are now face down (see Figure 5.14e).

6   Take the top line (edge) and fold it down to meet the base line (bottom edge), leaving the two peaks pointing away from you (see Figure 5.14f).

7   Take the bottom right-hand side and fold it under the flap on the left side. Make sure it tucks right under the flap for a snug fit (see Figure 5.14g).

8   Turn it completely over (see Figure 5.14h).

9   Again take the bottom right-hand side and fold it under the flap on the left side. Now stand the napkin up by pulling the sides of the base out until it is circular in shape (see Figure 5.14i).

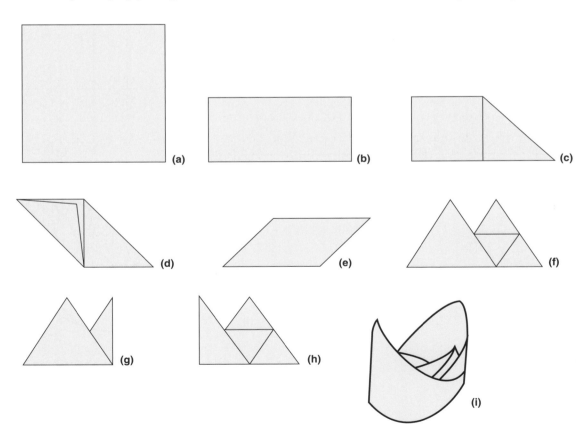

Fig 5.14. Bishop's mitre

Rose

1   Unfold the napkin and lay it out in a square (see Figure 5.15a).

2   Fold the corners into the centre of the napkin (see Figure 5.15b).

3   Fold the corners into the centre of the napkin for a second time (see Figure 5.15c).

4   Turn the whole napkin over so that all the corners folded into the centre are underneath (see Figure 5.15d).

5   Fold the corners into the centre once more (see Figure 5.15e).

6   Hold the four centre points down by means of an upturned 'Paris' goblet (see Figure 5.15f).

7   Holding the Paris goblet steady, place your hand under each corner and pull up a folded corner of the napkin (petal) on to the bowl of the glass. You now have four petals showing. Now place your hand under the napkin, but between each of the petals, and raise a further four petals. Place on an underplate (see Figure 5.15g).

Note: The napkin must be clean and well starched. Run the back of your hand over every fold to make the crease firm and sharp.

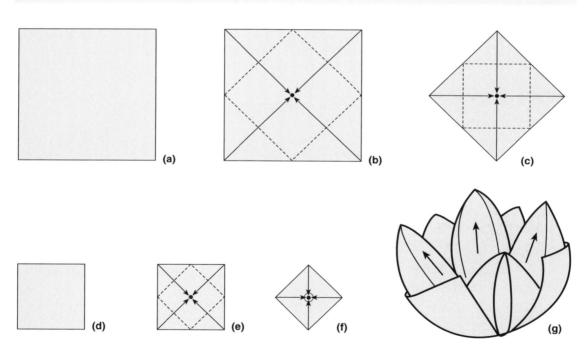

Fig 5.15. Rose

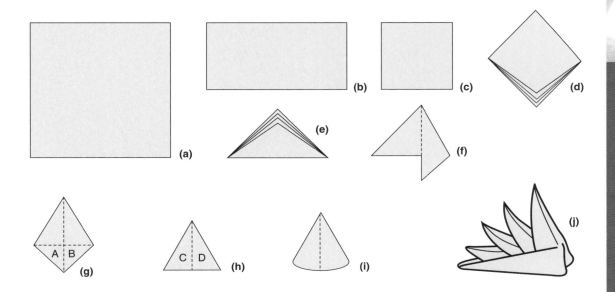

Fig 5.16. Cockscomb

Cockscomb

1 Open the napkin into a square shape (see Figure 5.16a).

2 Fold it in half (see Figure 5.16b).

3 Fold it in half again to make a square (see Figure 5.16c).

4 Rotate the square so that it now forms a diamond shape in front of you. Make sure the four single folds are at the bottom of the diamond (see Figure 5.16d).

5 Fold the bottom corner of the diamond to the top corner. You will then have a triangular shape in front of you, with the four single folds on top (see Figure 5.16e).

6 Take the right side of the triangle and fold it over on to the centre line (see Figure 5.16f).

7 Do the same with the left hand side (see Figure 5.16g).

8 Tuck the two lower triangles (A and B) under the main triangle (see Figure 5.16h).

9 Fold the two triangles (C and D) down from the centre line and hold it together. The four single folds should now be on top and at the peak of this fold (see Figure 5.16i).

10 Hold this narrow fold firmly, ensuring the four single folds are away from you. In turn, pull each single fold up and towards you (see Figure 5.16j).

Triple wave (French Fold)

1 Unfold the napkin and lay it out in a square.

2 Fold the napkin in three along the dotted lines to form a rectangle as in Figure 5.17a (for

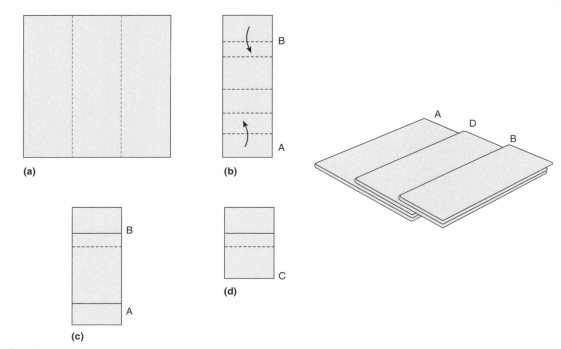

Fig 5.17. Triple wave

napkins that are already folded in three and then three again, just open the napkin out so that it is in the rectangle as in Figure 5.17)

3 Turn the napkin so that the narrow side is towards you

4 Fold each end of the napkin 'A' and 'B' inwards, along the dotted lines as indicated in Figure 5.17b.

5 Fold 'B' over once more.

6 Turn edge 'A' over so that it meets the edge of the top fold 'B'.

7 Turn edge 'C' under so that 'A' is now the top.

8 The final form for this napkin is shown in Figure 5.17.

9 The fold is laid with the steps of the folds away from the customer. A name card or menu may be placed in between the steps of the fold.

Laying covers for table service and assisted service

Cover

One of the technical terms often used in the foodservice industry is a 'cover' ('couvert'). The term originates from the custom, up to the fifteenth century, of serving 'under cover' ('a couvert'). This meant to cover the courses and dishes with a large white napkin in order to indicate that all precautions had been taken to avoid the poisoning of guests. In modern foodservice operations, the term cover has two definitions, according to the context in which it is being used.

1 When discussing how many customers a restaurant or dining room will seat, or how many customers will be attending a certain cocktail party, we refer to the total number of customers concerned as so many covers. For example, a restaurant or dining room will seat a maximum of 85 covers (customers); there will be 250 covers (customers) at a certain cocktail party; this table will seat a party of six covers (customers).

2 When laying a table in readiness for service there are a variety of place settings that may be laid according to the type of meal and service being offered. We refer to this place setting as a certain type of cover being laid. In other words, a cover refers to all the necessary cutlery, crockery, glassware and linen required to lay a certain type of place setting for a specific dish or meal.

When deciding on the laying of covers there are two basic service considerations. The first is where cutlery for the meal is to be laid before each course is served. The second is where the cutlery for the meal is to be laid prior to the start of that meal and for all the courses that are to be served. The first approach is known as the à la carte cover, and the second is known as the table d'hôte cover.

À la carte cover

The à la carte cover follows the principle that the cutlery for each course will be laid just before each course is served. The traditional cover, given below (and shown in Figure 5.18) therefore represents the cover for hors-d'oeuvre, which is the first course in a classic menu sequence (see Section 3.2 Classic menu sequence, page 70).

- Fish plate (centre of cover)
- Fish knife
- Fish fork
- Side plate
- Side knife
- Napkin
- Water glass
- Wine glass.

There are now a variety of approaches to what is laid for the à la carte form of service. This can include using large decorative cover plates and a side plate and knife only, or replacing the fish

Fig 5.18. À la carte cover

Fig 5.19. Classic or basic cover

knife and fork with a joint knife and fork. This is sometimes known as a classic or basic lay-up. An example of this type of lay-up is shown in Figure 5.19.

Where an à la carte cover has been laid, the cutlery required by the customer for the dishes she has chosen will be laid course by course. In other words, there should not, at any time during the meal, be more cutlery on the table than is required by the customer at that time.

If decorative cover plates are used for an à la carte cover it is common for the first course plates to be placed on this plate. The first course and the cover plate are then removed when the first course is cleared.

Table d'hôte cover

The table d'hôte cover follows the principle that the cutlery for the whole meal will be laid before the first course is served. The traditional cover is as follows.

- joint knife
- fish knife
- soup spoon
- joint fork
- fish fork
- sweet fork

- sweet spoon
- side plate
- side knife
- napkin
- water glass
- wine glass.

Again, there are some possible variations to this approach. The sweet spoon and fork may be omitted, for example.

Where a table d'hôte cover has been laid the waiter should remove, after the order has been taken, any unnecessary cutlery and relay any extra items that may be required. This means that before the customer commences the meal they should have all the cutlery required for the dishes chosen, set out as their place setting or cover.

Fig 5.20. Table d'hôte cover

Laying the table

Once the table is clothed-up it should be laid in readiness for service. The waiter must ensure that where applicable all cutlery is laid 1.25cm (½ in) from the edge of the table and that badged crockery has the badge or crest at the head or top of the cover. After polishing, the glasses should be placed upside down at the top right-hand corner of the cover. Once the covers have been laid the table accompaniments should be placed on the table according to the custom of the establishment.

Cutlery should be laid from a service salver or service plate. An alternative to this is to use a service cloth and to hold the items being laid in the service cloth, giving a final polish before setting the items on the table. In some establishments the service staff wear white gloves when laying cleaned and pre-polished tableware onto the tables in order to avoid finger marks.

When laying a cover, the cutlery should be laid from the inside to the outside of the cover.

This ensures even spacing of the cover and lessens the need to handle the items laid more than is necessary.

If an à la carte cover is being laid then the first item set on the table should be the fish plate in the centre of each cover.

If a table d'hôte cover is being laid then the first item to be set on the table should be the napkin or side plate in the centre of each cover. If the side plate is laid in the centre of each cover it would be moved to the left-hand side of the cover once all the cutlery had been laid. The purpose of initially placing something in the centre of the cover is to ensure that the covers are exactly opposite one another and that the cutlery of each cover are the same distance apart.

The order of laying these covers is as follows:

À la carte:

fish plate at the centre of the cover

fish knife

fish fork

side plate

side knife

napkin

water glass

wine glass.

Table d'hôte:

side plate at centre of cover

joint knife

fish knife

soup spoon

joint fork

fish fork

sweet fork

sweet spoon

move side plate to the left of cover

side knife

napkin

water glass

wine glass.

In some operations a trolley is used for storing cutlery. When laying-up, without customers in the restaurant, this trolley is pushed around the tables and the cutlery items are laid after the final polish with the waiter's cloth.

After the above covers have been laid, the table lay-up should be completed by the addition of the following items:

■ cruets

■ table numbers

■ table decorations

■ ashtrays (depending on the smoking policy of the establishment).

Polishing glassware

The following equipment is required to carry out this technique:

■ a container of near-boiling water

a   b

Fig 5.21. Polishing glasses: (a) allowing steam to enter the bowl of the glass, (b) polishing while rotating the glass

- a clean, dry teacloth
- the required glassware.

1 Using the base of the glass to be cleaned, hold the wine goblet over the steam from the boiling water so that the steam enters the bowl of the glass (see Figure 5.21a).

2 Rotate the wine goblet to allow the steam to circulate fully within the bowl of the glass and then hold the base of the glass over the steam.

3 Now hold the base of the wine goblet in the clean, dry teacloth.

4 Place the other hand underneath the teacloth in readiness to polish the bowl of the glass.

5 Place the thumb of the polishing hand inside the bowl of the glass and the fingers on the outside, holding the bowl of the wine goblet gently but firmly. Rotate the wine goblet with the hand holding the base of the glass (see Figure 5.21b).

6 When fully polished, hold the wine goblet up to the light to check that it is clean.

7 Ensure that the base of the glass is also clean.

The process described here is for single glasses. Larger quantities of glassware may be polished by first placing a glass rack full of inverted glasses over a sink of very hot water in order to steam the glasses. A number of people would then work together to polish the glassware.

Table accompaniments

The table accompaniments required to complete the table lay-up are the same whether an à la carte or table d'hôte cover has been laid:

- cruet: salt, pepper, mustard and mustard spoon
- ashtray (depending on the smoking policy of the establishment)
- table number
- floral table centre.

These are the basic items usually required to complete the table lay-up. In some establishments certain extra items will be placed on the table just prior to the service to complete its lay-up. These may include:

■ roll basket

■ Melba toast

■ gristicks

■ peppermill

■ butter and alternatives.

Preparing a simple floral table decoration

A simple centre table display can be made in a small shallow bowl, using oasis (a green coloured sponge-like material that holds moisture and is soft enough for greenery and flower stems to be pushed into it and to hold them secure).

Preparation

1   Using a sharp knife cut the oasis to size (unless it comes already cut and shaped as a round posy oasis). The oasis must be at least 5 cms higher than the rim of the bowl. This will allow enough room to fill it with greenery and flowers both on the top and round the side.

2   Soak the oasis (or foam) in water by placing it on the water and allowing it to sink of its own accord. Never push the oasis under, as this will leave air pockets in it and it will not fill with water properly. The oasis will be ready when bubbles stop forming and it has sunk to the bottom of the container.

3   Secure the moistened oasis into the posy bowl with oasis tape (green coloured, waterproof sticky tape) – if the bowl and secured oasis can be turned upside down without it moving then it is done correctly.

Foliage/greenery

4   'Greening up' the posy will help to make sure there are no gaps or holes in the arrangement.

5   The greenery used is often leather leaf, a type of fern, or sometimes Cupressus, known commonly as conifer. When using leather leaf it usually needs to be cut in half, making sure that the top half is left with a stem that can be inserted into the oasis.

6   Use the top sections of the greenery to create a skirt around the bowl, making sure the foliage is facing up to show the correct side. Leave at least a couple of centimetres for the stem, which needs to be free and clean, to create a good anchor so that the greenery does not come free. Make sure that the foliage is angled down to cover the bowl and continue to fill with the remainder of the foliage.

7   Allow room for the flowers (see Figure 5.22a). When dressing the arrangement remember to keep turning the arrangement as this will help to keep its shape round.

Flowers

8   The first step in using flowers is to grade them. This means choosing the flowers that will form the focal point of the arrangement (normally the largest in size or the most expensive). Examples are roses, large carnations, irises and lilies.

Fig 5.22a.

9   Prepare all flowers by stripping excess leaves to create clean stems, throwing away any marked or damaged flowers, and placing them in a size order, starting with the largest. Keeping the work area clear from cut stems and general mess will allow the full effect and shape of the arrangement to be seen as work progresses.

10 Decide which of the flowers will be used as a focal point from any of the flowers above, then use four of them. Place one in the posy as the central flower, with a height of usually two-thirds the width of the bowl, including the height of the oasis. Add on at least 5 centimetres and cut. Now push this into the centre of the arrangement.

11 With the three focal flowers that are left, angle these out at around 45° and at half the height of the top central flower.

12 Remember to leave a couple of centimetres for anchorage and cut the three focal flowers to the same height. Place them at equal distances around the top flower.

13 Once the focal flowers are in place, the hard work is done and all that is needed is to neatly fill the gaps.

14 Depending on the flower choice, proceed by using, for example, spray carnations around and through the arrangement. Always use buds for the outskirts and open, larger flowers further in and closer to the oasis.

Fig 5.22b.

15 Again, gauge one spray carnation from the oasis to the tip of the foliage, then cut a few to the same length (don't forget to leave some excess stem for anchorage). Place these at equal points around the base of the arrangement. Always work in odd numbers, otherwise the posy will look square (see Figure 5.22b).

16 Continue to fill. There may be a few buds poking between the focal flowers but never have these any higher than the top central flower. It is also useful to place a few open spray carnations, for instance close to the oasis around the top section.

17 Repeat this process with the other flowers. Whether using for example, chrysanthemums, alstromeria or other flowers, the same principle of using buds towards the outside and larger open flowers towards the top central section applies. Always remember to keep within the round dome shape.

18 Consider using filler flowers such as yellow Solidaster, blue or white September flower, gypsophilla, statice or limonium. These are very small flowers which don't have one head, but have branch-like stems. These can be used to fill gaps all over

Fig 5.22c.

a posy, making sure that they are displayed the right side up and that the stems are clean. Leave enough to anchor into the oasis and stay within the intended shape. Again, gauge one against the arrangement and cut more to the same length as this will help to keep the arrangement within the shape (see Figure 5.22c).

Note: The oasis should be kept moist to maximise the life of the flowers. Moisture content can be checked by lightly pressing the oasis – it should feel wet. The flowers can also be kept moist by lightly spraying them from time to time with a water gun.

Preparation of customer buffets and counters

Buffet service

There are various types of buffet, namely knife and fork, fork and finger buffets. The requirements of a particular occasion and the host's wishes will determine the exact format in setting up the room. Whatever the nature of the occasion there are certain basic principles to follow:

- The buffet should be set up in a prominent position in the room – the buffet may be one complete display or split into several separate displays around a room.
- There should be ample space on the buffet for display and presentation.
- The buffet should be within easy access of the stillroom and wash-up so that replenishment of the buffet and the clearing of dirties may be carried out without disturbing the customers.
- There must be ample space for customer circulation – buffets can be positioned and laid so that customers can access one or both sides of the buffet at once.
- Provision should be made for sufficient occasional tables and chairs within the room.
- The total presentation of the room should be attractive and promote a good atmosphere that is appropriate for the occasion.

Setting up the buffet

The exact equipment required when setting up the room will be determined by the occasion, for example, see Section 9.4 Weddings, page 379).

The buffet should be covered with suitable cloths, making sure that the drop of the cloth is within 1.25 cm (approx ½ in) from the ground all the way around the front and sides of the buffet. If more than one cloth is used, the creases should be lined up, and where the cloths overlap one another the overlap should be facing away from the entrance to the room. The ends of the buffet should be 'box' pleated, thereby giving a better overall presentation of the buffet.

To achieve a neat, crisp finish the procedure needs to be carried out with as little handling as possible. This may be achieved by adopting the following procedure:

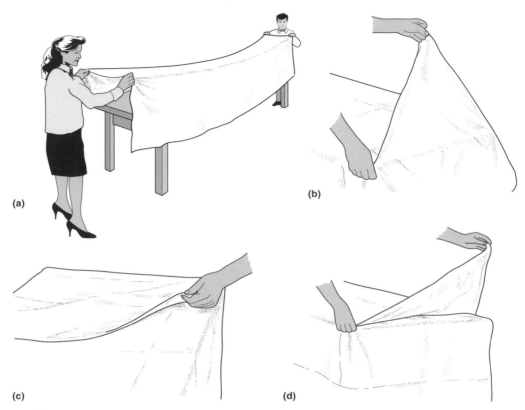

Fig 5.23. Boxing a buffet table

1   With assistance, open the screen fold along the buffet table from end to end (Figure 5.23a).

2   With a person at either end unfold the cloth so that the front and sides of the table are covered and the cloth is no more than 1.25 cm (½ in) from the ground.

3   Stand in front of the table and from the edge place your thumb on the front corner and take the far side of the cloth, lift and bring it back towards you in a semi circle motion (Figure 5.23b). This will bring the side of the cloth horizontal with the ground.

4   The fold on top of the table will now resemble a triangle (Figure 5.23c). This should be folded back towards the side of the table, ensuring that the folded edge is in line with the side of the table (Figure 5.23d).

5   Use the back of your hand to flatten the fold.

6   Repeat the procedure at the other end of the table.

All creases should be in line and slip cloths may be used to finish the top of the table.

Buffet displays may be enhanced by the introduction of a box that has been box-clothed. This can be placed on the buffet table to give extra height and to provide display space for special features.

Table skirting

Alternative methods of dressing a buffet table may include the use of table skirting. Although the initial outlay for such skirting may be high, the ease and simplicity of use makes it very popular for buffet and table decoration. One other feature of skirting is that it is made up of separate panels so that it is comfortable when customers are seated at a table.

A tablecloth is laid on top of the table and then the skirting is attached to the edge of the table by a plastic clip (Figure 5.24a),

Fig 5.24a.   b.

(a) Attaching table skirting in to a table edge and (b) a buffet table with table skirting attached (courtesy of Snap-Drape Europe Limited)

which is fitted to the top of the skirting. The skirting is attached to the table by sliding the clip into place over the lip of the table. The plastic clips are removable to allow the fabric to be cleaned.

Cafeteria service

This is a form of service where customers collect a tray from the beginning of the service counter, move along the counter to select their meal, pay and then collect the required cutlery for their meal, together with any accompaniments. (See also page 16 for different types of counter arrangements.)

Where customer turnover rate is particularly high in a very limited period of time, a variation on the cafeteria/counter (straight line) type service operates with a number of separate/staggered service points (échelon layout). Each of the service points offers a different main course dish, together with the appropriate vegetable dishes, sauces and accompaniments. Other service points offer hot and cold sweets, beverages, sandwiches, pastries, confectionery items and miscellaneous foods. In this way the customer, on entering the food service area, checks the menu to see what he requires and then goes immediately to the appropriate service point. The advantage of this system is that a person who requires just a sandwich and a hot drink is not held up by those selecting a full meal.

This service method will speed up the service as long as each of the service points is organised and staffed properly and there is no delay when foods and beverages need replenishing. The seating arrangements will depend on the:

- size and shape of the food service area
- design of tables and chairs used
- allowance made for gangways and clearing trolleys
- type of establishment.

As a guide, an allowance of 0.5–1 m² (3–10 sq ft) per person is sufficient. This takes account of table space, gangways and access to counters.

Menus

The menu offered may show a wide range of dishes from simple hot and cold snacks and beverages, all individually priced, to a limited table d'hôte menu with the set price of the meal being shown against the main course dishes offered.

The menus should be prominently displayed at the entrance to the cafeteria or foodservice area so that customers may decide as far as possible what meal they will purchase before arriving at the service points. This saves time later and ensures that the customer turnover is as quick as possible.

Layout

A tray stand should be placed at the beginning of the service counter or at the entrance to the service area, so that each customer can collect a tray before proceeding along the counter.

The layout of the dishes on the counter is most important and generally follows the order in which they appear on the menu. This could be as follows: hors-d'oeuvre, fruit juices, fruit cocktails, cold meats and salads, bread rolls, butter, soups, hot fish dishes, hot meat dishes, hot vegetables, hot sweets, cold sweets, ice-cream, assorted sandwiches, cakes and pastries, beverages and cold drinks. Such a layout will make it more convenient for the customer as the food items are in a logical order.

The length of the counter will generally be determined by the size of the menu offered, but should not be too long as this will restrict the speed of service. Cashiers should be sited at the end of the counter or at the exit to the service area so that customers can pay for their meal before they pass on to the seating area. Cutlery stands should be placed after the cashiers, along with accompaniments. They are placed here so that a customer can choose the item they require after making their food and beverage choices. Another advantage of placing the cutlery and accompaniments here is that the customer can return to collect these items, should they initially forget to do so, without interrupting the main queue of customers.

Service considerations

With this form of service, portion control equipment is used to ensure standardisation of the portion size served. Such equipment includes scoops, ladles, bowls, milk dispensers and cold beverage dispensers. Pre-portioned foods such as butter, sugars, jams, cream, cheeses and biscuits may also be used.

The meal may either be completely pre-plated or the main meat/fish dish may be plated with the potatoes, vegetables, sauces and other accompaniments added according to the customer's choice. If the former is carried out, it ensures a quicker turnover of customers through the various service points and requires less service top space. If the latter service is offered, then the turnover of customers is much slower as the necessary accompaniments must be added on request. More service top space is also required for the vegetable and potato dishes, sauces and accompaniments to be kept hot in readiness for service. This means more staff will be required for service and this in turn could increase the cost of the meal.

Checklists

Typical checklists for the preparation of a hot food counter, salad bar, dining area and take-away service may be as follows:

Hot food (counter preparation)

1 Turn on hot counter allowing enough time for it to heat up to the correct temperature.

2 Ensure that an adequate number of plates for the day's service are available:

  ■ on the hot food service counter or in plate lowerators

  ■ in an accessible place near the hot food counter as back-up stock.

3 Transfer regenerated hot food from oven to hot food counter.

   Important:

  ■ Use oven cloths when handling hot food to avoid accidents and spillages.

  ■ Always use a tray when transferring hot food to avoid accidents and spillages.

4 Check hot food menu items for the day and ensure that before service begins there is one dish of each menu item on the hot food counter.

5 Ensure that all hot food is properly covered to prevent any heat loss and deterioration in quality.

6 Have cleaning materials available to wipe any spills.

7 Ensure that for each dish on the hot food counter there is an appropriate service implement. The implements will depend on the dish but are likely to include the following:

  ■ large spoons for dishes such as vegetarian lasagne

  ■ perforated large spoons for dishes such as boiled vegetables (to drain off excess water)

  ■ ladles for dishes such as seafood mornay and aloo brinjal bhajee

  ■ food tongs for dishes such as fried plantain and Caribbean chicken

  ■ fish slices for dishes such as vegetarian pizza.

8 When service implements are not in use, remember to return each one to its designated position on the hot food service counter. This prevents any confusion during a busy service period, which may otherwise arise if service implements have been misplaced.

Salad bar (counter preparation)

1 Turn on the salad bar allowing enough time for it to chill to the correct temperature.

2 Ensure an adequate number of required salad bowls and plates are available for the day's service of salads, pâtés, cold meats, cold quiches and flans, cold pies, cheeses and items such as taramasalata/humous/tsatsiki. Remember that:

  ■ bowls are for salads only

  ■ plates should be used for the other cold items detailed above.

At any one time there should be enough salad bowls and plates on the cold counter for customer service, plus a back-up stock beneath the salad bar.

3 Ensure that the following service utensils are ready and placed in their designated places for service:

- salad tongs for dry salads such as freshly prepared green salad
- large spoons for wet salads such as champignons à la grecque
- fish slices for pâté, cold meats, cold quiches or flans and cold pies
- large spoons for taramasalata/humous/tsatsiki
- tongs for sliced French sticks and granary rolls.

4 Have cleaning materials ready to maintain appearance and cleanliness.

5 Transfer prepared salad items from the kitchen to the chilled salad bar.

6 Cover all food prior to service.

Dining area for cafeteria service (preparation)

1 Arrange tables and chairs, making sure they are all clean.

2 Wipe each table.

3 Ensure cutlery provisions for the day's service are in place, adequate and clean.

4 Ensure trays are clean and there is an adequate supply in the tray stack, ready for the customers' use.

5 Ensure all salt and pepper cruets are filled and that there is one pair on each table. If using sachets of salt and pepper, ensure that there are two bowls, containing salt and pepper respectively, at the counter by the cash till.

6 Fill drinking water jugs and place them in their designated place or make sure the water dispenser is in working order.

7 Ensure the napkin dispenser is filled up.

8 Ensure the clearing up trolley and lined bin are in position.

9 Have cleaning materials ready to wipe clean tables and used trays during service.

Take-away service (preparation)

Below is an example checklist for the setting up of a take-away prior to service.

1 Ensure all equipment is functioning correctly and switched on.

2 Check all temperature-controlled equipment is at the correct temperature.

3 Make sure adequate supplies of packaging, napkins and plates are available.

4 Ensure that the take-away menu and prices are clearly displayed.

5 Ensure that sufficient supplies of ready prepared food items and beverages are to hand to ensure minimum delay on receipt of orders.

6 Prepare foods on a 'batch cooking' basis to ensure the quality of the product at all times.

7 Ensure that the necessary uniforms, such as hats, overalls and aprons, are worn in all preparation areas.

8 For safety reasons, have available such items as oven cloths, tea towels and trays.

9 Have available and on show sales literature to assist in projecting the image of the establishment.

10 Have cleaning materials available for wiping down and in case of spillages.

11 Make sure all serving utensils are available and to hand.

12 Ensure that everything is in its place and therefore easily found as required. This will assist in an efficient work method.

13 Check that waste bins are available with clean plastic sacks in them.

14 Ensure that all working/serving surfaces are clean and have been wiped down prior to service with the appropriate cleaning materials.

Note: In a take-away service, extreme care must be taken at all times with regard to the quality of the product, hygiene, packaging, labelling and temperature control.

5.5 THE ORDER OF SERVICE (TABLE SERVICE)

Service conventions

Within food and beverage service there are traditional ways of doing things that have become established over time. These are known as the 'service conventions' and all have some logic behind them. Mostly this is to do with being effective and efficient in carrying out the service. The use of service conventions also ensures standardisation in the service sequence and the customer process (see page 15), both for staff and for customers. Some examples of general service conventions and the rationale for them is given in Table 5.1 (pages 220 to 224).

Procedure for service of a meal (table service)

Food and beverage service staff should be on duty with sufficient time before the service is due to commence in order to:

■ check the sideboards have all the equipment necessary for service

■ check that tables are laid correctly

■ check the menu and have a full understanding of the dishes, methods of cooking, garnishes, the correct covers, accompaniments and mode of service

■ ascertain the allocation of stations and other duties, if these are not already known

■ enable the headwaiter to check that all staff are dressed correctly in a clean and well presented uniform of the establishment.

The order of service presented below is for a party of customers having a four-course meal with wines. It describes the procedure for service from the moment they enter the establishment until they leave. This is a suggested order of service that will vary according to the establishment, the type of menu and service offered and the time available.

1 The customers enter and are greeted by the reception headwaiter. Check to see if they have a reservation. If not, allocate a table if one is available.

2 The reception headwaiter asks if the customers would like an apéritif in the lounge or reception area, or prefer to have one at the table.

3 The customers are taken to their table. The reception headwaiter indicates who is the host to the station waiter and then hands over to him. The station waiter makes polite conversation with the customers while they are settling at the table and helps to seat them.

4 The station waiter unfolds each customer's napkin and places it over his/her lap

5 The sommelier comes to the table to offer the wine list for the choice of apéritif. He/she takes the order and then serves the choices straight away.

6 Bread is offered, butter is placed on the table and any water is poured

7 Menus are presented to the host and his guests. Allow time for the party to make their choice.

8 Recognition of the host is most important. The station headwaiter provides explanations of any menu items and then takes the order of the party through the host. He/she stands to the left of the host and should be ready to offer suggestions and advice on the menu or translate any items if necessary.

9 The sommelier comes to the table to see if any wine is required with the meal, taking the order through the host. He/she should be able to advise suitable wines to accompany certain dishes.

10 The waiters change the covers where necessary for the service of the first course.

11 If wine is to be served with the first course, the correct glasses should be placed on the table and the wine served before the food.

12 The wine is presented to the host and opened. The host tastes the wine. The customers are served, ladies first, the host last. (The host may designate another customer to taste the wine, in which case they will be served last.) Remember that approximately three glasses of wine can be obtained from a half bottle and six glasses from a bottle. White wine should be served chilled and red wine at room temperature.

13 Lay the plates, serve the first course and offer any accompaniments.

14 Clear the first course.

15 Lay the covers for the fish course.

16 If wine is to be served with the fish course, the correct glasses should be placed on the table and the wine served before the food.

17 The wine is presented to the host, taking account of the notes on wine service as above, and the wine is opened and then tasted by the host. Serve the customers, ladies first, host last.

18 Lay the fish plates and serve the fish course.

19 Clear the fish course.

20 Lay the covers for the main course.

21 If a wine is to accompany the main course, the correct glasses should be placed on the table. Clear dirty wine glasses.

22 The wine is presented to the host, opened and then tasted by the host. Serve the customers, ladies first, host last.

23 Lay the joint plates and serve the main course. The station headwaiter must ensure everything required is on the sideboard before commencing service of this course. This is done to ensure that the service is not disrupted and that food does not go cold. Cold dishes should be served before hot dishes.

24 Underflats should be used under vegetable dishes and sauceboats. All hot food being served should be hot and served onto hot joint plates. The meat should be served first and placed on that part of the plate nearest the customer or at the bottom of the cover, i.e. at 6 o'clock. This should be followed by the potatoes, vegetables, and then any hot sauces and accompaniments.

25 The sommelier should top up the wine glasses when necessary. The station headwaiter should offer more rolls and butter as required and look at the table to ensure everything is satisfactory.

26 Clear the main course to include side plates and side knives, cruets, butter dishes, and accompaniments.

27 Crumb down.

28 Offer the menu for customers to choose a sweet dish. Take the order.

29 Lay the sweet covers and accompaniments.

30 The sommelier clears empty wine glasses and any empty wine bottles.

31 If a wine is to accompany the sweet course, the correct glasses should be placed on the table and the wine served before the food as previously.

32 Serve the sweet course. Cold dishes are served before hot dishes.

33 Clear the sweet course.

34 Take the tea/coffee order.

35 The sommelier presents the liqueur trolley. Serve brandies, ports and liqueurs as required.

36 The tea/coffee service is placed on the table. Serve the tea/coffee. Offer more tea/coffee as appropriate.

37 Place petits fours on the table.

38 Presentation of the bill. The waiter should receive the payment and have the bill receipted by the cashier. It is then returned with any change to the host.

39 The station headwaiter sees the customers out of the restaurant.

40 Clear down the table and re-lay if necessary.

Table 5.1 Some service conventions and the rationale for them

Convention	Rationale
Always work as part of a team	All members of the team should know and be able to do their own job well, to ensure a smooth, well-organised and disciplined operation.
Work hygienically and safely	For the protection of other staff and customers from harm and to avoid accidents.
Pass other members of staff by moving to the right	Having an establishment rule about each member of staff always moving to the right (or left) avoids confusion and accidents.
Hold glasses or cups at the base or by the handle	This is hygienic practice. Service staff should not hold glasses or cups etc., by the rim.
Avoid contact between fingers and mouth or hair	If contact between fingers and mouth or hair etc., is unavoidable, then hands must be washed before continuing with service. Always wash hands after using the toilet.
Cover cuts and sores	Covering cuts and sores with waterproof plasters or dressings is essential health and safety practice.
Use check lists for preparation tasks	Using checklists ensures that all members of staff complete all preparatory tasks in the same way. For example, housekeeping duties, furniture layouts, linen, paper, glassware, tableware, crockery, condiments, accompaniments, table decorations, menus, place cards, table plans, service sideboards/stations and service equipment.
Prepare service areas in sequence	Ensure service areas are laid out and housekeeping duties have been completed before the preparation for service begins. This can save time and unnecessary duplication of effort afterwards.
Consider using white gloves	In some establishments members of staff wear white cotton gloves when carrying out various preparation tasks instead of using service cloths. The gloves help to prevent the soiling of clean service items and avoid putting finger marks on cleaned and polished service equipment. White gloves are also used during service, instead of using service cloths, when serving plated foods that are presented on hot plates.
Use a model lay-up	Lay one initial full place setting (cover) to use as a model for all staff to measure against. A place setting is usually about 60 cm wide.

Table 5.1 continued

Convention	Rationale
Lay table place settings (covers) from the inside out	This makes table laying easier. Place a centre to the cover (a table mat or side plate for instance) then lay tableware in order from the inside of the cover outwards. When laying a number of covers it is more efficient to lay each piece of tableware for all covers in sequence, i.e. all side plates, then all side knives etc.
Use of standard lay-ups	Indicates the type of meals being taken, the sequence of the courses and also what stage customers are at within a meal.
Fully or partly lay the table before a meal begins	Most often tables are fully laid before a meal but this may vary, for instance, if the table is likely to become excessively cluttered or where there is not sufficient equipment to fully pre-lay all the tables.
Place items on the table consistently	Make sure that any crested or patterned crockery or glassware is always placed the same way round on the table and that it is evenly spaced.
Place items low to high	Lower items should be placed near to the customer and taller items behind or to the side of these. This makes items easily accessible by the customer and helps to avoid accidents.
Place items according to the customer's position at the table	Items placed on a table should be within reach of the customer. Handles etc., should be set for the customer's convenience.
Use checklists for reception and service requirements	For example, staff briefings, arrival and reception timings, service requirements at reception, seating of customers, service of courses, accompaniments and beverages, accident procedures, clearing during service and clearing following service. This helps to ensure that all information is complete and that procedures are carried out in the same way by all managers and staff.
Be aware of customers who may have special needs	Look out for, and be prepared to deal with, people with sight, hearing, speech, mobility and language difficulties. Also be able to deal with children.
Use order notation techniques	Use of such techniques helps any server to identify which member of a party is having a particular item of food or beverage.
Avoid leaning over customers	This shows courtesy and respect for physical space. Remember that no matter how clean service staff members are, food and beverage smells do tend to cling to service uniforms.

Table 5.1 continued

Convention	Rationale
Take food, wine and drink orders through hosts	This is common courtesy – agreement needs to be obtained for any items that are to be served. For larger parties, where there may be a choice, orders may be taken individually but it is useful to confirm what has actually been ordered with the host as this may save any disagreements later.
Serve cold food before hot food	When the hot food is served the service is complete and customers can enjoy the meal without waiting for additional items to be served. For the same reason, accompaniments should be automatically offered and served at the same time as the food item.
Serve wine before food	Similar to above. Customers will wish to enjoy the wine with their meal. They will not want to wait for the wine service as their hot food will go cold.
Use underplates (liners)	These are used (cold) for four main purposes: to improve presentation on the table; to make carrying of soup plates, bowls and other bowl-shaped dishes easier; to isolate the hand from hot dishes; to allow cutlery to be carried along with the item.
Use service salvers or service plates (with napkins on them to prevent items slipping)	Service salvers or service plates are used for five main purposes: to improve presentation of items to be served; to make carrying of bowl-shaped serving dishes easier and more secure (also avoids the thumb of the server being inside a service dish); to allow for more than one serving dish to be carried at a time; to isolate the hand from hot dishes; to allow service gear to be carried along with the item(s).
Hold flats, dishes and round trays on the palm of the hand	This is safer, makes for easier carrying and avoids the server's thumb being seen on the edge of flats, dishes and round trays. If the flats or dishes are hot then the service cloth can be underneath, folded and laid flat onto the palm to protect the hand.
Use doilies/dish papers on underplates (liners)	Doilies, dish papers (or linen or paper napkins) on underplates are used to improve presentation, to reduce noise and to prevent the dish from slipping on the underplate. Use doilies for sweet food items and dish papers for savoury food items.
Start service from the right hand side of the host, with the host last	Honoured guests are usually seated on the right of a host. The convention is to serve a table by moving clockwise to each customer, as this ensures that members of the serving staff are walking forwards to serve the next person. This also applies when serving beverages and when clearing during service.

Table 5.1 continued

Convention	Rationale
Serve women first	Often done if it does not slow the service. Particular care needs to be taken so as not to confuse things when the host is a woman. A host of either gender is still the host and should always be served last.
Silver serve food from the left hand side of a customer	Ensures that the service dish is nearer the plate for ease of service and to prevent food being spilt onto the person. Customers can more easily see the food being served and make choices if necessary, and members of the service staff are also able to see and control what they are doing.
Use separate service gear for different food items	This should be standard. It avoids different food items or sauces being transferred from one dish or plate to another and avoids messy presentation of foods on the customers' plates.
Serve foods onto plates consistently	For service of the whole main course onto a joint plate, place the main item at the 6 o'clock position with potatoes served next at the 10 past 2 position and vegetables last at the 10 to 2 position (this also follows the UK Royal National Institute for the Blind (RNIB) recommendations). For main courses with potatoes and vegetables and/or salads served on a separate plate or crescent, the main item is placed in the centre of the main plate with the separate plate or crescent of potatoes and vegetables and/or side salad to the left of the main plate.
Serve plated foods from the right hand side of a customer	Plates can be placed in front of the customer with the right hand and the stack of other plated food is then behind the customer's chair in the left hand. If there is an accident, the plates held in the left hand will go onto the floor rather than over the customer. Plated foods should be placed so that the food items are consistently in the same position for all customers.
For plated service consider the use of Carlton Club Service	Members of staff carry two plates, one in each hand with the hands crossed (which makes for steady carrying). On reaching the table one member of staff stands between each two customers. When a signal is given all members of staff bend forward, uncross their arms and place the two plates simultaneously in front of two customers, one plate to the left and one to the right.
Serve all beverages from the right hand side of a customer	Glasses are placed on the right hand side of a cover and the service of beverages follows from this. For individual drinks and other beverages, the tray is held behind a customer's seat in the server's left hand. Other beverages such as coffee and tea are also served from the right. All beverages should also be cleared from the right.

Table 5.1 continued

Convention	Rationale
Use trays	Use trays to bring foods and beverage items to the service areas and to clear during and following service. Trays can be brought to, or removed from, sideboards or service tables and also to serve plated foods from (or to clear plates onto) with service staff working as a pair.
Separate the serving at table from food/drink collection and sideboard clearing	Ensures that there is always someone in the room to attend to customers and to monitor the overall service, while others are bringing in food and drink orders or clearing items away from the service station. This approach allows for the training of new staff and ensures that customer contact is primarily through experienced staff.
Deal with complaints or other incidents quickly and discretely	Immediate attention, complying with standard establishment procedures, reduces the risk of problems escalating. Discretion reduces the potential for a simple problem to become a much larger one.
Sequence service staff line-ups for serving party bookings	Staff serving the main guests (top table) and the tables furthest from the service door should enter the room first. This is courtesy and operational sense as otherwise service staff could fall over each other. See also Section 9.3 Function organisation, page 364.
Consider the use of wave service at events where guests are seated at a number of separate tables	Wave service (see also Function organisation, page 364) may be used as an alternative to conventional silver service and/or to speed up plated service. The approach involves staff working together as a team serving one or more tables completely before going on to the next table. Adopting this approach means that tables are served throughout the room, over a period, but with the service on each individual table being completed quickly.
Clear from the right hand side of a customer	Plates can be removed from in front of the customer with the right hand and the stack of plates is then behind the customer's chair, in the server's left hand. If there is an accident, the plates held in the left hand will go onto the floor rather than over the customer. The exception to this is for side plates, which are on the left-hand side of the cover. These are more easily cleared from the left, thus avoiding stretching in front of the customer.
Use checklists for tasks required for clearing after service	In the same way as using checklists for preparatory tasks (see above), using checklists for clearing after service ensures that any member of staff completes all clearing tasks in the same way.

Removal of spare covers

In many instances the number of customers in a party is less than the table is laid for. The waiter must then remove the spare cover(s) laid on the table. Judgement must be used as to which cover is removed – this may depend on the actual position of the table. General considerations are that customers, where possible, should face into the room. The cover should be removed using a service plate or a service salver. When this has been done the position of the other covers should be adjusted if necessary and the table accompaniments re-positioned. The spare chair should also be removed. Where there is an uneven number of customers each side of a table, the covers should be positioned so that the full length of the table is used for both sides, by spacing the covers out on each side. This ensures that one customer is not left facing a space on the other side of the table.

Re-laying of tables

It is very often the case in a busy restaurant or dining room that a number of the tables have to be re-laid in order to cope with the inflow of customers. Where this is the case the table should first be completely cleared of all items of equipment and then crumbed down. At this stage, if the tablecloth is a little soiled or grubby a slip cloth should be placed over it or the cloth changed. It can then be re-laid.

5.6 TAKING CUSTOMER FOOD AND BEVERAGE ORDERS

Methods of order taking

Essentially there are four methods of taking food and beverage orders from customers. These are summarised in Table 5.2.

Table 5.2 Main methods of taking food and beverage orders

Method	Description
Triplicate	Order is taken; top copy goes to the supply point; second copy is sent to the cashier for billing; third copy is retained by the server as a means of reference during service.
Duplicate	Order is taken; top copy goes to the supply point; second copy is retained for service and billing purposes.
Service with order	Order is taken; customer is served and payment received according to that order, for example, bar service or take-away methods.
Pre-ordered	a) Individually, for example, room service breakfast (see Section 7.2, page 280) b) Hospital tray system (see Section 7.4, page 289) c) Functions (see Chapter 9, page 358)

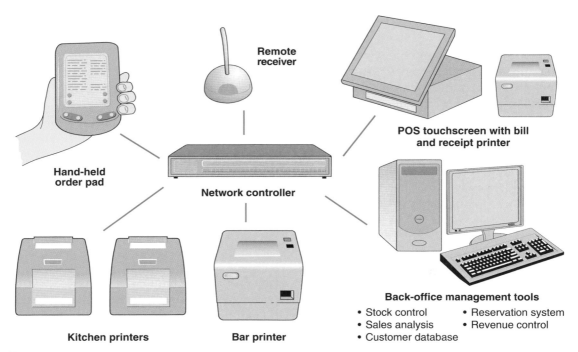

Fig 5.25. Radio-controlled electronic system for order taking and communication with food production and beverage dispense areas

All order taking methods are based upon these four basic concepts. Even the most sophisticated electronic system is based upon either the triplicate or duplicate method. Checks can be written on check pads or keyed in on handheld terminals. The order is then communicated by hand or electronically to visual display units (VDUs) or printout terminals in the food production or beverage provision areas. The main systems used are described in Section 10.2 Food and beverage revenue control, page 401.

Triplicate checking method

This is an order taking method used in the majority of medium and large first class establishments. As the name implies, the food check consists of three copies. To ensure efficient control the server must fill in the following information in the four corners of the check:

- table number
- number of covers
- date
- signature of server taking the order.

On taking the food order it is written from top to bottom of the food check. Where only a table d'hôte menu is in operation the customers would initially only order their first and main courses. The set price charged for this menu would be entered on the food check and circled.

A second new food check is written out for the sweet course, this being taken after the main course is finished. A third new check will be completed if any beverage such as coffee is required.

The operation for an à la carte menu is similar, although customers may order course by course according to their requirements.

All checks should be legible. Abbreviations may be used when taking the order as long as they are understood by everyone and not misinterpreted by the kitchen as the wrong order may be prepared.

When taking orders a note should be taken of who is having what order. This ensures that specific orders are identified and that they are served to the correct customer. A system for ensuring that the right customer receives the correct food is to identify on the order which customer is having which dish. A check pad design that might be used for this is shown in Figure 5.26. An electronic handheld order taking system is show in Figure 5.27

The food check

- The top copy of the food order goes to the kitchen and is handed to the aboyeur at the hotplate.

- The duplicate goes to the cashier who makes out the customer's bill.

- The flimsy, or third copy, is retained by the waiter at his/her sideboard as a means of reference.

- Any checks or bills that have to be cancelled should have the signature of either the headwaiter or supervisor on them, as should checks and bills which have alterations made on them.

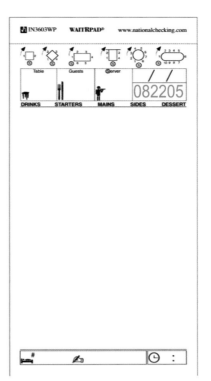

Fig 5.26. Check pad design enabling the waiter to identify specific orders (Image courtesy of National Checking Co)

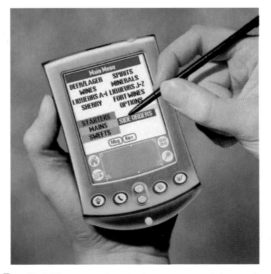

Fig 5.27. Handheld electronic pad for order taking (image courtesy of Uniwell Systems (UK) Ltd/PalmTEQ Ltd UK)

Special checks

In certain instances it is necessary to write out special checks. For example:

- Where it is necessary to write out more than one food check for a meal, such as where a sweet check is written out after the first and main course has been served. At the head of this check should be written the word 'Suivant' which means 'follow on' and shows that one check has already been written out for that particular table (see Figure 5.28)

- When an extra portion of food is required because insufficient has been sent from the kitchen, a special check must be written out headed 'Supplement' (see Figure 5.29). This means the food is a supplement to what has already been previously sent and should be signed by the headwaiter or supervisor. Normally there is no charge (n/c), but this depends on the policy of the establishment concerned.

- Where a wrong dish has been ordered and has to be sent back to the kitchen and replaced, a special check must again be made out (see Figure 5.30). Two main headings are used on this special check, 'Retour' (or 'return') and the name of the dish going back to the kitchen, and 'En place' (or 'in place') and the name of the new dish to be served.

- It occasionally happens that the waiter may have an accident in the room and perhaps some vegetables are dropped. These must be replaced without any extra charge to the customer. Here a check must be completed headed 'Accident' (see Figure 5.31). It will show the number of portions of vegetables required and should be signed by the headwaiter or supervisor in charge. No charge (n/c) is stated on the check to ensure that no charge is made to the customer.

Fig 5.28. Food check: Suivant / Follow on

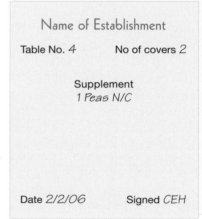

Fig 5.29. Food check: Supplement

Fig 5.30. Food check: Return / in place

Duplicate checking method

This is a control system that is more likely to be found in the smaller hotel, popular price restaurant and cafés and department store catering. It is generally used where a table d'hôte menu is in operation and sometimes a very limited à la carte menu.

As the name implies, there are two copies of each of these food checks, each set being serial numbered. A check pad, or bill pad as it is sometimes termed, usually contains a set of 50 or 100 food checks. The top copy of the food check is usually carbon-backed but, if not, a sheet of carbon must be placed between the top and duplicate copy every time a fresh order is taken.

For control purposes the top copy may have printed on it a server's number or letter. This should be the number or letter given to a waiter on joining the staff. The control and accounts department should be informed of the person to whom the number applies, and he retains it throughout his employment. On each set of food checks there should also be printed a serial number.

Sometimes the top copy of the set of food and drink checks is made up of a number of perforated slips, usually 4–5 in number. There is a section at the bottom of the food and drink check for the table number to be entered. The top copy sometimes has a cash column for entering the price of a meal or the dishes ordered but, if this is not the case, the waiter must enter them independently on the duplicate copy against the particular dish concerned.

When writing out a customer's order a different perforated slip should be used for each course. The server must remember to write out the number of covers and the price of the meal or dish concerned on each slip. Before sending each slip to the hotplate see that the details are entered correctly on the duplicate copy together with the price. Since the duplicate copy acts as the customer's bill, the waiter must ensure that everything served is charged and paid for.

As the service of a meal commences, the waiter tears off from the top copy of the food and drink check the perforated slip showing the first course ordered. This is taken to the hotplate

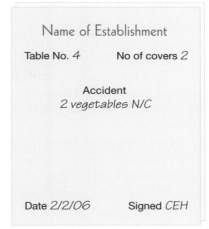

Name of Establishment

Table No. *4*   No of covers *2*

Accident
2 vegetables N/C

Date *2/2/06*   Signed *CEH*

Fig 5.31. Food check: Accident

Fig 5.32. Example of a duplicated order pad with perforated sections (courtesy of Wimpy International)

and the required dish is put up. As soon as this happens the aboyeur will tear off the server's number on the end of the slip and place it with the dish concerned. This then shows which waiter the dish is for. If there is no server number at the end of the perforated slip, then the perforated slip itself is left with the order until collected by the appropriate waiter. The aboyeur will then retain the slip showing the course just served. As soon as the first course is served, and allowing time for this course to be consumed, the second perforated slip is taken to the hotplate by the waiter. This dish will then be collected as required. This same procedure is carried on throughout the meal.

It may happen that there are insufficient perforated slips on the top copy of the food and drink check for a particular customer's requirements. Very often the waiter does their own drink service and thus takes the drink order and enters it on a separate perforated slip. When there are insufficient perforated slips, a supplementary check is used.

Other checking methods

As has already been mentioned, there are many variations to the basic manual checking control system. Three of these are briefly described below in order to give some idea of the possible variations available.

Menu order and customer bill

This shows the menu order and customer's bill combined on one sheet and would be allocated to each party of customers. When the order is taken each customer's requirements would be written down in the column next to the price column. Thus, if a party of two customers requested two cream soups, one mushroom omelette and chips and one fried cod and chips, it would be noted down as shown in Figure 5.33.

Soup		
Cream soup	2.60	2
Hot dishes		
Omelette served with chips and salad		
Plain		
Cheese		
Ham		
Mushroom	4.50	1
Tomato		
Fried cod and chips	4.75	1

Fig 5.33. Quick service menu and customer bill

Please note down your table number and choice of meals on this slip. Take it with you and place your order and pay at the food till	TABLE NUMBER	Main meals

Starters

Children's meals | Side orders | Drinks

Desserts, coffees and teas may be ordered at the food till at the end of your meal

Fig 5.34. Example of customer self-complete order sheet

Single order sheet

A further simple form of checking is used in cafés, quick turnover restaurants and department stores. It is a simple form of ordering which may be used, or adapted for use, in various forms of operation.

The menu is normally very limited. The server takes the order and marks down the customer's requirements, calls for the order verbally over the hotplate and, when the customer requests the bill, prices the order sheet and hands it to her. The customer then hands it to the cashier on leaving and pays the required amount. There is only one copy of this order and bill combined, and the cashier retains this for control purposes, after the customer has made the necessary payment.

Customer self-complete order

A modern trend is to ask customers to take their own food and drink order. This method is often found in bar operations and it allows staff to concentrate on the service of food (plate service) and beverages, and to accept payments. The customer order form may take the format as shown in Figure 5.34.

The order for the food and drink requirements, once complete, is taken by the customer to the food till and sent electronically by a member of staff to the kitchen where a printed copy is processed for the kitchen staff to produce the dishes required.

After submitting the initial food and beverage order at the food till, an account will be opened, under the table number, by processing the customer's credit card. This is so any additional items such as sweets, coffee or alcoholic beverages may be added to the bill. The customer may then pay the total bill at the conclusion of their meal. These additional items required may be ordered at the food till or at the customer's table.

Taking orders for dispense bar beverage service

An efficient system must operate here to ensure that:

■ the correct drinks are served at the right table

■ the service rendered is charged to the correct bill

- a record is kept of all drinks issued from the dispense bar
- management is able to assess sales over a financial period and make comparisons.

The usual system of control is a duplicate check pad. The colour of the check pad may be pink or white, but is generally pink or some other colour to distinguish it from a food check. This acts as an aid to the cashier and the control and accounts department in differentiating quickly between food (white) and drink (pink) checks (see Figure 5.35).

When the wine order is taken it is written in duplicate. The wine service staff must remember to fill in the four items of information required, one in each corner of the check. These are as follows:

- table number or room number
- number of covers
- date
- signature.

top copy to dispense bar

Name of Establishment

Table No. 10	Covers 3

2 sweet sherries
1 pale ale
1/2 x 16
1 x 40

Date 2/2/06	Signed CEH

Fig 5.35. Wine check

Abbreviations are allowed when writing the order as long as they are understood by the dispense bar staff and the cashier. When wines are ordered only the bin number, together with the number of bottles required, should be written down. The bin number is an aid to the dispense bar staff and cellar staff in finding, without delay, the wine required by a customer. Each wine in the wine list will have a bin number printed against it.

On taking the order the wine staff should hand both copies to the dispense bar staff, who retain the top copy, put up the order and leave the duplicate copy with the order. This enables the wine staff to see which is their order when they come to collect their wines and drinks. After serving the wines and drinks the duplicate copy is handed to the cashier.

Taking children's orders

Staff should pay special attention when taking orders for children. They need to be aware of the following points:

- The availability and choice of children's meals.
- What the children's meals consist of.
- Portion size, for example, the number of sausages.
- The cost per head.
- The need to make a special note of any specific requests, such as no baked beans.
- The need to serve young/small children first as they often become agitated when everyone else has been served and their meal is still to come.

- The importance of not overfilling cups, bowls or glasses.
- Provide children with the establishment 'give aways' in order to keep them occupied, for example, a place mat to be coloured in. This can also encourage sales.
- Always ensure children's plates are warm rather than hot to avoid mishaps.

Customers with special needs

Customers with special needs may require particular attention. These are customers who may be hard of hearing, blind or partially sighted (see page 187). In these instances consider the following:

- Where applicable, when taking the order, face the customer so he sees you full face.
- Speak normally but distinctly.
- Keep descriptions to a minimum.
- Indicate precisely any modifiers that are available with a specific dish, for example, a choice of dips being available with a starter, or the different degrees of cooking available for a grilled steak.
- Read back the order given for confirmation.

Other special needs may relate to vegetarians, those with particular religious or cultural restrictions and those with special dietary needs (see page 78).

5.7 SERVICE OF FOOD

In table and assisted service the general convention is to serve all food items from the left and to clear from the right. All beverages (both alcoholic and non-alcoholic) are served from the right. With the increase in plated service, it has become common to serve plated foods from the right. This is done for the same reason that dirties are cleared from the right: the left hand (normally) is used to stack dirties while the right clears the plates. This ensures that the stack of dirties is behind the customer. If a dirty plate falls, it will fall on the floor and not on the customer. With plated service, the additional plates of food are similarly held behind the seated customer.

It is also a convention to always serve cold food before hot food (irrespective of the host). This ensures that, once the hot food is served, the customer may eat immediately without having to wait while the cold food is collected and served. This allows all customers to receive their food at the correct serving/eating temperature.

For a more comprehensive listing of service conventions see Table 5.1, pages 220 to 224.

Service of soup

Soup may be served pre-plated, from a tureen at the sideboard, at a guéridon or from an individual tureen as shown in Figure 5.36. The waiter ensures that the soup is poured away from the customer. The underflat acts as a drip plate to prevent any spillage from going on the tablecloth.

Fig 5.36. Silver service of soup from an individual tureen

Consommé is traditionally served in a consommé cup on a consommé saucer with a fishplate underneath. It is traditional for this type of soup to be eaten with a sweet spoon. This is because consommé was originally taken before going home, after a function, as a warming beverage. It was originally drunk from this large cup. The garnish was eaten with the sweet spoon. The tradition of the sweet spoon has continued, but a soup spoon would also be acceptable.

Service from flats (meat/fish)

- The correct cover is laid prior to the food item ordered being served.
- The service cloth is folded neatly as a protection against heat from the serving dish.
- The fold of the cloth should be on the tips of the fingers.
- The dish is presented to the customer so he/she may see the complete dish as it has come from the kitchen. This is to show off the chef's artistry in presentation.
- The serving dish should be held a little above the hot joint plate with the front edge slightly overlapping the rim of the hot joint plate.
- The portion of food is placed in the 6 o'clock position (i.e. nearest to the customer) on the hot joint plate.
- When moving to serve the second portion, the flat should be rotated on the service cloth so the next meat portion to be served will be nearest the plate.
- Note that the portion of food served, on the plate nearest to the customer, allows ample room on the plate to serve and present the potatoes and vegetables attractively.
- If vegetables are being served onto separate plates, then the main food item is placed in the middle of the plate.

Service of potatoes and vegetables

- The general rule is for potatoes to be served before vegetables.

- When serving either potatoes or vegetables, the vegetable dish itself should always be placed on an underflat with a napkin on it. This is for presentation purposes.

- The purpose of the napkin is to prevent the vegetable dish slipping about on the underflat while the service is being carried out.

Fig 5.37. Silver service of potatoes and vegetables

- A separate service spoon and fork should be used for each different type of potato and vegetable dish to be served.

- Note again the use of the service cloth as protection against heat and to allow the easier rotation of the vegetable dish on its underflat.

- With the serving dish in its correct position the potato dish nearest the hot joint plate should be served.

- The potato dish served is placed on the hot joint plate on the far side, allowing the server to work towards herself as he/she serves the remaining food items ordered and making it easier to present the food attractively.

- Creamed potato is served by placing the fork into the spoon and then taking a scoop of potato from the dish. This is then carried to the plate and the fork moved slightly. The potato should then fall off onto the plate.

Note: Figure 5.37 shows the use of an underflat under the potato and vegetable dishes. It also indicates:

- how a variety of potatoes and vegetables can be served at one time by using a large underflat

- the use of a service cloth for protection from heat and to prevent the underflat from slipping

- the correct handling of the service spoon and fork

- the separate service spoon and fork for each variety of potato and vegetable served

- service from the left-hand side of the customer.

Service of accompanying sauces

- The sauce should be presented in a sauceboat on an underplate, with a sauce ladle.
- A ladleful of sauce should be lifted clear of the sauceboat.
- The underside of the sauce ladle should then be run over the edge of the sauceboat to avoid any drips falling on the tablecloth or over the edge of the hot joint plate.
- The sauce should be napped over the portion of meat already served or at the side of the meat depending on the customer's preference.

Service away from the table

Service of food away from the table includes service from trolleys, at buffets and counters. Tray service is considered in Chapter 7. Guéridon service is discussed in Section 8.2, page 303.

The main standard to be achieved in these forms of food service is that the server's hands should not touch the food. The food trolley should be between the staff and customer as if it were in a shop. Note that the food is not normally served by the spoon and fork technique. Instead, service is with one implement in one hand and another in the other hand with the service either on to plates on the buffet or on to a plate that the customer is holding.

Sweet and cheese trolleys

These should be attractively presented from the customer's point of view and well laid out from behind for the server. Plates for dirty service equipment should therefore be to the back of the trolley. Staff should explain food items to customers, either from behind the trolley, to the side of the trolley or standing by the table, but not in front of the trolley.

When the customer makes a selection, a plate should be positioned near the item to be served. Then, with a service spoon in one hand and a service fork in the other (or a gâteau slice etc.) food should be portioned and transferred neatly to the plate. The plate should then be placed in front of the customer from the right. For larger parties, two people will be required – one to take the orders and place the plate with food in front of the customer, the other to stand at the trolley and portion and plate the foods.

For temperature control purposes many sweet trolleys now come with ice pack compartments, which should be replenished before each service. For notes on the service of cheese and sweets see pages 94 and 100 respectively.

Fig 5.38. Sweet/cheese trolley (courtesy of Euroservice UK)

Service of food at buffets and counters

If food has not already been pre-plated, it should be served in a similar way to the procedures described for guéridon or trolley service above. Food should not be sloshed on to plates but served with a spoon (or some other service implement such as a chip shovel) in one hand and a fork in the other, and should be placed neatly on to the customer's plate. Additional items should be suitably arranged on to the plate and not piled on to other items already on the plate.

Checklists

Typical checklists for staff to adhere to in performance of service standards related to a hot buffet or counter, salad bar and dining areas are given below.

Hot food

■ Do not leave the hot food service counter unattended once service starts, as this will cause congestion in the flow of service.

■ Arrange for someone to take your place if you have to leave the service area for any reason.

■ Wipe up any spillages immediately. Spillages left on a hot counter for too long will harden and create problems later with cleaning.

■ When serving, it is important to adhere to portion control specifications.

■ When a dish of hot food is only one-third full inform the kitchen that more will be needed. Do not allow food items to run out during service. If the end of service time is approaching, check with the supervisor before requesting more.

■ Ensure plates are kept well stocked. If running low on plates on the service counter, replenish immediately from back-up stock.

Salad bar

■ Keep a constant eye on food levels in the salad bar.

■ Never re-fill bowls or replenish plates at the counter. Take a bowl or plate to the kitchen and fill or replenish it there.

■ Replace service spoons, slices etc., in their respective bowls, dishes and plates, if misplaced by customers.

■ Wipe up any spillages immediately.

■ Keep the salad bar tidy, well-arranged and well-presented at all times.

■ Keep a constant eye on the supply of bowls and plates for the salad counter service.

■ Remember: do not wait for a supply of salad bowls and plates to run out before replenishing from the back-up supply (beneath the cold counter). During a busy service period this will inevitably hinder the flow of service.

Dining areas

- Ensure the clearing station is ready and in place and ensure the following are available:
  - lined bin
  - bin liners
  - clearing trolley
  - wiping cloth
  - recommended cleaning materials.
- Keep a constant eye on tables and make sure they are clean and tidy at all times. Change table covers regularly, as and when required. An untidy and messy table is not pleasant for the customer.
- The dining area service should be self-clearing, i.e. customers are requested to return their trays containing used plates and cutlery to the clearing station. Failing this, promptly clear tables of any trays.
- At the clearing station:
  - empty the tray of used plates and cutlery etc., and stack ready for the dishwasher
  - empty disposable contents of a tray into a lined standing bin
  - wipe the tray clean with recommended cleaning materials.
- Return the stack of ready-cleaned trays to the tray stack, lining each tray with a paper liner (if used) before putting into place.
- Ensure there is always enough water in the drinking water jugs.
- Ensure there are enough napkins in the napkin dispenser.
- Check cutlery containers are adequately stocked.

Note: During service always ensure that at any one time there is an adequate supply of trays in the tray rack, ready for the customers' use.

5.8 SERVICE OF ALCOHOLIC BEVERAGES AND CIGARS

The cocktail/dispense bar may be said to be the shop window of an establishment as it is often the meeting point of customers prior to business and social events. The first impressions given here are therefore of prime importance in gaining further sales. The presentation of the bar personnel, together with a well-stocked, organised and efficiently run bar, are essential to give a good service to the customer. The bar personnel must have good technical skills, product knowledge, social skills and be able to work as part of a team, in order to meet the needs of the customers.

Service of aperitifs

The term apéritif covers a wide range of drinks that may be served before a meal. Apéritifs may be offered at the table once the customers have been seated, or may be offered in the lounge/reception area.

An indication of the glassware for a variety of beverages is given in Section 2.14 Glassware, page 62. The service of examples of popular bar drinks is shown in Table 5.3.

Table 5.3 Examples of popular drinks and their service

Drink	Service
Baileys	Either chilled or with crushed ice as frappé
Brandy	No additions to good brandies. Popular mixers for lesser brandies are lemonade or peppermint, together with ice
Campari	Soda water or lemonade together with ice and slice of orange
Dark rum	Lemonade or cola with ice and slice of lemon/lime or with blackcurrant and no ice
Sherries	Served chilled
Fruit juices	Served chilled or serve with lemonade, tonic water or sparkling mineral water. Also served with ice and a slice of lemon, orange or other fruit
Gin	Angostura Bitters and ice (Pink Gin) or with tonic water or bitter lemon together with ice and slice of lemon/lime
Liqueurs	May be served naturally or on crushed ice as frappé
Mineral water	Properly served chilled only, but can be with ice and lemon/lime at the request of the customer. Sometimes served with cordials or fruit juices
Aerated waters (e.g. cola)	Served chilled or with ice and slice of lemon/lime or orange. Sometimes served with cordials
Pernod	Water and with ice offered and sometimes with cordials or lemonade
Pimm's	Lemonade, ice and slice of lemon, cucumber, apple, orange and a sprig of mint. Sometimes also topped up with ginger ale, soda or tonic water
Port (white)	Serve chilled, sometimes with ice and slice of lemon/lime
Port (ruby)	Good port served naturally. Lesser port either by itself or with lemonade and ice
Sambucca	Coffee bean and set alight (For safety reasons this should be done at the table and the flame extinguished as soon as the oil from the bean is released into the drink)
Vermouths	With ice and slice of lemon/lime or sometimes with lemonade. Dry vermouths may alternatively be served with an olive; sweeter vermouths with a cocktail cherry
Vodka	Tonic water or lemonade, ice and slice of lemon/lime; orange cordial, ice and slice of orange; lime cordial, ice and slice of lemon/lime; tomato juice, ice, slice of lemon and Worcestershire sauce, sometimes with salt offered and also celery sticks

Table 5.3 continued

Drink	Service
Whisk(e)y	Natural or with water (often still mineral water), with ice offered or with dry ginger or Canada Dry or soda water and with ice offered
Wine	By the glass and sometimes, for white wine, with soda water or sparkling mineral water or lemonade, as spritzer
White rum	Natural with ice or with cola, ice and slice of lemon/lime

Many establishments now serve bar drinks with a glass coaster (often of paper) at the point of sale.

Service of cocktails

Cocktails should always be served well chilled in an appropriately sized glass with the correct garnish, straw and umbrella, according to the policy of the establishment. Many cocktails are served in the traditional V-shaped cocktail glass but, if the cocktail is a long drink, then a larger glass such as a Slim Jim will be better suited. The key consideration here should be the total presentation of the cocktail as seen visually by the customer. For further information on cocktails see Section 4.6, page 132 and Annex C, pages 470 to 482.

Service of wines

The sommelier or wine waiter should be able to advise and suggest wines to the host as required. This means that the wine waiter must have a good knowledge of the wines contained within the wine list and be able to identify examples of wines that will pair well with the menu dishes. Immediately the food order has been taken the wine list should again be presented to the host so that they may order wine for their party to accompany the meal they have ordered.

There are six key aspects to be taken into account when serving wines.

1 The wine waiter must be able to describe the wines and their characteristics honestly – bluffing should be avoided.

2 Always serve the wine before the food. Avoid waiting too long to serve the food after the wine has been served.

3 Serve wines properly temperatured – it is better to tell the customer that the wine is not at the right temperature for service, rather than resorting to quick heating or cooling methods as these can damage the wine.

4 Treat wine with respect and demonstrate a high level of technical skill, supported by the use of high quality service equipment. As the customer is paying for the wine and the service, they therefore have the right to expect their chosen wine to be treated with care.

5   Do not overfill glasses. Fill glasses to the right level, usually to the widest part of the bowl or to two-thirds full, whichever is the lesser. Sparkling wine served in a flûte is usually filled to about two-thirds to three-quarters of the glass. Doing so helps the wine to be better appreciated and looks better too.

6   Avoid unnecessary topping up – it does not sell more wine and it often irritates customers. Another reason for being cautious about topping up wine glasses is that the customer may be driving. If wine is constantly topped up the customer may not notice how much they are consuming. In general, it is preferable to ask the customer about topping up their wine.

Serving temperatures for wines

- *Red wines*: 15.5–18°C (60–65°F). Some young red wines may also be drunk cool at about 12.5–15.5°C (55–60°F).
- *White wines*: 10–12.5°C (50–55°F).
- Dessert wines, Champagne and other sparkling white wines: 4.5–10°C (40–50°F).

Wine glasses

Wines may be served in the types of glasses indicated below:

- Champagne and other sparkling wines: flûte or tulip-shaped glass.
- *German and Alsace wines*: traditionally a long-stemmed German wine glass but nowadays a medium-sized wine glass.
- *White wines*: medium-size wine glass.
- *Rosé wines*: flûte or medium-sized wine glass.
- *Red wines*: large wine glass

For examples of glassware see Section 2.14 Glassware, page 63.

Closures for wine bottles

There are now four main types of closures for wine bottles.

Natural corks	These closures are made from whole pieces of cork. Each is individual and unique and there can be quality variation. However, natural cork has a high degree of elasticity and compressibility and it can mould itself around tiny imperfections in the bottle neck. It is well proven for the long-term storage of wines. Natural cork is susceptible to trichloroanisole (TCA) (see Section 4.8, p.41) and if the cork dries out or is loose fitting the bottle can leak, and the wine can become oxidised through being exposed to the air.
Technical (or composite) corks	These are agglomerate corks made from small pieces of natural cork moulded into a cork shape and held with food-grade glue. The better quality closures are agglomerate with solid cork discs at either end. The solid end is the only part that comes into contact with the wine. However, as with natural cork, it is susceptible to TCA. The opening process is similar to natural corks.

Synthetics (plastics)	These are synthetic closures that may be used for wines that are to be drunk within about 18 months of bottling. After this time synthetic closures may lose their elasticity, resulting in the risk of the seal being broken and the wine becoming oxidised through exposure to the air. Although not susceptible to TCA, there are some risks of the closure taking up fruit flavours from the wine or adding 'plastic' flavours to the wine. The opening process is similar to traditional corks, although this type of closure can be more difficult to extract than cork and re-inserting the closure into the neck of the bottle is also difficult.
Screw caps	Various makes of screw cap and linings are used which are easy to open and reseal. The closure provides a tight seal for the bottle and TCA is unlikely. However, these closures are relatively new and the longer-term effects on wines for laying down (ageing) are yet to be determined. The opening procedure is to hold the whole length of the seal in the opening hand and to hold the base of the bottle in the other hand. The closure is held firmly in the opening hand with more pressure, from the thumb and first finger, around the cap itself. The bottle is then sharply twisted using the hand holding the base. There will be a click and then the upper part of the screw top can be removed.

A newer, fifth system is also being developed which is being referred to as 'glass on glass'. Essentially, this is a glass stopper that has the appearance of a decorative stopper, but it is guaranteed to hold firmly in the bottle neck and can also be used to reseal the bottle. An aluminium cap (similar to a standard bottle foil/cap) over the end of the bottle secures the glass stopper in the bottle and ensures the seal. In addition to the glass version, there will also be a more economical plexiglass version. The stopper is intended to:

■ provide the highest level of protection for the wine

■ ensure taste neutrality

■ look good

■ be recyclable.

The opening procedure is to first remove the end of the cap. Then hold the top of the bottle in the opening hand and the bottle by the base in the other hand. The edge of the closure is held firmly, by the thumb and first finger, around the closure itself. The bottle is then twisted using the hand holding the base. The stopper is then removed by lifting it slightly as the bottle rotates.

Sediment in wine

Tartrates of calcium and sodium are the two sources of sediment in both red and white wines. They are formed by a combination of tartaric acid (which occurs naturally in wine) and calcium or sodium. It is only the colours of red and white wine that cause the sediment to appear as different colours. Sugar is a natural ingredient of wine and will not form crystals within the wine.

On serving wine bits of cork may be found floating in the glass. This is a result of the opening process, where pieces of the cork have been broken off. This is not 'corked' wine, as it is often mistakenly termed. For an explanation of corked wine, see Section 4.8, page 141. The bits of cork should be removed with a teaspoon and the wine enjoyed. (If the cork breaks into fine pieces, the wine may require filtering through fine muslin.)

Pouring wine

When pouring wine, the neck of the bottle should be over the glass but not resting on the rim in case of an accident. Care should be taken to avoid splashing the wine and when pouring is complete, the bottle should be twisted and raised as it is taken away. This prevents drops of wine falling on the tablecloth or on a customer's clothes. Any drops on the rim of the bottle should be wiped away with a clean service cloth or napkin.

Service of white wines

1 Obtain the wine from the storage area. Check that the order is correct and that the wine is clear and properly temperatured.

2 Take to the table in an ice bucket and place the ice bucket in a stand.

3 Present the bottle to the host with the label showing – this allows him or her to check that the correct wine is to be served (Figure 5.39a).

4 Ensure the correct glasses are placed on the table for the wine to be served.

5 Make sure a clean napkin is tied to the handle of the ice bucket – this is used to wipe away condensation and water from the outside of the bottle before serving from it.

6 Using a wine knife, cut the foil all the way round, below or above the bottle rim at the top of the bottle (some bottles have small caps rather than foils). The top of the foil only is then removed and the top of the cork is wiped with the napkin (Figure 5.39b).

7 Remove the cork using a wine knife (Figure 5.39c). Smell the cork in case the wine is 'corked'.

8 Place the cork in the ice bucket. If the wine is a high quality vintage wine then the cork would generally be placed on a side plate at the head of the host's cover. This cork should have the name and year of the wine printed on it.

9 Wipe the inside of the neck of the bottle with the napkin.

10 Wipe the bottle dry.

11 Hold the bottle for pouring so that the label may be seen. Use the waiter's cloth in the other hand, folded, to catch any drips from the neck of the bottle (Figure 5.39d).

12 Give a taste of the wine to the host, pouring from the right hand side. He or she should acknowledge that the wine is suitable, i.e that it has the correct taste, bouquet and temperature.

13 Serve ladies first, then gentlemen and the host last, always commencing from the host's right. However, nowadays service often follows from one customer to the next, anti-clockwise.

14 Fill each glass two-thirds full or to the widest part of the bowl – whichever is the lower. This leaves room for an appreciation of the bouquet.

15 Replace the remaining wine in the wine bucket and refill the glasses when necessary.

a presenting the bottle

b removing the foil

c removing the cork

d pouring the wine

Fig 5.39. Service of wine

16 If a fresh bottle is required, then fresh glasses should be placed upon the table, and the host asked to taste the new wine before it is served.

17 On finishing pouring a glass of wine, twist the neck of the bottle and raise it at the same time to prevents drops from falling on the tablecloth

Service of red wine

The basic procedure for the opening and serving of red wines is the same as for white wines above. If the red wine to be opened is young the bottle may stand on an underplate or coaster on the table and be opened from this position. Although there is no technical reason why red wine should be served with the bottle in a wine basket or wine cradle, these are used in a number of establishments for display/presentation purposes.

The cork should be removed from the bottle of red wine as early as possible so that the wine may attain room temperature naturally. If the wine is of age and/or is likely to have a heavy sediment, then the wine should be decanted. It should be placed in a wine basket and first presented to the customer. Placing the bottle in a wine basket helps to keep the bottle as horizontal as possible, in order to prevent the sediment from being shaken up. The wine should then be decanted. Alternatively, if the wine is ordered in advance it can be left standing for a few days before opening (Figure 5.40a).

There is also a trend nowadays to decant younger red wines, simply because exposure to air improves the bouquet and softens and mellows the wine. Decanting also enhances the appearance of the wine, especially when presented in a fine wine decanter. However, the permission of the host should always be sought before decanting a wine in the restaurant.

Decanting is the movement of wine from its original container to a fresh glass receptacle, leaving the sediment behind.

1 Extract the cork carefully. The cork may disintegrate because of long contact with alcohol, so be careful.

2 Place a single point light behind the shoulder of the bottle, a candle if you are decanting in front of customers, but a torch, light bulb or any light source will do (Figure 5.40b).

3 Carefully pour the wine into an absolutely clean decanter. The light will reveal the first sign of sediment entering the neck of the bottle (Figure 5.40c).

4 As soon as sediment is seen, stop pouring into the decanter but continue pouring into a glass (Figure 5.40d). The latter wine, when it settles, can be used as a taster or for sauces in the kitchen.

5 The wine should always be checked to make sure that it is clear before being presented at the table for service.

6 If the wine is not clear after decanting then it should be decanted again into a fresh decanter, but this time using a wine funnel which has a piece of fine muslin in the mouth of the funnel. If the wine is still not clear it should not be served and a new bottle of the wine selected. (It is more common now for a wine funnel to be used as part of the decanting process generally, as shown in Figure 5.40.)

Very old red wine can break up with too much exposure to air. Such wines can be left to stand for a few days to allow the sediment to settle in the bottom. The bottle is then opened before the meal is served and the wine is poured very carefully straight into the glass, with the bottle

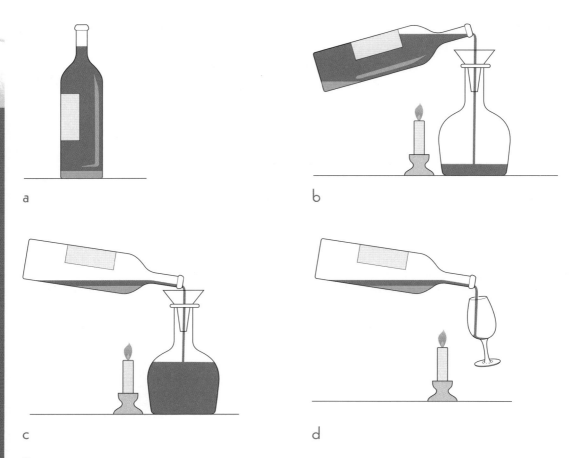

a   b   c   d

Fig 5.40. Decanting wine

held in the pouring position as each glass is approached. This prevents the wine slopping back to disturb the sediment. Sufficient glasses should be available to finish the bottle, thereby ensuring that the wine does not re-mingle with its sediment during the pouring process.

Service of Champagne and sparkling wine

The same method is used for opening all sparkling wines. The wine should be served well chilled in order to obtain the full effect of the secondary fermentation in the bottle, namely, effervescence and bouquet. The pressure in a Champagne bottle, due to its maturing and secondary fermentation, will be about 5 kg per cm^2 (about 70 lb per sq in). Great care must therefore be taken not to shake the bottle otherwise the pressure will build up and could cause an accident.

1   After presenting the bottle to the host the wine is ready for opening.
2   The neck of the bottle should be kept pointed towards a safe area in the restaurant during the opening process, in order to avoid any accidents to customers should the cork be released suddenly.

3   The thumb should be held over the cork with the remainder of the hand holding the neck of the bottle.

4   The foil around the top of the cork is separated from the foil around the neck of the bottle by pulling on the tab on the foil, or by using a wine knife to cut it. The foil is not removed.

5   The wine cage is carefully loosened, but not removed.

6   Then, holding the cork and the cage in one hand, the bottom of the bottle should be twisted with the other hand to slowly release the cork.

Sparkling wine should be served in flûtes or tulip-shaped glasses, from the right hand side of each customer. It is also worth considering lifting the glass from the table so as to pour the wine more easily and quickly, and to reduce the frothing of the wine.

Service of wine by the glass

Many establishments offer a range of wines for sale by the glass. Wines are mostly offered in 125 ml or 175 ml measures. With the exception of sparkling wines, it is often better to serve the wine in a glass larger than the measure. This allows the aroma to develop in the glass and the wine to be appreciated better.

Once a bottle is opened the wine can deteriorate quite quickly as it reacts with the air and oxidises. There are various methods of keeping wines once they have been opened. Some work by creating a vacuum within the bottle and then sealing the bottle with a removable closure (either manually or mechanically). Another system involves putting a layer of carbon dioxide gas (CO_2) on the surface of the wine, thus preventing air getting to it.

Service of beer

Beer should be served at a temperature of 12.5–15.5°C (55–60°F), with lagers generally cooler than other beers at 8.0–10.5°C (48–51°F). Many different varieties of bottled beers are also served chilled. Draught beer, on its route from the keg/cask to the pump, often passes through a chilling unit.

Types of beer glasses

All glasses used should be spotlessly clean with no finger marks, grease or lipstick on them. Pouring beer into a dirty glass will cause it to go flat very quickly.

The main types of beer glass are:

■   half pint/pint tankards for draught beer

■   pint tumblers for draught beer

■   tumblers for any bottled beer

■   short-stemmed 34.08 cl (12 fl oz) beer glass for Bass/Worthington/Guinness

■   lager glass for lager

■   Paris goblets in various sizes including 22.72, 28.40, 34.08 cl (8, 10, 12 fl oz) for brown/pale/strong ales.

Increasing sales of beers to be consumed with restaurant meals has encouraged changes in styles of glassware used. Generally these beer glasses, although often based on the listing above, are more elegant in style and made of higher quality glass.

Pouring beers

Draught or bottled beer should be poured slowly down the inside of the glass, with the glass held at a slight angle. This is especially important where a beer may produce a large head if it is not poured slowly and carefully, for example, Guinness or stouts.

Draught beers should have a small head on them, and the bar person should ensure that he/she serves the correct quantity of beer with a small head, and not a large head to make up the quantity required. A beer in a good condition will have the head, or froth of the beer, clinging to the inside of the glass as the beer is drunk (this is sometimes called lace on the glass).

For bottled beers, the neck of the bottle should not be placed in the beer when pouring, especially where two bottles are being held and poured from the same hand. If a bottled beer has a sediment, a little beer must be left in the base of the bottle to ensure that the sediment does not go into the poured beer.

Service of liqueurs

Liqueurs (sweetened and flavoured spirits) are generally offered from a liqueur trolley at the table. The wine butler should present the trolley immediately the sweet course is finished to ensure that any liqueurs required will be on the table by the time the coffee/tea is served. Again, the wine butler must have a good knowledge of liqueurs, their bases and flavours, and their correct mode of service. Traditionally all liqueurs were served in an Elgin-shaped liqueur glass (see page 64) but many alternatives are now used.

If a customer asks for a liqueur to be served frappé, for example Crème de Menthe frappé, it is served on crushed ice and a larger glass will be needed. The glass should be two-thirds filled with crushed ice and then the measure of liqueur poured over. Two short drinking straws should be placed into the glass before the liqueur is served.

If a liqueur is requested with cream, for example Tia Maria with cream, then the cream is slowly poured over the back of a teaspoon to settle on the top of the selected liqueur.

Fig 5.41. Bar trolley for the service of liqueurs (courtesy of Euroservice UK)

Basic equipment required on the liqueur trolley:

- assorted liqueurs
- assorted glasses – liqueur/brandy/port
- draining stand
- 25 and 50 ml measures
- service salver
- jug of double cream
- teaspoons
- drinking straws (short stemmed)
- cigars
- matches
- cigar cutter
- wine list and check pad.

Other items served from the liqueur trolley include brandies and fortified (liqueur) wines such as Port or Madeira.

Cigars

Where cigars are served it is often the sommelier's responsibility to sell these to the customer. However, some restaurants now discourage the sale of cigars.

The Havana is regarded as the best of all hand-made cigars, to be savoured like a rare wine. The Jamaican cigars come a close second but are milder than Havana and much less expensive. Nowadays, cigars are also made in other countries including the USA, Puerto Rico, the Philippines, Japan, the Dominican Republic and the East Indies.

There are classic measurements for cigars, which many cigar makers attempt to follow. However, the size of a cigar, when indicated by a name only such as Corona or Robusto, is not an indication of a universal standard. Cigars are now categorised by length and Ring Gauge (also spelt Ring Guage), which is measured in multiples of 64ths of an inch. A cigar with a 52 Ring Gauge, for example, measures 52/64ths of an inch in diameter. A Ring Gauge of 50 × 6 is 50/64ths of an inch in diameter by 6 inches long. If the Ring Gauge is

Fig 5.42. Example of cigar presentation box: humidor (courtesy of Hunters and Frankau)

Table 5.4 Cigar terms

Binder	A single leaf of tobacco that is wound around the filler of the cigar to hold it together.
Bunch	The term usually applied to the construction of the cigar when it consists of the binder tobacco wrapped around the filler leaves.
Curing	The process of drying the moisture out of newly harvested tobaccos.
Filler	The blended tobaccos, which form the inner core of the cigar. The filler is the most important part of the cigar as it is responsible for most of the flavour and smoking quality.
Long filler	Those fillers whose tobaccos run the entire length of the cigar. Long fillers are found in only the better cigars.
Shapes	Cigars are made in a variety of shapes and sizes to suit the individual's preferences for taste and style. Many smokers select different shapes for different times of the day.
Wrapper	The outer covering of the cigar is an important part of the cigar's flavour and smoking quality. The various shades of wrapper are: Claro (light, golden brown), Double Claro (the result of picking the leaves before reaching maturity), Candela (light green), Colorado (reddish mid-brown), Maduro (darkest) and English Market Selection/Natural (lighter in colour than Maduro).

stated 6 × 50 it is still 6 inches long and 50/64ths of an inch in diameter. Some examples of cigars are show in Table 5.5.

Storage

A fine cigar should be kept at between 15.5°C and 18°C (60°F and 65°F) and between 55% and 60% relative humidity, with as little variation as possible. A cigar will pick up any smell or moisture in the air, or dry up and smoke like tinder.

When a restaurant has a regular turnover, the best presentation and method of keeping cigars is in a humidor. This is a polished box with half a dozen sections, each holding a different size and type of cigar. On the inside of the lid is a pad which is kept damp, but not wet, to maintain the humidity (see Figure 5.42).

Where there is little turnover of cigar sales then the safest way to keep cigars in good condition is to buy, and offer them for sale, in tubes. These tubes are hermetically sealed and cigars stored in this way will retain their good condition for a long time.

Whether a cigar is stored in a tube, humidor or specially made box, all such containers are either made with, or lined with cedar wood. This is done because the aroma of cedar blends well with cigars and, as cedar wood is porous, it allows the cigar to breathe. A free circulation of air around these boxes is essential.

Table 5.5 Examples of cigar types and sizes

Type	Length in inches	Length in mm	Ring gauge
Torpedo and Pyramides	6–9	152–228	50–58
Belicoso	5–6	127–152	50–55
Robusto	4½–5	115–127	50–55
Hermoso	5	127	48
Double Corona	7½–8	190–203	47–52
Grand Corona and Montecrito A	9½	235	47
Churchill	7	178	46–50
Corona Gorda	5½–6	140–152	46–48
Lonsdale Corona	6½	165	32
Corona Grande	6	152	42
Corona	5	127	40–43
Petit Corona	5	127	40
Perla	4	102	40
Tres Petit	4½	115	40
Corona Culebras	5½	145	39
Especial	7½	190	38
Long Panetela	7	117	35–39
Demi Tasse	4	102	30–39
Panetela	4½	114	26–33

Service of cigars

- Cigar boxes should be opened carefully with a blunt instrument.

- To extract a cigar, press the rounded head and the cigar will tilt upwards for easy extraction.

- Customers should not be allowed to handle cigars before selection. In particular, they should not be allowed to roll a cigar near their ear (sometimes called 'listening to the band'). This tells nothing at all about the cigar and simply damages it.

- The appearance of a cigar should be smooth, firm and even to the touch. It should always be the same size and colour as its partners in the box. The wrapper (outer leaf) should have a healthy glow to it and the open or cut end should be smooth and even.

- The band or identification tag should only be removed if the customer requests it. If it is to be removed it should be done carefully as moving it up and down can damage the cigar. Even if peeled off gently, it can still rip the tobacco leaves.

- When cigars are not pre-cut a V-shaped cigar cutter if required to cut the end, thereby facilitating maximum free draught and ease of smoking. Do not make a small hole with a match or cocktail stick, as this will leave a moist tar concentrate, which imparts a very bitter flavour as the end of the smoke is approached.

■ To light a cigar for a customer, use the broad flame of a long match, a cedar wood spile, or a gas lighter, rotating the cigar to achieve even burning and periodically moving the cigar through the air to encourage burning.

5.9 SERVICE OF NON-ALCOHOLIC BEVERAGES

Coffee and tea

The following equipment is required for the service of coffee or tea:

Coffee tray

- tray or salver
- tray cloth/napkin
- teacup and saucer
- teaspoon
- sugar basin and tongs or a teaspoon according to the type of sugar offered

- coffee pot
- jug of cream or hot milk
- stands for the coffee pot and hot milk jug.

Tea tray

- tray or salver
- tray cloth/napkin
- teapot
- hot water jug
- jug of cold milk
- slop basin

- tea strainer
- stands for teapot and hot water jug
- sugar basin and tongs
- teacup and saucer
- teaspoon.

Variations of this basic equipment will depend on the type of coffee or tea that is being served. General points to note in laying up a coffee or tea tray are given below.

- Position the items to ensure an evenly balanced tray for carrying.

- Position the items for the convenience of the customer: beverage on the right with spouts facing inwards, and handles outwards and towards the customer for ease of access.

- Ensure the beverage is placed on the tray at the last moment so that it is served hot.

Service of coffee for table and assisted service

Placement of the coffee service

- When the coffee is served after lunch or dinner, the demi-tasse (capacity 9.5 cl (⅙ pint) is traditionally used. However, there is a modern trend away from the use of the demi-tasse, except at functions.

- Figure 5.43a shows the equipment required, positioned on the service salver, assuming a table of four customers is to be served. Using this method the waiter only has to make one journey from sideboard to the table.

- Note the coffee service for each customer is made up of a demi-tasse on its saucer, placed on a side plate, with its coffee spoon resting in the saucer and at right angles under the handle of the cup.

- The coffee service is placed on the table from the customer's right hand side, as the coffee will be served from the right.

- The coffee service is positioned on the right hand side of the customer with the handle to the right and the coffee spoon set at right angles to the handle.

- This procedure is then repeated until all the coffee services have been placed on the table for those customers requiring coffee (see Figure 5.43b).

Service of coffee from a tray

- Coffee is always served from the right hand side of the customer.

- The service salver rests on a neatly folded service cloth on the palm of the hand. This allows the server to rotate the service salver so that whoever is to be served is nearest the coffee service.

- The server asks the customer if he/she requires sugar, which is always offered first.

- The required amount of sugar is placed in the demi-tasse.

Fig 5.43a. Service salver before service of coffee

Fig 5.43b. Service salver by the time the second customer is reached

- The service salver is now rotated on the service cloth so that the hot coffee pot and cream jug are in their correct positions for serving.
- The customer is then asked if he/she requires coffee with or without milk or cream.
- Keeping the service salver level, the hot coffee pot is tilted using the service salver as a base, and the coffee served.
- The service salver is again rotated a little so that the cream jug is in its best position for serving.
- Again, keeping the service salver level, the cream jug is tilted using the service salver as a base, and the cream served.
- Having completed the service of the customer's coffee, the coffee service is eased into the centre of the place setting for the convenience of the customer.
- The server should always return to the table to see if the customers require their coffee to be topped up.

Note: In this method of service the pot and jugs are kept on the tray when being tilted. This is to enable the weight of the tray to remain balanced.

Some other methods of serving coffee are given below.

- Service from a pot of hot black coffee held on the sideboard on a hotplate. Milk or cream and sugar are placed on the table.
- Service of both hot milk (or cream or cold milk) and coffee from pots, one held in each of the waiter's hands. Sugar is placed on the table for the customers to help themselves.
- In function catering where larger numbers often have to be served, the hot milk or cream and sugar are placed on the table. Coffee is then served from a one litre plus capacity vacuum flask which may then be kept on the waiters' sideboard in readiness for replenishment should the customers require it. This method of holding and serving coffee ensures that it remains hot at all times (for examples of vacuum jugs for coffee or tea see Figure 4.4, page 118).

Also see Table 4.1 on page 119 for a listing of modern by-the-cup coffee styles.

Service of tea for table and assisted service

Placement of the tea service

The method for the placement of the tea service is similar to the placement of the coffee service described above.

- The tea service for each customer is made up of a teacup on its saucer, with a teaspoon resting in the saucer and at right angles under the handle of the cup.
- The tea service is placed on the table from the customer's right hand side.
- The tea service is positioned on the right hand side of the customer with the handle to the right and the tea spoon set at right angles to the handle.

Service of the tea

Tea is not usually served but the teapot is placed on the table for the customers to help themselves. The milk and sugar are also placed onto the table.

Some other methods of serving tea are shown below.

- Service from a pot of tea held on the sideboard on a hotplate. Milk and sugar are placed on the table.
- Service of both cold milk and tea from pots, one held in each of the waiter's hands. Sugar is placed on the table for the customers to help themselves.
- In function catering the milk and sugar are placed on the table. The tea is then served from a one litre plus capacity vacuum flask which may then be kept on the waiters' sideboard in readiness for replenishment should the customers require it. This means of holding and serving the tea ensures that it remains hot at all times (for examples of vacuum jugs for tea or coffee see Figure 4.4, page 118).

Note: When serving tea from multi-portion pots it is usual to remove the tea leaves once the tea has brewed, so that the tea does not become stewed. (Also see Section 4.1, pages 108 and 110 for the various types of tea and their service.)

Service of dispense bar beverages (non-alcoholic)

Non-alcoholic dispense bar beverages are categorised into five main groups:

- aerated waters
- natural spring water or mineral waters
- squashes
- juices
- syrups

Their correct service is essential in order that the customer may enjoy the beverage ordered to the full. This is where experienced bar personnel come into their own, ensuring that the drink ordered has the correct garnish, and is served at the correct temperature and in the correct glass.

Aerated waters

Aerated waters may be served on their own, chilled, in either Slim Jim tumblers, Paris goblets, Highball glasses or 34.08 cl (12 fl oz) short-stemmed beer glasses, depending on the requirements of the customer and the policy of the establishment. They may also accompany other drinks as mixers, for example:

- whisky and dry ginger
- gin and tonic
- vodka and bitter lemon
- rum and Coca-cola.

Natural spring waters/mineral waters

Natural spring or mineral waters are normally drunk on their own for medicinal purposes. However, as has been previously mentioned, some mineral waters may be mixed with alcoholic beverages to form an appetising drink. In all cases they should be drunk well chilled, at approximately 7–10°C (42–48°F). If drunk on their own they should be served in an 18.93 cl (6⅔ fl oz) wine goblet or a Slim Jim tumbler. Examples include Apollinaris, Buxton, Malvern, Perrier, Saint Galmier and Aix-la-Chapelle.

Squashes

Service from the bar: A measure of squash should be poured into a tumbler or 34.08 cl (12 fl oz) short-stemmed beer glass containing ice. This is topped up with iced water or the soda syphon. The edge of the glass should be decorated with a slice of fruit where applicable and drinking straws added.

Service from the lounge: The wine butler or lounge waiter must take all the items required to give efficient service on a service salver to the customer. Such items will include:

■ a measure of squash in a tumbler or 34.08 cl (12 fl oz) short-stemmed beer glass

■ straws

■ jug of iced water (on an underplate to prevent the condensation running onto the table)

■ small ice bucket and tongs (on an underplate because of condensation)

■ soda syphon

■ coaster to place the glass on in the lounge.

The coaster should be placed on the side table in the lounge and the glass containing the measure of squash placed on the coaster. The waiter should then add the ice and enquire whether the customer wishes iced water or soda to be added. The drinking straws should be placed in the glass at the last moment if required. It may be necessary to leave the iced water and ice bucket on the side table for the customer. If this is the case they should be left on underplates.

Juices

All juices should be served chilled in a 14.20 cl (5 fl oz) goblet or alternative glass.

■ *Tomato juice*: Should be served chilled in a 14.20 cl (5 fl oz) goblet or other glass, on a doily on an underplate with a teaspoon. The Worcestershire sauce should be shaken, the top removed, placed on an underplate and offered as an accompaniment. The goblet may have a slice of lemon placed over the edge as additional presentation.

■ *Fresh fruit juice*: If fresh fruit juice is to be served in the lounge, then the service should be similar to the service of squash described above, except that a small bowl of caster sugar on an underplate with a teaspoon should be taken to the table.

Syrups

Syrups are never served as drinks in their own right but generally as flavourings in such items as cocktails, fruit cups, long drinks and milk shakes.

Further information on non-alcoholic bar beverages may be found in Section 4.4, page 121.

5.10 CLEARING DURING SERVICE

The main methods for clearing in food service operations are summarised in Table 5.6.

Clearing tables in restaurants

Between courses and with customers in the room the procedures described below should be followed.

Clearing plates

The ability to clear correctly ensures speed and efficiency around the table, avoids the possibility of accidents and creates minimum inconvenience to customers. It also allows dirties to be stacked neatly and correctly on the sideboard. Use of the correct clearing techniques allows more to be cleared, in less time and in fewer journeys between sideboard and table.

All clearing techniques stem from the two main hand positions shown on page 175. Then, depending on what is being cleared, the technique is built up from there. Remember expertise comes with practice – so practice regularly.

Clearing first, joint and sweet plates

- Dirties should always be cleared from the right hand side of the customer.
- The waiter should position him/herself, taking up a sideways stance at the table.
- Figure 5.44a shows one of the two main hand positions previously mentioned, and the first dirty joint plate cleared.

Table 5.6 Clearing methods (Courtesy of Croner's Catering)

System	Description
Manual (1)	The collection of soiled ware by waiting staff and transportation to the dishwash area.
Manual (2)	The collection and sorting to trolleys by operators for transportation to the dishwash area.
Semi-self-clear	The placing of soiled ware by customers on strategically placed trolleys within the dining area for removal by operators.
Self-clear	The placing of soiled ware by customers on a conveyor or conveyor belt tray collecting system for mechanical transportation to the dishwash area.
Self-clear and strip	The placing of soiled ware into conveyor belt dishwash baskets by customers for direct entry of the baskets through the dishwashing machines.

- The dirty joint plate should be held firmly pushed up to the joint between the thumb and the first and second finger.

- Note the position of the cutlery: the fork held firmly with the thumb over the end of its handle and the blade of the joint knife placed under the arch in the handle of the fork.

- Any debris or crumbs will be pushed on to the bottom plate.

- Figure 5.44b shows the second dirty joint plate cleared and positioned on the holding hand.

- Figure 5.44c shows the second dirty joint knife positioned correctly and debris being cleared from the upper joint plate on to the lower joint plate using the second dirty joint fork cleared. This procedure is carried out as the waiter moves on to his next position in readiness to clear the third dirty joint plate.

- Figure 5.44d shows the holding hand with the already cleared items held correctly and ready to receive the next dirty joint plate to be cleared.

Fig 5.44a. Clearing joint plates
First joint plate is cleared

Fig 5.44b Second joint plate is cleared

Fig 5.44c Clearing debris from the upper plate

Fig 5.44d Preparing to clear the next dirty plate

- Figure 5.45 shows the joint plates correctly stacked, with the side plates being cleared in one journey to the table. This is an alternative to clearing the joint plates and then the side plates in two phases.

Clearing soup plates

- Dirties should always be cleared from the right hand side of the customer.

- The waiter should be positioned in a sideways stance at the table. Having picked up the first dirty soup plate on its underplate, this stance allows the waiter to pass the dirty plate from the clearing hand to the holding hand.

- Using this procedure ensures the dirty plates are held away from the table and the customers, reducing the likelihood of accidents to a minimum.

- Figure 5.46a shows one of the two main hand positions previously mentioned, and the first dirty soup plate cleared.

- This dirty soup plate should be held firmly on its underplate with the latter pushed up firmly between the thumb and the first and second fingers.

- It is important that this first dirty soup plate is held firmly as succeeding dirties are built up on this one, meaning there is a considerable weight to be held.

- Figure 5.46b shows the second dirty soup plate on its underplate cleared and about to be positioned on the holding hand.

- Figure 5.46c shows the position of the second dirty soup service on the holding hand. The soup spoon is taken from the lower soup plate to be placed in the upper soup plate.

Fig 5.45. Clearing joint and side plates in one journey

Fig 5.46 Clearing soup plates
(a) first soup plate is cleared

Fig 5.46
(b) First stage of clearing the second soup plate

Fig 5.46
(c) Second stage of clearing the second soup plate

- Figure 5.46d shows the upper soup plate with its two soup spoons now placed in the lower soup plate, leaving the upper underplate behind.

- The third dirty soup plate with its underplate is now cleared from the right and placed on the upper underplate on the holding hand. The above procedure is then repeated each time a dirty soup plate on its underplate is cleared.

Clearing side plates

- Side plates are cleared using a service salver or service plate. The purpose is to allow a larger working surface on which to clear the dirty side knives and any debris remaining.

Fig 5.46
(d) Second soup plate is cleared in preparation for the next

- Figure 5.47a illustrates the method of clearing debris from the upper dirty side plate and on to the service salver/plate.

- Figure 5.47b shows the holding hand having cleared four place settings with the dirty items and debris stacked correctly and safely.

Fig 5.47 Clearing side plates
(a) Clearing debris from the side plate to the service plate

Fig 5.47
(b) Hand position having cleared four side plates

- This method generally allows the waiter to clear more dirties in one journey between sideboard and table and is especially useful when working in a banqueting situation.

Crumbing down

The process of crumbing down usually takes place after the main course has been cleared and before the sweet order is taken and served. The purpose is to remove any crumbs or debris left on the tablecloth at this stage of the meal (see Figure 5.3, page 178).

The items of equipment used to crumb down are:

- a service plate (a joint plate with a napkin on it)
- the waiter's cloth or service cloth.

Alternatively a small pan and brush or metal crumber may be used.

On the assumption that a table d'hôte cover has previously been laid, the sweet spoon and fork, prior to crumbing down, should normally be positioned at the head of the cover. However, if an à la carte cover has initially been laid, then, after the main course has been cleared, there should be no tableware on the table prior to crumbing down.

- Crumbing down commences from the left hand side of the first customer. The service plate is placed just beneath the lip of the table. Crumbs are brushed towards the plate using a folded napkin, a specialist crumber brush or a metal crumber.
- This having been completed, the sweet fork is moved from the head of the place setting to the left hand side of the cover.
- The waiter now moves to the right hand side of the same customer and completes the crumbing down of this place setting.
- The sweet spoon is then moved from the head of the place setting to the right hand side of the cover.
- While the sweet spoon and sweet fork are being moved to their correct positions, the service cloth is held under the service plate by the fingers of the holding hand.
- Having completed the crumbing down procedure for one place setting the waiter is now correctly positioned to commence again the crumbing down of the next place setting, i.e. to the left of the next customer.

This method of crumbing down ensures that the waiter does not, at any time, stretch across the front of a customer to complete any one place setting in readiness for the sweet course.

Changing a dirty ashtray

This procedure may be carried out as required and according to the establishment policy.

- Figure 5.48a shows a dirty ashtray on the table.

Fig 5.48. Changing a dirty ashtray (a) Stage one   (b) Stage two   (c) Stage three

- Figure 5.48b: a clean ashtray is held over the dirty ashtray.
- The clean ashtray is placed upside down directly on top of the dirty ashtray.
- The dirty ashtray covered by the clean ashtray is lifted away from the customer's table. This cover is necessary to ensure no fine cigar or cigarette ash is blown on to the tablecloth.
- The dirty ashtray with its cover is transferred to the holding hand away from the table.
- The clean ashtray is then placed on the table (Figure 5.48c).

This service procedure may also be carried out by bringing two clean ashtrays on a service plate or salver to the table. This ensures there is always a second ashtray to cover the dirty ashtray being removed.

5.11 BILLING

The seven basic billing methods are described in Table 5.7.

Table 5.7 Billing methods

Method	Description
Bill as check	Second copy of order used as bill.
Separate bill	Bill made up from duplicate check and presented to customer.
Bill with order	Service to order and billing at same time, for example, bar or take-away service methods.
Pre-paid	Customer purchases ticket or card in advance, either for specific meal or specific value.
Voucher	Customer has credit issued by third party for either specific meal or specific value, for example, a luncheon voucher or tourist agency voucher.
No charge	Customer not paying – credit transaction.
Deferred	Refers to, for example, function catering where the bill is to be paid by the organiser, or customers who have an account.

Note: All billing methods are based upon these seven concepts. The main systems used to support these methods are listed in Section 10.2 Food and beverage revenue control, page 402. The different payment methods are also identified in Section 10.2, page 406.

Bill as check

When a customer requires the bill, the waiter checks everything is entered on the duplicate copy of the food and drink check and then totals the bill. It is then presented to the customer. One of two methods of payment may now occur. The customer may pay at the cash desk on the way out, or pay direct to the waiter who will give any change if payment is made by cash. The cashier usually keeps a copy of the bill on payment and the customer gets a receipt and a copy of the bill if requested.

Depending on the system used, a waiter may enter the details of his bills from the stubs on his check pads into an account slip. This account slip plus the stubs and payments received are then passed on to the control and accounts department who marry them all up.

If the waiter makes out and presents the bill to the customer, who then pays the cashier on leaving the establishment, then the cashier will draw up a daily summary sheet or analysis sheet.

Fig 5.49. Electronic point of sale billing and payment system

This shows the daily takings and also an analysis sheet showing each individual waiter's takings.

Control is effected by the control and accounts department marrying up the checks used to order food and drink from the bars, stillroom and kitchen against the bills issued by each waiter.

Separate bill

This billing method is usually run in conjunction with the triplicate checking system. The basic differences between the duplicate and triplicate billing methods are set out in Table 5.8.

On receiving the duplicate copy of the food check from the waiter, the cashier opens a bill according to the table number on the food check. All the sets of manual bills are serial numbered for control purposes. The number of an electronic bill is recorded as it is opened. The cashier enters the items ordered onto the bill together with the prices, as checks are received from the food or wine waiters. When this is done the bill and duplicate checks are pinned together (with electronic systems only the checks are pinned together) and may be placed into a special book or file that has its pages numbered according to the number of tables in the room. As further checks are received the items are entered onto the bill and the checks then stored with the others for that table.

When the customer requests the bill, the waiter must collect it from the cashier who must first check that all items are entered and priced correctly and then total it up. The top copy of the bill is presented to the customer, on a side plate and folded in half, or in a bill folder. On

Table 5.8 Basic differences between duplicate and triplicate checking and billing methods

Differences	Duplicate	Triplicate
Type of establishment	Popular price restaurants, cafés, department stores where a table d'hôte menu is in operation with possibly a limited à la carte menu	First-class establishments usually operating an à la carte menu
Number of copies of food/beverage check	Two	Three
The bill	The bill is the duplicate copy of the food and drink check and is made out by the waiter	The cashier makes out the bill, which is in duplicate
Payment of the bill	The guest may make payment directly with the cashier or with the waiter according to the policy of the establishment	The guest makes payment via the waiter who returns the receipted bill together with any change to the customer
At the end of service	The account slip and stubs from the waiter's check pad must be handed in, together with the cash received. The cashier completes the summary sheet and hands it in with any payment receipts including cash together with the duplicate bills and order checks to the control and accounts department	The cashier completes the summary sheet and hands it in with any payment receipts including cash and the duplicate bills and order checks to the control and accounts department

receiving the necessary payment from the customer, the waiter returns the bill and payment to the cashier who will receipt both copies of the bill and return the receipted top copy plus any change to the waiter. The waiter then returns this to the customer. The receipted duplicate copy with the duplicate checks pinned to it is then removed from the special book or file and put on one side until service is completed.

Bill with order

This billing method may take a variety of forms depending upon the requirements of the establishment and the depth of management control information required. See also Section 5.6: Menu order and customer bill (page 230) and The single order sheet (page 231).

This principle of billing may also be used in bars where the customer's order is rung up as requested on a pre-set (electronic) keyboard. Here, each key relates to a specified drink and its cost. A VDU shows the customer the order as it is rung up and the prices being charged. When the order has been completed, the total sum owing is displayed. On receipt of cash for the order dispensed, the VDU displays the change to be returned to the customer. A receipt or itemised bill can be printed out for the customer if required.

This system speeds up the process of billing the customer and allows specific control over payment received, and change given where appropriate, as well as controlling all stock items held.

Pre-paid

This billing method happens when pre-payment is required for a specific occasion or event. The organiser must determine the exact number of customers prior to the event. Upon arrival at the event, admission and/or the receipt of food or beverages is obtained by the customer handing in a ticket or card.

Voucher

This method involves a customer being issued credit by a third party. This could be by his/her employer, in the form of a luncheon voucher. A luncheon voucher can be exchanged for like goods, food and non-alcoholic beverages to the maximum value indicated on the voucher. Should the goods requested come to less than the sum shown on the voucher, no cash may exchange hands to make up the difference to the purchaser. However, should the cost of the goods requested exceed the sum shown on the voucher, then the customer must pay the difference to the supplier of the goods.

Other types of credit vouchers may be issued to a specific value, to be given in exchange or part exchange for goods or services received. The supplier of the goods or services then uses these credit vouchers as the basis of the claim for the payment owing from the employer, firm, or agency that issued them.

No charge

If no charge is to be made to a customer receiving goods or services, he/she should be asked only to sign for the goods and services received and the bill should then be sent to the firm or company supplying the hospitality. In some instances the customer will be required to show some type of official form or letter authorising the provision of the service. This method of billing is also used if the establishment, for whatever reason, decides not to charge the customer. This is called 'comping'. The procedure is the same but in this case the bill is sent to the person who authorised the comping.

Deferred/account billing

In deferred or account billing a service has been requested by an individual, firm or company, which has been confirmed and taken place. The bill for the total services provided is then sent after the event to the organising person or body for payment. Payment in this manner often relates to special party bookings or function catering. This method of payment is also available to customers who have accounts with the establishment, where an invoice for payment is sent to the customer, usually once a month. In these cases the customer is normally presented with the bill to sign, before the bill is sent to the control department for adding to the customer's account. This arrangement is similar to those for the resident guests of an hotel.

5.12 CLEARING FOLLOWING SERVICE

At the end of service a range of duties need to be completed, as shown below. These duties are carried out without customers in the service areas.

- Clear the cold buffet to the larder. Collect and wash all carving knives and assist generally in clearing the restaurant.

- Collect all linen, both clean and dirty, and check that the correct quantities of each item of linen are returned. Used napkins should be tied in bundles of ten. All linen should be placed in the linen basket and returned with the linen list to the linen room or according to the establishment policy.

- Switch off the hotplate. Clear away any service silver or other service dishes remaining and restock the hotplate with clean crockery.

- Return cutlery and hollow-ware, together with the tableware and trolleys to the store.

- Collect all cruets and accompaniments and return them to their correct storage place. Where appropriate, return sauces etc., to their original containers.

- Check all the sideboards/workstations are completely empty. Hotplates should be switched off and the dirty linen compartment emptied.

- Clear down the bar top, put all the equipment away and wash and polish used glasses. These should be put away in their correct storage place. Remove all empty bottles etc. Complete consumption and stock sheets. Lock up.

- Put away all equipment that has been used. Empty all beverage service equipment and wash and put away. All perishable materials should be put away in their correct storage places. Still sets and milk urns should be emptied, washed out and then left standing with cold water in them.

- Empty and clean all trolleys and return them to their storage places. Any unused food items from the trolleys should be returned to the necessary department. Any service equipment used on the trolleys should be cleaned and returned to storage areas.

- Empty the liqueur trolley. Return stock to the bar storage and restock the bar from the cellar. Bar shutters and doors should be properly locked.

Specific after service duties

At the completion of service certain after service duties will need to be carried out by different members of the food and beverage service staff. The allocation of specific responsibilities helps to ensure that all areas are left safe, clean and replenished in readiness for the next service. Examples of what might be involved for specific members of staff are shown in the checklists below.

Headwaiter/supervisor

1   Ensure gas and electrical appliances are switched off and plugs removed from sockets.
2   Return any special equipment to the appropriate work area.
3   Secure all windows and check fire exits.
4   Check that all tasks are completed in a satisfactory manner prior to staff completing their shift.

Station waiter/server

1   Replace all equipment in the sideboard according to the sideboard checklist.
2   Wipe down the sideboard and trolleys, clearing all dirty equipment to the wash-up area.
3   Clear down tables and crumb down. Relay tablecloths and slip cloths as appropriate.
4   Switch off and clean sideboard hotplates.
5   Return special equipment to work areas.
6   Return to store cupboards any surplus crockery and silver.
7   Remove plugs having switched off all electrical sockets.
8   Return food/drink check pads and menus to the drawer in the headwaiter's desk.
9   Check area of responsibility with the head waiter/supervisor.

Bar person

1   All working surfaces to be wiped down.
2   Ensure that all equipment is washed, dried and put away in its correct place for future use.
3   Make sure all glassware is washed, rinsed, dried and then stored correctly.
4   Empty the bottle trolley and waste bin. Replace the bin liner in the waste bin.
5   Place surplus orange/lemon slices on to plates and cover with cling film. Store in the chilling unit or fridge.
6   Sweep and mop the floor.
7   Return the liqueur trolley to the bar.
8   Drain the glass-washing machine.
9   Turn off the chiller lights.

10 Complete the control system.

11 Replenish bar stock.

12 Make the bar secure.

13 Check area of responsibility with headwaiter/supervisor.

Stillroom staff

1 Ensure the correct storage of such food items as bread, butter, milk, teabags and ground coffee.

2 Wipe down all working surfaces.

3 Clean and tidy the stillroom fridge and check its working temperature.

4 Check that all equipment is left clean and stored in its correct place.

5 Left over foods to be placed into clean containers and stored correctly.

6 All surplus accompaniments to be stored correctly in proprietary jars and their lids to be wiped down.

7 Switch off applicable electrical appliances.

8 Make sure all carrying trays are wiped down and stacked correctly.

9 All surplus teapots/coffee pots etc. to be stored in the appropriate storage area.

10 Check area of responsibility with the head waiter/supervisor, or the person taking over the area, prior to leaving.

Buffet or counter staff

1 Turn off the electricity supply to the hot-food and cold-food counter.

2 Clear the hot-food counter and cold-food counters and return all leftover food to the kitchen.

3 Turn off the power supply to the oven at the wall.

4 Clear the oven of any remaining food.

5 Important: write down on the day sheet the number of portions of each type of regenerated meal that is left over as waste. This exercise is essential for portion control monitoring and gives an indication of the popularity or otherwise of any one particular dish. Hand in the daily sheet to the supervisor who will then prepare a consumption sheet (see page 419) to show what was taken out and what is now left. This will then be entered into the sales analysis book.

6 Clean all service utensils such as serving spoons, ladles, fish slices, knives and trays that have been used during the course of the day in hot food preparation and service. Wipe them dry.

7 Return all cleaned and dried service utensils to the appropriate storage places ready for the next day's use.

8 Check the stock of plates needed for the next day's service of food.

THE SERVICE OF BREAKFAST AND AFTERNOON TEA

CHAPTER 6

6.1 BREAKFAST SERVICE

The current trend is for breakfasts to be offered in a variety of establishments. Hotels are tending towards offering room-only rates or to serve a continental breakfast inclusive in the room rate, and to offer the full breakfast at an extra charge.

Breakfast in hotels may be served in the hotel restaurant or dining room, in a breakfast room set aside for this meal, or in the hotel guest's bedroom or suite. The service of breakfast in rooms or suites is dealt with in Section 7.2, page 280.

Types of breakfast

Café complet

The term 'café complet' is widely used in continental Europe and means a continental breakfast with coffee as the beverage. The term 'thé complet' is also used, with tea provided as the beverage.

Café simple or thé simple

Café simple or thé simple is the beverage (coffee or tea) with nothing to eat.

Continental breakfast

The traditional continental breakfast consisted of hot croissant, brioche or toast, butter and preserves and coffee as the beverage. The current trend in the continental breakfast menu is towards offering a wider variety of choice, including cereals, fruits, juices, yoghurts, ham, cheese, assorted bread items and a wider selection of beverages.

Full breakfast

A full breakfast menu may consist of from two to eight courses and usually includes a cooked main course. Traditionally this was a very substantial meal and included such items as chops, liver, game, steak, kippers and porridge as the main part of the meal. This type of breakfast was traditionally known as an English Breakfast, but is now also known as Scottish, Irish, Welsh or more simply British Breakfast. The term 'Full Breakfast' is also becoming more common.

To meet the needs of the modern-day customer, the menu content of the full breakfast has changed to include a much more varied choice of items to suit all tastes. Today customers expect to see such items as fresh orange juice, fresh fruit, yoghurts, muesli, continental pastries, homemade preserves, margarines, decaffeinated coffee and mineral waters on the full breakfast menu. Examples of breakfast menu items are given in Table 6.1.

Table 6.1 Examples of breakfast menu items

Menu	Examples of food items
Juices	Orange, pineapple, grapefruit, tomato, prune, carrot, apple.
Fresh and stewed fruit	Melon, strawberries, grapefruit (half or segments), pineapple, apricots, peaches, mango, paw paw, lychees, figs, prunes (fresh and stewed).
Cereals	Cornflakes, Weetabix, Special K, Alpen, muesli, bran flakes, Rice Krispies, porridge.
Yoghurts	Natural and fruit, regular and low fat.
Fish	Fried or grilled kippers, poached smoked haddock (sometimes with poached eggs), grilled herring, fried or grilled plaice, fried or grilled sole, Kedgeree, smoked fish (sometimes including dishes like smoked salmon with scrambled eggs), marinated fish such as gravadlax.
Eggs	Fried, poached, scrambled, boiled, plain or savoury filled omelette, Eggs Benedict.
Meats	Bacon in various styles, various sausages, kidney, steak, gammon.
Potatoes and vegetables	Hash browns, sauté potatoes, home fries, mushrooms, baked beans, fresh or grilled tomato.
Pancakes and waffles	Regular pancakes or waffles, with maple syrup or other toppings, blueberry pancakes, wholemeal pancakes, griddle cakes.
Cold buffet	Hams, tongue, chicken, smoked cold meats, salamis, cheeses (often accompanied by fresh salad items).
Bread items	Toast, rolls, croissants, brioches, crisp breads, plain sliced white or brown bread, Danish pastries, American muffins, English muffins, spiced scones, tea cakes, doughnuts.
Preserves	Jams, marmalade, honey.
Beverages	Tea, coffee (including decaffeinated), chocolate, tisanes, proprietary beverages, milk, mineral waters.

Breakfast covers

The breakfast cover may be divided into two types:

- continental breakfast cover
- full breakfast cover.

Fig 6.1. Example of a continental breakfast (courtesy of Six Continents Hotels)

Cover for a continental breakfast

For a continental breakfast consisting of hot croissant/brioches or hot toast, butter, preserves and coffee or tea, the cover would be as follows:

- napkin
- side plate with side knife
- sugar basin and tongs or individual sugar packets in a bowl
- tea or breakfast cup and saucer and a teaspoon

- stands or underplates for coffee/tea pot and hot milk/hot water jug
- ashtray (depending on smoking policy)
- table number.

If the beverage is tea then the following additional items will be needed:

- slop basin
- tea strainer.

Cover for a full breakfast

The full breakfast consists of a number of courses, usually three or four, with a choice of dishes within each course, as shown on the specimen full breakfast menu below. The cover will therefore include some or all of the following:

- napkin
- side plate and side knife
- fish knife and fork
- joint knife and fork
- sweet spoon and fork
- tea or breakfast cup, saucer and teaspoon
- sugar basin and tongs or individual sugar packets in a bowl

- slop basin
- tea strainer
- stands or underplates for teapot/coffee pot and hot water jug/hot milk jug
- salt and pepper
- caster sugar in shaker
- ashtray (depending on smoking policy)
- table number.

The majority of the items listed above for the two types of breakfast are often placed on the table as part of the mise-en-place, before the customer is seated. A number of items are then placed on the table when the customer is seated. These include:

- butter dish with butter and alternatives
- preserve dish with preserves
- jug of cold milk
- toast rack with toast and/or bread basket with hot rolls
- other items according to the customer's choice
- tea pot/coffee pot/hot or cold milk/hot water jug.

Fig 6.2. Full breakfast cover

Breakfast served in the restaurant (table service)

The basic mise-en-place for the service of breakfast is normally carried out the evening before, after the service of dinners has finished. To ensure protection against dust until the breakfast staff come on duty, the corners of the cloths may be lifted up and over the basic mise-en-place. It will be completed the following morning before the actual service of breakfast commences. This will include turning breakfast cups the right way up and laying the breakfast buffet with items usually served for the first course, such as chilled fruit juices, cereals and fruit compôte, together with all the necessary glasses, plates and tableware required for the service. The breakfast buffet should also contain preserves and butter and alternatives. Jugs of iced water and glasses should be ready on the buffet throughout the meal, especially if the establishment is catering for American visitors. Preserves are usually now served in individual pots.

Summary of the order of service for breakfasts (table service)

1 Greet and seat the customer. The customer should be escorted to a particular table and seated. The breakfast menu should then be presented and the customer given time to make his choice.

2 Take the customer's order. The food order is written on one check and sent to the kitchen and the beverage on another check which is sent to the stillroom.

3 Ensure the correct cover as per the customer's order. While the orders are being attended to in the various departments, the waiter must remember to remove any unwanted cutlery from the cover and, where appropriate, to lay fresh cutlery together with any accompaniments that may be required, for example, Worcestershire sauce if the first course is to be tomato juice.

4 Serve the first course plus accompaniments.

5 After the first course is cleared serve the following:

- *Beverage*: The teapot and hot water jug or the coffee pot and hot milk jug should be placed on the stands or underplates to the right of the lady (or the elder if more than one) in the party or, in the case of an all-male party, by the senior gentleman present. The handles of the pots should be placed in the most convenient position for pouring.

- *Croissant, brioche, rolls, toast*: Hot fresh toast and/or hot rolls should then be placed on the table together with preserves and butter before serving the main course.

6   Serve the main course (plated) plus accompaniments. (The main course at full breakfast is usually plated and all necessary accompaniments should be on the table before it is served.)

7   Check any other requirements.

8   On clearing the main course the waiter should move the side plate and knife in front of the customer and then enquire if more toast, butter, preserves or beverage is required.

Buffet or American breakfast

Of all hotel meals, it is very often the service of breakfast which seems to give management the most problems. This is perhaps because it seems that the majority of hotel guests arrive for breakfast within a very few minutes of one another, all requiring fast service. However well planned the service may be, this sudden influx of customers can create havoc. To add to this, the situation may be aggravated by staff shortages. To overcome these problems and to meet the needs of their hotel guests, many hotels have in recent years introduced a self-service breakfast buffet, which has successfully provided a fast breakfast service.

The change towards buffet style of service for breakfast has also increased the range of foods on offer. The buffet can be used for any type of breakfast, with the most extensive often called American Buffet Breakfast. Examples of the full range of menu items that may be found are given in Table 6.1 on page 271.

Buffet breakfast menus are often priced and offered at three main levels:

■   *Continental*: Including juices, bread items and beverages.

■   *Cold buffet*: Including those items of continental breakfast plus a selection of cold items from the buffet.

■   *Full breakfast*: Full selection from the buffet including hot cooked items.

For the service of this style of breakfast meal customers are presented with the breakfast menu when they sit down and from that they make their choice of either the full breakfast or other types of breakfast. With the buffet breakfast all items are self-served from the buffet, with perhaps the exception of any egg dishes or other cooked to order items and the beverages required.

6.2 AFTERNOON TEA SERVICE

The old English tradition of taking afternoon tea at 4 o'clock is slowly dying out and in its place is the trend towards tea and pastries only, with the venue changing from the hotel lounge to coffee shops, cafés and food courts. With the advent of all-day dining menus, the traditional division of mealtimes is also changing.

Types of afternoon teas

Afternoon tea is served in many establishments and in a variety of forms. Afternoon tea may be classified into two main types:

■ Full afternoon tea as served in a first-class hotel or restaurant.

■ High tea as served in a popular price restaurant, department store or café.

Full afternoon tea

The menu for a full afternoon tea usually consists of some or all of the following items, which are generally served in the order in which they are listed. Note that beverages are served first.

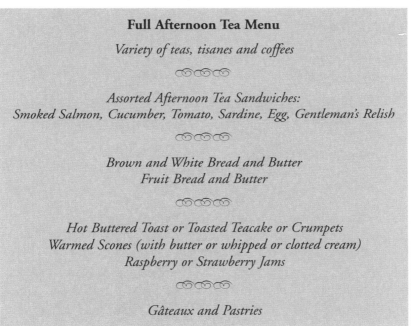

Full Afternoon Tea Menu

Variety of teas, tisanes and coffees

Assorted Afternoon Tea Sandwiches:
Smoked Salmon, Cucumber, Tomato, Sardine, Egg, Gentleman's Relish

Brown and White Bread and Butter
Fruit Bread and Butter

Hot Buttered Toast or Toasted Teacake or Crumpets
Warmed Scones (with butter or whipped or clotted cream)
Raspberry or Strawberry Jams

Gâteaux and Pastries

Cover for full afternoon tea

The following cover will normally be laid for a full afternoon tea:

■ napkin

■ side plate with side or tea knife

■ pastry fork

■ teacup and saucer and a teaspoon

■ jug of cold milk and or side plate with lemon slices (depending on the tea taken)

■ teapot and hot water jug stands or underplates

■ sugar basin and tongs or individual packets of sugar

■ slop basin and tea strainer

■ butter dish with butter and alternatives

■ preserve dish on an underplate with a preserve spoon, or side plate with small individual preserve pots

■ ashtray (depending on smoking policy)

■ table number.

Note: The beverage, jug of cold milk, preserve dish and butter dish are only brought to the table when the customers are seated, and are not part of the mise-en-place.

High tea

A high tea may be available in addition to the full afternoon tea. It is usually in a modified à la carte form and the menu will offer, in addition to the normal full afternoon tea menu, such items as grills, toasted snacks, fish and meat dishes, salads, cold sweets and ices. The meat dishes normally consist in the main of pies and pastries, whereas the fish dishes are usually fried or grilled.

The following accompaniments (proprietary sauces) may be offered with high tea:

Fig 6.3. Cover for full afternoon tea after the order has been taken

- tomato ketchup
- brown sauce (e.g. 'HP')
- Worcestershire sauce
- vinegar
- mustards.

Cover for high tea

The cover for high tea may include:

- napkin
- joint knife and fork
- side plate and side knife
- cruet: salt, pepper, mustard and mustard spoon
- teacup, saucer and teaspoon
- jug of cold milk and or side plate with lemon slices (depending on the tea taken)
- teapot and hot water jug stands or underplates

- slop basin and tea strainer
- sugar basin and tongs or individual packets of sugar
- butter dish with butter and alternatives
- preserve dish on an underplate with a preserve spoon or side plate with small individual preserve pots
- ashtray (depending on smoking policy)
- table number.

Note: As for the full afternoon tea cover, the jug of cold milk, butter dish and the preserve dish are not part of the mise-en-place and should only be brought to the table when the customers are seated. Any other items of tableware that may be required are brought to the table as for à la carte service.

Order of service for afternoon tea (table service)

The general order of service for afternoon tea is:

1. beverages
2. hot snacks – bread and butter (sometimes salads)*
3. sandwiches
4. assorted bread items with butter and alternatives and preserves
5. hot toasted items
6. scones, with butter or cream and preserves
7. cakes and pastries.

Fig 6.4. Cover for high tea

Notes:

*High tea only: For the service of a high tea, the beverage should again be served first, followed by the hot snack ordered, which is often accompanied by bread and butter. When this has been consumed and cleared, the service then follows that of a full afternoon tea.

a. Order taking is usually carried out using the duplicate checking method.

b. The sandwiches may be dressed on silver flats and are set out on the buffet prior to service. Alternatively, sandwiches are pre-plated with a predetermined selection and then served to the customer at the table as required.

c. Toast, teacakes and crumpets are often served in a soup plate or welled dish with a silver cover on an underplate. An alternative to this is the use of a muffin dish, which is a covered silver dish with an inner lining and hot water in the lower part of the container. When serving hot buttered toast for afternoon tea, the crusts from three sides only are removed and the toast is then cut into fingers with part of the crust remaining attached to each finger – this makes it easier for the customer to hold the toast when eating it.

d. The scones and assorted buttered breads are often dressed on dish papers on flats and are also set out on the buffet or brought from the still room as required.

e. Preserves are served either in individual pots or in preserve dishes, both of which are often served on a doily on an underplate with a preserve spoon.

f. Gâteaux and pastries can be presented on cake boards, which are placed on plates or on round silver flats or salvers. An alternative to this is the use of a pastry trolley.

g. Ice creams and other sweet dishes are becoming more popular now and are usually served last.

Note: Afternoon tea may also be served in the lounge (see Section 7.3, page 284).

Reception or buffet tea

A reception or buffet tea is offered for special functions and private parties only and, as the name implies, the food and beverage are served from a buffet table and not at individual tables. The foods that will be available might be a selection from either the full afternoon tea or the high tea.

The buffet should be set up in a prominent position in the room, making sure that there is ample space for display and presentation and for the customers to make their choice. The buffet should have easy access to the stillroom and wash-up so that replenishment of the buffet and the clearing of dirties (used tableware items and serving dishes) may be carried out without disturbing the customers.

When setting up the buffet it is necessary to ensure there is ample space for customer circulation and that a number of occasional tables and chairs are placed round the room. These occasional tables may be covered with clean, well-starched linen cloths, and have a small vase of flowers and an ashtray on them (depending on the smoking policy of the establishment).

Setting up the buffet

The afternoon tea tableware, crockery and napkins should be laid along the front of the buffet in groups with the teacups, saucers and teaspoons concentrated in one or more tea service points as required. Sugar bowls may be placed on the buffet or on the occasional tables that are spread round the room. The tea should be served from urns which should be kept hot, at the separate tea service points along the buffet. Milk should be available in milk jugs. Non-dairy creamers and a range of sugars (sometimes in packets) may also be offered. Tisanes in packets together with hot water and slices of lemon might also be available.

A raised floral centrepiece can be the focal point around which the dishes of food are placed. Cake stands may also be used for presentation and display purposes.

Fig 6.5. A cake stand for afternoon tea (courtesy of Six Continents Hotels)

Service

During the reception some of the staff must be positioned behind the buffet for the service and replenishment of the dishes of food and beverages. Other members of staff should circulate the room with the food and to clear away the dirties. As the dishes on the buffet become depleted, they should be quickly replenished or cleared away so that the buffet looks neat and tidy at all times.

SPECIALISED FORMS OF SERVICE

CHAPTER 7

7.1 INTRODUCTION

In Chapter 1 five groups of service methods were identified (see pages 17–19). In the first four of these methods (table service, assisted service, self-service and single point service) the customer comes to where the food and beverage service is provided. In the last group (specialised) the food and drink is taken to the customer, i.e. the customer is served in situ. This method of service also takes place in areas not conventionally designed for food and beverage service. It includes tray methods found in hospitals and aircraft and sometimes in off-premises catering, as well as lounge service, room service and home delivery.

This chapter gives more information on the specialised method of service and identifies the additional tasks and duties associated with it.

7.2 FLOOR/ROOM SERVICE

Floor or room service varies from basic tea and coffee making facilities in the room and possibly a mini-bar, to vending machines on floors, or the service of a variety of meals in rooms. The extent of service in hotel guest rooms will depend on the nature of the establishment. In five-star hotels 24-hour room service is expected, whereas in two- and three-star hotels service may be limited to tea and coffee making facilities in the room and only continental breakfast available to be served in the room.

Fig 7.1. Room service (courtesy of Six Continents Hotels)

Full and partial room service

An example of a room service menu is shown in Figure 7.2. In this establishment full room service is offered and the room service staff are employed to provide 24 hour service.

Service may be operated from a floor pantry – there may be one on each floor of an establishment or one sited to service two or three floors. An alternative system is where all food and beverages come from a central kitchen and are sent to the different floors by lift, before being taken to the rooms, possibly in a hot trolley.

Floor service staff must have considerable experience as they have to deal with the service of all types of meals. They also have to deal with the service of all alcoholic beverages and so must a have good knowledge of both the product and the licensing laws. The floor service staff tend to work on a shift system, as the service has to be provided 24 hours a day.

The hotel guest may call for service by pressing a button that lights up a series of coloured lights in the corridor or lights up a panel in the floor pantry, which is divided into numbered sections denoting the rooms. The guest may telephone direct to the floor pantry or telephone their request to reception or the restaurant or dining room.

NIGHT MENU

Served from 11.00pm to 9.00am

SOUPS £9.90

❶ New Forest Wild Mushroom Soup
❶ Minestrone Vegetable Soup with Basil and Pine Kernels
Cream of Chicken Soup

SANDWICHES

Please choose from our daily menu selection on page 8

STARTERS

❶ **The Real Caesar salad £13.00**
An all-time favourite with romaine lettuce,
tossed with garlic and anchovy dressing

Served with Grilled Chicken £19.00
Served with Grilled Prawns £21.50
Served with Smoked Salmon £19.50

❶ **Marinated Feta Cheese and Ripe Beef Tomato £14.90**
Served with a lebanese salad and croûtons of pitta bread

Avocado and Shrimp Salad £16.50
Avocado and fresh shrimps, served with a light sauce and lemon, herb salad

❶ **Mixed Green Salad with a Light Olive Oil Lemon Dressing £9.90**

Premium Scottish Smoked Salmon £19.50
Served with brown bread, capers, onions, parsley and lemon

❶ **Mozzarella and Plum Tomato with Fresh Basil £15.50**
Served with wild rocket, cherry sun blush tomato and focaccia crostini

❶ **Deep Fried Vegetable Spring Roll £14.50**
Served with a sweet ginger-chilli dip and a light Oriental salad

❶ *denotes vegetarian dishes*

All prices are inclusive of V.A.T.
A £1.95 cover charge is applicable

9

MAIN COURSES

CLASSIC PASTA

Your choice of fresh pasta - Spaghetti / Penne / Linguini

Bolognese £17.50
With beef and tomato

❶ **Napoletana £15.50**
With tomato and fresh basil

❶ **Arrabbiata £15.50**
With tomato, chilli and garlic

FROM THE OCEAN

❶ **Whole Dover Sole £27.50**
Served meunière or grilled – with fresh parsley, new potatoes and lemon

❶ **Traditional Battered Fish and Chips £21.50**
Served with potato fries, lemon and tartar sauce

Fresh Water King Prawn "Alleyppey" Curry £23.50
Served with curry leaf lemon sauce

FROM THE GRILL

❶ **Aberdeen Fillet of Beef £26.90**
Served with watercress and grilled tomato with
your choice of béarnaise of pepper sauce

Whole Lobster Grilled Provençale £ market price
Lobster grilled with garlic butter and tomato served with basmati rice

Classic Beef Burger £16.95
Served with coleslaw and potato fries

Rump of Lamb Niçoise £24.95
Served with Fresh ratatouille and olives

❶ **Vegetable Side Orders £6.95**

Daily Mixed Fresh Vegetables
French Beans, Mange Tout, Broccoli
Jacket Potato, Potato Fries, New Potatoes
Plain Basmati Rice, Saffron Basmati Rice

❶ *denotes vegetarian dishes*
❷ *authentically prepared local dish*

All prices are inclusive of V.A.T.
A £1.95 cover charge is applicable

10

Fig 7.2. Part of a room service menu (courtesy of The Sheraton Park Tower, London)

A food or wine check is made out for all requests from the hotel guests or, in the event of special luncheon or dinner parties, a bill made out and presented to the host who will sign it to show that the services listed have been received. It is most important that a signature is obtained in case of any query or complaint when the bill is presented to a hotel guest on leaving an establishment. All checks, once signed by the hotel guest, should be passed immediately to reception or control so that the services rendered may be charged to his/her account. All orders are usually taken in triplicate, the top copy going to the department supplying the food or beverage required, a duplicate going to control or reception (after being signed by the hotel guest) and the third copy kept by the floor service staff as a means of reference.

The pantry from which the floor service staff operate may be likened to a mini stillroom and holds the equipment required for the preparation and service of any meal. This equipment can include:

- gas or electric rings
- salamander
- hotplate
- hot cupboard
- small still set or other coffee making machine
- sink unit
- refrigerator
- ice making machine
- lift to central kitchen
- cutting boards
- knives

- storage shelves and cupboards
- crockery
- cutlery and hollow-ware
- glassware
- sugars, cruets, proprietary sauces and other accompaniments
- linen
- guéridon trolley
- chafing lamps and Suzette pans
- wine service equipment, wine buckets, stands baskets etc.
- trays.

Sufficient equipment must be available to maintain a high standard and to enable efficient service to be given at all times.

The service staff carry out all their own pre-service preparation (mise-en-place) before the service of meals. This includes the checking and refilling of cruets and other accompaniments, laying up of breakfast trays, changing of linen, laying up of tables, washing and polishing of glasses, cleaning of trays and so on. Some establishments provide a different style and design of crockery etc., for the service of meals on the floors.

Floor service staff must also co-operate with other staff within the establishment. The floor service staff should ensure that all rooms are cleared as soon as meals are finished so that the meals are not in the way when rooms are being cleaned.

Breakfast only service

In some hotels only breakfast service is available, which is often provided by the housekeeping staff. An example of a breakfast menu is shown in Figure 7.3. This menu also acts as an order which, when completed, is hung on the outside of the hotel guest's bedroom door. The bottom portion of the card is detached and sent to the billing office for charging to the guest's account. The remaining portion goes to the floor service pantry or to the central kitchen. Trays are then made up and delivered to the room within the appropriate time range.

The laying up of a breakfast tray involves the same procedure, with a few exceptions, as laying up a table for a full or continental breakfast in the restaurant. As most orders for the service of breakfast in the room are known in advance the tray may be laid according to the order. The main differences between laying a tray and a table for the service of breakfast are as follows:

- A tray cloth replaces the tablecloth.
- Underplates are usually left out because of lack of space and to reduce the weight of the tray.
- There will be no ashtray or table number on the tray.

With standing orders for breakfast in the rooms, the trays are often laid up the night before, placed in the pantry and covered with a clean cloth. The beverage, toast, rolls etc. and first course, together with the preserves and other accompaniments that may be required according to the order given, will normally be prepared by the floor service staff in the service or floor pantry. The main course is sent up already plated from the kitchen in the service lift. Before taking the tray to the room it is important to check that nothing is missing and that the hot food is hot. For this reason, the beverage and toast should be the last items placed on the tray.

The positioning of the items on the tray is important – they should be placed so that everything is to hand for the guest. For example, the beverage and breakfast cup, saucer and teaspoon should be placed to the top centre-right of the tray as this is in the correct position for pouring and helps balance the tray. Any bottled proprietary sauce required should be laid flat to avoid accidents when carrying the tray. The spouts of hot beverage pots or jugs should face inwards, to avoid spillages, which may cause scalding to the server or slippages on wet floors. On arriving at the door of the room, the member of staff should knock loudly, wait for a reply, and then enter, placing the tray on a table and then adjusting the items on the tray as appropriate.

If there are two or more people taking breakfast in the apartment, it may be necessary to lay up a table or trolley and to serve the breakfast in the same way as in the restaurant. After approximately 45 minutes the floor service staff should return to the room, knock and wait for a reply, enter and ask if it is convenient to clear the breakfast tray away. It is

---

PLEASE HANG YOUR ORDER OUTSIDE YOUR DOOR BEFORE 2:30am

FROM 04:30AM UNTIL 06:00AM
CONTINENTAL BREAKFAST ONLY

06:00 - 06:15 ❑	07:00 - 07:15 ❑	08:00 - 08:15 ❑	09:00 - 09:15 ❑
06:15 - 06:30 ❑	07:15 - 07:30 ❑	08:15 - 08:30 ❑	09:15 - 09:30 ❑
06:30 - 06:45 ❑	07:30 - 07:45 ❑	08:30 - 08:45 ❑	09:30 - 09:45 ❑
06:45 - 07:00 ❑	07:45 - 08:00 ❑	08:45 - 09:00 ❑	09:45 - 10:00 ❑

Other .... ❑

CONTINENTAL BREAKFAST No. of persons.................... @£13.95pp

FRUIT JUICES
A B
❑ ❑ Orange
❑ ❑ Grapefruit
❑ ❑ Tomato

BAKERY
A B
❑ ❑ Croissants
❑ ❑ Danish Pastry
❑ ❑ Toast (Wholemeal or White)
 (delete as necessary)

BEVERAGES
A B
❑ ❑ Coffee
❑ ❑ Tea*
❑ ❑ Hot Chocolate

CEREALS
A B
❑ ❑ Weetabix
❑ ❑ Alpen
❑ ❑ Cornflakes
❑ ❑ Rice Crispies
❑ ❑ Branflakes
❑ ❑ Porridge

❑ ❑ Grapefruit Segments
❑ ❑ Orange Segments

❑ ❑ Natural Yoghurt
❑ ❑ Fruit Yoghurt

A B
❑ ❑ Decaffeinated Coffee
❑ ❑ Hot Milk
❑ ❑ Cold Milk

*Darjeeling, Earl Grey, Jasmine, Assam, Ceylon, Traditional English, Lapsang Souchong, Green, Camomille, Rose Hip, Mint, Lemon

SCOTTISH BREAKFAST No. of persons .... @£17.50pp
Please make your choice from the above Continental Breakfast in addition to the selection below. Choose one of the following:
FRESH FARM EGGS served
A B
❑ ❑ Scrambled
❑ ❑ Fried
❑ ❑ Poached
❑ ❑ Boiled...................Minutes
❑ ❑ Omelette

A B
❑ ❑ Bacon
❑ ❑ Pork Sausage
❑ ❑ Beef Sausage
❑ ❑ Black Pudding
❑ ❑ Baked Beans
❑ ❑ Haggis
❑ ❑ Mushrooms
❑ ❑ Tomatoes

Fish dishes are not included in the Scottish Breakfast but can be ordered at a supplement of £3.50.
A B
❑ ❑ Smoked Salmon and Scrambled Eggs
❑ ❑ Loch Fyne Grilled Kipper Fillet

Please Note: Supplement of £6 per person applies if breakfast is included in the room rate.

CELEBRATION BREAKFAST No. of persons .... @£29.95pp
Includes your choice of breakfast from above plus:
❑ ❑ Fresh Fruit Salad or ❑ ❑ Fresh Strawberries or ❑ ❑ Seasonal Berries with Cream
and
❑ ❑ Scottish Oak Smoked Salmon with Scrambled Eggs
or
❑ ❑ Smoked Haddock with Poached Eggs or ❑ ❑ Grilled Kippers
and half bottle of Taittinger Champagne 375ml.

Please Note: Supplement of £19.95 per person applies if breakfast is included in the room rate.

GUEST NAME... N° OF BREAKFASTS..........................

SIGNATURE .... ROOM N° ....

*Tray charge of £2.50 per person is applicable to all room service deliveries.
The above prices are inclusive of V.A.T.*

Fig 7.3. Example of breakfast tray laid for a continental breakfast

Fig 7.4. Room service breakfast menu and order card (courtesy of the Glasgow Hilton Hotel)

 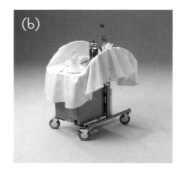 

Fig 7.5. Room service tables: (a) opened, (b) laid and folded for transportation, (c) laid and opened for service, with detachable hot cupboard fitted (courtesy of Burgess Furniture Ltd, London, UK)

important to note that all trays and trolleys should be cleared from the rooms and corridors as soon as possible, as they may impede the housekeeping staff in their work, and may also inconvenience the hotel guests.

When breakfast service is finished all equipment must be washed up in the floor pantry and foodstuffs such as milk, cream, butter, rolls and preserves should be returned to the refrigerator or store cupboard. The pantry is then cleaned and the mise-en-place carried out for the day.

In-room facilities

Mini bar

An example of a mini bar menu is shown in Figure 7.6. This card also acts as a hotel guest self-completion bill. Mini bars are restocked each day and the consumption reconciled with the billing office.

Tea and coffee making facilities

The standard stock for these (usually complimentary) facilities includes a teacup and saucer, a teaspoon (one per person), tea/coffee pot (or both), kettle (self-switching) and a selection of tea, coffee, sugar, chocolate, creamer, non-sugar sweetener and, possibly, biscuits. The stock should be a standard stock, replaced each day by the room attendants.

7.3 LOUNGE SERVICE

Lounge service may include the service of continental breakfast, morning coffee, luncheon, snacks, afternoon tea, dinner or late evening snacks as well as alcoholic beverages. Although mainly associated with hotels, it is also found in public houses, wine bars and on ships. Examples of lounge service menus are given in Figure 7.7.

THE RITZ LONDON

PRIVATE BAR

IN ORDER TO FACILITATE YOUR DEPARTURE AND AVOID LATE CHARGES PLEASE INDICATE
YOUR PRIVATE BAR CONSUMPTION IN THE BOX AND HAND IT TO THE CASHIER
WHEN SETTLING YOUR BILL

2 RITZ CHAMPAGNE	37.5CL	£30.00	☐	2 ORANGE JUICE	20CL £3.50	☐
1 CHATEAU ST. BONNET	37.5CL	£16.00	☐	1 TOMATO JUICE	20CL £3.50	☐
1 RITZ CHABLIS	37.5CL	£16.00	☐	2 7UP	20CL £3.00	☐
2 GLENMORANGIE	5CL	£9.00	☐	1 DIET COCA COLA	20CL £3.00	☐
2 XO FOR MEN COGNAC	5CL	£16.00	☐	2 COCA COLA	20CL £3.00	☐
2 JOHNNIE WALKER	5CL	£9.00	☐	2 GINGER ALE	20CL £2.00	☐
2 JACK DANIELS	5CL	£10.00	☐	2 TONIC WATER	20CL £2.00	☐
2 GORDONS GIN	5CL	£9.00	☐	2 RITZ SWEET JARS	200G £5.00	☐
2 VODKA CRISTAL	5CL	£9.00	☐	1 SMOKED ALMONDS	60G £4.50	☐
2 BACARDI RUM	5CL	£9.00	☐	1 MINT THINS BOX	200G £6.50	☐
2 REMY MARTIN. V.S.O.P.	5CL	£12.00	☐	1 LONDON POST BOX (WITH TOFFEE)	200G £10.00	☐
1 BECKS BEER	33CL	£6.00	☐	1 SALTED PEANUTS	60G £2.00	☐
2 BUDVAR BEER	33CL	£6.00	☐	1 ARLINGTON BEAR	£20.00	☐
2 STILL MINERAL WATER	33CL	£3.00	☐	1 RITZ LONDON BUS	£12.50	☐
2 SPARKLING MINERAL WATER	33CL	£3.00	☐	1 RITZ DISPOSABLE CAMERA	£12.00	☐
				1 ORANGE PEEL CHOCOLATE	150G £6.00	☐
SPORT MINERAL WATER	33CL	£3.00	☐	1 HINT MINT	£3.00	☐
				PLAYING CARDS	£15.00	☐

PRICES INCLUDE VALUE ADDED TAX

ROOM NUMBER: _____   NAME: _____

DATE _____   SIGNATURE: _____

Fig 7.6. Example of a mini bar menu (courtesy of The Ritz Hotel, London)

Organisation of lounge service

The lounge is very often the 'front window' of the establishment, so the standards of service should be high to reflect the overall standards. This responsibility rests with the lounge staff and they must therefore be of smart appearance, efficient and attentive to the hotel guests. They should have a good knowledge of food and beverage service, especially the licensing laws and their obligations to both hotel guests and management. Throughout the day the lounge staff must ensure that the areas are presentable at all times. Before luncheon and dinner, cocktail snacks may be placed on the coffee tables and, after lunch, the tables must be prepared for the service of afternoon tea.

In a first class establishment lounge service staff may possibly operate from their own service pantry. However, in most instances the lounge staff work and liaise with the stillroom, or one of the dispense bars, for the service of all types of beverages required, both alcoholic and non-alcoholic. The lounge staff may have access to a dedicated storage area that holds a basic stock of items they may need in case of emergency. These items may be as follows:

- small stock of linen
- salvers
- ashtrays (depending on smoking policy)
- assorted glasses
- cups, saucers and teaspoons for the service of hot beverages
- dry goods: coffees, teas and sugars
- check pads, bill pads and stock sheets for alcoholic drinks

- basic alcoholic drink stock (for use when hotel guests must be served in the lounge because the bars are closed) to include spirits, brandies, mineral waters, aperitifs, liqueurs, soft drinks and wines
- cocktail snacks – cocktail onions, salted peanuts, gherkins, cocktail cherries, olives, cheese sticks etc.
- Other beverages – Horlicks, Bovril, cocoa, Ovaltine, tisanes and chocolate.

The lounge staff must be prepared for the following types of service in the lounge:

- various breakfast foods
- morning coffee
- apéritifs and cocktails before luncheon
- coffee, liqueurs and brandy after luncheon
- afternoon tea

- apéritifs and cocktails before dinner
- coffee, liqueurs and brandy after dinner
- service of late night beverages, both alcoholic and non-alcoholic
- other snacks throughout the day, depending on the type of establishment.

The triplicate checking method is normally used for lounge service (or the electronic equivalent), with the top copy going to the supplying department – the stillroom or dispense bar. The second copy should either stay with the lounge staff if they have to make out a bill for a chance customer, or go to reception or control so the resident's account can be charged accordingly. The flimsy or third copy remains with the lounge staff as a means of reference.

Chance customers usually pay for the service at the time. Resident hotel guests may not wish to pay in the lounge and staff must then ensure that the hotel guest signs the check to confirm the services received. The check must show the correct room number. The amount should then be charged to the guest's hotel account.

Stocktaking should be held at regular intervals with the occasional spot check on certain items. Stock sheets should be completed daily and are often in the form of a daily consumption sheet (see page 416) showing the daily sales and the cash received, which may be compared with the checks showing the orders taken.

Buffets and trolleys

For some types of lounge service, afternoon tea for example, a buffet may be set up to display the range of foods on offer. Alternatively, a guéridon (trolley) may be used to offer a selection of foods to customers seated within the lounge areas.

KNIGHTSBRIDGE LOUNGE
EXPRESS MENU

SANDWICHES
Please Select Your Own Favourite Bread "Onion, White, Wholemeal, Freshly Baked Baguette Or Our Delicious Healthy Carrot Bread"

Sheraton Park Tower Club Sandwich   £16.50
Roasted Chicken, Pan-Fried Egg, Bacon,
Lettuce And Tomato With French Fries

Roast Beef And Tangy Horseradish   £9.50

Honey Roast   £8.50
Ham And Cheddar Cheese

Smoked Salmon   £9.80

Norwegian Prawns   £9.50
With Lettuce And Cocktail Sauce

ITALIAN TOASTED PANINIS

IL Pollo   £11.50
Roasted Chicken, Lemon Mayonnaise,
Rocket Leaves, Sun Blush Tomato And Olives

IL Parma   £11.95
Mozzarella Cheese, Parma Ham,
Tomato, Olive Oil And Wild Rocket

❤ IL Caprese   £9.95
Mozzarella Cheese, Basil, Tomato,
Olive Oil And Wild Rocket

A Full Beverage List Can Be Requested From Your Waiter
SERVICE NOT INCLUDED
Value Added Tax Is Included In All Prices

Menu Available From 12 Pm To 8 Pm Daily

Fig 7.7a. Part of a lounge service menu, courtesy of The Sheraton Park Tower, London

MAIN COURSES

The Classic Beef Burger   £16.00
Served With Coleslaw And Potato Fries

| With Cheese | With Bacon | With Egg | With Cheese And Bacon |
| £16.50 | £16.50 | £16.50 | £17.50 |

With Cheese, Bacon And Egg
£18.50

Grilled Chicken Burger   £16.50
Served With Coleslaw And Potato Fries

| With Cheese | With Bacon | With Egg | With Cheese And Bacon |
| £16.50 | £16.50 | £16.50 | £17.50 |

With Cheese, Bacon And Egg
£18.50

Sirloin Steak   £19.50
Served With Watercress And Grilled Tomato,
With Your Choice Of Bearnaise Or Pepper Sauce

Lamb Biryani   £22.00
Lamb Cooked In Spicy Arabic Sauce Served With Rice

Chicken Curry   £22.00
Chicken Cooked In A Mild Curry Sauce Served With Rice

Ⓐ Organic Salmon Sauce Mousseline   £19.00
Served With Parsley New Potato And Grilled Tomato

CLASSIC PASTA
Your Choice Of Fresh Pasta, Spaghetti/ Penne

Bolognese   Ⓥ Napolitana
With Beef And Tomato   *With Tomato And Fresh Basil*
£15.95   £14.95

Ⓥ Arrabbiata   Tiger Prawns
With Tomato, Chilli And Garlic   *Sauteed With Olive Oil, Garlic And Lemon*
£15.50   £18.50

Fig 7.7b. Part of a lounge service menu, continued, courtesy of The Sheraton Park Tower, London

7.4 HOSPITAL TRAY SERVICE

Hospital catering services have major foodservice goals, as all meals should reach the patient quickly, look attractive and be of specific nutritional value. Patients in hospital often have special dietary needs (see pages 77–79) and their likes and dislikes are also of importance. They may also have particular needs because of their medical condition.

Patients in hospital generally fall into one of six categories:

- medical
- surgical
- geriatric (older people who may have special needs)
- orthopaedic (these patients may have difficulty in moving as a result of their medical condition)
- maternity (expectant and new mothers)
- paediatric (children).

Meal times in hospitals

The timing of patients' meals generally follows the same pattern:

Breakfast	7.30–8.00 a.m.
Lunch	12 noon
Tea	3.00–3.30 p.m.
Supper	6.00–6.30 p.m.
Later hot drink	Anytime between 8.00 and 10.00 p.m.

Order taking

Menu order forms are used to take orders from patients in the main wards of hospitals. The menu contains a choice for lunch, dinner and breakfast and is given to each patient the day before. The patient marks off their requirements for lunch, dinner and breakfast for the following day. They may also indicate on the card whether they require a large or small portion. The menus are then collected and sent to the catering manager.

When the order cards have been collected menu reader terminals are used to scan the hand marked menu cards. The menu reader terminals are used to transmit food and beverage requirements to production areas, print records and control the individual meal assembly for the hospital conveyor systems. The menu reader terminals can also be interfaced with computer systems for dietary and recipe analysis.

Tray systems

There are a number of commercially available tray service methods used in hospital catering. Individual patient trays are made up on a conveyor system according to the patients' pre-ordered requirements. Various methods are used to keep the food hot or cold, ranging from the heated or chilled pellet method to specially insulated trays. Trays, once completed, are transported to the wards in ambient cabinets. At service time, depending on the type of dish, extra portions are available in case they are required. Beverages may be added at ward sites before presentation to the patient.

The advantages of this system are as follows:

- the patient is able to select the meal items required from a menu
- over the period of a week or a fortnight, the patient has a wide and varied selection of dishes from which to choose
- patients receive their meal presented appetisingly on the plate and at the correct temperature
- labour and administration costs can be reduced
- time originally spent in the ward plating up meals may now be used for other duties.

Microwave ovens are also used in hospitals to provide quick re-heating facilities for food at certain periods of the day and night. All forms of dishes required can be prepared the day before during off peak hours in a central kitchen and blast-frozen or chilled. When required the following day, the dishes can quickly be ready for service.

Note: Private patients' choice of food and beverages is usually larger and more varied than in the main wards, and here the service is similar to hotel room service.

7.5 HOME DELIVERY

The 'Meals on Wheels' service, provided by local authorities, was perhaps the first type of home delivery and is certainly one of the most well known. More recently home delivery service has become a part of the profit sector. Services range from Indian and Chinese takeaway deliveries, to restaurants providing full meals (hot, or cold for customers to re-heat). One chain of pizza restaurants was specifically designed to be primarily a home delivery operation and was based upon an American concept.

Methods of delivery vary, but all endeavour to preserve the product in heat retention presentation packages. The most simple, but nevertheless effective, is the pizza home delivery system, which utilises thick cardboard with internal corrugations to provide a form of insulation to keep the pizza hot. The time required for heat retention is limited by the extent of the delivery area. Indeed, the companies who operate these services endeavour to deliver the pizza within 30 minutes.

7.6 AIRLINE TRAY SERVICE

Most airlines now operate using a catering commissary. A commissary is a term used to cover the catering, cabin requirements, bonded stores, cleaning and other passenger requirements. It is now accepted that on many short-haul routes, only snack-type meals or sandwiches and beverages are offered. For some operators the provision of food and beverages is provided for

A cuisine truly worth adopting should at its heart have the longer term health of its followers in mind. This is why we have introduced exclusively to our FIRST customers world-class spa cuisine from Chiva-Som, Thailand's award-winning health resort.

In addition, the British Airways Culinary Council is an elite group of established and well-known restaurateurs. Each chef is recognised individually for his own unique specialties, skills and dedication to his craft. The Culinary Council works with British Airways' own menu development team to provide a range of British and International dishes that will delight your palate and please the eye.

The British Airways Culinary Council

Michel Roux, OBE – The Waterside Inn, Bray; Vineet Bhatia – Rasoi, Sloane Square; Richard Corrigan – Lindsay House, Soho; Shaun Hill – The Merchant House, Ludlow; Jancis Robinson, OBE, M.W.; Nicholas Lander – The Financial Times, London; Mark Edwards – London

FIRST

LUNCH

Welcome to the FIRST dining experience, where you are in control of when and what you eat. Please create your own menu combination, from a light snack to a complete meal.

Starters

Loch Fyne kinglas smoked salmon and caviar crème fraîche

Chiva-Som's Thai tempeh cakes with sweet chilli dipping sauce

Parsnip and stem ginger soup

Fresh salad leaves with your choice of tomato and basil oil or mustard mayonnaise

Main

Fillet steak with freshly-seared foie gras, glazed shallots and Madeira jus

Chiva-Som's yellow lobster and green papaya curry with cucumber relish and lemon grass brown rice

Duchy of Cornwall free-range sausages, red onion jus and mashed potatoes

Salad of spicy chicken with warm tomato and cumin dressing

Please feel free to request an alternative selection of vegetables from the menu.

Snacks

Bacon roll served with tomato ketchup

Parsnip and stem ginger soup and a side salad

Penne pasta with your choice of cherry tomato and basil sauce or quattro formaggio cheese sauce

Duchy of Cornwall biscuits

A selection of cheese and fruit

Dessert and Cheese

Cox's Orange Pippin apple crumble with crème anglaise

White chocolate and strawberry terrine with chunky strawberry coulis and shortbread biscuits

Cheese plate featuring –

Quickes Cheddar – This full-bodied cheese is made of cow's milk by one of the famous cheesemakers in England.

Oxford Blue – Soft and creamy with a mild flavour, this cheese is made from cow's milk.

Tornegus – This semi-hard unpasteurised cheese is made from cow's milk and herbs.

Unpasteurised cheese may pose a health risk to certain groups of people including pregnant women, the elderly, the very young and those whose systems may be immunocompromised.

A basket of fresh fruit

Your choice of
Espresso, cappuccino, coffee, decaffeinated coffee, tea or herbal tea

AFTERNOON TEA

Sandwiches

Selection of sandwiches featuring prawn with dill, free-range egg salad, honey mustard chicken with spinach and mature Cheddar cheese with tomato and red onion marmalade

Pâtisserie

Warm plain or fruit scones served with clotted cream and strawberry jam

Dundee cake, chocolate and orange victoria sponge and coconut macaroon

---

Champagne

Charles de Cazenove Grand Apparat Brut Champagne
This is a first rate, buttery, Chardonnay-dominated deluxe Champagne – vinous, serious and demanding with a pronounced toasty aroma and a rich, mouth-filling flavour.

White Wines

Chablis 1er Cru Les Vaillons 2003, Domaine Billaud-Simon
A fantastic Chablis from one of the great modern producers – rich and concentrated with a refreshingly clean citrus finish and great intensity.

Riesling Herrenweg de Turckheim 2002, Domaine Zind-Humbrecht
This superb Alsace Riesling, from top bio-dynamic producer Olivier Humbrecht, has an extravagant aroma of intense citrus peel and an opulent, throat-tingling flavour.

Renwood Select Series Viognier 2004
The Viognier grape originated in the Rhône valley but is now one of California's trendiest varieties. It is hand-picked from selected sites to give a rich style with a dominant flavour of fresh white peach.

Red Wines

Château Branaire Ducru 1995, Grand Cru Classé St Julien
1995 was a glorious vintage for the commune of St Julien and its wines are now at the peak of perfection. Branaire has an open blackberry nose, is well-structured with a ripe soft fruit flavour and a real touch of class.

Chinon, Clos de l'Olive, 2003, Couly-Dutheil
2003 was another lovely vintage in the Loire Valley and the Cabernet Franc grape achieved full maturity. This wine is soft and rounded with beautiful primary fruit aromas and flavours.

Gordon Brothers Syrah 2001, Columbia Valley
Washington State is a very serious wine producer nowadays and the Gordon Brothers sun-drenched vineyards overlooking the Snake River are some of the best, producing deliciously rich but balanced wines.

Dessert Wines

Opitz Goldackerl Trockenbeerenauslese 2002, Austria
Austria makes some of the finest sweet wines in the world. The effervescent Willi Opitz, from his tiny vineyards in Illmitz near the Hungarian border, produces some of the very best in the country.

Warre's 1988 Colheita Port
Complex, sweet, nutty flavours offer an admirable after-dinner glass.

Spirits, Digestifs and Liqueurs

We offer a complete range of classic and timeless spirits, digestifs and liqueurs including Gonzalez Byass Sherries, Johnnie Walker Blue Label Scotch Whisky, Tanqueray No. Ten Gin, The Glenlivet 18-year-old Single Malt Whisky, Smirnoff Black Label Vodka, Camus XO Cognac and Woodford Reserve Kentucky Whiskey.

Soft Drinks

A selection of traditional and modern drinks including Coca-Cola, Highland Spring still or sparkling mineral water

---

Fig 7.8a. Example of First Class in-flight menus and wine list (Courtesy of British Airways Plc)

STARTERS

* Ballottine of salmon with herb crème fraîche
  or
  Artichoke and roast vegetable salad with tomato and basil dressing

* Fresh seasonal salad served with vinaigrette

MAIN

Pan-seared fillet of beef with cracked black pepper sauce
and potatoes dauphinoise

King prawn masala

Three cheese tortellini with wild mushrooms
and creamy pesto sauce

* Marinated corn-fed chicken and roast Mediterranean vegetable
  salad with lemon tarragon dressing

DESSERT

Mango and passion fruit parfait

Keen's Cheddar and Stilton cheese

Chocolates

* Well Being selection – refer to High Life for details.

067,093,175,177,189,203,207,
209,213,217,229,297 CW
1   220C005-ROT1

LUNCH

SNACKS

Sandwiches of kippered salmon with horseradish crème fraîche
and free-range egg mayonnaise with cress
or
Sandwiches of grilled Mediterranean vegetables with cream cheese
and gammon ham with tomato

SWEETS

Warm fruit scone with clotted cream and strawberry preserve

Moist ginger cake

DRINKS

Tea, ground coffee or decaffeinated coffee

Selection of herbal teas – peppermint, blackcurrant,
apple or camomile and honey

AFTERNOON TEA

3   220C005-ROT1

WINES

CHAMPAGNE COCKTAILS

Kir Royale – Crème de Cassis gives this cocktail
its distinctive taste.

Buck's Fizz – Crisp, dry Champagne and naturally sweet
orange juice.

CHAMPAGNE
Charles Heidsieck Brut Reserve
This classic Champagne has complex flavours and aromas
of brioche, almonds and apricots together with perfectly-judged
acidity. Refreshing and complete.

WHITE
Raymond Reserve Chardonnay 2002, Napa Valley
The experience of five generations of Napa Valley winemakers
can be seen in this lovely creamy wine with great fruit
and well-integrated oak.

Pouilly-Fumé 2003, Pascal Jolivet
A crisp, clean and refreshingly racy dry white wine
from the Central Vineyards region of the Loire Valley.

RED
Beringer Knights Valley Cabernet Sauvignon 2000
The grapes for this excellent wine come from the unique volcanic
soils of the Knights Valley. Aged in oak for twenty months, it is
rich and complex with black cherry and cassis flavours.

Rioja Urbina Reserva Especial 1996
A classic, old-style Rioja with an aromatic, perfumed nose
and lots of vanilla notes from its time spent maturing
in American oak barrels.

A selection of traditional and modern drinks to suit all tastes
including Coca-Cola.

There will be a complimentary bar available
serving alcoholic beverages and soft drinks.

002W624   10/05   220C005-ROT1   4

BRITISH AIRWAYS

WORLD TRAVELLER

MENU

Hot smoked salmon, potato and dill
salad with mustard seeds

Chicken tikka masala
or
Braised beef with dumplings
and winter vegetables

Blackberry and apple pie with custard

Coffee or tea

Fig 7.8b. Example of Club World (business class) and World Traveller (economy) in-flight menus and wine list (Courtesy of British Airways Plc)

by an additional charge to the customer. On long-haul flights, airlines provide a more extensive service of food and beverages. The airline will provide dishes to meet its passengers' particular needs, for example, meals that meet religious requirements, as well as meals for vegetarians, children and invalids.

Service on airlines is often a combination of trolley service, as used for beverages, and tray service with the trays being distributed from the trolley in which they are stacked.

For economy and tourist flights all meals tend to be of the same size, with identical portions. The meals are arranged in individual portion containers, sealed, chilled and then stored until required. The economy or tourist class meal is often served on a plastic or melamine tray and uses disposable place mats, cutlery, tableware and napkins, together with disposable glasses for any drinks required.

Business and first class passengers will often receive a food and beverage service equivalent to that of a first class hotel or restaurant and there is little portion control. The first class service may offer joints of meat that are served from a trolley as it moves up the aisle, and served with the appropriate garnish. This, combined with the use of fine bone china, glassware and silver plated tableware, creates an atmosphere of content and well being while the meal is being served. Great use is also made of pre-portioned foods, such as salt, pepper, mustards, sugars, cream, cheeses, dry biscuits and preserves.

When all the food has been prepared the required quantities of each dish are placed on trays. These are then put into hot cupboards and kept hot until transported to the plane, or chilled and stored in the catering unit until required to be re-heated on board the aircraft. Each airline will supply its own equipment such as tableware, crockery and glassware.

High-speed ovens can heat meals in 20 minutes. The tray containing the meal is then given to the passenger on a pull-down table. In between meals, tea, coffee, biscuits, cakes and other snacks are served, together with cold drinks.

All alcoholic beverages and cigarettes are drawn from the bonded stores on the catering premises under the watchful eye of a representative of Customs and Excise.

When the aircraft is in the air the cabin crew will provide the service to the passengers. Their job can be very difficult, especially if the flight is of a short duration, as this can leave little time for a meal to be served.

7.7 RAIL SERVICE

Food and beverage operations on trains generally fall into one of three categories:

- conventional restaurant
- kiosk (take away)
- trolley service operations.

On sleeper services a limited type of room service is provided. However, all these services are provided on the move and away from the home base and suppliers. The logistics of providing on-train catering are therefore similar in organisation to off-premises catering (see page 385).

Rail catering has also seen the introduction of a tray service system, similar to airlines. The food and drink is served on trays to passengers at their seat, rather than in a restaurant car where tables are laid as in a restaurant.

Fig 7.9a. Example of an on-train buffet shop menu and first class Travelling Chef at seat service menu (Courtesy of Great Western Trains Company Limited)

Fig 7.9b. Example of an on-train Pullman Dining menu and wine list (Courtesy of Great Western Trains Company Limited)

GUÉRIDON SERVICE

CHAPTER 8

8.1 INTRODUCTION

The definition of the term guéridon is a movable service table, or trolley, from which food may be served. This may include serving foods that have to be carved, jointed or filleted, foods that have to be flambéed, foods that have to be prepared and served or simply foods that are being served from the guéridon. In other words, it is a movable sideboard carrying sufficient equipment for the service requirements, together with any spare equipment that may be necessary. The guéridon itself may come in various forms, for example, a Calor gas trolley specially made for the purpose, a plain trolley or even a small table. This form of service may also refer to a carving trolley, cheese trolley or a sweet trolley.

Guéridon service is normally found in high-class establishments with an à la carte menu and service. It is more costly as it requires a higher level of service skills, the use of more expensive and elaborate equipment, and a larger area for the movement of trolleys.

Flambé dishes first became popular in Britain during the Edwardian era. Crêpes Suzette claims to be the first flambé dish, which was supposedly invented by Henri Charpentier when working as a commis at the Café de Paris in Monte Carlo in 1894.

The Japanese art of cooking at the table, known as Tepanyaki, is another more modern and specialist approach, with great visual appeal for the customer. It involves the service of Teryaki, a Japanese dish of meat or fish that is grilled or broiled after being soaked in a seasoned soy sauce marinade. It is prepared on a tepan or hibachi table where the Japanese chef prepares teryaki meat together with shrimp, rice and vegetables immediately in front of the customers. This creates a dining experience that combines cooking, dining and entertainment in one.

Special equipment

Flare lamps

These are an essential item of equipment for guéridon service and are used in cooking and flambéing dishes. The maintenance of the flare lamp is very important to maximise the life of the lamp and to minimise the possibility of accidents.

The main types of lamp used today are fuelled in one of three ways:

- *Methylated spirits*: these have a good flame but care must be taken to trim the wick, which will help to avoid fumes. All components must fit together well as any leakage of the spirit can cause a serious fire hazard. The use of these lamps is on the decline.

- *Flammable gel*: this is very clean and safe to refill as the gel either comes in individual lamp size containers, which fit directly into the lamp, or in a large container with a dispenser. However, the flame can be fairly weak.

- *Calor gas*: these lamps are very popular and replacement canisters can be obtained that fit directly into the lamp. The gas is odourless and excellent control of the flame can be achieved. These lamps are often used in purpose-built trolleys where the lamp is incorporated into the structure, thus giving the same working height all along the trolley top. This is much safer and there is less chance of accidents. The top of the trolley is stainless steel, which allows for easy cleaning. The guéridon will normally also have a control switch for the gas lamp, a drawer for surplus service equipment, a cutting board for

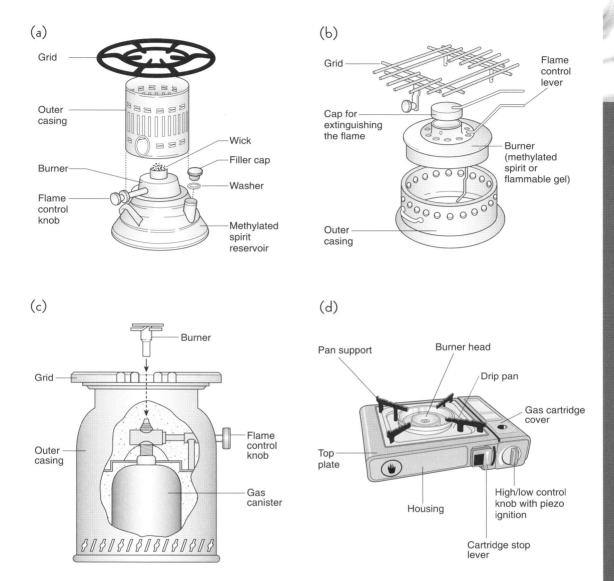

Fig 8.1. Four types of Guéridon lamp: (a) traditional methylated spirit lamp, (b) modern methylated spirit or flammable gel lamp, (c) gas lamp and (d) gas stove

use when cooking dishes at the table, a bracket on the lower shelf used for holding bottles of spirit and liqueurs and an indentation on the top to hold accompaniments.

In recent years portable gas stoves, which were first produced as camping stoves, have begun to be used for cooking purposes on the guéridon trolley. These are lightweight, self-contained, portable stoves with their own carry case. They have an automatic push button ignition and built-in safety features. The stove will operate for up to two hours on a Sunngas P220 cartridge. In addition these stoves are considerably less expensive than the average flare lamp.

Chafing dishes and Suzette pans

The true chafing dish is deep, has a lid and is designed to fit onto its own individual heating unit. Larger versions of these are now found on buffets. The shallower pans, which are used for lamp cookery, are called Suzette pans. They resemble frying pans in shape and size and have a diameter of 23–30 cm (9–12 in), with or without a lip. The lip is usually found on the left hand side. The pans are generally made of silver-plated copper as this gives an even distribution of heat.

Hotplates

The main function of a hotplate is to keep food hot before it is served to the customer. They are usually positioned on the sideboard, but may often be found on both the sideboard and the guéridon. They come in a vast range of sizes and may be heated by gas, electricity, methylated spirits or flammable gel; infrared ones are also available.

Care and maintenance of equipment

It is the visual display of preparing food at the table that is attractive to many customers. All actions must therefore meet the highest hygiene and safety standards and good planning and organisation can achieve this. The hygiene and safety factors relating to guéridon service are given below.

- Hygiene and appearance of staff should be of the highest standard (see Section 1.8, page 25).
- All equipment should be spotlessly clean and polished daily.
- Food should not be handled with bare hands.
- Trolleys should be wiped down between each use.
- The hotplate or lamp should never be placed outside the trolley legs.
- The trolley should not be positioned for use close to curtains or soft furnishings.
- Spirits should never be left near heated trolleys or naked flames.
- Spirits should be handled carefully when flaming dishes.
- The trolley should not be moved around the restaurant with food or equipment on it.
- Lamps should be checked on a daily basis to ensure they are in good working order.

A daily safety inspection and cleaning programme should be enforced through the use of a cleaning rota or schedule. The food service personnel should carry out this work as part of the normal mise-en-place period and under the supervision of a senior member of the team.

All items of small silver equipment should be checked on a daily basis using the appropriate method of cleaning, such as:

- burnishing machine
- plate powder
- silver dip.

(a)

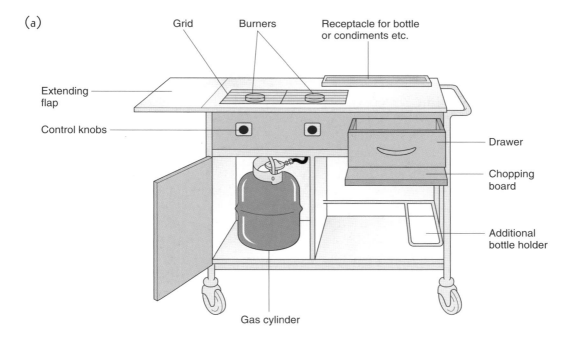

Grid Burners Receptacle for bottle or condiments etc.

Extending flap

Control knobs

Drawer

Chopping board

Additional bottle holder

Gas cylinder

(b)

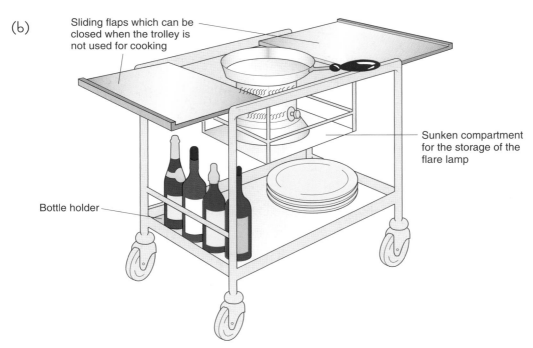

Sliding flaps which can be closed when the trolley is not used for cooking

Sunken compartment for the storage of the flare lamp

Bottle holder

Fig 8.2. Examples of flambé trolleys: (a) gas-fuelled flambé trolley and (b) flambé trolley with flare lamp

All large equipment such as flambé lamps, Suzette pans, hotplates and trolleys should be hand-cleaned with the correct cleaners, again on a daily basis. Remember always to use the least abrasive cleaner otherwise the surface of the equipment will become scratched. For copper-based items a mixture of salt, lemon and a little vinegar is generally sufficient.

Specific maintenance of certain parts of the equipment is essential. This might include the lubrication of castors on trolleys and also any moving parts of equipment that are used, such as hinges and drawer runners. Three-in-one oil or WD40 may be used.

Checklists

To ensure efficiency and safety in the care and maintenance of equipment a checklist should be drawn up for all staff to follow as required. An example is given below.

Gas lamps

- Check that all moving parts move freely.
- Ensure both the jet and burner are free from soot and dirt.
- Clean by the correct methods, using Silvo or Goddard's plate powder for example, but remember never to immerse in water.

Gas bottles

When changing a gas bottle the following factors should be considered:

- Ensure at all times there is no heated equipment or naked flames near the lamp.
- Follow the manufacturer's instructions and directions and use the correct spanner.
- Check all taps are in the 'off' position.
- All gas bottles should be kept cool during storage.

Spirit lamps

- Check the amount of methylated spirit.
- Ensure the air hole is free.
- Trim the wick and check it for length.
- Clean off any excessive dirt and spent matches.
- Ensure all moving parts move freely.
- Clean by the appropriate method, but remember not to immerse in water.

Any elaborate decoration on equipment should be checked carefully and, if necessary, cleaned with a toothbrush.

8.2 GUÉRIDON SERVICE

For guéridon service the taking of food orders is similar to that detailed in Chapter 5, pages 225 to 228. In addition, the carving trolley, sweet trolley and cheese trolley may be used as selling aids.

When guéridon service is being undertaken all dishes must be presented to the customers at the table before the actual service of the food and especially before the filleting, jointing and carving of any dish. This is so that the customers can see the dishes as the kitchen has presented them before the dishes are to be served. Customers can also confirm that the orders are correct.

Mise-en-place for guéridon service

In many establishments where guéridon service is carried out it is policy to standardise the basic layout of the guéridon. This is to ensure that the required standards of service are met and that safety is a prime consideration of all the service staff. There are many designs of guéridon available on the market today, but the basic format for the lay-up of the top of the guéridon may be as shown in Figure 8.3.

Where necessary, the top and undershelf of the guéridon should be covered with a folded slip cloth, although this will of course depend on the nature of the guéridon and its general appearance. For convenience of working, the cutlery layout should be similar to that of a sideboard as this saves time and speeds up the service. This may include:

- service spoons and forks (joint)
- sweet spoons and forks
- soup, tea and coffee spoons
- fish knives and forks
- special equipment including a soup and sauce ladle
- joint and side knives.

The hotplates or table heaters are generally placed on the left hand side on the top of the guéridon. These heaters may be gas, electric or methylated spirit. Also on the top may be a carving board, knives for carving, jointing and filleting and a selection of basic accompaniments such as oil and vinegar, Worcestershire sauce, English and French mustard and caster sugar.

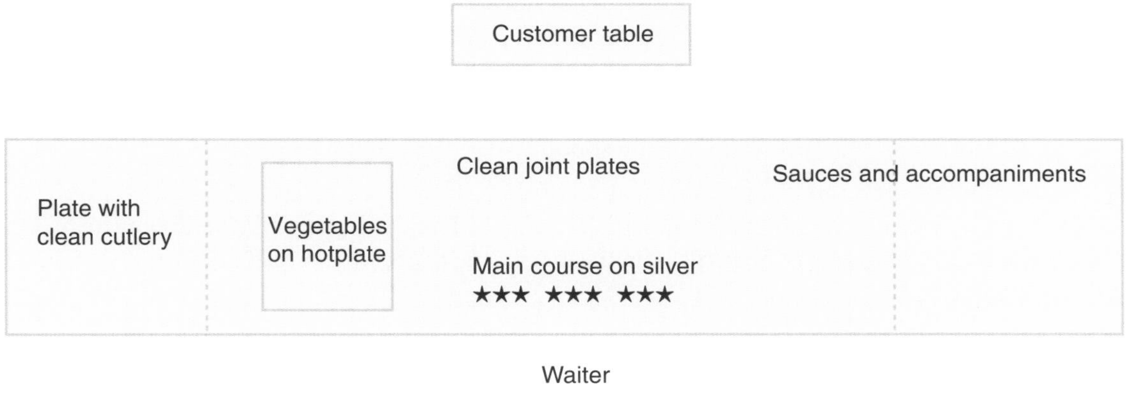

Fig 8.3. Example of a basic guéridon lay-up

Underneath will be found a service plate and service salver, side plates and some joint plates for dirty cutlery as the service is being carried out. There should also be some underflats of assorted sizes for the service of vegetables and sauces. A selection of doilies or dish papers may be useful for the presentation of sauces and other accompaniments. Any other mise-en-place required, such as coffee saucers, accompaniments and check pads, will be on the waiter's sideboard or workstation, together with a surplus of all the guéridon equipment in case of emergency.

Procedure for guéridon service

- Guéridon service is essentially a chef and commis service. There must therefore be complete liaison and teamwork between them and the other members of the team.

- Always push the guéridon, never pull it. This helps to avoid accidents, as one is able to see more easily where one is going.

- The guéridon should be kept in one position for the service of a complete course and not moved from customer to customer.

- Unlike silver service, when the service spoon and fork are used together in one hand, guéridon service requires that the spoon and fork are used one in each hand. This gives more control and is a quicker procedure.

- The dish is first presented to the customer and the name of the dish is stated for example, 'Your Dover sole, madam'. The dish is then returned to the guéridon.

- Hot serving plates are placed on the side of the trolley, with the food being served placed onto the hotplate.

- The food being served is then carved, jointed or filleted if necessary, and is placed onto the customer's plate.

- The waiter then places the potatoes and vegetables onto the plates while the plates are still on the guéridon. The waiter also serves the sauces onto the plates.

- The plates are then placed in front of the customers.

- Where more than two covers are being served from the guéridon, only the main dish of each customer should be served from the guéridon, with potatoes and vegetables, sauces and accompaniments being passed in the usual manner. This speeds up the service as generally there is not sufficient room on the guéridon for the service of the complete meal.

- When transferring foods and liquids from the service flats and dishes to the plate, always run the fork along the underside of the spoon to avoid drips marking the plate.

- Never fillet or carve on a silver dish as it can ruin it. Use either a carving board or a hot joint plate. When using a fork in carving, always work with the curved side downwards, otherwise the prongs will puncture the meat.

- The commis must always keep the guéridon clear of dirties.

- When the service is finished at one table wipe down the guéridon and move on to the next table immediately. It will then be ready for the commis coming from the kitchen with a loaded tray.

Service considerations for different foods

Hors d'oeuvre or other appetisers	These are served in the usual way except for various speciality dishes (see also Chapter 3, pages 85 to 88).
Soups	Always served from the guéridon, whether in individual soup tureens or in larger soup tureens requiring a ladle.
Egg dishes	Unless there is any special treatment required these dishes are served straight to the table.
Pasta and rice dishes	Served onto the customers' plates at the guéridon. The pasta is served by lifting the pasta high from the serving dish using a service spoon and fork, and then moving this over to the customer's plate and lowering the pasta onto the plate.
Fish dishes	Filleted when necessary and served at the guéridon.
Meats	Carved or jointed where necessary, and always on a board, and then served onto the customer's plate at the guéridon.
Potatoes and vegetables	Either served onto the customers' plates at the guéridon, or served as in silver service, after the main courses have been put onto the customers' plates and placed in front of them. Sauces and accompaniments are served in the same way.
Cheese	Most often served from a cheese trolley, but may also be served from a service (such as a cheese board), which is presented on the guéridon.
Sweet	Served from the guéridon if a flambé type dish or from the cold sweet trolley.
Savoury	Served from the guéridon or pre-plated.
Coffee and tea	Usual service at the table unless speciality coffees are required.

Liquors used in lamp cookery and flambé work

There are many different types of liquors used for various purposes in lamp cookery and flambé work. Some examples are shown below.

Types	Purposes
Spirits and liqueurs Fortified (liqueur) wines Sparkling wines Still (light) wines Beer Cider Syrups	To flambé, sweeten, colour, balance flavours, to achieve the correct consistency and to remove excessive fat/grease.

8.3 INTRODUCTION TO CARVING, JOINTING AND FILLETING

Knowledge together with practical and social skills are necessary to project a professional image as a carver (trancheur). Carving techniques are craft skills of real value to the foodservice trade. They will be required in those restaurants using a carving trolley, in carvery-type operations, for serving at a buffet and for special occasions.

All customers have their likes and dislikes – the meat to be medium or well done, some fat or very little fat, a portion carved from the end of the joint, sliced thinly or thickly, white meat only, a mix of white and brown meat and so on. The trancheur has to acknowledge all of these requests while remaining organised and efficient. He must have all the correct equipment to hand for the joint to be carved together with the appropriate accompaniments and sauces. The professional trancheur will also maximise the number of portions from the joint being carved and keep wastage to a minimum.

Carving, jointing and filleting skills

Carving, jointing and filleting are skilled arts only perfected by continual practice. General considerations are as follows:

- Always use a very sharp knife, making sure it is sharpened beforehand and not in front of the customer. Remember you are going to carve a joint, not cut it to pieces.
- Carving is best achieved by pulling the knife back towards you and not by pushing the knife forwards.
- Cut economically and correctly to maximise the portions obtained and at the same time work quickly to avoid hold ups in the room.
- Meat is carved across the grain, with the exception of saddle of mutton or lamb, which is sometimes cut at right angles to the ribs.
- The carving fork must hold the joint firmly to prevent accidents. This is the only time the fork pierces the meat.
- Practise as much as possible to acquire expertise in the art of carving and to develop confidence in front of the customer.

Selection of tools

- For most joints a knife with a blade 25–30 cm (10–12 in) long and about 2.5 cm (1 in) wide is required.
- For poultry or game a knife with a blade 20 cm (8 in) long is more suitable.
- For ham a carving knife with a long flexible blade is preferred. This is often referred to as a ham knife.
- Serrated knives do not always cut better than the plain bladed knife, with the latter giving a cleaner cut.

- A carving fork is needed to hold the joint firmly in position when carving.
- Carve on a board, either wooden or plastic. Avoid carving on china plates or metal. Apart from the damage this can cause (especially to silver), small splinters of metal can become attached to the food.

Cleanliness and hygiene

The standard of cleanliness of the trancheur and his equipment during the practical application of the craft are of the utmost importance. Good service practices are listed below.

- Always wear spotlessly clean protective clothing. Remember customers are watching a demonstration of the craft.
- Ensure that personal cleanliness is given priority as you are working in the vicinity of your customers as well as handling food.
- Always pre-check work areas and equipment to ensure good hygiene practices.
- Do not handle meat, poultry or game excessively.
- Carve as required and do not pre-carve too much or too early.
- Keep all meat, poultry or game under cover, be it hot or cold, and at the correct serving temperature.
- Be constantly vigilant for any sign of deterioration in the food being offered.
- At the conclusion of each service ensure all equipment is thoroughly cleaned and well rinsed.

Methods of carving, jointing and filleting

The carving of all hot food must be performed quickly so that there is minimum heat loss.

Beef and ham	Always cut very thinly.
Rib of beef	May either be carved on the bone or by being first removed from the bone and then sliced.
Steaks	Chateaubriand or entrecôte double are sliced at angles, either in half or into more slices, depending on the customer's preferences.
Lamb, mutton, pork, tongue and veal	Carved at double the thickness of beef and ham.
Saddle of lamb	Carved along the loin in long, fairly thick slices.
Shoulder of lamb	This has an awkward bone formation. Starting from the top, cut down to the bone, then work from top to bottom, then turn the piece over and work gradually round.
Lamb best ends	These are sliced between the cutlet bones and can also be double cut by cutting close to each side of the bone.

Boiled beef and pressed meats	Generally carved slightly thicker than roast meats and each portion will include some fat. Boiled beef should be carved with the grain to avoid the meat shredding.
Cold ham	Carved onto the bone from top to bottom in very thin slices.
Whole chicken	A medium-sized bird is often dissected into eight pieces, making up four portions.
Poussin and small feathered game	May be either offered whole or split into two portions.
Duckling	May be carved into four/six portions, two legs, two wings and the breast cut into long strips.
Turkey and other large birds	Often portioned into legs, wings and breast and then carved into slices separately. Make up portions with white meat from the wings or breast together with a slice of brown meat off the leg and a share of the stuffing. Alternatively, the bird may be left whole with the joints separated from the main carcass so as to allow for carving without jointing first.
Salmon	This is first skinned whether it is hot or cold. It is then served in fillets, one from each side of the bone. Cut slices up to 10 cm (4 in) long and 2.5 cm (1 in) thick.
Lobster and crayfish	Hold firmly. Pierce vertically with a strong knife and cut with a levering motion towards tail and head. Hold shell down with a spoon on a dish, slowly lifting out the meat with a fork. Slice the meat diagonally.
Sole	First remove the bones along either edge. Then draw the fillets apart with the aid of two large forks. Serve a top and bottom fillet per portion.

Carving trolley

The carving trolley is a very expensive item of equipment. Because of this, great care must always be taken with the maintenance and use of the carving trolley to ensure that it functions correctly.

Function

The function of the carving trolley is to act as an aid to selling. At all times the waiting staff must be salespeople and sell the dishes on the menu by brief and accurate description. The carving trolley supplements this by being a visual aid to selling and should be at the table as the waiter takes orders so that he may suggest and show particular items to the customer. Always remember to push the trolley and not pull it. This enables the trolley to be steered and moved safely and helps to avoid accidents.

Maintenance

The carving trolley should be cleaned at regular intervals with the aid of plate powder, ensuring that all the powder is finally polished off so that none comes into contact with any foodstuffs. A toothbrush may be used for cleaning any intricate design work.

Safety factors

There are certain safety factors to observe in the handling of the carving trolley and these must be carefully adhered to.

■ The container on which the carving board rests contains hot water. Ensure the base is filled with hot water before the burners are lit.

■ Make sure the safety valve on the base is set on correctly and screwed down tight. There is a small hole set in the safety valve which allows the surplus steam to escape. This valve must be placed so it is on the opposite side of the trolley from where the trancheur works, to avoid the hands being scalded by the escaping steam. The safety valve must never be blocked or covered over. If it is, pressure will build up within the base, which can buckle the trolley and may cause an accident.

Fig 8.4. Carving trolley
(courtesy of Euroservice UK)

■ Two methylated spirit or flammable gel lamps heat the carving trolley. Ensure the lamps are functioning properly, with trimmed wicks and the spirit holders filled with methylated spirit or the gel holders filled. There must be sufficient fuel to last throughout the service period.

■ The lower shelf should be used for carrying the service plate, spare service cutlery and a clean joint plate.

■ Handle the carving implements correctly and safely and sharpen a knife using a steel safely.

Mise en place

For its satisfactory operation in the restaurant, the correct equipment must be placed on the carving trolley before service. This includes:

■ carving board

■ carving knives/forks

■ sauce ladles

■ service spoons and forks

■ joint plates for dirty cutlery

■ spare napkin and service cloth.

Preparation of joints

The correct preparation of joints before cooking is very important and any bones which may make carving difficult should be removed prior to cooking. At the same time, the person carving must have knowledge of the bone structure of a joint in order to carve correctly and thus acquire the maximum number of portions. Therefore the carver must be able to:

■ recognise the joint, poultry or game to be carved

■ be aware of the bone structure and muscle fibre of the product being carved

■ recognise the correct carving implements required.

Presentation of the trolley

■ The trancheur must always ensure that the carving trolley is correctly laid up before it is taken to the table.

■ The plate rest for the hot joint plates should be extended and the two containers for gravy and sauces should be already filled. These two containers should always be placed at the end nearest the plate rest. This is for ease of service and also provides the shortest distance between the containers and the plates.

■ When being used the carving trolley should be placed next to the customer's table, in between the customer and the trancheur. This ensures that the customer can see every operation performed by the trancheur and appreciate the skills involved.

■ The trolley should be positioned to ensure that the safety valve is on the side away from the trancheur. This is to ensure that the trancheur will not be scalded when using the trolley.

■ The trolley should be positioned in such a way that the lid is drawn back from the trolley towards the trancheur so as to reveal the foods to the customer.

8.4 DISHES INVOLVING WORK ON THE GUÉRIDON

Hors d'oeuvre and other starters

For the service of traditional hors d'oeuvres see page 85.

Smoked eel (anguille fumée)

Equipment

■ carving board

■ small sharp knife

■ joint fork

■ spare plate for skin and bone

■ spare plate for dirty cutlery

■ service spoon and fork.

Ingredients

■ whole smoked eel.

Accompaniments

■ creamed horseradish sauce

■ cayenne pepper

■ peppermill

■ segment of lemon

■ traditionally brown bread and butter.

Cover

■ fish knife and fork

■ cold fish plate.

Method

1 Ensure all ingredients and equipment are organised before commencing.

2 Start at the tail end.

3 Cut a section about 10 cm (4 in) long.

4 Insert the knife between skin and flesh on one side and loosen the skin.

5 Insert the skin between the prongs of the fork and roll up on the fork towards the backbone.

6 Cut round the backbone.

7 Roll the skin off the other side and cut free with the knife

8 Fillet each side removing the backbone.

9 Place on to a cold fish plate and serve.

10 Offer horseradish sauce separately.

Note: Eel is very often carved on the buffet rather than on the guéridon because of the length of the whole eel and the space required in order lay it out on a flat surface for carving.

Smoked trout (truite fumée)

Equipment

- service spoons and forks on a service plate
- spare plate for dirty cutlery
- cold joint plate.

Ingredients

- smoked trout dressed on a silver flat.

Accompaniments

- creamed horseradish sauce
- cayenne pepper
- peppermill
- segment of lemon
- traditionally brown bread and butter.

Cover

- fish knife and fork
- cold fish plate.

Method

1 Ensure all ingredients and equipment are organised before commencing.

2 Present the dish to the customer then return to the guéridon.

3 Place little crisp lettuce leaves and tomato on the fish plate.

4 Place the smoked trout onto a cold joint plate before removing the head and tail.

5 With the aid of a service spoon and fork, remove both the head and tail.

6 Set the smoked trout neatly onto the cold fish plate and serve.

7 Offer horseradish sauce separately.

Smoked salmon (saumon fumé)

Equipment

- carving knife (usually a ham or long thin flat knife)
- joint fork
- service spoon and fork
- spare plate for dirty cutlery.

Ingredients

- side of smoked salmon on a board.

Accompaniments

- cayenne pepper
- peppermill
- half of lemon wrapped in muslin or segment of lemon
- traditionally brown bread and butter
- sometimes chopped shallots and capers are offered together with soured cream.

Cover

- fish knife and fork
- cold fish plate.

Method

1 Ensure all ingredients and equipment are organised before commencing.

2 Present the salmon on the board to the customer, or the trolley with the salmon and board on it.

3 Ensure that the side of smoked salmon has been prepared for service with the skin being trimmed and any small bones removed using a small pair of fish pliers.

4 Carve from the head towards the tail and start about half way down so that slices will not be too long when laid onto the fish plate for service.

5 Remove the black line in the middle of each slice by making a small V-shaped incision at the centre of the side of smoked salmon before carving each slice.

6 Carve each slice wafer thin, giving 2–3 slices per portion.

7 Insert the edge of the slice of smoked salmon between the prongs of the joint fork and roll up.

8 Lift over to the cold fish plate and unroll neatly onto the fish plate.

9 Serve and offer accompaniments.

Note: Because of the size of a side of smoked salmon it is often carved on the buffet or on a dedicated service trolley.

Caviar (Caviare – roe of the sturgeon)

Equipment

- sweet spoon or two teaspoons for service
- spare plate for dirty cutlery.

Ingredients

- caviar pot(s) in a dish of crushed ice on an underflat

Accompaniments

- blinis (buckwheat pancakes) or hot breakfast toast
- butter
- segments of lemon
- sieved hard boiled white and yolk of egg
- chopped shallots
- sometimes soured cream.

Cover

- caviar knife on the right hand side of the cover
- cold fish plate.

Note: If a caviar knife is not available then a side knife can be used.

Method

1 Ensure all ingredients and equipment are organised before commencing.

2 Present the guéridon at the table.

3 If a sweet spoon is used then generally one spoonful weighing approximately 30 grams is recognised as being a portion.

4 If two teaspoons are used, the caviar is moulded in the two spoons (quenelle), 3–4 teaspoonfuls per portion.

5 When served direct from the pot(s), the caviar is usually weighed before and after service and then the amount used is charged according to the amount served.

Note: Caviar may also be served in small glass bowls set on crushed ice. These are usually placed on the table at the top of the cold fish plate and the accompaniments are then offered at the table. The larder may also serve the caviar already pre-plated.

Whole melon (melon frappé)

Equipment

- cutting board
- sharp knife
- clean napkin
- spare plate for debris from the melon
- spare plate for dirty cutlery
- soup plate for pips from the melon
- service spoons and forks on a service plate
- cocktail sticks in a holder.

Ingredients

- melon in a small container of crushed ice
- cocktail cherries in a small silver or glass dish.

Accompaniments

- ground ginger
- caster sugar.

Cover

- sweet spoon and fork or a small (side) knife and fork (especially if the melon is a little unripe)
- cold fish plate.

Method

1 Ensure all ingredients and equipment are organised before commencing.

2 The melon should be in a small container of crushed ice.

3 Present the melon to the customer then return to the guéridon.

4 Lift the melon with the aid of a clean napkin onto a carving board.

5 Trim both ends.

6 Stand the melon on end and cut out the required portion or portions. Use your judgement as to the size of a portion but, as a guide, there should be approximately six portions to one whole melon.

7 Place the cut portion on a clean napkin and hold it firmly in the left hand. Scoop out any pips with the aid of a service spoon into the remainder of the whole melon. If there is less than half the melon left then scoop the pips straight into a soup plate.

8 Trim the base of each portion so it stands squarely on the cold fish plate and will not roll or slide about.

9 If required the waiter may cut the flesh of the melon from the rind and slice.

10 Decorate with a cocktail cherry on a stick and serve.

Note: Charentais melon, which is usually served half to a portion, is often served in a bowl on crushed ice. A sweet spoon (or teaspoon) is placed on the under plate or on the right hand side of the cover.

Globe artichoke (artichaut)

A globe artichoke may be served either hot or cold, and either as an appetiser or as a separate vegetable course.

Equipment

- lamp if served hot
- service spoons and forks on a service plate
- spare plate for dirty cutlery
- sauce ladle.

Ingredients

- globe artichoke on a silver flat.
- sauceboat of sauce on an underflat.

Accompaniments

- if served hot: sauce Hollandaise or beurre fondue
- if served cold: sauce vinaigrette.

Cover

- large (joint) fork on the right hand side of the cover (used to consume the heart)
- hot or cold fish plate as appropriate

- fingerbowl containing lukewarm water and a slice of lemon, on a napkin on an underplate
- spare napkin.

Method

1 Ensure all ingredients and equipment are organised before commencing.
2 Present the dish to the customer then return to the guéridon.
3 With the service spoon and fork transfer the globe artichoke from the silver flat to the hot or cold fish plate.
4 Lift out the centre leaves and arrange neatly on the edge of the hot or cold fish plate.
5 Pour the required sauce into the space left in the centre. Sometimes additional sauce is put in a small ramekin on an underplate, together with a teaspoon, and placed on the table.
6 Serve, ensuring that the cover and accompaniments are already on the table, including the finger bowl placed and positioned at the top left hand corner of the cover together with the spare napkin.

Pâté de foie gras

Foie gras is made from the goose's liver and the geese are specially bred and fattened for this purpose. However, there is a wide range of pâtés more commonly offered. These are sometimes known as pâté maison (pâté of the house or establishment), where each recipe may vary.

Equipment

- two teaspoons
- silver jug of very hot water
- if pâté maison is being offered, then a side knife will be required

- service spoons and forks on a service plate
- spare plate for dirty cutlery.

Ingredients

- terrine (pot) of foie gras or terrine of pâté.

Accompaniments

- hot breakfast toast, with crusts removed, cut into triangles and served in a napkin on a side plate
- alternatives are various breads, often warmed, including brioche.

Cover

- small side knife and a sweet fork
- cold fish plate.

Method

1 Ensure all ingredients and equipment are organised before commencing.

2 Present the dish to the customer then return to the guéridon.

3 If foie gras is being offered, place the two teaspoons in the silver jug of very hot water.

4 Using each in turn, draw the teaspoon across the surface of the foie gras so that curls of the foie gras may be formed.

5 Give four or five curls per portion and, as they are formed, place them on the cold fish plate.

6 Decorate with little crisp lettuce leaves and some segments of tomato. Serve.

7 If pâté maison is being offered, the waiter must use the side knife, frequently dipped in hot water, to cut two or three slices per portion. Decorate as above and serve.

Note: In some instances the pâté may come already sliced from the larder and dressed on to a flat. In this case serve as for silver service or guéridon service.

Shellfish cocktail (cocktail de crevettes)

Equipment

- small glass dishes, with teaspoons, to hold the ingredients, all placed on a silver salver.
- soup plate for mixing the sauce
- service spoons and forks on a service plate
- spare plate for dirty cutlery.

Ingredients

- shellfish
- shredded lettuce
- tomato concassé
- sieved hard-boiled white and yolk of egg
- mayonnaise
- tomato ketchup
- Worcestershire sauce
- lemon juice
- chopped parsley
- slice of lemon.

Accompaniments

- lemon wedge
- traditionally brown bread and butter.

Cover

- teaspoon
- sweet fork or oyster fork
- shellfish cocktail holder on a dish paper on an underplate.

Note: The oyster fork and teaspoon may be placed to the right and left of the cover or on the dish paper on the side plate on either side of the shellfish cocktail holder*.

Method

1 Ensure all ingredients and equipment are organised before commencing.

2 Present the guéridon at the table.

3 Ensure there is some crushed ice around the base of the shellfish cocktail holder and that it is well chilled.

4   Place the tomato concassé in the base of the shellfish cocktail holder.

5   On top of this place some shredded lettuce followed by the shellfish, which may be prawns or shrimps. Keep one or two shellfish by for decorating the finished dish.

6   Make up the sauce by mixing together the mayonnaise, tomato ketchup, Worcestershire sauce and a little lemon juice in the soup plate.

7   Coat the shellfish with the tomato flavoured mayonnaise. Be careful not to put too much mayonnaise in as this can overpower the rest of the ingredients.

8   Now decorate the top with the sieved hard-boiled yolk and white of egg and chopped parsley.

9   Place the remaining shellfish and slice of lemon over the edge of the holder and serve.

*A shellfish cocktail holder has an insert, which is placed into the holder that contains crushed ice. An alternative would be to use a small glass bowl set on a soup plate of crushed ice.

Dressing and serving salads from the guéridon

Salads may be served:

■ as part of a selection for hors d'oeuvres (see page 85 for the service of hors d'oeuvres)

■ as a starter course (see page 94 for examples of salad appetisers)

■ to accompany a roast or other main course

■ as a separate course usually after the main course (see page 93 for the general service of salads).

General points in salad making

When mixing salads either at the guéridon or within the stillroom or kitchen, always ensure that:

■ hands and utensils are scrupulous clean

■ ingredients are fresh, crisp, cool and moisture free to avoid impairing the dressing by dilution

■ there is a contrast of colour and flavour even for plain, green salads

■ the mixing bowl is large enough – do not attempt to overload it with salad leaves. To mix well, salad must lie loosely and be capable of free movement within the bowl.

Basic equipment and ingredients

■ Salad bowl.

■ Fresh, clean, dry salad ingredients in the bowl or on a separate plate ready for moving to the bowl when the salad is to be made.

■ Soup plate for mixing dressing.

■ Dressing ingredients.

■ Salad servers (metal or wood) for mixing after dressing the salad and serving onto salad crescents (saladiers – quarter-moon shaped dishes), plates or bowls.

- Salad crescents, plates or bowls for the number of covers to be served.
- Garlic press (if required).

- Teaspoons for tasting.
- Joint plate for dirty cutlery.

General method

1 Ensure all ingredients and equipment are organised before commencing.

2 Present the guéridon at the table.

3 Place salad ingredients into the salad bowl.

4 Use a service spoon and fork or salad servers (one in each hand) to break the leaves if required.

5 Make dressing (see pages 319 to 320 for a selection of dressings).

6 Pour the dressing over the salad in the bowl.

7 Use salad servers to thoroughly blend the salad with the dressing by turning over the leaves from top to bottom.

Note: Dressings are usually blended together before being added to the salad but if ingredients are to be added separately to the salad, then these steps should be followed:

- oil first until all leaves glisten softly with a film of oil
- followed by vinegar or lemon juice (sparingly)
- then seasoning.

Service of salad

1 Place the dressed salad onto the salad crescents.

2 Serve the salad crescent to the top left of the customer's cover.

3 Place a sweet fork with the prongs facing down on the left hand edge of the salad crescent with the handle at an angle of 45° to the cover for service.

4 Now serve the course that the salad is to accompany (for example, hot roast poultry, game) as quickly as possible.

Note: If salad is to be served alone the cover is a small knife and fork, with the salad served onto a plate (rather than a salad crescent) or into a bowl or a soup plate.

Caesar salad

Equipment

- salad bowl
- service spoon and fork
- plates or bowls for numbers of covers to be served
- garlic press.

Ingredients

- fresh clean, dry cos (or Romaine) salad leaves on separate joint plate
- croûtons
- grated or shaved Parmesan cheese.

Dressing

- olive oil
- white wine vinegar
- Dijon mustard
- raw egg yolk*
- Worcestershire sauce
- salt and pepper mill
- peeled garlic cloves
- chopped anchovy fillets.

*Some establishments may substitute pasteurised egg for fresh egg yolk.

Accompaniments

- none.

Cover

- small knife and fork
- cold plates or bowls with underplates.

Method

1 Ensure all ingredients and equipment are organised before commencing.

2 Present the guéridon at the table.

3 Mix the ingredients for the dressing in the salad mixing bowl using a service fork: crushed garlic (depending on the customer's requirements) mustard, dash of Worcestershire sauce, vinegar and raw egg yolk.

4 Blend in the oil using the service fork as a whisk.

5 Add chopped anchovies.

6 Add seasonings to taste (according to the customer's requirements) and stir.

7 Put the lettuce leaves into the mixing bowl and break into smaller pieces (largish fragments) using a spoon and fork (one in each hand).

8 Add the croûtons and fold in.

9 Move the salad in the bowl with the service spoon and fork to ensure that it is fully covered by the dressing.

10 Present the salad onto the cold plates for service.

11 Sprinkle with grated (or shaved) Parmesan.

12 Serve.

There are many variations to this salad. One specific variation replaces the egg that is incorporated into the dressing with a one-minute boiled egg broken over the salad just before serving. Other variants include making the dressing by incorporating two or three chopped anchovy fillets into a basic vinaigrette that has been seasoned with garlic and some horseradish cream. Some recipes substitute English mustard for Dijon. Garlic is usually used but some variants involve rubbing this over the wooden bowl before making the salad, while others use chapons (garlic croûtons). Other ingredients that might be used include Roquefort cheese and seasonings such as Tabasco. Some recipes keep the anchovy fillets separate and then decorate the salad with them rather than incorporating them, chopped, into the dressing. As well as finishing with the sprinkling of grated Parmesan, some variations also sprinkle with ground pepper and lemon juice.

Salad dressings

Standard equipment

The standard equipment required on the guéridon when preparing a salad dressing is:

- soup plate in which to mix the dressing
- service cloth
- service spoons and forks on a service plate
- teaspoons in a small jug of water (for tasting the dressing as it is being made)
- spare plate for dirty cutlery.

The ingredients are dependant upon the type of dressing required. Examples of seven different dressings are given below:

French dressing

Ingredients

- French or Dijon mustard
- seasonings of salt, pepper, cayenne pepper (sometimes caster sugar)
- four to six parts olive oil to one part vinegar.

Method

1 Place the mustard and seasonings in a soup plate which is resting on the folded service cloth at an angle, thus retaining the mixture in one part of the soup plate to make mixing easier.

2 Blend the seasonings together with a service fork.

3 Add the measure of vinegar to the seasonings and mix well to form a smooth mixture.

4 Now add the oil and blend together with the service fork.

5 Taste and adjust seasonings if required.

English dressing

As for French dressing with the exception that English mustard replaces the French mustard,

the proportions of oil to vinegar are one to two, and one teaspoon of caster sugar is added to the seasonings.

Sauce vinaigrette

Ingredients

- one teaspoonful French, Dijon or English mustard
- seasoning of salt and peppermill
- one tablespoon of vinegar
- two tablespoons of oil.

Method

1 Place the mustard, seasoning and vinegar in a soup plate and mix together using a fork.

2 Add the oil, mixing slowly.

3 The proportions of vinegar and oil used are according to individual taste.

Roquefort dressing

Ingredients

- Roquefort cheese
- wine vinegar (see Method A)
- olive oil (see Method A)
- sauce mayonnaise (see Method B)
- seasoning (salt)
- jug of single cream
- lemon juice.

Method A

1 Break down the Roquefort cheese into small lumps or cream it right down by mixing in a soup plate with a little wine vinegar or lemon juice.

2 Add the olive oil and season with salt. This will help to bring out the full flavour of the cheese. A little single cream may be added.

Method B

1   Break down the Roquefort cheese into small pieces in a soup plate.

2   With the aid of a large fork, fold the pieces of Roquefort cheese into some sauce mayonnaise.

3   Season with salt to help bring out the flavour.

Acidulated cream dressing

This form of dressing is mainly offered with salads containing fruit, such as orange salad (*salade d'orange*).

Ingredients

■   lemon juice

■   seasoning (salt)

■   jug of single cream

■   paprika.

Method

1   Mix the lemon juice with the seasoning.

2   Add the single cream.

3   Check the taste.

Note: For the preparation of a fresh orange for orange salad, see Fresh Fruit, page 362.

Mustard cream

Ingredients

■   ⅓ litre (½ pt) single cream

■   tablespoon of mustard

■   juice of a lemon

■   seasonings.

Method

1   Place the dry ingredients into the soup plate and blend together.

2   Mix the single cream in slowly and thoroughly to avoid lumps.

3   Add juice of the lemon to taste.

4   Adjust seasoning if necessary.

Lemon dressing

Ingredients

■   two tablespoons of oil

■   fresh lemon juice to taste

■   seasonings.

Method

1   Blend the oil and seasonings well together in a soup plate.

2   Add the fresh lemon juice sparingly.

3   Taste as the dressing is made; the dressing should produce a 'bite' at the back of the throat.

Soups

Clear soup with sherry (consommé aux xérés)

Equipment

■   lamp

■   sauce ladle (but more often a soup ladle as this has more visual appeal).

Ingredients

■   portion of soup in a soup tureen

■   measure of warm sherry (or Madeira etc.) added by the waiter at the guéridon.

Accompaniments

- segments of lemon in a lemon press, placed on a side plate at the head of the cover
- cheese straws are offered and traditionally brown bread and butter.

Cover

- sweet spoon (this is traditional when eating consommé – see Chapter 3, page 88)
- hot consommé cup on consommé saucer on an underplate.

Method

1 Ensure all the mise-en-place is completed before commencing.

2 Present the guéridon at the table and serve from the guéridon.

3 Keep the soup hot on a lamp or hotplate and then ladle/pour into the consommé cups which will be sitting on the consommé saucer on an underplate.

4 The measure of sherry may be warmed and added to the soup at the last moment in the kitchen, or it may be heated in a sauce (or soup) ladle over the lamp, flambéd and then poured over the soup.

5 Serve immediately.

Fish dishes

Grilled or shallow fried sole (sole grillée ou meunière)

Equipment

- lamp
- service spoons and forks on a service plate
- hot joint plate for filleting
- spare plate for dirty cutlery
- spare plate for fish debris.

Ingredients

- silver flat with the sole together with lemon wedges.

Accompaniments

- lemon wedge.

Cover

- fish knife and fork
- hot joint plate.

Method A

1 Ensure all the mise-en-place is completed before commencing.

2 Present the dish to the customer then return to the hot plate or lamp on the guéridon.

3 Remove the fish from the silver flat on to the hot joint plate.

4 With the aid of a service spoon and fork remove the side bones (Figure 8.5a).

5 Run the tip of the spoon down the backbone.

6 Place two large forks back to back at the head of the fish and on the backbone. Press the forks down so that the tips of the forks pierce the flesh on either side of the backbone (Figure 8.5b). Now ease the fillets slowly away from the backbone.

7 Continue to do this working the forks gradually down the backbone towards the tail.

8 Lift out the bone (Figure 8.5c).

9 Place the fillets back together in their original shape on the silver flat. Re-heat as necessary.

10 Coat with beurre fondue or replace garnish and serve.

Method B

1 Steps 1–5 as in A above.

2 Start at the head of the fish and, with the aid of a service spoon and fork, loosen the two top fillets.

3 Hold the fish firmly with the spoon and run the fork down from head to tail between the two top fillets and the backbone.

4 Repeat this with the other two fillets, placing the fork between the bottom fillets and the backbone.

5 Lift out the backbone.

6 Proceed as in steps 9 and 10 in A above.

(a)

(b)

(c)

Fig 8.5. Preparation of a Dover sole

Poached sole (sole pochée)

Equipment

- lamp
- hot joint plate for filleting
- service spoons and forks on a service plate
- two joint forks
- spare plate for dirty cutlery

Ingredients

- sole on a silver flat together with garnishes.

Accompaniments

- according to garnish.

Cover

- fish knife and fork
- hot fish plate or hot joint plate if to be served as a main course.

Method

1 Ensure all the mise-en-place is completed before commencing.

2 Present the dish to the customer then return to the guéridon.

3 Remove the sole from the silver flat on to the hot joint plate.

4   Remove the side bones with the aid of the joint fork.

5   Run the tip of the service spoon down backbone of the sole

6   With the aid of two joint forks, fillet the sole as for sole grillée or meunière,

disturbing the glazed sauce coating the fillets as little as possible.

7   Replace the fillets together in the shape of the fish on the silver flat.

8   Recoat with sauce and serve.

Deep fried sole (sole frite)

Equipment

- lamp
- service spoons and forks on a service plate
- hot joint plate for filleting
- spare plate for debris
- spare plate for dirty cutlery.

Ingredients

- deep fried sole on a dish paper on a silver flat.

Accompaniments

- sauce tartare
- segments of lemon.

Cover

- fish knife and fork
- hot joint plate.

Method

1   Ensure the guéridon is laid up fully before commencing.

2   Present the dish to the customer then return to the guéridon.

3   Lift the sole onto the hot joint plate.

4   Remove the side bones as for grilled sole.

5   Run the point of the spoon down the centre of the sole, from head to tail, making a slight incision.

6   Cut off the tail approximately 2.5 cm (1 in) from the end.

7   Hold the spoon curved side upwards and insert the point between the fillet and the bone at the tail end of the fish.

8   Hold the sole firmly with the fork and push the spoon up towards the head, lifting off one top fillet.

9   Repeat for the other top fillet, and then lift the two loosened top fillets off the backbone.

10   Lift out the backbone.

11   Replace the top fillets on the bottom ones on the silver flat and re-heat and then place onto a hot joint plate for service.

12   Add a garnish of lemon and serve.

Poached or grilled salmon cutlet (darne de saumon poché ou grillé)

Equipment

- lamp
- spare plate for debris
- service spoons and forks on a service plate

- spare plate for dirty cutlery.

Ingredients

- poached or grilled salmon in an earthenware dish plus garnishes.

Accompaniments

■ according to the garnish, for example, Hollandaise, Doria.

Cover

■ fish knife and fork
■ hot fish plate or hot joint plate if to be served as a main course.

Method

This type of dish is generally served in an earthenware dish, and therefore it is not necessary to remove it to a hot joint plate for the skinning and filleting of the darne (thick slice across the bone).

1 Ensure all the mise-en-place is completed before commencing.

2 Present the dish to the customer then return to the lamp or hotplate on the guéridon.

3 Hold the salmon firmly in place with the fork.

4 With the point of the spoon curved side outwards, run round the edge of the darne removing the skin.

5 As an alternative to this method of removing the outer black skin a joint fork may be used, inserting the skin between the prongs of the fork. Twist the fork around the outer edge of the darne and roll the skin up on the fork as you proceed.

6 Insert the point of the spoon between the flesh and the centre bone and push the fillets away from the bone.

7 Remove the bone.

8 Lift the two fillets on to the hot fish plate or joint plate, being careful not to break the flesh, and add the garnish. Serve.

Whole sea bass cooked in a crust of Brittany rock salt (Le bar cuit en crôute de sel du Bretagne)

Equipment

■ hotplate
■ service spoons and forks on a service plate
■ joint knife
■ large fish serving knife (or palate knife)
■ depending on the size of the fish, a hot joint plate or, for larger fish, a board for filleting (the filleting can be done on the serving dish but be careful not to cut down onto the silver)
■ spare plate for dirty cutlery
■ spare plate for fish debris
■ gourmet spoons.

Ingredients

■ serving flat with the sea bass.

Accompaniments

■ none.

Cover

■ fish knife and fork
■ hot joint plate.

Service

1 Ensure all the mise-en-place is completed before commencing.

2 Present the fish to the customer then return to the guéridon and place on the hotplate.

3 Using a joint knife and fork gently break away the salt, being very careful not to touch the skin of the fish. The fork is for leverage and the heel of the knife is used to repeatedly tap the salt hard, in a

straight line along the backbone and belly of the fish. This helps to remove the salt in one single piece.

4   Neatly scrape the salt away making sure that there is clear access to the backbone and belly.

5   Place a service spoon at the top of the sea bass between the head and the body and place the service fork with the prongs inverted under the head (or in the mouth of the fish). Bring the fork upward and the spoon down through the neck to remove the head. Do not discard the head – see below.

6   Using a joint knife, make an incision along the back of the fish from head to tail above the bones and then repeat this around the gut. Trap the tail between the prongs of the fork, flip it upward so that it separates from the body, then discard.

7   Remove the skin by placing the spoon under the top incision, holding the fork on top of the spoon and lifting the skin back towards the belly. Alternatively, use the tip of the knife, loosen the skin from the tail and slightly forward under the rear of the belly, then trap the tail skin between the prongs of the fork, roll to the side and the skin will peel off.

8   Run the serving knife down the line of the fish above the bones to separate the top side and belly fillets, then push the serving knife slightly forwards and the fillet should loosen itself from the main bone – it is then easy to slide the serving knife under to lift.

9   Cut across the fillet at an angle to the size of the portion required.

10 A service spoon and fork may then be used to lift the flesh from the bones.

11 Repeat this process until all the flesh has been removed from the top side and belly fillets.

12 When all the top and belly fillets have been removed, use the joint knife to gently scrape away any gut stuffing and any loose bones, and then use a service spoon and fork to completely remove the bone away from the bottom fillets. To ensure a clean removal of the bone, run the knife along the bone first.

13 Using a service spoon and fork remove any bones that may be left lying on the bottom fillets.

14 Run a knife down the centre of the fish to separate the bottom side and belly fillets.

15 Portion the bottom fillets following the same process as for the top fillets.

16 Arrange the fish portions on joint plates and serve.

17 An additional touch is to remove and serve the cheek meat to the customer. Taking the head, and using the fork for leverage, flip open the gill and remove the cheek meat and place on a gourmet spoon. Then repeat with the other side of the head. Coat the cheek meat with just a touch of the sauce and offer the tasting spoons to the customers.

Note: Although this example is for sea bass, the same method can be applied to all large round fish served whole. In the case of cold whole salmon, points 5 to 16 may be followed, although it is normal practice to present cold salmon, or other round fish served whole, with the skin removed in which case points 8 to 16 should be followed. Although cold salmon and other round cold fish may be presented on their belly, and not their side, the process for filleting and portioning the fish is similar.

Sometimes excess bones can be difficult to see. Resting the blade of the joint knife on the fillet and gently dragging it along the surface can check for this, as the knife will detect any bones.

Blue trout (truite au bleu)

Equipment

- lamp
- filleting knife
- service spoon and fork
- spare plate for dirty cutlery
- spare plate for debris.

Ingredients

- blue trout in an individual copper fish kettle.

Accompaniments

- Hollandaise sauce or beurre fondue.

Cover

- fish knife and fork
- hot fish plate or a hot joint plate if to be served as a main course.

Method

1   Ensure the guéridon is correctly laid up – this dish is normally presented from the kitchen in an individual copper fish kettle.

2   Present the dish to the customer and return to the guéridon.

3   Lift out on a draining tray.

4   Remove the garnish of sliced carrots and onions.

5   With the point of the filleting knife make an incision from the head to tail on the thin line showing on the side of the trout. Cut only the skin, not the flesh.

6   Lift off the skin below that line with the knife and also above the line to the backbone.

7   Turn the fish over and repeat the process of removing the skin on the second side, remembering to remove the fins.

8   Lift the trout carefully onto a hot fish plate or joint plate and decorate with a few slices of carrot and onion. Moisten with a little stock.

9   Serve and then offer the accompaniment.

Flambéed scampi with a cream sauce (scampi à la crème flambée)

Equipment

- lamp
- pan on an underplate
- service plate with service spoons and forks
- spare plate for dirty cutlery.

Ingredients

- dishes of sliced mushrooms and chopped onions
- portion of floured scampi
- glass of sherry, white wine, vermouth or spirit, e.g. brandy, Pernod or whisky, depending on the specific dish
- butter
- oil
- seasonings: salt, peppermill, cayenne pepper and Tabasco sauce on a service plate
- sauce boat of single cream.

Accompaniments

- peppermill.

Cover

- fish knife and fork
- hot fish plate or joint plate if to be served as a main course.

Method

1 Ensure all ingredients and equipment are organised before commencing.
2 Present the guéridon at the table.
3 Place the pan on a slow heat to melt the butter; add a little oil.
4 Sauté the onions lightly and add the mushrooms.
5 Add the scampi and cover. After a short while add the flavouring liquor.
6 Season with salt, peppermill, Tabasco and cayenne.

7 When the scampi are cooked, quickly flambé and then douse with acidulated cream.
8 Reduce the cream and thicken the sauce.
9 Serve onto a hot fish plate or joint plate and offer to the customer.
10 Often the scampi is served on a nest of rice pilaff.

Note:

- This dish has many variations by using different flavouring liquor and flambé spirits.
- It can be combined with fresh fruit to offer a subtle blend of foods – fresh black grapes, pineapple chunks, peaches etc.
- Variations include Scampi Boulvarde, au Pastis or Crêpes.

Steaks

Double Entrecôte steak (Entrecôte double)

Obtained from the boned sirloin.

Equipment

- lamp or hotplate
- pan
- board for portioning the Entrecôte steak
- sharp knife for carving
- service spoons and forks on a service plate
- two side plates for pressing the trimmed ends to extract all the juices
- spare plate for dirty cutlery.

Ingredients

- silver flat with the double Entrecôte steak on it.

Accompaniments

- English and French mustard or alternatively sauce béarnaise.

Cover

- steak knife and joint fork
- hot joint plate.

Method

1 Ensure all the mise-en-place is completed before commencing.
2 Present the dish to the customer then return to the guéridon.
3 Lift the double Entrecôte steak from the silver flat onto the board.
4 Trim the ends.

5   Cut on the slant into two portions. Place back onto the silver flat on the lamp.

6   Press the trimmed ends between two hot side plates, allowing juices extracted to fall over the two portions of steak.

7   Place the portions of steak onto the hot joint plates and add the garnish. Set out attractively.

8   Serve.

9   Offer accompaniments.

Note: This dish is normally offered for two customers. When taking the order the waiter should ask how the customers wish the steak to be cooked. If one customer wants their steak to be rare and the other customer medium, then the steak will come in from the kitchen rare and, once carved, one portion may be cooked a little longer in a pan on the lamp at the table.

Double fillet steak (Chateaubriand)

Method

The cover, accompaniments, equipment required for the guéridon and the method are as for Entrecôte double. However, each portion of the Chateaubriand is carved into approximately two or three slices, each 15 mm (¾ in) thick, rather than being left in one whole piece per portion, as is the case with an Entrecôte double.

Note: Although the Chateaubriand is commonly termed a double fillet steak, it may be large enough to serve a party of two, three, four or five customers as required.

Fig 8.6. Carving of Chateaubriand

'T' bone steak/Porterhouse steak

This is a steak made up of part sirloin and part fillet, the whole being held together by the backbone, with a rib separating the sirloin from the fillet.

Equipment

■ lamp

■ board for carving

■ sharp knife

■ spare plate for debris

■ service spoons and forks on a service plate

■ spare plate for dirty cutlery.

Ingredients

- silver flat containing the Porterhouse steak.

Accompaniments

- English and French mustard.

Cover

- steak knife and joint fork
- hot joint plate.

Method

1 Ensure all the mise-en-place is completed before commencing.

2 Present the dish to the customer then return to the guéridon.

3 Remove from the silver flat onto the carving board.

4 Cut out the 'T' bone to give two separate pieces of meat: one of sirloin and one of fillet.

5 Return the two pieces of meat to the silver flat and place on the lamp to keep hot.

6 Dress attractively on the hot joint plate with the garnish.

7 Serve.

8 Offer accompaniments.

Note: If the Porterhouse steak is for more than one person then carve the fillets as for a chateaubriand and the sirloin as for the double entrecôte.

Steak tartare

Equipment

- soup plate
- service spoons and forks on a service plate
- spare plate for debris
- spare plate for dirty cutlery
- containers for the various ingredients.

Ingredients

- portion of chopped raw fillet steak, moulded into a cake shape and presented on a round silver flat
- one egg yolk
- salt
- chopped gherkins, capers, parsley and shallots
- oil and vinegar
- peppermill
- French mustard
- Worcestershire sauce.

Note: The portion of raw fillet steak is usually welled in the centre to hold a half eggshell with the egg yolk inside. (Some establishments may substitute pasteurised egg for fresh egg yolk.)

Accompaniments

- cayenne pepper
- peppermill.

Cover

- joint knife and fork
- cold joint plate.

Method

1 Ensure the guéridon has all the necessary mise-en-place before proceeding.

2 Present the guéridon at the table.

3 Begin by making the sauce in the bowl in which the dish is to be completed.

4 Put the seasoning of salt, pepper and

French mustard in the soup plate. Mix well.

5 Place the yolk in the soup plate and beat the yolk and seasoning together using a service fork.

6 Add vinegar and mix in, then add a little oil, according to the amount of sauce you wish to make, and mix in.

7 Be careful of the quantity of sauce being made as the finished product should be moist but not runny or too liquid.

8 Add the chopped gherkins, capers, parsley and shallots and bind together well.

9 Now place in the raw chopped fillet steak together with a dash of Worcestershire sauce, incorporating the sauce and fillet steak together well.

10 Taste and adjust seasoning as appropriate.

11 Shape into a round flat cake and place on the cold joint plate.

12 Serve.

Steak Diane

Equipment

- lamp
- pan on an underplate
- service spoons and forks on a service plate
- teaspoons
- plate for dirty cutlery.

Ingredients

- minute steak on a plate
- chopped shallots
- chopped parsley
- fines herbes
- cayenne pepper
- peppermill
- cruet
- oil and butter
- Worcestershire sauce
- measure of brandy
- jug of double cream.

Accompaniments

- Usually none.

Cover

- steak knife and joint fork
- hot joint plate.

Method

1 Ensure the guéridon is correctly laid up with all the mise-en-place.

2 Present the guéridon at the table.

3 Ask the customer how they would like their steak cooked.

4 Place some butter and a little oil in the pan and allow to melt. The oil will prevent the butter from burning.

5 Season the steak with cruet, cayenne pepper and peppermill.

6 Place the chopped shallots in the pan and sweat without colouring until cooked.

7 Place the steak in the pan and cook as required.

8 Add a dash of Worcestershire sauce and then sprinkle with some chopped parsley and fines herbes.

9 Add a measure of brandy and flambé.

10 Serve immediately from the pan onto a hot joint plate at the table.

11 Before serving, if requested, a thickened sauce may be made by the addition of a little double cream. Bring up to simmering point but do not boil.

12 If a sauce is made, the steak must be kept on a hot joint plate on the hotplate and covered while the sauce is being prepared.

13 Coat the steak with the sauce and serve, ensuring it is piping hot.

Note: There are many variations in the making of Steak Diane, each done to an establishment's traditional recipe or being a speciality of the waiter who is making the dish.

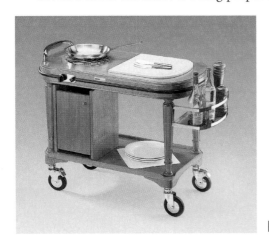

Flambé trolley (courtesy of Steelite International)

Alternative recipe and method for Steak Diane

Equipment

- lamp
- pan on an underplate
- service spoons and forks on a service plate
- teaspoon for the parsley
- plate for placing dirty cutlery.

Ingredients

- olive oil
- butter
- sirloin steak batted out thinly
- French mustard
- Worcestershire sauce
- salt and pepper
- chopped shallots
- sliced mushrooms

- chopped parsley
- small jug of double cream
- one measure of brandy.

Accompaniments

- Usually none.

Cover

- joint knife and fork
- hot joint plate.

Method

1 Ensure the guéridon is correctly laid up with all the mise-en-place.

2 Present the guéridon at the table.

3 Ask the customer how they would like their steak cooked.

4 Season the steak and smear both sides with French mustard.

5 Heat about one sweet spoon of olive oil in a pan.

6 Add a knob of butter just before adding the shallots and mushrooms.

7 Cook shallots and mushrooms until part done.

8 Season the dish with Worcestershire sauce.

9 Move the shallots and mushrooms to the side of the pan.

10 Add the steak and cook on both sides.

11 Flame the dish with the brandy.

12 Add cream to enhance the sauce.

13 Serve from the pan onto a hot joint plate and use a teaspoon to sprinkle the chopped parsley.

Monkey gland steak

Equipment

- lamp
- pan on an underplate
- service spoon and forks
- plate for dirty cutlery
- teaspoons
- timbales for ingredients on a large salver.

Ingredients

- flattened fillet steak on a plate
- chopped shallots
- chopped parsley
- jug of double cream
- measure of whisky
- mustards (French and English)
- garlic (optional)
- salt and pepper
- peppermill
- cayenne pepper
- olive oil
- butter
- Worcestershire sauce.

Accompaniments

- mustards
- tossed salad.

Cover

- joint knife and fork
- hot joint plate.

Method

1 Ensure the mise-en-place is completed before commencing.

2 Present the guéridon at the table.

3 Explain the seasonings to the customer.

4 Melt the butter in the pan and add a little oil.

5 Season the steak and spread with mustard on both sides.

6 Sauté shallots to the 'pearl' stage; add garlic if required.

7 Sauté the steak as required.

8 Season with Worcestershire sauce.

9 Flambé with whisky.

10 Finish with cream and chopped parsley.

11 Serve onto a hot joint plate and place in front of the customer.

12 Offer mustards.

Meat dishes

Beef stroganoff (filet de boeuf stroganoff)

Equipment

- lamp
- pan on an underplate
- service spoons and forks on a service plate
- plate for dirty cutlery
- teaspoons
- timbales for ingredients on a large silver flat.

Ingredients

- fillet steak cut into baton shapes
- chopped shallots
- chopped parsley
- sliced button mushrooms
- chopped chutney (mango)
- jug of double cream
- cayenne pepper
- peppermill
- salt and pepper
- olive oil
- butter
- Worcestershire sauce
- measure of brandy
- garlic (optional)
- fried rice.

Accompaniments

- none.

Cover

- joint knife and fork
- hot joint plate.

Method

1 Ensure the mise-en-place is correct before commencing.
2 Present the guéridon at the table.
3 Explain the seasonings to the customer.
4 Melt the butter in a pan with a little oil.
5 Season the steak.
6 Sauté the shallots to the 'pearl' stage; add garlic if required and the mushrooms.
7 Sauté the steak; season with Worcestershire sauce.
8 Add mango chutney to the desired taste.
9 Flambé with brandy.
10 Finish with double cream and chopped parsley.
11 Serve onto a hot joint plate and place in front of the customer.
12 If fried or savoury rice is to be served then make a nest of rice and place the stroganoff in the centre.

Veal escalope suédoise (escalope de veau suédoise)

Equipment

- lamp
- pan on an underplate
- service spoons and forks on a service plate
- plate for dirty cutlery.

Ingredients

- escalope on a plate
- chopped shallots
- chopped parsley
- French mustard

- orange curaçao
- Worcestershire sauce
- butter
- olive oil
- salt and pepper
- peppermill
- cayenne pepper
- sliced mushrooms
- measure of brandy
- double cream.

Accompaniments

- none.

Cover

- joint knife and fork
- hot joint plate.

Method

1 Ensure the mise-en-place is complete before commencing.

2 Present the guéridon at the table.

3 Melt the butter and add a little oil.

4 Season the escalope.

5 Sauté the onions without colouring, then add the mushrooms.

6 Add the escalope and cook.

7 Season with salt, pepper, cayenne pepper and Worcestershire sauce.

8 Add curaçao without flambéing.

9 Ensure the escalope is cooked and flame with spirit (brandy).

10 Add double cream and adjust the consistency.

11 Serve onto a hot plate and finish with a little chopped parsley.

Joints

All the descriptions for joints are for carving from a carving trolley. Before commencing carving the trolley must be checked to ensure all the mise-en-place has been completed. The trolley is then presented at the table.

For all the joints listed the cover is a joint knife and fork and a joint plate.

Boned sirloin of beef (contrefilet de boeuf)

Accompaniments

- roast gravy (from the trolley)
- Yorkshire pudding (from the trolley)
- English and French mustard and horseradish sauce (placed on the table by the waiter or offered to the customer and served as required).

Note:

- The beef is normally cooked to be a little underdone.
- Beef is carved in thin slices giving mainly lean meat and a little fat per portion.

Sirloin of beef on the bone (aloyau de boeuf)

The accompaniments offered are as for a boned sirloin of beef. The sirloin is comprised of two parts:

- The undercut, which can be removed from the sirloin and may be served separately, either as fillets or tournedos, or larded and roasted. If it is to be carved then this should be done across the joint and not parallel to the side with the grain. A piece of fat should be served with each portion.

■ The uppercut, where the portions should be carved in thin slices down towards the ribs. On reaching a rib-bone the waiter must release the meat attached to the bone by running the knife along and between the bone and the sirloin. This then allows the slices of meat carved to fall free.

Note:

■ Boiled beef is carved with the grain as this prevents shredding. A little cooking liquor should accompany each portion.

■ Ribs of beef are carved in a similar fashion to the uppercut of the sirloin.

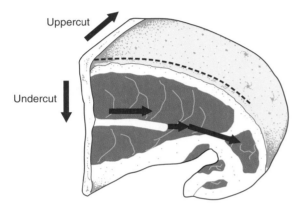

Fig 8.7. Carving a sirloin of beef

Best end of lamb (carré d'agneau)

Accompaniments

■ roast gravy

■ mint sauce

■ redcurrant jelly.

Note: Carve two/three cutlets per portion.

Method A

1 Hold the best end firmly on the board by inserting a service fork into the base at one end.

2 Turn the best end upright.

3 Carve into cutlets using the exposed end of the ribs as a guide to the correct amount per portion.

Method B

1 Lay the best end flat on the board with the exposed end of the ribs pointing downwards.

2 Holding the best end firmly with a service fork and using the exposed ends of the ribs as a guide, carve into cutlets.

Saddle of lamb (selle d'agneau)

Note:

- The loin may be roasted, boned, stuffed, rolled and roasted or may be cut into chops.
- The two loins undivided make up a saddle.

Accompaniments

- roast gravy
- mint sauce
- redcurrant jelly.

Note: There are **two** alternative methods of carving the saddle.

Method A

1 Remove the whole side loin from the saddle.
2 Carve into slices parallel with the ribs and approximately 6 mm (½ in) thick.
3 Serve some lean meat and some fat per portion.

Method B

1 Cut down one side of the backbone reaching approximately halfway along the length of the saddle.

2 Cut right down the side of the backbone to the short ribs.
3 At the point where cutting finishes, halfway along the backbone, turn the knife at right angles and cut down through the meat and fat.
4 Cut out lengths of meat from the saddle, commencing at the backbone, parallel to the backbone where the initial incision was made.
5 Work outwards to the edge of the saddle.
6 Each wedge of meat should then be carved into thin slices lengthwise.

Note:

- With Method A, each customer is given a portion of some lean meat and a little fat.
- With Method B, if the waiter is not careful it is possible for one customer to have a portion of all lean meat and another to receive nearly all fat and very little lean meat.

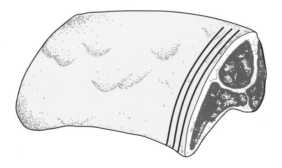

Fig 8.8. Carving a saddle of lamb (method A)

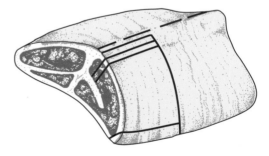

Fig 8.9. Carving a saddle of lamb (method B)

Leg of lamb (gigot d'agneau)

Accompaniments

- roast gravy
- mint sauce
- redcurrant jelly.

Method

1 The waiter should remember that initially he/she should carve onto the bone.

2 Take out a small V-shaped portion of meat just above the knuckle.

3 Proceed to carve the portions of meat by carving on to the bone from the V-shaped cut. This part of the joint is known as the 'nut' and is the most choice part.

4 After the initial portions have been carved from the nut of meat, the succeeding portions should be carved – a slice from the nut and a slice from the underside.

Note:

- When carving a leg of lamb, the waiter should hold the knuckle in a clean napkin to keep it steady on the board.
- The flesh of lamb should be cooked evenly and be rosé (pink) in colour.
- Always cut generously.

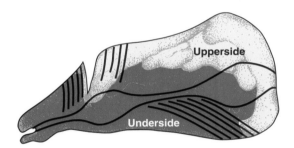

Fig 8.10. Carving a leg of lamb

Leg of pork (cuissot de porc)

Accompaniments

- roast gravy
- apple sauce
- sage and onion stuffing.

Method

- Carved in a similar fashion to a leg of lamb, but the slices carved should be thin.

Ham (jambon)

There are two methods of carving hams:

- *French*: the ham is cut into very thin slices down the length of the ham.
- *English*: the ham is carved at the thick end where the meat is at its most tender.

Note: If the ham is boned and rolled it will then be carved in slices across the fibre of the meat.

Poultry

Roast chicken (poulet rôti)

Equipment

- lamp
- carving board
- sharp carving knife (a filleting knife can also be used)
- service spoons and forks on a service plate
- spare plate for dirty cutlery
- spare plate for debris.

Ingredients

- roast chicken on a silver flat.

Accompaniments

- bread sauce
- roast gravy
- parsley and thyme stuffing
- bacon rolls
- game chips
- watercress.

Cover

- joint knife and fork
- hot joint plate.

Method

1 Ensure all the mise-en-place is completed before commencing.

2 Present the whole chicken to the host at the table, then return to the lamp or hotplate on the guéridon.

3 With the service spoon and fork lift the chicken from the silver flat onto the carving board, draining off any liquid that may be inside.

4 Lay the chicken on its side on the board from right to left in front of you, with a leg uppermost.

5 Holding the bird firmly on the board with the flat of the knife, insert the service fork beneath the leg joint and raise the leg until the skin surrounding it is taut.

6 Cut round the taut skin surrounding the leg with the tip of the knife, at the same time pulling the leg away from the joint and cutting the flesh where necessary.

7 Cut the leg into two pieces through the joint, also removing the claw end.

8 Place the two pieces of leg onto the silver flat.

9 Proceed in the same manner with the other leg.

10 Turn the chicken onto its back. Insert the joint fork into the base of the carcass to hold it firmly.

11 Carve part of the breast and down through the wing joint, giving one piece made up of the wing and a little breast.

12 If necessary turn the chicken on its side and, with the aid of the service fork, lever the wing away from the carcass, at the same time holding the chicken firmly with the flat of the knife.

13 Proceed in the same manner with the other wing.

14 Position the bird on its back. Cut down one side of the breastbone and lever off half the breast.

15 Proceed in the same manner with the other side of the breast.

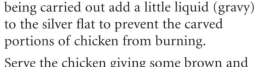

16 An alternative method of removing the breast is by turning the chicken on its side and cutting through the wishbone joints.

17 Turn the chicken onto its breast, holding it firmly in place with the service fork.

18 Insert the knife between the flesh and the wishbone. Holding the whole breast on the board with the knife, lever the carcass away with the aid of the service fork.

19 Cut the whole breast into two portions lengthways.

20 Replace the carved chicken on the lamp. If necessary, while the carving operation is being carried out add a little liquid (gravy) to the silver flat to prevent the carved portions of chicken from burning.

21 Serve the chicken giving some brown and some white meat per portion. Remember to add some game chips, bacon rolls and watercress if these make up the garnish.

Note: Having completed the carving of the chicken, the carcass should be turned over. The 'oyster' piece is found on the underside of the carcass and is a small brown portion of meat found on either side of the back.

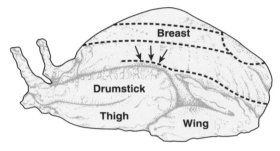

Fig 8.11. Carving a roast chicken

Poussin (young [baby] chicken, six weeks old)

Equipment

- lamp
- carving board
- 16 cm jointing knife
- plate for debris
- service spoons and forks on a service plate
- plate for dirty cutlery.

Ingredients

- Poussin on a silver flat together with the garnish.

Accompaniments

- As per the menu garnish.

Cover

- joint knife and fork
- hot joint plate.

Method

1 Ensure all the mise-en-place is completed before commencing.

2 Present the dish to the customer then return to the guéridon.

3 Lift the poussin from the silver flat onto the carving board with the aid of the service spoon and fork.

4 Insert the service fork into the base of the carcass and hold firmly on the board with the breast uppermost.

5 Using the length of the blade and through the hip joint cut around the carcass keeping the whole side of the poussin intact.

6 Repeat this process on the opposite side.

7 If necessary place the two portions of poussin on the silver flat and re-heat.

8 Present on a hot joint plate, adding and arranging the garnish.

9 Serve accompanying gravy/sauces.

Roast duck (canard rôti)

Equipment

- lamp
- carving board
- sharp carving knife
- service spoons and forks on a service plate
- spare plate for dirty cutlery
- spare plate for debris.

Ingredients

- roast duck on a silver flat.

Accompaniments

- apple sauce
- sage and onion stuffing
- roast gravy.

Cover

- joint knife and fork
- hot joint plate.

Note: Before beginning to carve a duck, remember that the joints are much tighter and more compact than those of a chicken and are therefore more difficult to find and cut through when carving. Also, the wing joints lie a little further under the base of the carcass than those on a chicken.

The initial stages in carving a duck are the same as for a chicken until the legs and wings have been removed.

Method

1 Ensure all the mise-en-place is completed before commencing.

2 Present the dish to the customer then return to the guéridon.

3 Transfer the duck to the carving board using a service spoon and fork.

4 Hold the duck firmly on the carving board with the aid of a joint fork in the base of the carcass.

5 The breastbone on a duck is wide and flat in comparison with that of the chicken. It is therefore easier to remove the complete half breast from the breastbone.

6 Now cut into long thin slices (aiguillettes) on the carving board.

7 Repeat with the other half breast.

8 Dress back onto the silver flat. Reheat if necessary. Serve with the appropriate accompaniments.

Note:

- In the case of a duckling, very often the wing and breast are carved all in one portion.

- When carving the breast, a cut on an angle should be made with the carving knife along the length of the breast. This is because the meat is shallow and to carve straight down onto the flat breastbone would take the edge off the carving knife. This method allows aiguillettes to be carved with the breast still on the carcass.

Note: The carving of wild duck (canard sauvage) is similar to the above, but the accompaniments are orange salad with acidulated cream dressing.

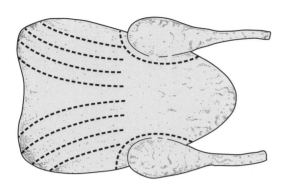

Fig 8.12. Carving a duck

Roast turkey (dindonneau rôti)

Equipment

- lamp
- carving board
- sharp carving knife
- service spoons and forks on a service plate
- spare plate for dirty equipment
- spare plate for debris.

Ingredients

- roast turkey on a silver flat.

Accompaniments

- cranberry sauce
- bread sauce
- chestnut stuffing
- chipolatas
- gravy
- game chips
- watercress.

Cover

- joint knife and fork
- hot joint plate.

Method

1 Ensure all the mise-en-place is completed before commencing.

2 Larger birds are normally served from a carving trolley. The trolley is presented at the table before carving. For smaller birds, which are served on a flat, present the whole turkey to the host at the table then return to the lamp or hotplate on the guéridon. Using the service spoon and fork lift the turkey from the silver flat onto the carving board, draining off any liquid that may be inside.

3 The legs and wings should be separated but not entirely removed from the carcass (i.e. pulled to one side). This is to allow the trancheur to carve thin slices the full length of the body on either side.

4 If possible, carve and serve the stuffing with the slices.

5 As with roast chicken, the dark meat from the legs should be carved and a portion made up of both white and dark meat.

6 Serve with accompaniments.

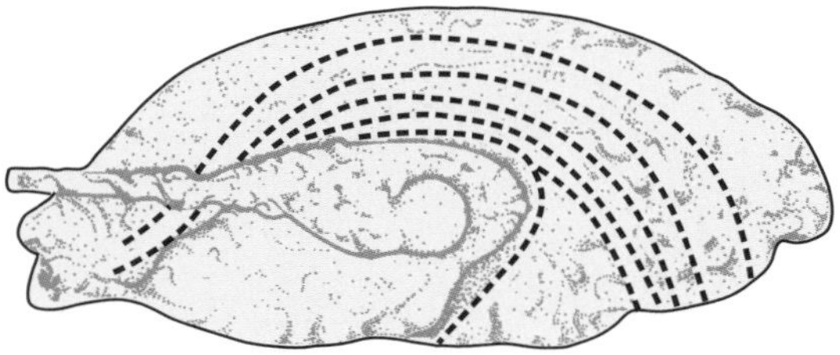

Fig 8.13. Carving a turkey

Flambéed chicken breast (suprême de volaille flambée)

Equipment

- lamp
- pan on an underplate
- service spoons and forks on a service plate
- spare plate for dirty equipment
- butter knife
- sauce ladle.

Ingredients

- prepared suprêmes on a silver flat (if required the suprêmes may be marinated in wine or liqueur beforehand)
- glass of red or white wine
- Drambuie
- double cream in a sauceboat
- butter
- olive oil
- tomato concassé (in a small glass bowl)
- sliced mushrooms (in a small glass bowl)
- finely chopped onions (in a small glass bowl)
- seasonings of salt, pepper, cayenne pepper.

Accompaniments

- none or possibly a side salad.

Cover

- joint knife and fork
- hot joint plate.

Method

1 Ensure all the mise-en-place is completed before commencing.

2 Present the guéridon at the table.

3 Place the pan on a low heat to melt the butter and add a little oil.

4 Season the suprêmes.

5 Sauté the onions to the pearl stage without colouring and add the mushrooms.

6 Add the suprêmes and cook as quickly as possible without browning too much.

7 Add the wine and reduce the liquor.

8 Flambé with Drambuie and add the double cream.

9 Reduce the cream as quickly as possible and finish by combining the tomato concassé with the cream sauce.

10 Serve onto the hot joint plate and offer to the customer.

Note:

- During the cooking time a salad dressing could be prepared, ready to add to the salad once the main course is served.

- There are many variations to this dish, for example, ingredients such as curry powder and other seasonings may be added, and alternative wines and flambé spirit may be used.

Game

Grouse (grouse)

The grouse season is from 12 August to 12 December. Grouse is regarded as a particularly choice dish and if small it is generally served whole. Otherwise it should be split into two portions by carving down through the middle of the breastbone.

Note:

- A larger bird may be carved into three portions as indicated – from either side of the bird remove a leg or wing in one piece. This gives two portions. The third portion is made up of the remainder of the breast separated from the carcass.

- Partridge may be carved in the same fashion (see below).

Partridge (perdeau)

The partridge season is from 1 September to 1 February. Depending on its size the partridge may be carved into two or three portions. If large, the three portions would consist of:

1 one leg and one wing with a little of the breast attached

2 as above

3 the breast left on the bone.

If small the partridge should be split into two portions by carving down through the breast-bone.

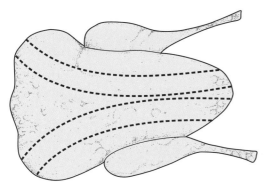

Fig 8.14. Carving a partridge or grouse

Woodcock (bécasse)

The woodcock season is from 1 August to 1 March. It is split into two portions as for grouse or partridge. Generally woodcock is served on a croûte spread with a pâté made from the giblets of the woodcock.

Snipe (bécassine)

The snipe season is from 1 August to 1 March. Snipe are served whole as they are too small for carving into portions.

Pheasant (faisan)

The pheasant season is from 1 October to 1 February. The flesh of the pheasant is very dry and the waiter should use a very sharp knife. Remove the legs as for chicken or duck. These are normally not served. Carve in thin slices on either side of the breast down to the wing joint. The wing is not normally removed as a separate portion.

Wood pigeon (pigeon)

The wood pigeon season is from 1 August to 15 March. Wood pigeon is carved in half through the breast to give two portions.

Saddle of hare (selle de lièvre)

The season is from 1 August to 28 February. Saddle of hare is carved in slices lengthwise as in a saddle of lamb. The flesh is dark in colour.

Sweet dishes

Peach flambé (pêche flambée)

Equipment

- lamp
- pan on an underplate
- matches
- spare plate for dirty cutlery
- service spoons and forks on a service plate.

Ingredients

- measure of brandy
- caster sugar
- portions of warmed peaches in peach syrup in a timbale.

Accompaniments

- caster sugar.

Cover

- sweet spoon and fork
- hot sweet plate.

Method

1 Ensure all the mise-en-place is completed before commencing.
2 Present the guéridon at the table.
3 Place the peach syrup in the pan and heat.
4 Add the portion of peaches.
5 Pierce the peaches with a fork to allow the heat to penetrate more quickly.

6 Baste the peaches occasionally, allowing the peach syrup to reduce right down until it is almost caramelised.
7 At this stage sprinkle with caster sugar. This speeds up the caramelising effect and aids flambéing.
8 Ensure the hot sweet plate is now placed in front of the customer.
9 Pour over the brandy and flambé.
10 Serve from the pan onto hot sweet plates at the table, or serve onto hot sweet plates at the flambé trolley.

Pear flambé (poire flambée)

As above but using pears and pear syrup.

Banana flambé (banane flambée)

Method A

Equipment

- lamp
- pan on an underplate
- service spoons and forks on a service plate
- spare plate for dirty cutlery
- carving board
- small carving knife (12.5 cm/5 in).

Ingredients

- banana
- measure of rum (or Pernod depending on the specific dish)
- butter
- caster sugar
- fresh orange juice (optional).

Accompaniments

- caster sugar.

Cover

- sweet spoon and fork
- hot sweet plate.

Method

1 Ensure all the mise-en-place is completed before commencing.
2 Present the guéridon at the table.
3 Prepare the banana as explained on page 362.
4 Place the butter in the pan and melt.
5 Pierce both halves of the banana with a fork to allow the heat to penetrate more quickly.
6 Place the banana round side down in the pan and heat. Baste with the butter occasionally and then turn the banana over.
7 When golden brown add a little fresh orange juice and blend well. This produces the sauce and removes the surplus fat from within the sauce.

8 At this stage place the hot sweet plate on the table in front of the customer.

9 When heated sufficiently, flambé with the rum.

10 Serve at the table from the pan onto the hot sweet plate, or serve onto a hot sweet plate on the flambé trolley.

Note: Be careful not to overheat the banana at any stage, as it will become too soft.

Method B

Equipment

- lamp
- pan on an underplate
- matches
- service spoons and forks on a service plate
- spare napkins
- sauce ladle
- spare plate for dirty equipment
- small carving board
- small sharp knife.

Ingredients

- one portion of banana
- three sauce ladles full of fresh orange juice in a sauceboat
- creamed mixture: 40 g Demerara sugar and 40 g butter
- one measure of dark rum.

Accompaniments

- caster sugar.

Cover

- sweet spoon and fork
- hot sweet plate.

Method

1 Ensure all the mise-en-place is complete before commencing.

2 Present the guéridon at the table.

3 Place the pan on a low heat, add the creamed mixture and allow to melt and colour slightly.

4 Place the banana on a carving board and remove the skin, as described on page 362.

5 Split the banana in two lengthways.

6 Pierce the banana to allow the heat to penetrate.

7 Add the orange juice to the pan and blend together well to produce a clear smooth sauce.

8 Place the banana in a pan – rounded side down.

9 Heat quickly, baste and turn over.

10 Sprinkle with caster sugar and heat well.

11 Place the hot sweet plate in front of the customer.

12 Flambé with rum.

13 Serve from the pan onto the hot sweet plate at the guéridon or at the table.

Cherries flambé with Kirsch (cerises flambées au Kirsch)

Equipment

- lamp
- pan on an underplate
- service spoons and forks on a service plate
- spare plate for dirty cutlery.

Ingredients

- portion of cherries in syrup in a timbale
- measure of Kirsch
- caster sugar.

Accompaniments

■ caster sugar.

Cover

■ sweet spoon and fork

■ hot sweet plate.

Method

1 Ensure all the mise-en-place is completed before commencing.

2 Present the guéridon at the table.

3 Place the cherries and cherry syrup into the pan and heat.

4 Reduce the cherry syrup to a minimum.

5 Sprinkle with caster sugar to help caramelise the remaining syrup and as an aid to flambéing.

6 Place the hot sweet plate on the table in front of the customer.

7 Add the Kirsch and flambé.

8 Serve at the table from the pan onto a hot sweet plate or serve onto a hot sweet plate on the flambé trolley.

Cerises flambées au glace vanille

As above with the vanilla ice cream served immediately before the cerises flambées.

Cherries jubilées (cerises jubilées)

Equipment

■ lamp

■ pan on an underplate

■ service spoons and forks on a service plate

■ spare plate for dirty cutlery.

Ingredients

■ portion of cherries in syrup in a timbale

■ measure of brandy

■ caster sugar.

Accompaniments

■ caster sugar.

Cover

■ sweet spoon and fork

■ hot sweet plate.

Method

1 Exact timing is required to serve this dish correctly, so it is important to ensure that the flambé trolley has the correct mise-en-place before commencing.

2 Present the guéridon at the table.

3 Light the lamp. Place the portion of cherries in the syrup in the pan and heat up to simmering point.

4 Allow the syrup to reduce quickly until almost caramelised.

5 When the syrup is reduced to a minimum, sprinkle with caster sugar. This is an aid to flambéing and speeds up caramelisation.

6 The measure of brandy is now added to the cherries and they are flambéed.

7 Serve immediately from the pan onto a hot sweet plate, either at the guéridon or at the table.

Rum omelette (omelette au rhum)

Equipment

- lamp
- pan on an underplate
- matches
- service spoons and forks on a service plate
- spare plate for dirty cutlery.

Ingredients

- measure of rum
- caster sugar
- omelette received from the kitchen on a silver flat at the last moment. The omelette should be cooked baveuse (firm outside and runny inside).

Accompaniments

- caster sugar.

Cover

- sweet spoon and fork
- hot sweet plate.

Method

1 Ensure all the mise-en-place is completed before commencing.
2 Present the omelette to the customer then return to the lamp on the guéridon.
3 Trim the ends of the omelette with the aid of a service spoon and fork.
4 Sprinkle with caster sugar.
5 Pour a measure of rum round the edge of the flat.
6 Heat quickly and light with a match.
7 Serve immediately onto a hot sweet plate at the table or the guéridon trolley.

Strawberries Romanoff (fraises Romanoff)

Equipment

- two large glass bowls
- service spoons and forks on a service plate
- spare plate for dirty cutlery.

Ingredients

- portion of strawberries (250 gms for two portions)
- measure of Curaçao (or Cointreau or Grand Marnier)
- 25 g caster sugar
- half a lemon (or orange)
- 200 ml double cream (or Chantilly cream).

Accompaniments

- caster sugar.

Cover

- sweet spoon and fork
- glass bowl on an underplate or cold sweet plate.

Method A

Preparation

1 Rinse the strawberries and pat dry with kitchen paper or cloth.
2 Taste a strawberry to see how sweet it is – this will help in determining how much lemon juice to add.
3 Reserve two whole strawberries.
4 Halve and hull the remainder of the strawberries.
5 Put the cut strawberries into a bowl and sprinkle with the liqueur, a little fresh

lemon juice and 25 g of caster sugar, then set aside to chill and macerate.

6 Whip the double cream in a glass bowl (with vanilla essence and caster sugar for Chantilly cream) to firm peaks.

At the guéridon

7 Ensure all the mise-en-place is completed before commencing.

8 Present the guéridon at the table.

9 At the guéridon, stir the strawberries in the bowl to make sure they are fully coated in the marinade.

10 Spoon the strawberries into two small glass bowls (cooled) and top with whipped cream and a decorative strawberry.

Method B
Preparation
As for Method A stages 1 to 4.

At the guéridon

5 Ensure all the mise-en-place is completed before commencing.

6 Present the guéridon at the table.

7 In a glass bowl, pour the liqueur to be used together with the lemon juice (depending on the sweetness of the strawberries) over the strawberries and allow to macerate for a few minutes.

8 Whisk the double cream in a glass bowl with two forks until it thickens.

9 Remove two-thirds of the strawberries plus the liquid into a glass bowl.

10 Add the thickened double cream a little at a time until the mixture is firm.

11 Set on to a cold sweet plate and decorate the top with the remaining strawberries. Sprinkle with a little caster sugar and serve.

Note: Alternatives are:

- Eton Mess – flavoured with curaçao and lemon juice, strawberries are cut in smaller pieces and folded into the whipped cream.

- Fraises royale – flavoured with Van der Hum, Kirsch and orange juice.

- Pêches à la royale – strawberries and peaches combined with brandy and cream.

Pineapple flambé (ananas rafraîchi au Kirsch flambé)

Equipment

- lamp
- pan on an underplate
- service spoons and forks on a service plate
- spare plate for dirty cutlery
- carving board
- carving knife (at least 20 cm/8 in).

Ingredients

- fresh whole pineapple with a small jug of sugar syrup or tinned pineapple slices with jug of syrup from the tin

- cherries for garnish
- measure of Kirsch
- butter
- caster sugar.

Accompaniments

- caster sugar.

Cover

- hot fruit plate or sweet plate
- fruit knife and fork or a sweet spoon and fork.

Method

1 Ensure all the mise-en-place is completed before commencing.

2 Present the guéridon at the table.

3 If the pineapple is fresh, prepare as per instructions on page 354.

4 Place the sugar syrup in the pan and heat.

5 Pierce the pineapple with a fork to allow the heat to penetrate more quickly.

6 Place the portion of prepared pineapple into the heated sugar syrup.

7 Allow to heat quickly, reducing the liquid to the stage where it is almost caramelised.

8 At this point sprinkle well with caster sugar. This helps caramelise the sugar syrup and aids flambéing.

9 Place the hot fruit or sweet plate in front of the customer on the table.

10 Pour Kirsch over the pineapple, allow to heat, then flambé.

11 Serve onto the hot fruit or sweet plate from the pan, at the table.

Crêpes Suzette

Equipment

- lamp
- pan on an underplate
- service spoons and forks on a service plate
- two teaspoons on a side plate
- two sweet forks on a side plate
- oval flat with three sauceboats for the creamed mixture, orange juice and lemon juice
- brandy and liqueur glass on an underplate
- one bottle of Orange Curaçao
- one bottle of brandy
- two hot sweet plates.

Ingredients
(For two portions)

- 85 g (3 oz) caster sugar
- 85 g (3 oz) butter
- half lemon
- zest of two oranges
- one measure of Orange Curaçao
- one measure of brandy
- four pancakes on an oval flat.

Accompaniments

- none.

Cover

- sweet spoon and fork
- hot sweet plate.

Method

1 Ensure all the mise-en-place is completed before commencing.

2 Present the guéridon at the table.

3 Pour out the required measure of liqueur and spirit.

4 Place the creamed mixture of caster sugar, butter and zest into the pan and melt. Allow to colour slightly to a light golden shade.

5 Add three sauce ladles of orange juice and blend well.

6 Add the juice of half a lemon if required, according to taste.

7 Add one measure of Orange Curaçao.

8 Mix well, stirring with a large fork, then taste.

9 Add the pancakes, one at a time, heat well, turn over and then fold.

10 During this process the sauce should be reducing all the time and thickening.

11 When the sauce is reduced sufficiently, add the measure of brandy and flambé.

12 Serve onto the hot sweet plates from the pan, at the table or at the guéridon trolley.

Fresh fruit

Prepared on the guéridon at the table. For the preparation of fresh melon see page 313.

Equipment

- small very sharp knife
- sweet fork
- fruit plate
- spare plate for dirty cutlery
- small glass dish
- cutting board
- service spoons and forks on a service plate
- spare plate for debris
- spare napkin
- apple corer.

Ingredients

Will depend on the fruit being prepared, for example:

- fresh dessert apples or pears on a plate

or

- fresh ripe but firm bananas on a plate

or

- two oranges on a plate

or

- whole fresh pineapple on a plate.

Accompaniments

- caster sugar
- measure of dark rum, Kirsch or other spirits or liqueurs as requested by the customer and to accompany the dish ordered.

Cover

- fruit knife and fork or sweet spoon and fork or small (sweet) fork depending on how and when to be served
- fruit plate
- finger bowl on a doily on a side plate and filled with lukewarm water and a slice of lemon
- spare napkin.

Service notes

1 The equipment, ingredients and accompaniments listed above, together with the cover, may vary slightly depending on the specific requirements of the customer.

2 Before commencing ensure that all the mise-en-place is completed.

3 Present the guéridon at the table.

4 Present the fruit to the customer at the table then return to the guéridon.

Apple or pear (pomme ou poire)

Method

1 Cut a cone from the top of the apple or pear around the stalk approximately 2.5 cm in diameter and put aside for later use (Figure 8.15a).

2 Cut the base of the apple or pear.

3 Place a fork into the top of the apple or pear where the stalk cone was removed from.

4 Peel the apple in strips from top to bottom or in a spiral from top to bottom (Figure 8.15b or c).

5 Cut the apple into two then into quarters (Figure 8.15d).

6 Remove the core from each quarter (Figure 8.15e).

7 Decorate on the plate using the stalk cone to garnish (Figure 8.15f).

8 Dress with spirit or liqueur should the customer request it.

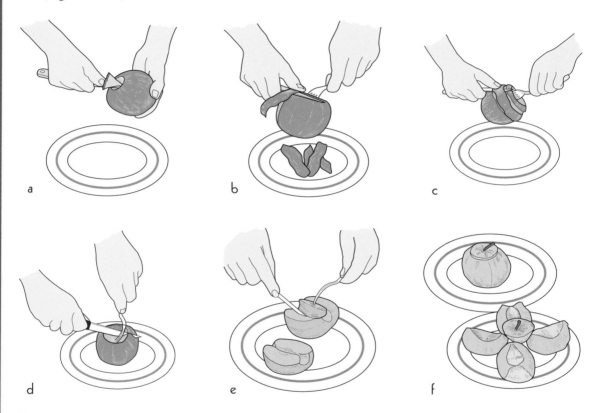

a   b   c

d   e   f

Fig 8.15. Preparation of an apple

Banana (banane)

Method

1 Remove the end of the banana (Figure 8.16a).

2 Slice through the banana and through the stalk lengthways, using the fork to steady the banana, to give two even slices (Figure 8.16b).

3 Insert the end of the banana skin between the prongs of a joint fork and carefully roll back away from the flesh, using your knife on the outside of the skin to keep the half banana firmly held on the board. (Figure 8.16c). Care should be taken here to ensure the flesh of the banana does not become broken.

4   Dress with dark rum if requested. Present
    neatly on the cold fruit plate.

a   b   c

Fig 8.16. Preparation of a banana

Orange (orange)

Method

1   Cut a slice from one end of the orange
    with the aid of the sharp knife.

2   Pierce the cut slice with the fork to act as a
    guard when sectioning the whole orange.

3   Now pierce the whole orange with the fork
    from the uncut end, so that it is firmly
    held on the fork.

4   Make an incision around the uncut end of
    the whole orange through the skin to the
    flesh (through the rind and pith).

5   Remove the peel and pith by cutting strips
    from the cut end to the incision made
    around the orange (Figures 8.17a and b).

6   At this stage you should have a whole
    orange on the fork with the peel and pith
    removed.

7   Holding the orange over the glass bowl,
    cut out each segment of the orange
    leaving the pith on the fork. Let the
    segments of orange fall into the glass bowl
    (Figure 8.17c).

8   With the aid of a second fork, squeeze the
    pith over the glass bowl to remove all the
    juice.

9   Sprinkle with caster sugar.

10 Dress onto the fruit plate and serve
    (Figure 8.17d).

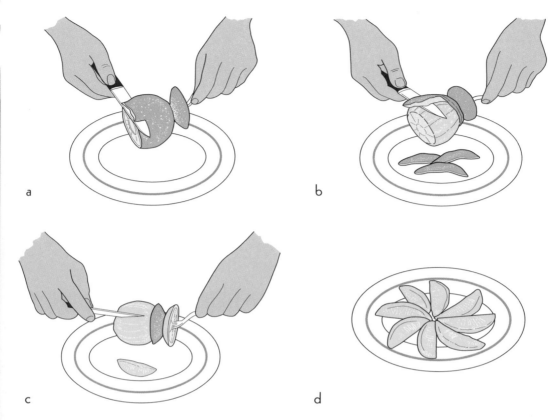

Fig 8.17. Preparation of a orange

Pineapple (ananas)

Method

1 Hold the pineapple by the stem and remove the base of the pineapple.

2 Peel the pineapple in strips from top to bottom (Figure 8.18a) or cut the pineapple peel in a spiral from bottom to top (Figure 8.18b).

3 Remove the eyes by cutting a V-shaped channel. Note that each channel should go from left to right as this will give a less complex spiral that does not all run into one (Figure 8.18c).

4 Cut round the core using the point of a paring knife, either before slicing the pineapple (Figure 8.18d) or after slicing it (Figure 8.18e).

5 Remove the core from the sliced pineapple (Figure 8.18f).

6 Dress with Kirsch if requested. Present neatly onto the cold fruit plate.

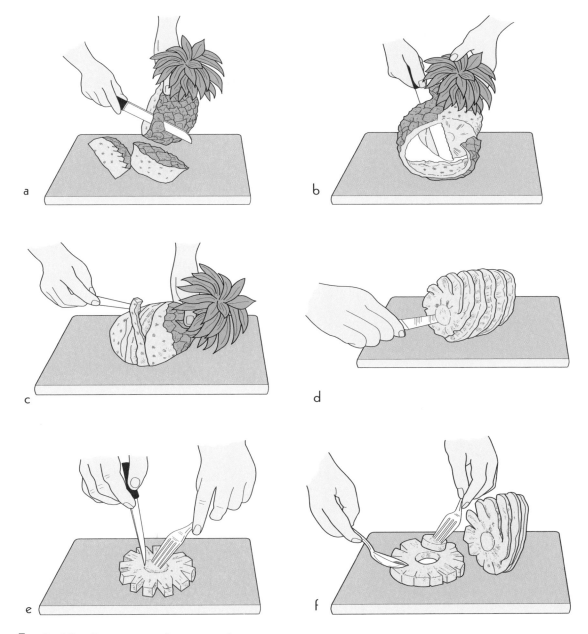

a

b

c

d

e

f

Fig 8.18. Preparation of a pineapple

FUNCTION CATERING

9.1 INTRODUCTION

Function catering is the term used for the service of special events for specific groups of people at pre-set times, with the food and beverages provided being pre-determined. It includes occasions such as luncheon parties, conferences, cocktail parties, weddings and dinner-dances. In larger establishments all functions take place within the banqueting suites and are under the administrative control of the banqueting manager. In the smaller operation these functions normally take place in rooms set aside for the purpose and come under the jurisdiction of the manager or assistant manager. There are also specialist banqueting conference centres. Most of the staff available for functions are employed on a casual basis. At busy periods there may be a number of functions running at the same time.

Fig 9.1. The Palm Court at the Waldorf Hilton Hotel, London, laid for a function (courtesy of FCSI, UK)

Functions are as popular as ever but their purpose and style is changing. Theme evenings, for example, are becoming increasingly popular. There is also a trend towards less formality. At the same time, guests have higher expectations of the overall standard of décor, lighting effects and tableware used, as well as higher standards of food, beverages and comfort.

Types of function

There are two main types of function:

Formal meals (sometimes called banquets)

- luncheons
- dinners
- wedding breakfasts.

Buffet receptions

- wedding receptions
- dances
- cocktail parties
- anniversary parties
- buffet teas
- conferences.

A further breakdown of the types of function may be as follows:

- *Social*
  - dinners (trade associations)
  - luncheons (Rotarians)
  - receptions
  - cocktail parties
  - charity dinners.

- *Conferences*
  - political conferences
  - trade union
  - training seminars
  - sales conferences
  - academic conferences.

- *Public relations*
  - – press party to launch a new product
  - – fashion parade
  - – exhibition
  - – dealer's meetings
  - – seminars.

Function service staff and responsibilities

In larger establishments there is generally a small number of permanent staff dealing solely with functions. This often includes a sales manager, banqueting/function manager, assistant managers, banqueting/function headwaiters, service staff, technical staff and porters together with an administration office. In smaller establishments, where there are fewer functions, the manager, assistant manager and food and beverage service staff undertake the administrative and organisational work as part of their regular duties.

Sales manager

The main role of the sales manager is to promote the function facilities of an establishment and, where necessary, to make the initial approaches and contacts. The sales manager must have an extensive knowledge of room specifications, size, light switches, electric points, height of doorways, maximum floor loads and so on. This enables him/her to respond quickly to any requests at the initial meeting with a client. Most establishments have various forms of banqueting and/or meetings and conference sales packages (see page 360) and these provide a range of information about the facilities available and the charges for them.

Banqueting/conference manager

The banqueting/conference manager is responsible for all administration, including meeting prospective clients and discussing the arrangements for the menu, table plans, costs, wines, band, toastmaster and so on. He/she must communicate to all the departments concerned the date of a function, numbers expected and any other details that might be required by a particular department.

Administration office staff

The administration staff work with the managers and are responsible for handling all incoming and outgoing mail, ensuring that information about a function is passed to the relevant internal departments and for record keeping. The administrative staff handle inquiries and may take provisional bookings for functions, ensuring the details are entered on the function booking form (see page 361).

Banqueting/function headwaiter

The banqueting/function headwaiter is in charge of the function rooms plus the organisation required to prepare the rooms for various functions. He/she may also be responsible for engaging staff, on a casual basis, to cover the various duties at a function.

Dispense bar staff

The dispense bar staff are responsible for the allocation of bar stock for the various functions, setting up the bars, organisation of the bar staff, control of stock and cash during service and stocktaking after a function has taken place. They are also responsible for restocking the function bars.

Banqueting head wine waiter

The banqueting head wine waiter may work in conjunction with the dispense bar staff and is often responsible for organising and employing (if on a casual basis) the banqueting wine waiters. He/she will allocate the wine waiters' stations, give them floats if there are cash wines and discuss the service with them.

Permanent service staff

The permanent service staff are usually experienced staff who can turn their hand to any job concerning functions and banqueting. They generally do most of the mise-en-place before the function (the laying of tables etc.).

Casual staff

Casual staff are brought in on a part-time basis to work at the functions as needed.

Porters

There are generally a number of porters on the permanent function staff. They are essential members of staff as there is often a great deal of work involved in preparing room layouts before and after functions.

9.2 FUNCTION ADMINISTRATION

Function sales

In order to promote the sale of functions (meetings/conferences/banquets etc.) most establishments now have banqueting and/or meetings and conference sales packages. These range from the very simple to the elaborate and complex, depending on the nature of the establishment. Examples of the content often included in these types of packages are:

- Location and contact details of the establishment and the staff involved.
- Examples and descriptions of the type of functions that can be accommodated.
- Information on how to get to the establishment, local attractions and availability of car parking.
- Examples and costs of set packages, for example, for conference delegates this might be day rates, overnight rates and meal rates.

- Room plans indicating size, possible layouts, availability of services (electric sockets, telephone points), air conditioning, access points, maximum weight the floor will take etc.
- Provision for disabled visitors.
- Room hire charges.
- List and description of styles of tables and chairs and other equipment available (e.g. meeting tables, conference chairs, lounge areas, technical equipment such as public address systems, video players and TV monitors, flip chart stands and paper, lecterns, overhead, slide and data projectors, computers, white boards, blackout curtains, double glazing and sound proofing).
- Charges for additional equipment such as projectors etc.
- Availability of room decoration, flowers, lighting systems.
- Availability of disco, resident bands, presenters, Masters of Ceremony, Toast Masters etc.
- Examples of meal packages such as a range of set menus, snack menus, conference lunches, and also details of the service methods available, such as formal table service, buffets, in-room service etc.
- Other services such as car rental, limousine services, private bus services, catwalks, business services and other services of the establishment such as restaurants and fitness and leisure facilities.
- Standard terms and conditions of bookings.

Booking and administrative procedures

When the client is ready to make a booking a file is opened. The file will contain the client's details and will be used to hold all the requirements for the particular function, as well as all correspondence sent and received. At the meeting when the booking is confirmed a function booking form will be completed. The basic information that is recorded is shown below.

- Date and time of function (including access and clear down times).
- Client details.
- Type of function.
- Location of function within the establishment.
- Food and beverage requirements.
- Service methods (including wines and drinks being inclusive or cash).
- Expected number of people attending (and confirmation of final deadline for actual numbers attending).
- Table plan.
- Price being charged (e.g. inclusive or per head).
- Inclusive or cash bar and wines.
- Provision for guests with special needs.

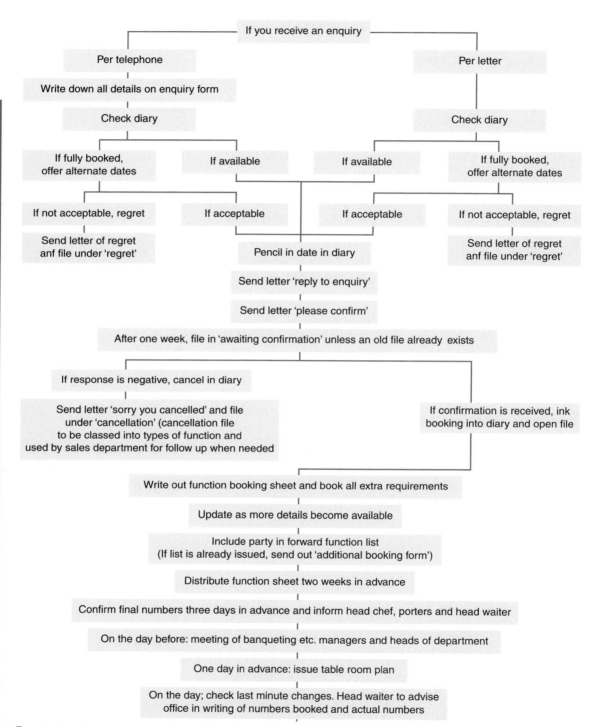

Fig 9.2. Summary of function administration procedures

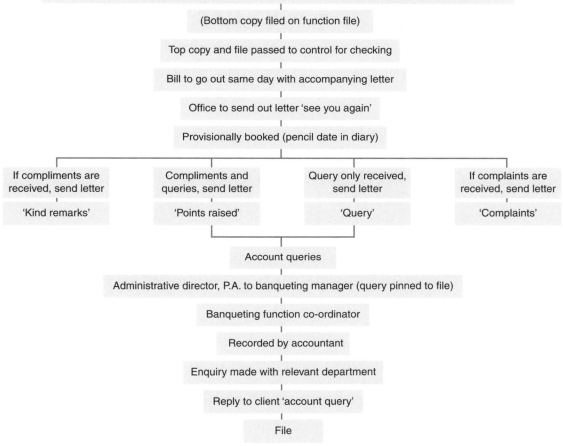

On the day after: invoice to be handed to the banqueting function co-ordinator plus function checks from: manager, head waiter, bar man: checks from flower shop; charges for audio/visual; charges for security and other charges. Used to compile and complete function account

(Bottom copy filed on function file)

Top copy and file passed to control for checking

Bill to go out same day with accompanying letter

Office to send out letter 'see you again'

Provisionally booked (pencil date in diary)

If compliments are received, send letter	Compliments and queries, send letter	Query only received, send letter	If complaints are received, send letter
'Kind remarks'	'Points raised'	'Query'	'Complaints'

Account queries

Administrative director, P.A. to banqueting manager (query pinned to file)

Banqueting function co-ordinator

Recorded by accountant

Enquiry made with relevant department

Reply to client 'account query'

File

Fig 9.2. continued

- Additional charges for equipment hire etc.
- Contractual requirements (deposit payments, payment in advance etc.).

The requirements for a function will depend upon the nature of the function and it is useful to have a checklist of these. In addition to the information listed above, the following might also be considered:

- overnight accommodation
- list of toasts
- date for final inspection visit by client
- floral decor for the tables, rooms, reception area and button holes

- telephones
- security
- lectern
- marketing
- secretarial facilities

- toastmaster
- audio-visual equipment
- syndicate/breakout/interview rooms
- band, cabaret, dancing (and meal requirements)
- photographer
- place cards
- special liquor licence

- music, dancing or entertainment licences
- sign-posting
- seating plan
- car parking
- private bar facilities
- cloakrooms
- function cancellation policies.

An example of a summary of the administrative procedures for functions is given in Figure 9.2.

9.3 FUNCTION ORGANISATION

Function menus

There should be a varied choice of menu within a wide price range, with special menus available for occasions such as weddings, twenty-first birthday parties and New Year's Eve. The number of courses at a banquet is normally four, plus beverages, but can be many more, and often include:

1 hors-d'oeuvre or other appetisers

2 soup or fish

3 meat – with a selection of seasonal vegetables

4 sweet

5 coffee or tea – with a selection of petits fours.

This approach is generally popular, but extra or alternative courses such as entrées, cheese or savouries may be added. The sequencing of courses is detailed in Chapter 3, pages 70–72.

Wines

The banqueting wine list is often smaller than the main wine list of an establishment but usually contains a selection of good wines from the main wine list. Wines may be inclusive with the meal or on a cash basis, the money being payable to the sommeliers who may work on a float system. Very often the apéritif served before a function is also inclusive with the meal but if not, there may be a cash bar set up in the reception area.

Service methods in function catering

For functions the service method may take any of the following forms (see pages 17–19 for definitions of service methods):

- silver
- plate
- self-service

- family
- assisted service.

The type of service method chosen is usually determined by the:

- host's wishes
- equipment available
- type of function
- foods and beverages to be served
- time available for the function
- skills of the service staff available.

Formal seating arrangements

Of the total number of people attending a function it must be determined how many will be seated on the top table and how many on the sprigs, round or oblong tables that make up the full table plan. It must be known whether the number on the top table includes the ends of the table, and care is normally taken to avoid seating 13 people on this table.

All tables, with the exception of the top table, are numbered, again usually avoiding using the number 13. In its place 12A may be used or the number 13 just left out. Using letters of the alphabet for the table designation rather than numbers can avoid this problem. The table numbers themselves are usually on stands of such a height that they may all be seen from the entrance of the banqueting room, the approximate height of the stands being 75 cm (30 in). After the guests are seated, and before the service commences, these stands are usually removed. However, if they are left on the table then they can provide an aid to the sommeliers when checking for cash wines.

Table seating plans

It is common now for table seating plans to be produced in two main ways:

- An alphabetical list of the people attending, giving an indication of the table, or location on a sprig, where the person has been seated.
- A listing of the people attending by table, showing all the people seated on a particular table or section of a sprig.

Before the function three copies of each of the two-table seating plans are made. These go to:

- *The organiser*: before the function so that he/she may check all necessary arrangements.
- *The guests*: the table seating plans should be placed in a prominent position in the entrance of the banqueting suite so that all guests may see where they have been seated, the position of their table in the room, and who else is sitting at the same table or section of a sprig.
- *The banqueting manager*: for reference purposes.

Table layout

The type of table layout used for a particular function will depend upon a number of factors, including the:

- organiser's wishes
- nature of the function
- size and shape of the room where the function is to be held
- number of covers attending.

For the smaller type of function a U- or T-shaped table may be used. Where the luncheon or dinner party is more formal there may be a top table and separate tables (round or rectangular) for the various parties of guests. Where the function to be held has a very large number of covers, then the generally accepted form of table plan is a top table and sprigs.

However, before these various table plans can be shown to the organiser when a function is being booked, careful consideration must be given to spacing, i.e. widths of covers, gangways, size of chairs and so on. This is to allow a reasonably comfortable seating space for each guest and, at the same time, to give the waiters sufficient room for the service of the meal. Also the gangway space must be such that two waiters may pass one another during the service without fear of any accident occurring.

The general considerations for table spacing are:

- Minimum space between sprigs should be 2 m (6 ft). This is made up of two chair widths (from the edge of the table to the back of the chair (46 cm or 18 in)) plus a gangway of 1 m (3 ft), allowing each waiter sufficient passing space: total of 2 m (6 ft).
- Table widths are approximately 75 cm (2 ft 6 in).
- The length along the table per cover should be 50–60 cm (20–24 in).
- The space from the wall to the edge of the table should be a minimum of 1.4 m (4 ft 6 in). This is made up of a 1 m (3 ft) gangway, plus one chair of width 46 cm (18 in).
- The height of the chair from the ground will vary according to the style and design, but is approximately 46–50 cm (18–20 in).
- The length of the table used is generally 2 m (6 ft) but 1.2 and 1.5 m lengths (4 and 5 ft) may be used to make up a sprig.
- Round tables are 1.0, 1.5 or 2 m (3, 5 or 6 ft) in diameter with the appropriate extensions.
- Suggested area allowance for sit-down functions per person is approximately $1.0–1.4$ m^2 (12–15 sq ft); for buffets the allowance is $0.9–1.0$ m^2 (10–12 sq ft).

Examples of banquet layouts

Top table and sprigs

Function for 110 covers: 15 guests on top table; 3 sprigs required.
Dimension of room $=$ 18 m (60 ft) long by 11 m (36 ft) wide.

Method of working

1 Length of table required for top table:
   15 guests $\times$ 60 cm (2 ft) cover width $=$ 9 m (30 ft) or 5 $\times$ 2 m (6 ft) tables.

2 Number of covers on each sprig:
   110 covers $-$ 15 covers on top table $=$ 95 covers
   95 covers $\div$ 3 sprigs $=$ sprigs of 32, 32 and 31 covers
   Therefore, each side of a sprig will have 16 covers, except one, which will have 15 covers.

3 Length of sprig:
   16 covers $\times$ 60 cm (2 ft) cover width $=$ 9.7 m (32 ft) or 5 $\times$ 2 m (6 ft) tables.

4 To check if three sprigs may be fitted on top table:
   3 sprigs × 75 cm (2 ft 6 in) (width) = 2.25 m (7 ft 6 in)
   2 gangways × 1 m (3 ft) (width) = 2 m (6 ft)
   4 chair depths 46 cm (18 in) = 2 m (6 ft)
   Total = 6.25 m (19 ft 6 in)
   Thus, there is plenty of room (see Figure 9.3).

This layout also allows for five extra covers in case of emergency. These are located:

   1 either end of the top table = 2
   1 either end of the sprigs = 3
   Total = 5

If the host had so wished, could a similar plan be developed making the layout more compact, for use in a slightly smaller room? In other words would it be possible to get four sprigs on a 10 m (30 ft) long top table? The answer is yes.

   4 sprigs × 75 cm (2 ft 6 in) width = 3 m (10 ft)
   3 gangways × 1 m (3 ft) width = 3 m (9 ft)
   6 chair depths = 46 cm (1 ft 6 in) = 3 m (9 ft)
   Total = 9 m (approx. 30 ft)

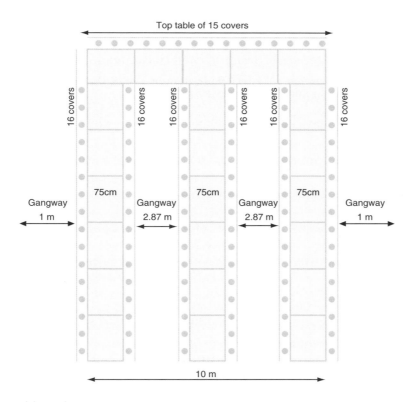

Fig 9.3. Top table and sprigs

Four sprigs would give a more compact layout and bring everyone closer to the speakers on the top table. This alternative plan allows for 12 covers on each side of the four sprigs and additional seating at the top table ends and sprig ends if required.

Top table and round tables

Function for 110 covers: 15 guests on top table, 95 covers on round tables.
Dimension of room = 18 m (60 ft) long by 12 m (36 ft) wide.

> **Note:** When using round tables it is first necessary to calculate the number of covers that could be seated at round tables of different diameters. In all cases it is necessary first to calculate the circumference of the round table. This is done by multiplying the diameter of the table by pi (π) (where π = 22 ÷ 7). Therefore, circumference is the diameter of the table × 22 ÷ 7. A cover would normally require 60 cm (2 ft) width on the circumference of a round table.

The calculations for 1 m, 1.5 m and 2 m diameter tables are as follows:

Circumference of a round table 1 m (3 ft) in diameter:
1 m × 22 ÷ 7   = 3.1 m
Number of covers available per round table (allowing 60 cm (2 ft) per person):
3m ÷ 0.6m   = 5
Therefore the number of covers will be 5 per 1 m diameter round table.

Circumference of a round table of diameter 1.5 m (5 ft):
1.5 m × 22 ÷ 7   = 4.7 m
Number of covers available per round table (allowing 60 cm (2 ft) per person):
4.7 m ÷ 0.6 m   = 7.9
Therefore the number of covers could be up to 8 per 1.5 m diameter round table.

Circumference of a round table of diameter 2 m (7 ft):
2 m × 22 ÷ 7   = 6.3 m
Number of covers available per round table (allowing 60 cm (2 ft) per person):
6.3 m ÷ 0.6 m   = 10.5
Therefore the number of covers could be up to 11 per 2 m diameter round table.

Method of working

1 Length of table required for top:
   15 guests × 60 cm (2 ft) cover width = 9 m (30 ft) or 5 × 2 m (6 ft) tables.

2 Number of round tables required:
   110 covers – 15 top table covers = 95 covers to be laid on round tables.
   Assuming using tables all same diameter (1.5 m/5 ft), i.e. 8 covers per table.
   Number of tables required is 95 covers ÷ 8 covers per table = 11.875 tables.
   Therefore 12 tables will be required (11 × 8 covers and 1 × 7 covers).

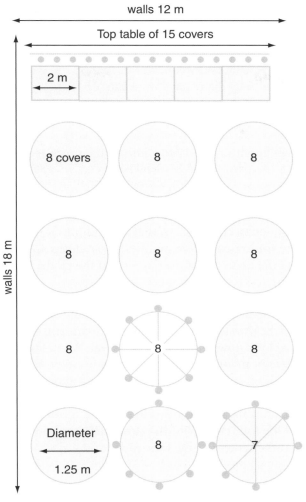

walls 12 m

Top table of 15 covers

2 m

8 covers

8

8

8

8

8

8

8

8

Diameter

1.25 m

8

7

walls 18 m

Fig 9.4. Top table and round tables

3   To check if the tables will fit in the length of the room (i.e. 18 m (60 ft), as per the table plan:
   For top table:

Gangway behind top table to wall	= 1 m (3 ft)
Top table chair depth	= 0.46 m (1 ft 6 in)
Top table width	= 0.75 m (2 ft 6 in)
Gangway below top table	= <u>1 m (3 ft)</u>
Total for top table	= 3 m approx (10 ft)

   For round tables:

Round table diameter	= 1.5 m (5 ft) diameter
Chairs depth × 2 per table	= 1 m (3 ft)
Gangways (allow below each table)	= <u>1 m (3 ft)</u>
Total	= 3.5 m (11 ft)
Total for round tables × 4	= 14 m (46 ft)

Total length required = 3 m (10 ft) for top table plus 14 m (46 ft) for four round tables = 17 m (56 ft).
The length of the room is 18 m (60 ft) so the proposed table plan fits.

4 To check if the tables, as per the table plan, will fit in the 12 m width of the room:
3 round tables each 1.5 m (5 ft) diameter   = 4.5 m (15 ft)
6 chair widths each 0.46 m (1 ft 6 in)   = 3 m (9 ft)
4 gangways each at 1 m (3 ft)   = 4 m (12 ft)
Total   =11.5 m (36 ft)
Thus the table plan will fit within the 12 m width of the room (see Figure 9.4).

Clothing up

The minimum size of banqueting cloths is 2 m (6 ft) in width by 4 m (12 ft) in length. They are available in longer lengths, for example, 6 m or 18 ft. These cloths are used on top tables and sprigs, thus often avoiding the necessity of overlapping of the cloths that will occur when smaller-sized tablecloths are used.

When laid, the centre crease should run straight down the centre of the table, with the overlap the same all round the table. All cloths should be in the same fold and have the same pattern. Any overlap of cloths should face away from the main entrance so that the join is not visible to the guests as they look down the room on arrival. When laying the cloth it may require three or four waiters to manipulate it (depending on size), to ensure it is laid correctly, with the minimum of handling, and without creasing or becoming dirty.

For round tables square cloths are often used. The cloth will normally be 1.4 m larger diagonally than the diameter of the table. This is to ensure a maximum drop of 70 cm where the cloth hangs lowest (at the four corners of the cloth) and a minimum drop of 20 cm where the cloth hangs highest (at the centres of the four edges of the cloth).

The calculation for this is made as follows:

Diameter of table plus the maximum drop each side of the table = diagonal measurement of tablecloth, corner to corner.

For example, a 200 cm diameter table plus 2 × 70 cm maximum drop = 340 cm.

Therefore the diagonal measurement of the tablecloth corner to corner = 340 cm.

To find the size of the square cloth then the formula is:
Length of edge = $\sqrt{(\text{diameter}^2 \div 2)}$

For example:
(340 cm diameter × 340 diameter cm) ÷ 2 = 57800 cm

The square root of 57800 cm = 240 cm

Therefore the cloth will be 240 cm by 240 cm.

A cloth of 240 cm by 240 cm will ensure that:

- the longest drop will be 70 cm ((340 cm – 200 cm) ÷ 2) at each of the four corners of the cloth (so that the corners of the cloth do not touch the floor)
- the shortest drop will be 20 cm ((240 cm – 200 cm) ÷ 2) at the centre of each of the four sides of the cloth (so that the table will be covered where the cloth has the shortest drop).

Using this approach for tables of 1 m, 1.5 m and 2 m the tablecloth will be as follows:

Table diameter	Cloth size	Longest drop at the four corners of the cloth	Shortest drop at the centre of the four sides of the cloth
1 m	170 × 170 cm	70 cm	35 cm
1.5 m	205 × 205 cm	70 cm	27 cm
2 m	240 × 240 cm	70 cm	20 cm

Service organisation

Traditional

For formal functions it is normal practice that the top table service staff always commence to serve/clear first. Therefore, the banqueting headwaiter will organise their staff so that, at a given signal, the top table service staff can commence to serve, immediately followed by all the other service staff. The banqueting headwaiter will not give any signal to clear a course until all guests have finished eating.

All staff should leave and enter the room led by the top table staff and followed by the other service staff in a pre-determined order. This pre-determined order generally means that those staff with stations furthest from the service doors should be nearer the top table service staff in the line-up (see Allocating stations, page 373). Theoretically this means that, when entering the room, all service staff reach their stations at more or less the same time. Each member of staff then serves his/her own table using the pre-determined service method – either full silver service or a combination of plate and silver service and so on. However, when deciding on the pre-determined order, another factor that should influence the final decision is that of safety. In other words, as far as is possible, any cross-flow of staff and bottlenecks in their movement to and from the room should be avoided.

Wave service

Wave service can be used mainly when meals are plated, although some establishments also use this style of service organisation for silver service and other forms of service. It is a way of saving on staffing for conventional service and/or speeding up service for plated systems. The term wave comes from the approach where tables are not served or cleared altogether but are served over a period of time, with guests on some tables being served quickly at one time before the service on other tables is started. There are two basic approaches to this:

- For both plated service and traditional silver service the staff from two tables next to each other will work together as a team. This happens throughout the room. The pair work together to serve one of the tables completely and then will assist each other to completely serve the other table.

- The alternative is for a larger group of staff to work as a team, serving one table completely at a time before going on to the next. This is especially useful when plated service is being used for the food.

The resulting effect of adopting these approaches is that tables are served throughout the room, over a period, but with each individual table's service being completed quickly.

Wave service may also be used for functions where guests are seated on a top table and sprigs (see page 366). In this case, sections of the banquet tables are served before moving to another section of the table layout.

For plated service, one of the difficulties is ensuring that the food is hot when being served. For table service the speed of the transfer of the plate from the kitchen can ensure that the food is hot when reaching the table, assuming of course that the food has always been first presented onto hot plates.

Carlton Club Service

Carlton Club Service (named after the members' club in St James's, London, where it was first used) is an enhancement of plated service. This is used for both restaurant table service and for functions. Members of the service staff carry two plates from the kitchen, one in each hand, with the hands crossed (which makes for steady carrying). On reaching the table one member of staff stands between each two guests. When a signal is given all members of staff bend forward, uncross their arms and place the two plates simultaneously in front of two guests, one plate to the left and one to the right. Care is also taken to ensure that the plated foods are placed so that the food items are consistently in the same position for all guests.

Buffet functions

There are three types of buffet:

- *Finger buffets*: the guests select and consume the food with their fingers. The foods and beverages may be available at a buffet or on trays that are carried by the waiters. Usually napkins are available on the passed trays too. The room is organised to ensure there is ample space for the guests to circulate and that a number of occasional tables and chairs are placed round the room. These occasional tables may be covered with linen cloths and may have a small vase of flowers placed on them. Any dirties are then removed from these tables by clearing staff as required.

- *Fork buffets*: the guests select foods which are transferred onto a plate and they then eat the food using only a fork. In this case, the food should be of such a shape and size that this is easily accomplished. Glass holders are usually available which clip to the side of the plate, in which a wine glass may be secured. Napkins are also available on the buffet. The room organisation is similar to that used for finger buffets above.

- *Display buffets*: the guests select their food and then eat at a table. Here the guests approach the buffet at its various service points to select their requirements course by course. Most ancillary items may also be collected, if needed, at the buffet. These might include rolls, butter, sauces, napkins, tableware and the like. The guests then return to their tables to consume the different parts of the meal. The table layouts are similar to the standard banquet layouts. The clearing of the tables takes place in the same way as for formal banquets.

Staff organisation

The general considerations for service staff for functions are given below.

■ A waiter at a banquet is generally expected to serve between 10 and 12 covers on a station but this may be up to 20 depending on the service organisation (see above).

■ A wine waiter will serve approximately 25 covers, but this depends on the type of function, the number of wines on offer and whether any wine is inclusive in the price of the menu or if cash drinks are being served. The wine waiters will also often assist the food waiters with the service of vegetables and sauces for the main course.

■ The wine waiters may also be required to serve apéritifs at a reception before a meal. If so, they will be required to do the necessary mise-en-place to ensure the reception area is ready, for example, ashtrays, cocktail snacks, setting-up of portable bar, polishing glasses etc.

■ When cash wine and drinks are served the wine waiters are normally given a float with which they may pay the cashier or bar person as drinks are ordered and collected from the bar. The responsibility then rests with the wine waiter to collect the payments for any drinks served.

Using white gloves

In some establishments members of staff wear white cotton gloves when carrying out various preparation tasks. The gloves help to prevent the soiling of clean service items and also avoid putting finger marks on cleaned and polished service equipment.

White gloves may also be used during service, instead of service cloths, when serving plated foods that are presented on hot plates. If white gloves are to be used then there must be a clean edge on the plate so that the food or sauces on the plates do not easily soil the gloves.

Allocating stations

When all the necessary mise-en-place has been completed and all the staff are assembled together, the stations are allocated to the waiters and wine waiters. More experienced and proficient members of staff are usually allocated to the top table.

The waiters should queue up in an orderly fashion at the hotplate for each course, with the waiter for the top table at the head of the queue and then the various waiters in order according to the distance of their station from the service hotplate. This order must be maintained throughout the service.

After the service of each course the brigade should remain outside the banqueting room and in readiness to clear and serve the next course.

Example of allocating stations, staff required and the order at the hotplate for a dinner of 84 covers (silver service)
12 covers on the top table and 24 covers on each sprig (12 on each side).

Table requirements (see plan in Figure 9.5):
Top: 4 × 2 m (6 ft) tables = 8m this allows for 60 cm (24 in) table width per cover.
Sprigs: 4 × 2 m (6 ft) tables = 8 m allowing for 60 cm (24 in) table width per cover. This will mean a total of 3 sprigs in all: 12 covers on each side.

Stations will be: Top table: 12 covers   12 covers
                     Sprigs: 6 × 12 covers   72 covers

There will be 7 stations of 12 covers = total 84 covers. For the plan given in Figure 9.5, the order of staff at the hotplate, by station number, will be: 1, 2, 3, 4, 5, 6, and 7.

The staff for stations 2, 4 and 6 will enter the room through the service doors and proceed down the room to their right. The staff for stations 3, 5 and 7 will enter through the service doors and proceed down the room to their left. See the plan in Figure 9.5.

Staff instruction sheets

Staff instruction sheets are provided for each function. These sheets give detailed instructions for all staff working on the function. Their purpose is to ensure that all the required duties are covered, that a particular function is laid up correctly and everything is in order in the shortest possible time and to provide guidance to casual staff.

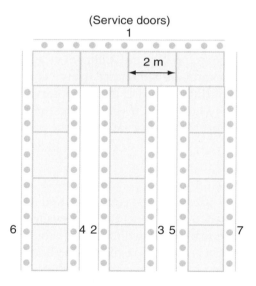

Fig 9.5. Example of allocating stations and the order at the hotplate

Forms of address

For all functions, formal and informal, etiquette is very important and great care should be taken to ensure the correct forms of address are used to suit the occasion. At very formal functions, royalty or other dignitaries may be attending as guests. Etiquette therefore demands a certain order of precedence when proposing and replying to toasts, and the correct mode of address should be adhered to.

Table 9.1 gives some examples of the correct modes of introduction, address and place cards for both formal and social occasions.

Note:

■ Formality is always followed on occasions involving members of the Royal Family.

■ The social forms of address are given for Peers, Baronets and Knights. For details related to more formal events, *Debrett's Peerage and Baronetage* or *Debrett's Correct Form* should be consulted.

■ The members of the Royal Family listed in Table 9.1 are shown in order of precedence.

Table 9.1 Precedence and forms of address

Title	Introduction	Verbal address	Place cards
The Royal Family *The Queen*	'Her Majesty the Queen'	'Your Majesty' and subsequently 'Ma'am'	
The Duke of Edinburgh	'His Royal Highness, Prince Philip, The Duke of Edinburgh'	'Your Royal Highness' and subsequently 'Sir'	
A Royal Prince	'His Royal Highness, Prince Charles, The Prince of Wales' 'His Royal Highness, Prince Andrew, The Duke of York' 'His Royal Highness, The Prince Edward'	'Your Royal Highness' and subsequently 'Sir' 'Your Royal Highness' and subsequently 'Sir' 'Your Royal Highness' and subsequently 'Sir'	His Royal Highness, The Prince of Wales His Royal Highness, The Duke of York His Royal Highness, The Prince Edward
A Royal Princess	'Her Royal Highness, The Princess Anne'	'Your Royal Highness' and subsequently 'Ma'am'	Her Royal Highness, The Princess Anne

Table 9.1 continued

Title	Introduction	Verbal address	Place cards
A Royal Duke	'His Royal Highness, The Duke of Gloucester'	'Your Royal Highness' and subsequently 'Sir'	His Royal Highness, The Duke of Gloucester
A Royal Duchess	'Her Royal Highness, The Duchess of Gloucester'	'Your Royal Highness' and subsequently 'Ma'am'	Her Royal Highness, The Duchess of Gloucester
Peers, Baronets and Knights			
Duke	'The Duke of Somerset'	'Duke'	The Duke of Somerset
Duchess	'The Duchess of Somerset'	'Duchess'	The Duchess of Somerset
Earl	'Lord Salisbury'	'Lord Salisbury'	Lord Salisbury
Countess	'Lady Salisbury'	'Lady Salisbury'	Lady Salisbury
Viscount	'Lord Wilton'	'Lord Wilton'	Lord Wilton
Viscountess	'Lady Wilton'	'Lady Wilton'	Lady Wilton
Government members			
The Prime Minister	By appointment or by name	By appointment or by name	The Prime Minister
Chancellor of the Exchequer	By appointment or by name	'Chancellor' or by name	Chancellor of the Exchequer
Ministers	'Mr Salmon'	'Minister' or 'Mr Salmon'	Mr Roy Salmon
The Clergy			
Archbishops	'The Archbishop of York'	'Archbishop' (socially)	His Grace, The Archbishop of York
Bishop	'The Bishop of Downton'	'Bishop' (socially)	The Lord Bishop of Downton

Table 9.1 continued

Title	Introduction	Verbal address	Place cards
Local Government *Lord/Lady Mayor*	By appointment or appointment and name	'My Lord/Lady Mayor' or 'Lord/Lady Mayor'	The Lord/Lady Mayor
Mayor	By appointment or appointment and name	'Mr/Madam Mayor'	The Mayor of Woodfalls
Mayor's Consort	By appointment or appointment and name	'Mayoress'	The Mayoress of Woodfalls

The Loyal Toast

At any formal function it is common for the Loyal Toast to be made. The toastmaster generally announces this toast as soon as the sweet course has been cleared, but before the coffee/tea is to be served. Staff should ensure before this time that all glasses have been 'charged' in readiness for the coming toasts.

The Loyal Toast should be announced by the toastmaster and is then normally proposed by the host for the evening, for example, the Chairman or President of an Association. The Loyal Toast is a toast to the reigning monarch: the Queen.

Traditionally at formal functions, no guest would smoke until after the Loyal Toast. Increasingly it has now become common for smoking not to be allowed at any time within a function room. If smoking is to be allowed, then the toastmaster indicates immediately after the Loyal Toast that the company present has the 'Chair's permission to smoke'. Staff should then ensure that ashtrays are placed on the tables.

Example of an order of service for a formal function (table service)

1. The toastmaster announces the luncheon or dinner.
2. Guests proceed to their places in the room.
3. Grace is said.
4. Guests are seated. Chairs pulled out by waiters. The waiters place napkins across the guests' laps.
5. Water and first wine is served.
6. If first course is not already on the table, proceed to hotplate to collect first course.
7. Line up according to the conventional system (see page 371), top table first.
8. Serve first course – top table waiter to commence service first.
9. All waiters (food) to leave room after each course is served.

10 Take in fish course plates.

11 Clear first course.

12 Second wine is served.

13 Lay fish plates.

14 Take out dirties and collect fish course.

15 Serve fish course. Leave room taking dirty silver.

16 Take in meat plates.

17 Third wine is served.

18 Clear fish course.

19 Lay meat plates.

20 Take out dirties and collect potato and other vegetable dishes.

21 Place on a hotplate on a sideboard or side table.

22 Return to hotplate and collect main meat dish.

23 Present on each table and serve together with sauces if appropriate.

24 Serve accompanying potatoes and vegetables.

25 Leave room taking dirty silver.

26 Continue with a similar process for the remaining courses of the meal through to the beverages.

Note: The headwaiter will control all the food waiters at the hotplate although variations on this service may be adopted according to the situation. The headwaiter also controls the exit from the hotplate into the banqueting room.

The order of service on the top table at functions, especially very formal occasions, is the one time when the host might be served first or at exactly the same time as the Guest of Honour, should they be seated on different stations.

At formal functions there may be speeches and toasts. These often take place at the end of a meal. However, it has become more common for these to take place at different times during the meal.

Ordering of drinks and wines

If required, a bar must be set up in the reception area away from the main entrance, so as to avoid overcrowding in one area as the guests are arriving and being announced by the toastmaster. The bar should be clothed up as a buffet, with the cloth within 1.3 cm (½ in) of the ground in the front, and with both ends boxed in. Keep the rear of the bar open so it may be used for storing extra supplies of drink, glasses and any necessary equipment such as glass jugs, soda syphons, extra ice and so on. Always allow ample working space behind the bar. The top of the bar is generally higher from the ground than the average table and, if no shelves are available for storage purposes, then sometimes smaller tables may be incorporated under the bar to be used for storage.

There should always be a good stock of drink, which is generally brought from the cellar approximately 45 minutes before the reception is due to commence. Once the drink is at the bar there should always be one barman on duty at all times. Depending on the function, drinks may be served either 'cash' or 'inclusive'. Whichever may be the case, stocktaking should be undertaken when the service is completed. Where necessary, do not forget to have on hand price lists, till, floats, notices regarding size of measures and liquor licence (if required).

When the drinks are to be served on a cash basis, this can very often be a lengthy process. To speed this up there should be wine waiters on duty near the table plan in the reception area together with commis. They should have:

- menus
- wine lists
- check pads

- table plan
- list of stations
- wine waiters' names

Note: The objective here is to get as many orders as possible for wine to accompany the meal, prior to the meal service commencing.

The order should be written in duplicate with the guest's name at the top of the check to assist in identifying customer's orders at the tables. One copy should go to the cellar or dispense bar and the duplicate to the correct wine waiter. The order should be prepared by the dispense barman or cellarman and when the wine waiter shows the duplicate he should be given the required order. Do not open the wine until the guests arrive at the table – red wine should be at room temperature and white wine should be chilled. At a cash reception the wine waiters very often act as lounge waiters and therefore are always to hand to receive any orders in readiness for the service.

As for food service, the top table must always be served first with drink. The toasts very often commence immediately the coffee is served. By this stage the wine waiters should have taken all the liqueur orders, served them and collected all the cash outstanding in the case of cash drinks. While the speeches are going on all the food waiters should be out of the room. The wine waiters may circulate if necessary.

On completion of the function, and when the food and wine waiters have cleared their stations and the latter returned any floats, they should be paid off after returning service cloths, jackets and other equipment provided for the service.

9.4 WEDDINGS

Wedding functions are usually of two main types:

- wedding breakfast
- wedding reception (buffet).

Fig 9.6. A function room laid out for a wedding (courtesy of Six Continents Hotels)

At the initial meeting between the client and the banqueting manager to arrange a wedding function, the approaches are similar to those detailed in Section 9.2 Function administration (see pages 360–364).

The requirements of the client will depend on the type of wedding function, the number of guests attending and the cost per head to be paid. The type of wedding (civil or religious) will also affect the arrangements and have implications for the specific requirements for the wedding breakfast/reception. Some additional considerations are requirements concerning a wedding cake stand and knife, whether a room should be available for the bride and bridegroom to change prior to leaving the function to go on their honeymoon, whether the wedding presents will be displayed and, if so, how much space will be needed and whether the services of a photographer will be required. The menu is often printed in silver, together with the names of the couple and the date, as the menus are often kept as souvenirs. For a wedding the content of the menu and beverages will be affected by cultural and religious dietary influences, as well as any special dietary needs (see pages 77–79).

Wedding breakfast (banquet)

When the wedding breakfast is to be a formal banquet then the details given in Section 9.3 Function organisation will apply. This includes the same considerations for:

- seating arrangements
- table plans
- table layouts
- clothing up
- service organisation
- staff organisation
- order of service.

In addition to the customary toasts there will also usually be the need to organise the cutting of the wedding cake at the end of the meal.

Wedding reception (buffet)

Where the reception is to be a buffet then the buffet itself should be placed in such a position that it is on view to all guests as they enter the room, but within access of the service doors for ease of clearing and re-stocking. The buffet should be clothed up so that the buffet cloth reaches within 1.3 cm (½ in) of the floor and both ends should be boxed neatly. The creases along the top and front of the buffet should be lined up. Adequate room should be left between the buffet and wall to allow two people to pass and for any extra supplies and equipment required.

If the function is being carried out in a marquee in private grounds then the ground should be covered with canvas or a form of corded matting. Behind the buffet and in the service areas duckboards may be used on canvas to avoid walking on wet ground or in mud and carrying it into the main part of the marquee.

The buffet itself may be split into three sections for ease of service:

Section	Requirements
Service of food	Should be presented appetisingly and attractively on the buffet with the cutlery and crockery required placed in a decorative manner, conveniently near the service points. Food for replenishing the buffet should be close to hand. The centre of the buffet may be raised in order to show off the dishes to greater effect.
Service of tea and coffee	This section should have all the necessary equipment close to hand. This will include teacups and saucers, teaspoons, sugar basins, cold milk jugs, tea and coffee urns and hotplates for the pots of hot milk. The service of beverages does not normally take place until after all the toasts have been completed. It is advisable to allow a little more in quantity than is actually required.
Service of alcoholic and non-alcoholic drinks	This section of the buffet should have all the correct size glasses for the drinks to be served (spirits, soft drinks and mineral waters, cocktails, wines and Champagne), plus ice buckets for the white, sparkling and rosé wines to be chilled, service salvers, waiters' cloths and all the ancillary equipment required for mixing drinks and cocktails to give the correct form of service. Any Champagne or other sparkling wine used for the toasts must be well chilled to approximately 7°C (45°F). A surplus of glasses should be kept under the buffet in their appropriate boxes. Diet, low calorie and low alcohol drinks should be on hand if required.

As an alternative the buffet itself may be used entirely for displaying the food and separate service points may be set up for the service of beverages, both alcoholic and non-alcoholic. This depends upon the exact nature of the function, the room available, number of guests, requirements of the client and the type and amount of drinks to be served.

Floral arrangements

The floral arrangements are an important aspect of the decoration and help show off the room to best effect. A large vase of flowers should normally be placed near the entrance to be noted on arrival by all the guests. A further large centrepiece of flowers may be placed in the centre of the buffet and other smaller arrangements of flowers placed at intervals around the room on the occasional tables. The final floral arrangements will depend on the cost involved. The front of the buffet cloth may be decorated with some greenery (smilac) of some sort, or some coloured velvet may be draped along in order to take away the plainness of the white buffet cloth. Purpose-made pleating can also be used to enhance the front and overall appearance of the buffet. This pleating may be purchased in a variety of colours.

The wedding cake

The wedding cake may be used as a separate focal point away from the buffet and should be placed upon its stand with a knife on a special table clothed-up for the purpose. This is a very important aspect of the dressing of the room, as the main formalities of the function take place, at a certain stage of the proceedings, around the wedding cake. It must, therefore, be in full view to everyone in the room. The bride's and bridesmaid's bouquets are often placed on the table around the base of the wedding cake, together with any telegrams of congratulations that are to be read out by the best man or toastmaster.

Arrangement of the room

Occasional tables should be placed at regular intervals around the room and clothed up in a suitable manner. Groups of chairs should be placed around each table, ensuring there is still space left for people to walk around and meet.

All the ancillary items required for the efficient service of the meal should be placed upon the occasional tables. Items might include butter, rolls/French bread, side plates, side knives, napkins, sugar basins and tongs, accompaniments for cold meats and salads and ashtrays (depending on the smoking policy of the establishment). Thus, the majority of the brigade on duty can be either serving drinks or clearing, and not be involved in the service of food which will be done from the buffet by other members of the brigade or one or two chefs if there is any carving involved.

Other requirements

The client may request that you arrange for a photographer to be present and this then is a further charge that has to be made. The photographer will probably take photographs of the bride and bridegroom on arrival at the reception, together with a group photo of those in the receiving line, one of the bride and bridegroom cutting the cake and maybe one or two of the buffet while it is complete.

Fully attended cloakrooms must be available for all guests on arrival.

Staffing

The number of staff required will depend on the nature and requirements of a particular function. As a guide, at a buffet type reception, the following staffing would be required:

Brigade: 1 head waiter/banqueting head waiter
1 waiter to every 25–30 covers
1 wine waiter to every 40 covers
1 barman to every 3 wine waiters
1–2 commis for fetching, carrying and clearing
1 chef to every 35–40 guests for service

Procedure at a wedding buffet reception

1 Any casual staff required should report approximately one hour beforehand to complete the necessary mise-en-place, to be allocated duties and to be briefed on the procedure to be carried out.

2 If a toastmaster is required, he should arrive approximately 30 minutes before the arrival of the bride and bridegroom to acquaint himself with the room where the function is being

held and to enquire what his duties will be with regard to announcing the guests on arrival. He must liaise with the best man to discuss the timing of cutting the cake and the toasts and who is to give them. If there is to be a social evening afterwards then the toastmaster may act as master of ceremonies (MC) for the duration of the function.

3 The bride and bridegroom should arrive first. Some photographs may be taken at this stage and an apéritif offered or a glass of Champagne.

4 Immediately following the bride and bridegroom should be the parents of the bride and bridegroom and bridesmaids and/or pages. These people will generally make up the 'receiving line' to greet the guests as they are announced by the toastmaster.

5 All the guests should generally arrive together. Cloakrooms at this stage must be fully staffed. Guests announced by the toastmaster then pass down the receiving line and enter the room.

6 The toastmaster should count guests entering the room. This is a help to management for costing purposes.

7 The wine waiters should be placed at strategic points in the reception area for the service of apéritifs or Champagne to the guests as they move on from the receiving line (see page 384). These trays should be replenished with full, fresh glasses. The wine waiters at the initial briefing should be allocated different sections of the room for service after the reception so as to ensure efficient service for all guests in the room.

8 After the reception the buffet should be open for service. The turnover on the buffet should be quick and efficient to avoid any major delays that may cause congestion. The wine waiter should be going round serving drinks and topping up glasses. An important factor to note during the service of the food and drink is to ensure that there are always some members of staff circulating, keeping the tables clear of any dirty equipment. Ashtrays should be changed as and when necessary.

9 At the agreed time the toastmaster should announce the cutting of the cake by the bride and bridegroom. Portions of the cake should then be passed around to all guests and Champagne taken round by the wine waiters. When this has been done the toastmaster will begin the toasts. All the principal people concerned should be in a group by the wedding cake or in a central position so they can be seen and heard by everyone present.

10 After the toasts any remaining cake and tiers must be packed, ready to be taken away by the host. The top tier is sometimes kept for a christening.

11 The bride and bridegroom may then change. If required, food and Champagne should be placed in the changing rooms. Here, liaison is required between floor service, housekeeping and banqueting staff to ensure that timing is correct as far as the movements of the bride and bridegroom are concerned.

12 When the bride and bridegroom have left the reception the flowers should be packed up for the host to take away.

Family line-up to greet guests at a wedding breakfast or wedding reception

There are two basic approaches for the family line-up:

Approach A

Toastmaster
Entrance

1 Bride's mother
2 Bride's father
3 Bridegroom's mother
4 Bridegroom's father
5 Bride
6 Bridegroom
7 Best man
8 Bridesmaid/Matron of honour

Approach B

Toastmaster
Entrance

1 Bride's mother
2 Bride's father
3 Bride
4 Bridegroom
5 Bridegroom's mother
6 Bridegroom's father
7 Bridesmaid/Matron of honour
8 Best man

Note: The best man is responsible for ensuring that everyone leaves the place where the wedding ceremony has taken place and that no one is left behind. He therefore does not always arrive in time for the beginning of the reception.

Table arrangement for the top table at a wedding

Below is a general arrangement for the seating for the top table.

Looking from the front of the table left to right:

Approach A

1 Best man
2 Groom's mother
3 Groom's father
4 Bride
5 Bridegroom
6 Bride's mother
7 Bride's father
8 Matron of Honour/Principal Bridesmaid

Approach B

1 Best man
2 Groom's mother
3 Bride's father
4 Bride
5 Bridegroom
6 Bride's mother
7 Groom's father
8 Matron of Honour/Principal Bridesmaid

Procedure for toasts at a wedding

Method A

1   Cutting of the cake.
2   While it is being cut the best man may read out telegrams.
3   Pass the cake and Champagne or alternative for toasts.
4   Toastmaster announces a toast to the bride and bridegroom, proposed by the bride's father or near relation.
5   Response of the bridegroom who also proposes a toast to the best man and bridesmaids.
6   Response of the best man who also replies on behalf of the bridesmaids.
7   Any other toasts: close relative of bride or bridegroom.

Method B

1   Pass the Champagne or alternative for toasts.
2   Toastmaster announces a toast to the bride and bridegroom, proposed by the bride's father or near relation.
3   Response by the bridegroom who also proposes a toast to the best man and bridesmaids.
4   Response by the best man who also replies on behalf of the bridesmaids.
5   Any other toasts: close relative of the bride or bridegroom.
6   Cutting of the cake: telegrams of congratulations read by the best man. Pass cake and more Champagne.

9.5 OUTDOOR CATERING (OFF PREMISES CATERING)

The business of an outdoor catering firm should, as far as possible, continue throughout the year to ensure the plant (equipment provided for a particular function) and staff are used to the full. At each function carried out the organiser should aim to give a fully comprehensive sales service, covering not only meals and drinks but also such things as confectionery and snack kiosks. As in function catering the organisation must be planned to the last detail and an initial survey should be exact and thorough. The following points are usually included in the initial survey:

■   Type of function.
■   Date of function.
■   Site and distance from depot/premises.
■   Local transport.
■   Local commodity purchase.

- Staff recruitment.
- Layout of site.
- Number of people expected to attend.
- Provision for people with special needs.
- Availability of water, gas, electricity, drainage and refrigeration.
- Spending power of people attending.
- Kiosk and stand details.
- Time allowed for setting up and dismantling catering units.
- Type of licence (if required).
- Mobile units adaptable to hot and cold food.
- Lines of communication to ensure control of staff and continuous supplies.
- Photographers.
- Press.
- Changing room and toilets.
- Insurance against weather/fire.
- First aid.
- Cost of overheads on a particular site.
- Type of service (the one most suited to each particular catering operation will need to be decided), for example:
  - buffet-style service may be preferred to restaurant service
  - provision of the take-away meal service in disposable containers
  - supply of some simple hot dishes – soup, fish and chips and so on
  - flexibility of drink service: hot or cold – according to weather.
- Washing-up facilities.
- Containers supplied for litter and disposable items.

Each outdoor catering operation is different and so the main points to be noted during the initial survey will vary. From the basic list shown above it is clear that organisation beforehand is the key to success. The person in charge needs to be decisive, quick-thinking, able to command, adaptable to varying situations and circumstances and, above all, needs to have the respect of the staff working under him/her.

The majority of staff employed at outdoor catering functions are taken on as casual staff. This involves a high administration load for the organisers and also the scrutiny checks of the staff must be very thorough to ensure the quality of the personnel.

The organisation of outdoor catering functions must be very thorough too, because once on site it is often virtually impossible to rectify errors. Any items forgotten or not packed on the transport will have to be gone without. This can affect the success of the function and can also damage the reputation of the service provider.

SUPERVISORY ASPECTS OF FOOD AND BEVERAGE SERVICE

10.1 LEGAL CONSIDERATIONS

There are a wide variety of legal requirements for food and beverage operations. These include company law, licensing regulations and employment law. In a book of this kind, which aims to provide a foundation in food and beverage service, it is not possible to cover all legal aspects that affect food and beverage operations. We have, however, attempted to provide a summary of the principal legal requirements as they affect the relationship between the food and beverage operator and the customer.

Licensing

There are four fundamental licensing objectives that underpin everything within the *Licensing Act 2003*. These are:

- the prevention of crime and disorder
- public safety
- the prevention of public nuisance
- the protection of children from harm.

Local authorities have a statutory duty to publish a licensing policy detailing how they will promote the licensing objectives in their area.

24-hour licensing

The law does not set permitted hours and applications may be made to local authorities for up to 24-hours-a-day trading. However, each application is subject to the views of the police, local residents and environmental health amongst others, and the authorities will take these views into consideration when deciding what hours are set.

Dual licenses

Separate licences are required for the person and for the premises.

- *Personal licence*: required for those who are going to authorise sales of alcohol at the premises, either as designated premises supervisor or in the absence of the designated premises supervisor. They must pass a new licensing qualification based on the 2003 Act and will have to obtain a Criminal Records Bureau certificate. Those wanting to supply liquor in a members club, provide regulated entertainment or supply hot food between 11:00 p.m. and 5:00 a.m. will not need a personal licence.
- *Premises licence*: required for the provision of alcohol and entertainment. This allows 'licensable activities' to be provided at the premises. Licensable activities for which a premises licence is required are:
  - the sale of alcohol
  - the supply of alcohol in a qualifying club (previously a registered club)
  - the provision of regulated entertainment
  - the provision of late night refreshment.

One or all of these activities can be contained on the premises licence. In order to provide licensable activities to the public, there is also a need for one of three types of permission:

- *Premises licence*: the most common type of licence. It may authorise the sale by retail of alcohol, the provision of regulated entertainment and the sale of hot food between 11 p.m. and 5 a.m. These licences are held by pubs and nightclubs, restaurants, off licences, supermarkets, theatres, cinemas etc.
- *Premises certificate*: necessary for the supply of alcohol to members and guests of the club and the provision of regulated entertainment within the club.
- *Temporary event notice*: necessary for the sale by retail of alcohol, the provision of regulated entertainment, the supply of hot food or drink between 11 p.m. and 5 a.m. on a temporary basis. There are limitations on the frequency with which these can be used.

Regulatory crime

The running of licensed premises is regulated by the Licensing Authority and other bodies concerned with regulatory crime issues, including Health and Safety, Food Safety, Trading Standards (see Sale of goods and trades descriptions, page 400), Disability Discrimination and Door Security. In addition, the Licensing Authority or Police are concerned with issues such as underage sales, permitting drunkenness on licensed premises and the breach of any conditions of a licence. All of these matters can give rise to prosecutions in the Magistrates Court with potential fines.

Health and safety

The Environmental Health department of a local authority will carry out inspections of licensed premises. Issues investigated include the cleanliness of the premises and the presence or otherwise of risk assessments in relation to certain parts of the operation and following an accident of any description. (See also Health, safety and security, page 395.)

Food safety

Environmental Health Officers are concerned with the cleanliness of kitchens, the storage of food and the temperatures at which the food is maintained. In addition, products used to clean premises are subject to regulations concerning the Control of Substances Hazardous to Health (COSHH). Not having proper risk assessments in place is a criminal offence.

Under the terms of the *Food Safety Act*, severe penalties can be imposed if there are food and beverage items for sale that are not of the substance or quality demanded by the purchaser. This can include spirits that have been inadvertently (or deliberately) watered down. For example, the use of speed pourers effectively leaves bottles open for long periods of time, which leads to evaporation of the alcohol. Equally, if the pourers are washed and then replaced in the bottles when they are wet, the water can become introduced to the spirit and cause a reduction in the percentage of alcohol by volume (abv).

Underage sales

It is an offence to serve children on licensed premises. Children who are under the age of 16 are not allowed in premises that exclusively or primarily sell alcohol for consumption on the premises, when they are open, unless they are accompanied by a person who is over 18. This means that children under 16 will still be allowed into supermarkets or off licences unaccompanied. Children under 16 are also not permitted in premises licensed to sell alcohol for consumption on the premises when they are open after midnight, whether accompanied or not. Under the Act, children cannot consume alcohol in licensed premises. The only exception is if the young person is 16 or 17 and is having a table meal and is accompanied by an adult. In those circumstances, a 16- or 17-year-old may consume beer, wine or cider only.

Permitting drunkenness in licensed premises

It is an offence to serve people who are drunk or to permit people who are drunk to remain on licensed premises.

Disability discrimination

It is now a requirement to make 'reasonable adjustments' to premises to afford access to disabled persons. Failure to do so may leave an operator open to a civil claim by a disabled person who feels that they have been unduly prejudiced. (See also Discrimination on page 393.)

Door security

All door staff must be trained and registered. Failure to do so leaves not only the door supervisors, but also those employing and supervising them, open to potential prosecution.

Licensing qualifications

Under the licensing system there are now requirements for various qualifications to be held by particular members of staff. Examples are:

- National Certificate for Personal Licence Holders (NCPLH)

Accredited qualification satisfying the training criteria defined by the Licensing Magistrates as evidence of the applicant's knowledge and understanding of the new licensing laws and the social responsibilities attached to running licensed premises.

- National Certificate for Door Supervisors

Accredited and nationally recognised qualification awarded to those who pass two examinations covering the basic knowledge and responsibilities of the occupation. This qualification is a requirement for a door supervisor who wants to apply for a Security Industry Authority (SIA) licence.

- National Certificate for Licensees (Drugs Awareness)

Accredited and nationally recognised qualification designed for licensees and managers of licensed premises to provide operational guidelines to deal effectively with, and prevent, any drug-related problems.

■ Professional Barperson's Qualification

This qualification is designed for barpersons working in licensed premises. The qualification comprises two units: The Barperson's National Certificate – which covers the licensing law, and The Customer and Drinks Service – which covers the skills and knowledge necessary to work professionally in a bar.

Note: The licensing system outlined above is for England and Wales. The licensing system for Scotland is to be broadly similar.

Weights and measures

Beer or cider

Unless sold in a pre-packed container (quantity must be stated), beer and cider may only be sold in quantities of ⅓ pint, ½ pint or multiples of ½ pint. It must be provided in a capacity measure (such as a lined glass) unless sold through a dispensing meter. The ⅓ and ½ pint measures do not apply to mixtures of two or more liquids, for example, shandy or lager and lime.

Spirits

Whisky, gin, vodka and rum must be sold in 25 mls or 35 mls or multiples thereof (measures of other spirits are usually based on these quantities, too). A notice must be displayed indicating the measure being used in the establishment. The restriction does not apply to the mixtures of three or more liquids, for example, cocktails.

Table 10.1 Examples of measures per bottle

Beverage	Bottle size	Metric measure
Spirits	75 cl	30 × 25 ml or 21 × 35 ml
Spirits	70 cl	28 × 25 ml or 20 × 35 ml
Spirits	65 cl	26 × 25 ml or 18 × 35 ml
Vermouths (aromatised wines)	75 cl	15 × 50 ml
Fortified (liqueur) wines	75 cl	15 × 50 ml
Liqueurs		Varies according to bottle size but likely to be in measures of 25 ml or 35 ml.

Table 10.1 gives a guide to the number of measures that may be obtained from the various bottles.

Wines

There is no specific quantity if the wine is sold in sealed containers. Open carafes, however, must be 25, 50 or 75 cl or 1 litre. Wine by the glass must be sold in quantities of 125 ml and/or 175 ml or multiples of either quantity.

Contracts

A contract is made when one party agrees to the terms of an offer made by another party. In food and beverage service there are essentially two types of customer: those who pre-book and those who do not (often called chance or casual customers).

For those who pre-book the offer is made by them, for example, a requirement for a table for four at 1 p.m.. If the restaurant suggests an alternative, for example, 'We do not have a table at 1 p.m., but we have one at 1.30 p.m.', then the offer is made by the restaurant.

There is a requirement for a price list to be shown (see page 394). In operations where the customer may not have or is not required to pre-book (such as fast food operations) it is likely to be considered, in law, that the price list constitutes an offer.

If customers fail to turn up on time, then the table need not be held. Similarly, if the party is only two and not the four previously booked, then restaurants may seek compensation. Alternatively, if the food and drink is not as expected then the customer can refuse to pay but must provide proof of identity and their home address. Only if fraud is suspected may the police be involved, as fraud is a criminal offence.

However, contracts may be broken if one party is induced to enter into a contract by false statement, for example, if promised a certain menu which is not available. In this case there is no obligation for the customer to continue with the contract. Also, if either party is unable to meet the terms of the original contract due to unforeseen circumstances, such as the customer falling ill or the restaurant burning down, then the contract becomes 'frustrated', as it cannot be fulfilled.

Care should be taken with contracts with minors: contracts cannot be made with persons under 18 unless it is for 'goods and services suitable to the minor's needs and his station in life'.

Sale of goods and trades descriptions

The *Sale and Supply of Goods Act 1994* applies to the sale of goods by description. It clarifies that there is an implicit contract when the caterer accepts the order of a customer.

According to the Act, the customer can refuse to pay or can demand replacement if:

- the goods supplied do not correspond with the description, for example, roast chicken which is in fact poached and then quick grilled
- a displayed item is not what it seems, for example, a sweet trolley where the cream, which

one would reasonably expect to be fresh, is in fact artificial. (It makes no difference if the customer has partly or entirely consumed the purchase)

■ the goods are inedible.

The *Trades Description Acts 1968/1972* make it a criminal offence to mis-describe goods or services. Care must therefore be taken when:

■ wording menus and wine lists

■ describing menu and beverage items to customers

■ describing conditions, such as cover and service charges or extras

■ describing the service provision.

A person charged under the Act will have to prove that reasonable precautions were taken to ensure that descriptions were not misleading. However, the Act also provides the following defence of such a charge if the description was:

■ the result of pure mistake

■ the result of information from another person

■ the fault of someone else

■ the result of accident or other cause beyond the control of the person concerned

■ misleading but the person charged could not reasonably have known that.

Discrimination

The *Sex Discrimination Act 1975*, the *Race Relations Act 1976/2000* and the *Disability Discrimination Act 1995* seek, among other things, to legislate against discrimination on grounds of ethnic origin, race, creed, sex or disability. The Acts also define what such discrimination might be:

■ *Direct discrimination*: for example, refusing service to customers of particular ethnic origin, race, creed, sex or disability.

■ *Indirect discrimination*: for example, denying consumer services by imposing unjustifiable conditions or requirements which have ethnic origin, sex or disability implications.

■ *Discrimination through victimisation*: for example, by (a) refusal of provision, that is refusal of admission on the basis of ethnic origins, sex or disability; or (b) omission of provision, that is providing services to ethnic customers that are markedly inferior to those available to the public in general or which may only be available at a price premium.

Providing services

The food and beverage operator is under no specific requirement to serve anyone unless the food and beverage operation is within an establishment covered by the *Hotel Proprietors Act (HPA) 1956* and the customers seeking food and beverage service provision are resident in the hotel. Reasons for refusal to provide provision might be as follows:

■ there is no space left on the premises

- the person is intoxicated
- the person is under the influence of drugs
- the person does not comply with the dress requirements of the operation
- the person is unable to pay the admission charge
- the person is a known troublemaker
- the person is an associate of a known troublemaker
- the person is under legal minimum age for licensed premises or does not comply with an age policy set by local management.

Under the *Licensing Act 2003*, the licensee has the right to refuse any person who is drunk, violent, quarrelsome or disorderly and the police may be brought in to assist. The Act also makes it an offence to sell intoxicating liquor to a drunken person or those less than 18 years of age. Under the provision of the *Hotel Proprietors Act 1956*, innkeepers are relieved of the obligation to serve if a customer is not in a fit state or appears to be unable to pay. In addition, an exclusion order can be made against a particular person.

Price lists

Under the terms of the *Price Marking (Food and Drink Services) Order 2003*, prices of food and drink must be displayed in a clear and legible way by persons selling by retail for consumption on the premises. However, this does not apply:

- where the supply is only to members of a bona fide club or their guests
- at staff restaurants or works canteens
- at guest houses where the supply is only to people staying there.

Also excluded from the requirements are specially agreed menus at prices agreed in advance, for example, in function catering.

The main provisions of the Order are:

- Prices must be displayed so as to be able to be seen by customers before reaching the eating area. If access is from the street then the list must be at the entrance or be able to be read from the street. If this area is part of a complex then the list must be at the entrance to the eating area.
- For self-service premises the list must be at the place where the customer chooses food and at the entrance, unless it can otherwise be seen from there.
- Both food and drink must be included.
- Table d'hôte menu prices must be given.
- VAT must be included and service and/or cover charge must be prominently shown as an amount or a percentage.

Service, cover and minimum charges

Part III of the *Consumer Protection Act 1987* deals with misleading prices and among its provisions it states that it is an offence to give misleading price information and authorises the issue of a Code of Practice. The 'Code of Practice for Traders on Price Indications' gives recommendations on service, cover and minimum charges in hotels, restaurants and similar establishments, as detailed below.

Cover charges and minimum charges should be 'shown as prominently as other prices on any list or menu, whether displayed inside or outside'. Also, it is not appropriate to suggest optional sums, whether for service or any other item, in the bill presented to the customer. If a customer in hotels, restaurants or similar places must pay a non-optional extra charge, for example, a 'service charge' then:

i) incorporate the charge within fully inclusive prices wherever practicable, and

ii) display the fact clearly on any price list or priced menu, whether displayed inside or outside (e.g. by using statements like 'all prices include service').

While compliance with the Code is not obligatory, failure to do so can be relied on by a prosecutor as evidence that an offence has been committed. Copies of the Code are available from the Department of Trade and Industry.

Customer property and customer debt

Under the terms of the *Hotel Proprietors Act 1956* establishments have liability for guests' property for those who have booked overnight accommodation. Other than this, establishments have no automatic liability for guests' property unless the customer can prove negligence. However, care should be taken by staff so as to minimise potential loss or damage. Notices warning guests of 'no responsibility' may help in defence but do not guarantee exemption from liability for the food and beverage operator.

If customers are unable to pay, no *right of lien* exists except in inns (the right to hold property against non-payment of an account under the terms of the *Hotel Proprietors Act 1956*). The only action for the foodservice operator is civil proceedings, unless the proprietor believes that fraud has been attempted in which case the police should be called.

Health, safety and security

There is a common law duty to care for all lawful visitors. The Acts which affect health and safety issues include the *Occupiers Liability Act 1957*, the *Health and Safety at Work Act 1974* and the *Fire Precaution Act 1971* and *Regulations 1997 and 1999*.

In addition, the *Food Safety Act 1990* makes it clear that establishments must not:

■ sell (or keep for sale) food that is unfit for people to eat

■ cause food to be dangerous to health

■ sell food that isn't what the customer is entitled to expect, in terms of content or quality

■ describe or present food in a way that is false or misleading.

It is important for a foodservice operator to be able to demonstrate that steps have been taken to ensure good food hygiene. If prosecuted under the *Food Safety Act 1990*, the foodservice operator would need to convince the court that they had taken all reasonable steps to avoid the offence (this is called a 'due diligence defence').

Essentially safety is a civil duty and negligence is a criminal offence. The implications for staff under the above legislation are that they should:

■ understand the food hygiene regulations and that it is their responsibility to act within the bounds of these regulations

■ notify management of any major illnesses

■ perform duties in any area concerned with the handling of food in a hygienic manner and keep within food and hygiene regulations

■ make themselves familiar with all escape routes and fire exits in the building

■ ensure that fire exits remain clear at all times

■ participate in fire evacuation drills and practices

■ take reasonable care for the health and safety of themselves and of others, and ensure that health and safety regulations are followed

■ report to heads of department or duty managers any hazards which may cause injury or ill-health to customers and/or staff

■ not interfere with or misuse anything provided in the interests of health, safety and welfare

■ cooperate with employers in order to carry out duties within the context of the Acts.

Maintaining a safe environment

One of the responsibilities of all employees, to themselves, to work colleagues and to customers, is to be aware of hazards that may arise when working. Many accidents occur through carelessness or through lack of thought, for example:

■ not having the correct protective clothing such as an apron

■ not wearing sensible (stable and properly fitted) shoes

■ delay in clearing spillages or picking up items of equipment that have fallen on the floor

■ not being aware of customers' bags placed on the floor

■ items of equipment not stored correctly

■ broken glass or crockery not wrapped up sufficiently before being placed in the bin

■ forgetting to unplug electrical appliances prior to cleaning

■ putting ashtray debris into rubbish bins containing paper (a fire hazard)

■ forgetting to switch off and unplug an appliance after use, or at the end of the service

■ not being observant with table lamps or lit candles on a buffet

■ overfilling coffee pots, soup tureens, glasses etc.

■ using cups, glasses, soup bowls etc., for storing cleaning agents

■ stacking trays incorrectly

- carrying a mix of equipment on a tray, such as cutlery, crockery and glassware
- carpet edges turned up
- faulty wheels on trolleys or castors on sideboards
- being unaware of customers' walking sticks and crutches
- lack of adequate space for the 'safe' service of food and drink due to bad planning
- lack of knowledge in carrying out certain tasks, for example, opening a bottle of sparkling wine.

Procedure in the event of an accident

All employers must be able to provide first aid should such a need arise. In the event of an accident the first course of action should be to call for the assistance of a trained and qualified first aid person.

Under the terms of the *Health and Safety at Work Act* employers must keep a record of all accidents that occur in the workplace. If you are involved in or witness an accident you will be required to give information and/or to complete an accident form. For this reason it is wise to make notes on the event at your earliest convenience. The information should include:

- the location of the accident
- the time of the accident
- a statement of the event
- details of witnesses
- treatment administered.

Procedure in case of fire

All employees should be given fire drill training within their induction programme. This initial training should then be followed up by regular training sessions on the procedures to be followed in the event of fire. This training should include:

- fire procedures in own specific area of work
- fire drill instructions for both customers and staff
- the location of fire points (safe places where staff and customers should assemble after an evacuation) nearest to own particular area of work
- the location of the fire exits
- the correct type of fire extinguisher to be used in relation to the type of fire (see Table 10.2, page 398).
- an identification of own specific responsibilities in the event of fire.

In the event of the fire alarm ringing all employees must:

1 Follow the fire instructions as laid down for the establishment.

2 Usher all customers and staff out of the work area promptly and calmly.

3 Pay special attention to customers with special needs such as those with mobility problems.

4 Walk quickly but do not run. Display a sense of urgency.

5 Do not panic; remain calm as composure will be imitated by others.

Table 10.2 Fire extinguishers and their uses

Contents	Water	Foam	CO$_2$	Dry powder	Halon
Label colour:*	White on red	Cream on red	Black on red	Blue on red	Green on red
Electrical suitability:	Danger – electrically conductive		Safe – non-electrically conductive		
Suitable for:	Solids	Some liquids	Electrical	Liquid	Liquid
Unsuitable for:	Oil	Electrical	Solids	Very little	Solids

* Under European Union standards the body of every extinguisher must be coloured red. However, a colour zone is used to indicate what the extinguishing medium is – the colours used for these mediums are the ones given here, and they are the same as the previous whole body colour coding system.

6 Proceed as promptly as possible to the nearest assembly point.

7 Ensure that someone watches to see that there are no stragglers.

8 Follow the exit route as laid down in the establishment fire instructions.

9 Never use a lift.

10 Never re-enter the building until told it is safe to do so.

11 Do not waste time to collect personal items.

Employees have a responsibility to assist in fire prevention, control and safety. They must therefore ensure that:

■ fire exits are not obstructed

■ fire-fighting equipment is not damaged or misused

■ no smoking rules are observed at all times

■ as far as is possible all electrical and gas equipment is switched off

■ all doors and windows are closed when not being used for evacuation purposes

■ fire doors are not locked or wedged open

■ sufficient ashtrays/stands are available for the disposal of cigarette ends and used matches

■ the procedure for making an emergency fire call is known.

Cleaning programmes

All food and beverage service staff should be made aware of the importance of cleaning programmes to reduce and minimise the build up of dust, bacteria and other forms of debris. For this reason, together with the considerations needed for safety and hygiene, full attention needs to be paid by all concerned to cleaning tasks and when they should be carried out. Overall, regular maintenance makes the service area look attractive and will project the right image for the establishment.

A cleaning programme should be set up for any cleaning tasks that must be done in any area. Some tasks are done daily, even twice daily, for instance, the washing and polishing of crockery before each service period. Other tasks might be done weekly, monthly or every six months. Certain items of equipment will need cleaning immediately after each service period is finished.

Examples of tasks are as follows:

Immediately after use:	● carving trolley ● sweet trolley ● copper pans ● refrigerated trolleys ● flare lamps.
Daily:	● vacuuming ● damp dusting chairs ● polishing sideboard tops ● cleaning brasses ● clearing ashtrays.
Weekly:	● silver cleaning ● cleaning pictures ● defrosting fridges ● wipe down doorframes and all high ledges ● washing cellar/crockery store ● floors.
Monthly plus:	● shampoo carpets ● dry clean curtains ● maintenance checks on still set, chilling units, fridges, air conditioning systems ● all lighting.

Points to note:

■ Always use the correct cleaning materials for the task in hand.

■ Clean frequently.

■ Rinse all surfaces well.

■ Dusters should only be used for dusting and not other cleaning tasks.

■ Use cleaning procedures that are adequate and efficient.

■ Cloths used for cleaning toilets must not be used for any other purpose.

■ Clean and store equipment safely and in its correct place.

■ Do not use cleaning cloths for wiping down food preparation surfaces.

■ Consider safety at all times and do not stretch or stand on chairs to reach high points – use a stepladder.

Maintaining a secure environment

Depending upon the nature of the establishment, the security measures that are laid down may vary considerably. As employees, staff should be aware of all such measures as they relate to their own work environment. Consideration needs to be given to the aspects of security outlined below.

- The importance of wearing some form of recognised identity badge.
- Being observant and reporting 'suspicious' persons and/or packages.
- Not discussing work duties with customers or outside of the workplace.
- Allowing bags, packages and one's person to be searched upon request when either entering or leaving the workplace.
- Being aware of the security procedures for the establishment, should sudden and urgent action have to be taken.
- Ensuring external fire doors are kept shut but not locked, nor left ajar in error.
- Ensuring that all areas have been vacated when responsible for 'locking up' duties. All toilets/cloakrooms must be very carefully checked and at the same time all windows and doors should be checked to ensure they are locked.
- Keys should only be handled by someone in authority. A signing out book should be available when staff request keys.
- Keys are never to be left unattended.
- When handling cash, all large denomination notes should be checked carefully as well as all cheque and credit card payments, to prevent fraud, the passing of illegal notes and the acceptance of altered credit cards.
- Being alert and observant at all times and not hesitating in reporting anything suspicious to the immediate superior.

Dealing with a suspicious item or package

All employees should be constantly alert for suspicious items or packages.

- If an object is found then it must immediately be reported to the security officer, manager or supervisor.
- Do not touch or attempt to move the object.
- If there are customers in the immediate vicinity, discreetly attempt to establish ownership of the object.
- If the ownership is established then ask the customer to keep the object with them, or to hand it in for safe keeping.
- If no immediate ownership is established, then the area should be cleared and the authorities notified without delay.

Dealing with a bomb threat

Immediate action needs to be taken as a bomb could go off at any moment. As a result staff should:

- be aware of and follow establishment policy with regard to bomb threats and evacuation procedures
- evacuate the immediate work area
- search the work area to ensure it is cleared, if this is part of their own responsibility
- evacuate the premises and usher all customers/staff through the nearest usable exits to specified assembly areas
- count all persons present to determine their safety and minimise the risk of fatal accidents.

10.2 FOOD AND BEVERAGE REVENUE CONTROL

A control system covering the sale of all food and beverages in a foodservice operation is essential to maximise returns. The type of control system used will vary from one operation to another.

In a large establishment a control and accounts department would be in overall charge of the efficient running and working of the control systems used. In a smaller establishment this may be taken over by an assistant manager, who would personally carry out the daily and weekly checks that were necessary. All control systems should be as simple as possible, making it easier for the food and beverage service staff to operate, and for the control and accounts department staff to check for any errors and omissions and have them rectified.

Purpose of a revenue control system

A control system essentially monitors areas where selling takes place.

- There must be efficient control of all food and beverage items issued from the various departments.
- The system should reduce any pilfering and wastage to a minimum.
- Management should be provided with any information they require for costing purposes and so that they may estimate accurately for the coming financial period.
- The cashier should be able to make out the customer's bill correctly so that the customer is neither overcharged nor undercharged.
- The system should show a breakdown of sales and income received in order that adjustments and improvements may be made.

The main control methods in use in foodservice establishments are:

- Order taking methods (see Section 5.6, page 225).
- Billing methods (see Section 5.11, page 262).
- Sales summary sheets (see page 410).
- Operational statistics (see Section 10.4, page 418).

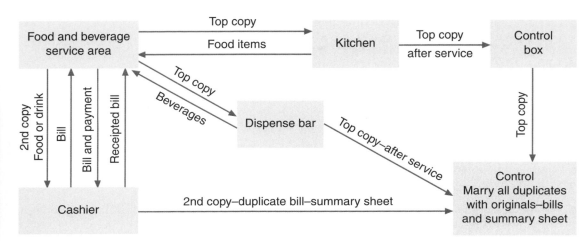

Fig 10.1. Flow chart of food and beverage checks

The process of food and beverage revenue control is summarised in Figure 10.1. This chart is based upon the triplicate method for food and the duplicate method for the dispense bar. The chart indicates that all top copies go to the dispense points (bar, kitchen) and follows the flow of information through until top and second copies are matched up by control.

Systems for revenue control

The four basic methods for order taking are identified in Table 5.2 (page 225). The seven basic methods of billing are identified in Table 5.7 (page 262). The systems that are used to support the various order taking and billing methods are summarised below.

- *Manual systems*: using hand-written duplicate or triplicate checks for ordering from kitchen and bar and for informing the cashier. Often used with a cash till or cash register. This system is found in many high-level restaurants and in popular catering.

- *Pre-checking system*: orders are entered directly onto a keyboard that then prints each order check with a duplicate and retains a record of all transactions. The keyboard may be pre-set or pre-priced. This system may be found in many full-service restaurants and in popular catering.

- *Electronic cash registers*: allows for a wider range of functions including sales analysis. ECRs may be installed as stand-alone or linked systems. These systems are found in store restaurants, cafeterias and bars.

- *Point-of-sale control systems*: have separate keyboard terminals in the various service areas, which are linked to remote printers or visual display units (VDUs) in the kitchen, bar etc. The terminals can be fixed or set in docking stations for hand-held use. In hotels, this equipment may also be linked to the hotel accounting systems. This system is also found in many modern restaurants.

- *Computerised systems*: enable a number of serving terminals, intelligent tills and remote printers to be controlled by a master unit compatible with standard computer hardware (see Figure 5.25, page 226). Depending on software, the functions may also include a variety of performance measures such as planning and costing, sales analysis, gross profit reporting, stock control, re-ordering and forecasting, VAT returns, payroll, staff scheduling and account information. These systems are often found in hotels, fast food and chain restaurants.

■ *Satellite stations*: remote terminals linked by telephone to a central processor to enable sales performance to be analysed (usually overnight) and reported back. These systems are found in fast food and chain restaurant operations.

Electronic point of sale control (EPOS)

The more sophisticated of the systems (point-of-sale, computerised and satellite) provide for increasingly efficient service at the point of sale, as well as improving the flow and quality of information to management for control purposes. The advantages will vary from one system to another, but may be summarised as follows:

■ *Fewer errors*: sales information entered will be more accurate because mistakes in the sequence of entries required for a particular transaction are not permitted. Automatic price look-up or pre-set keys are available rather than the potentially less reliable manual entry.

■ *Faster processing*: transactions can be processed more quickly and this may be achieved by:
  – the automatic reading of price-tags using a hand-held wand or moving the item over a fixed reader set in a counter top
  – single key entry of prices
  – eliminating any manual calculation or hand-writing by the assistant.

■ *Training time*: may be reduced from days on the conventional cash register to hours with the electronic systems. This is because many systems have a sequencing feature, which takes the user through each transaction step by step, giving instructions on a VDU.

■ *Instant credit checking*: a customer's credit rating can be checked by having terminals compare the account number with a central computer file or through on-line connections to card providers.

■ *Detailed management information*: electronic systems provide more direct information in a computer-readable form. This improves both the detail and quality of computerised stock control and accounting systems and makes them more economic for relatively small establishments.

■ *Additional security features:* includes such things as:
  – locks which permit the ECR to be operated only by authorised personnel or totals etc. to be altered and reset only by supervisors and managers
  – not disclosing at the end of the day the sum of the receipts that should be accounted for.

■ *Advanced calculating facilities*: systems can be programmed to calculate the total price when a number of items of the same price are purchased, there are a number of items at various prices or if VAT has to be added.

■ *Improved printouts*: in terms of quality and the amount of information contained on the customer's receipt. This may also include facilities where:
  – receipts may be overprinted with sales and VAT
  – both alphabetic and numeric information can be presented in black and white or colours

- the receipt can contain the names of the goods purchased as well as, or instead of, a simple reference number.
- ■ *Improved appearance*: modern systems are styled to fit in with the décor of present day foodservice environments.

Individual foodservice operators will determine which system best suits their needs and gives them the information they require.

The cashier

Before the start of service the cashier should have made all relevant checks and have the required materials to hand. Each establishment will have its own procedure but will generally include the following:

- ■ Check the float: if it is incorrect follow the company procedure.
- ■ Ensure the cash drawer is properly organised with notes and coins in the relevant compartments.
- ■ Ensure there are enough credit/debit card vouchers, till rolls, promotional items, bill folders, stapler or paper clips and pens etc.

The cashier's duties for table and assisted service may be summarised as follows:

- ■ issuing and recording of check books
- ■ counter-signing spoilt checks
- ■ receiving all unused checks
- ■ maintaining cash floats
- ■ preparation of bills

- ■ receiving payments (which may include cash, credit card and cheque payments as well as luncheon vouchers or other forms of prepaid voucher)
- ■ producing sales summaries
- ■ banking receipts.

Note: Alternatively, individual servers may take payments. Cashiers on cafeteria checkouts may have similar duties but excluding the tasks regarding checks.

On receiving the duplicate copy of the food check from the server, the cashier opens a bill in duplicate according to the table number on the food check. All the sets of bills are serial numbered for control purposes. As the cashier receives the checks from the food or wine waiter, the items ordered are entered on to the bill, either manually or electronically. When this is done the bill and duplicate checks are pinned together and may be placed into a special book or file, which has its pages numbered according to the number of tables in the service area. The bill and duplicate checks are placed in the page corresponding to the table number. As further checks are received the items are entered onto the bill and the checks then pinned with the others to the bill.

When the customer requests the bill the waiter must collect it from the cashier who must first check that all items are entered and priced correctly and that the bill is totalled up. The top copy of the bill is presented to the customer on a side plate and folded in half with one corner turned up, or in a bill folder. On receiving the necessary payment from the customer the waiter returns the bill and payment to the cashier who will receipt both copies of the bill and return the receipted top copy plus any change to the waiter. The latter then returns this to the customer. The receipted duplicate copy with the duplicate checks pinned to it is then removed from the special book or file and put on one side until service is completed.

At the conclusion of service a sales summary sheet (see page 410) is created. This shows an analysis of all payments taken and must be balanced against sales by the cashier before going off duty. Once it is balanced it should be handed to the control and accounts department, together with all the duplicate bills and their checks, and the money and other payments received plus the float. A receipt must be obtained for the monies and payments handed in.

Where services are provided to residents in the lounges and on the floors, payments might not be taken at the same time. Therefore, all bills must be signed by the resident concerned to show he/she has received a particular service. When a resident signs a bill for a service rendered the waiter must ensure the correct room number is obtained so that the charge can be made on the right bill. These bills should then be immediately passed to the control and accounts

Fig 10.2. Example of a bill

department. It is their job to ensure that the bills are posted onto the guest's account. In this way all residents' bills are kept up to date and all services provided are charged for.

Methods of payment

There are various ways of making payment for goods or services received, some of which have already been indicated under Billing methods (see page 262). The main methods of payment are described below.

Cash

The amount of cash received by the operator should always be checked in front of the customer and when change is given it should be counted back to the customer. Any notes received by the operator should be checked to ensure they are not forgeries. An itemised and receipted bill should always accompany the change.

Cheque

A cheque guarantee card should always accompany payment by cheque. The operator receiving the cheque should make sure:

- it is dated correctly
- it is made payable to the correct firm or company
- the correct amount is filled in
- it is signed by the person indicated on the cheque
- the signature on the cheque is the same as that on the cheque guarantee card
- the bank sort code is the same as on the cheque card
- the cheque guarantee card is valid – it has not expired in relation to the dates indicated.

The cheque guarantee card indicates that the bank concerned will meet the cheque payment (up to the limit indicated on the back of the card). This will be the case even if the person writing the cheque has insufficient monies in his/her account. Some credit and debit cards also act as cheque guarantee cards. An example of this is a Barclaycard.

Credit cards/debit cards/charge cards

- *Credit cards*: allow customers to spend up to a pre-determined limit. The customer receives a statement of payments at the end of a month, which he can then pay off in full or in part. Interest is charged on any remaining balance.
- *Debit cards*: used in a similar way to a credit card but the amount due is immediately deducted from the customer's bank account. Examples include the Switch and Connect cards.
- *Charge cards*: work in a similar way to credit cards but the customer is invoiced once a month. The account must then be paid up in full. Examples include the American Express and Diners Club cards.

On receipt of a credit, debit or charge card the operator should check that it is still valid by looking at the dates on the card. There are now two systems for accepting payments with these types of cards: signature verified and chip and PIN.

Signature verified

This is a manual system in which the validity of the card is checked, often through an on-line or dial-up connection to the card issuer, by passing it through an electronic card reader. Once verified, the details of the transaction are printed in the form of an itemised bill which the customer is then asked to sign. A copy of this itemised bill is then given as a receipt. Some establishments also make out a sales voucher. The customer is then requested to sign the voucher after which the operator should check the signature with that on the card. The customer receives a copy of the voucher as a receipt.

Chip and PIN

Chip and PIN means that the customer enters their PIN (personal identification number) into a hand-sized keypad when they use a credit or charge card for face-to-face transactions such as in shops, hotels or restaurants.

Receiving chip and PIN payments

- Dealing with Chip and PIN is very similar to previous processes used for card transactions.
- The POS (point of sale) terminals used provide step-by-step instructions to complete a transaction.
- First the transaction total is displayed on the POS terminal display.
- The customer is then asked for their card.
- In most cases the customer will hand the card to the member of staff, but sometimes customers may be asked to insert the card into the reader themselves.
- The chip and PIN card is inserted into the reader.
- Once the card is verified, the customer is asked to enter their PIN.
- The machine will then check the PIN number entered against the PIN held on the chip in the card.
- Be prepared to show customers how to enter their PIN. Be patient – customers using chip and PIN for the first time may need reassurance.
- Customers *must* enter their own PIN – it is not secure for a member of staff to do it and customers are required not to reveal their PIN to anyone.
- If necessary remind customers that their PIN may be the same as the one that they use at a cash machine.
- Suggest that the customer shields the PIN pad from other customers as they enter their PIN.
- If the customer says they can't remember their PIN, then they may be allowed to sign the payment slip in the traditional way (depending on establishment policy). If this does happen then pay particular attention to the card and signature.

- The prompts on the POS terminal screen are followed and the payment is processed.

- The card is then removed from the card reader.

- The receipt is issued and the receipt and the card are returned to the customer.

Payment in restaurants

There are two ways of dealing with payments in restaurants:

- The first is to ask the customer to come to the cash desk, or workstation, to complete the payment transaction there – some customers may prefer this.

- The second is to have hand-held self-powered terminals that can be taken to the table.

Locked PIN

- If the customer enters the wrong PIN three times in a row, the card will become temporarily unusable.

- The POS terminal prompt will indicate whether payment on this card can be made using signature or whether the customer needs to provide a different method of payment.

Fig 10.3. Example of a hand held credit/debit card payment terminal with printer

- Advise customers that they can unlock their PIN:
  - by contacting their card issuer. Contact numbers are on the back of most cards or on statements
  - at most cash machines which have an unlock PIN facility.

People with disabilities

The procedures are generally the same. However, some additional considerations are given below.

- Offer to assist when needed and most importantly exercise patience to ensure that a customer has enough time to complete a stress-free transaction.

- Make sure all customers, including those in wheelchairs, can easily reach the desk or table to sign the bill or to access the PIN pad.

- Follow the terminal prompts – some cardholders may have chip and signature cards instead of chip and PIN cards. Chip and PIN terminals will recognise this type of card and automatically ask for a signature.

- Encourage, or help, the customer to pick up the PIN pad (from the cradle if appropriate).

- Suggest that the customer shields the PIN pad from other customers as they enter their PIN.

Declined transactions

Procedures for declined transactions are the same for any credit card/debit card/charge card payments, whether signature verified or chip and PIN. Where the card is declined, always ask for an alternative method of payment.

Traveller's cheques

These may be issued by either a travel agent or bank in the traveller's own country. They may be issued in sterling, US dollars, Euros and other currencies.

The traveller's cheque must be signed once when issued and again when used to pay for something or when exchanging for cash. The rate of exchange will be that at the time of the transaction.

All traveller's cheques come in different values and this value is guaranteed as long as the two signatures match. When a payment is made by traveller's cheque the customer must:

■ date the cheque or cheques required

■ make them payable to the establishment concerned

■ sign the cheque or cheques for a second time in the appropriate place.

The cashier will then:

■ match the two signatures

■ ask for other identification to check the two signatures against. Such identification might be the customer's passport

■ give change where needed in the currency of the traveller's cheque.

Vouchers and tokens

Vouchers, such as Luncheon Vouchers, may be offered in exchange for food in those establishments that accept them. The vouchers have an expiry date. Should food be purchased above the value of the voucher, the difference must be paid for in cash.

Tokens might be exchanged for specific meals or for certain values. If food purchased is more than the value of the token then the difference is again paid in cash. No change can be given for purchases valued at less than the token being exchanged.

Dealing with discrepancies

Prevention is better than cure! When dealing with cash, do not allow anyone to interrupt you during the transaction or get involved with the counting of money. This will only serve to confuse things.

■ Always double check cash received before placing it in the till and any change before giving it out.

■ If you make a mistake always apologise and remain polite. If you feel you cannot deal with a situation ask for assistance from your supervisor or manager.

■ Bank notes should be checked for forgeries and if found to be fake then they must not be accepted. You should explain why you cannot accept them, advising the customer to take the note to the police station.

■ If credit card fraud is suspected the credit card company may request that the card be retained. Suggest to the customer that they contact the company to discuss the matter. You may wish to offer the use of a telephone with some privacy.

Sales summary sheets

Sales summary sheets are sometimes also called restaurant analysis sheets, bill summaries or records of restaurant sales. They provide for:

■ the reconciliation of items with different gross profits
■ sales mix information
■ records of popular/unpopular items
■ records for stock control.

There are many different formats for sales summaries, which are often electronically produced. Depending on the needs of the establishment, the information often includes:

■ date
■ food and beverage outlet (if more than one)
■ period of service
■ bill numbers
■ table numbers
■ number of covers per table

■ bill totals
■ analysis of sales e.g. food, beverages, or more detailed, e.g. per menu and wine and drink list items
■ various performance measures (see page 418)
■ cashier's name.

They may also include individual staff or till sales breakdowns.

Consumption control

In food and beverage service areas there may be food and beverage items displayed on:

■ cold tables
■ buffets
■ carving trolleys

■ sweet trolleys
■ liqueur trolleys
■ food and beverage counters.

A consumption control method is used for these services that identifies the number of portions/measures etc., issued to the area. Following service, returns are deducted and the final total equals the consumption. The consumption is then checked with actual sales to identify shortages/surpluses. This method of control is also found in room and lounge service.

Consumption control sheet		Date: 22/2/2006			Service period: Luncheon	
Item	Portions issued	Portions returned	Portions consumed	Billed portions	Difference +	−
Fruit salad	24	6	18	15		3
Gateau	20	5	15	14		1
Flan	30	10	20	16		4

Fig 10.4. Example of a consumption sheet

10.3 BEVERAGE CONTROL

The system of beverage control is basically the same as for food. However, for beverages the cellar is the focal point for the storage of alcoholic and non-alcoholic liquor.

Determining stock levels

All the individual outlets within an establishment such as the lounge, lounge bar, cocktail bar, saloon bar, brasserie, dispense bars and floor service, should draw their stock on a daily or weekly basis from the cellar. Each outlet will hold a set stock (or 'par stock') of liquor, which is sufficient for a service period or for a day or week etc. The level of the par stock will be determined mainly by the amount of storage space available in the service areas and also taking account of the expected sales demand. At the end of this service period each individual outlet will requisition for the amount of drink consumed in that one service period, day or week, thus bringing their total stock back up to the par stock level.

For the establishment as a whole, the central stock levels that are required in order to meet expected sales demand may be determined by using past sales data. A useful formula is:

$$M = W(T + L) + S$$

Where:
M is the maximum stock level
W is the average usage rate (over the review period)
T is the review period (time interval between orders)
L is the lead time (time it takes for the order to arrive), and
S is the safety stock (buffer or minimum stock level).

For example:
W = 24 bottles per week
T = 4 weeks
L = 1 week
S = 1 week's usage of 24 bottles

Therefore:
$$M = 24 \times (4 + 1) + 24 = 144 \text{ bottles}$$

Minimum stock (buffer or safety stock) may also be calculated as follows:
$$L \times W = 1 \times 24 = 24 \text{ bottles}$$

ROL (reorder level) may also be calculated as follows:
$$(W \times L) + S = (24 \times 1) + 24 = 48 \text{ bottles}$$

The same basic approaches can be applied for all types of alcoholic and non-alcoholic beverages, whether based on purchasing units such as bottles above, or quantities such as litres/gallons.

Using this approach can enable foodservice operations to determine the stock holding that will meet the needs of the expected demand, while at the same time minimising the amount of capital tied up in the stock being held. Good stock control can also be supported by the application of a 'just in time' (JIT) approach to purchasing. JIT involves only ordering stock as required in order to meet forecasted demand, rather than holding unnecessarily high stock levels just in case.

Beverage control procedures

In any foodservice establishment where income is received from the sale of wine and drink, a system of control and costing must be put into operation. The system used will depend entirely on the policy of the establishment. Some or all of the books listed below may be necessary, depending upon the requirements of the particular foodservice operation.

Book	Used to record
Order book	Orders made to suppliers
Goods inwards/goods received book	Goods received from suppliers
Goods returned book	Goods that are sent back to suppliers.
Returnable containers book	Returnable containers sent back to suppliers
Cellar stock ledger	Stock movement in and out of the cellar
Bin cards	Stock of individual lines in the cellar
Requisition book	Re-stocking orders for individual service areas
Daily consumption sheets	Usage of stock in individual service areas
Ullage book	Breakage, spillage and wastage
Off-sales book	Items sold at the off-sale prices
Transfers book	Movement of stock between different service areas

Although referred to as books here, most modern-day systems are computer-based. However, the basic processes are the same whatever the method being used to record the data.

A summary of the basic steps in bar and cellar control is given in Figure 10.5.

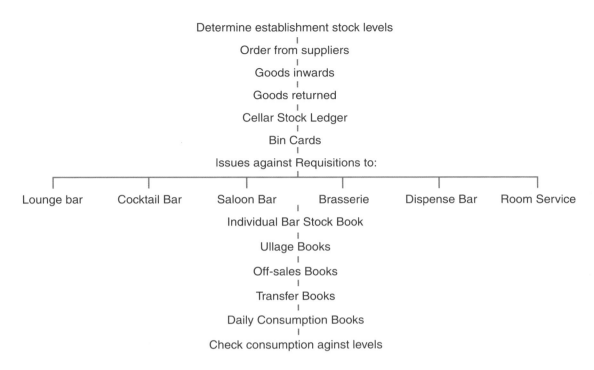

Fig 10.5. Summary of basic steps in bar and cellar control

Order book

The cellarperson is responsible for purchasing all alcoholic and non-alcoholic drinks needed to maintain the level of stock in an establishment. The order should be written in duplicate on an official order form. The top copy is then sent to the supplier and the duplicate remains in the order book for control purposes when the goods are delivered. In some instances there may be three copies of the order sheet. If so, they are distributed as follows:

- *Top copy*: supplier.
- *Duplicate copy*: control and accounts department.
- *Third copy*: remains in the order book.

Goods inwards/goods received book

All deliveries should be recorded in full detail in the goods received book. Each delivery entry should show the following:

- delivery note/invoice number
- name and address of supplier
- order number
- date of delivery
- list of items delivered

- quantity
- unit
- item price
- discounts if applicable
- total price.

413

When the goods are delivered to an establishment they should be accompanied by either a delivery note or an invoice. Whichever document it may be, the information contained should be exactly the same, with one exception: invoices show the price of all goods delivered whereas delivery notes do not. The goods delivered must first be counted and checked against the delivery note to ensure that all the goods listed have been delivered. The cellarperson may carry out an extra check by checking the delivery note against the copy of the original order in the order book. This is to ensure that the items ordered have been sent, in the correct quantities, and that extra items have not been sent which were not requested on the order sheet, thereby incurring extra cost.

Goods returned book

Records of any returns made to suppliers are recorded in the good inwards book or in a separate goods returned book. This may also include records of returnable containers such as kegs, casks and CO_2 cylinders, or these may be recorded in a separate returnable containers book.

Cellar stock ledger

The cellar stock ledger is an essential part of beverage control and may be used as either an extension of, or in place of, the goods received book. It therefore shows movement of all stock into the establishment and issues out to the bars or dispensing points. All movement of stock in and out of the cellar is often shown at cost and selling price.

Bin cards

Bin cards (see Figure 10.7) are used to indicate the physical stock of each separate stock line held in the cellar. The movement of all stock in and out of the cellar should be recorded on each individual bin card.

Every time an item is received or issued it must be entered on the corresponding bin card and the remaining total balance shown. Thus, the bin cards should show, at any given time, the total amount of each particular line currently held in stock.

Name of drink	Bin no.	Opening stock	Received	Total	Closing stock	Consumption	Price per unit	£

Fig 10.6. Cellar stock ledger

Name of wine			Bin No.
Date	Received	Balance	Issued

Fig 10.7. Bin card

The bin cards are also often used to show the maximum stock and minimum stock levels, thus providing a guide to the cellarperson when reordering. The minimum stock indicates the reorder level, leaving sufficient stock in hand to carry over until the new delivery arrives. The maximum stock indicates how much to reorder and is determined by such considerations as storage space available, the turnover of a particular item and to some extent, by the amount of cash available within the establishment budget (see Determining stock levels, page 411).

Requisition

Each unit dispensing alcoholic beverages should use some form of requisition to draw items from the cellar. These requisitions may be controlled either by colour or serial number, and are normally in triplicate. The copies are sent as follows.

- *Top copy*: to the cellar.
- *Duplicate copy*: to the beverage control department.
- *Triplicate copy*: used by each unit to check its goods when they have been received from the cellar.

The following information is listed on the requisition:

- name of the dispensing unit
- date
- list of items required
- quantity and unit of each item required
- signature of the authorised person who may both order and receive the goods.

The purpose of the requisition is to control the movement of items from the cellar into the dispensing unit and to avoid too much stock being taken at one time, thus overstocking the bar. The level of stock held in the bar is known as 'par' stock. The amount ordered on the requisition each day should bring the stock back up to par. The amount to reorder is determined by taking account of the following equation:

Opening stock *plus* additions (requisition) *less* closing stock *equals* consumption (the amount to reorder of each item to the nearest whole unit).

No items should be issued by the cellarperson unless he receives an official requisition form, correctly filled in, dated and signed by a person in authority from the department concerned. The cellarperson should have a list of such signatures and should not issue any stock unless a person on the list signs the requisition sheet. To aid the cellarperson, all requisitions should be handed into him at a set time each day, when all issues will be made. In certain instances, however, depending on the organisation of an establishment, it may be necessary to issue twice per day, once before opening time in the morning and again before opening time in the evening.

Ullage book

Each sales point must have a ullage book for recording the amount of beer wasted in cleaning the pipes, broken bottles, measures spilt or anything that needs a credit.

Off-sales book

The off-sales book contains a record of the number of bottles, whether beers, spirits or wines, sold at off-sales prices and the difference in price between the off-sales price and the on-sales price (this is the price if the item was sold within the establishment by measure). This difference will be allowed against the gross profit.

Transfer book

With multi-bar units it is necessary to minimise the movement of stock between bars with different prices otherwise this can create shortages. If this does happen then all such stock movements must be recorded in a transfer book.

Daily consumption sheet

The daily consumption sheet lists all of the sales in an individual service area, such as number of spirit measures, number of bottles of wine or beers by quantity. This information is then used to calculate what receipts should have been received for the items used.

Name of drink	Bin no.	Mon	Tues	Wed	Thurs	Fri	Sat	Sun	Total

Fig 10.8. Daily consumption sheet

Beverage gross profit

An analysis of non-alcoholic and alcoholic beverage sales and the stock held allows for two performance measures to be obtained:

- the gross profit
- the overage or shortage of the estimated monetary revenue and stock in hand.

The data can then be analysed to identify the reasons for any variations in beverage gross profit.

Calculating gross profit

Gross profit is determined by deducting the beverage cost from the sales. It is essential that a physical alcoholic beverage stock be taken at least on a monthly basis, and more often if it is felt necessary.

To determine the overage or shortage it is necessary to estimate how much money should have been taken during a given period of time, based on the consumption at selling price. The consumption must be priced out bottle-by-bottle, keg-by-keg.

For example, a bar has sold 12 bottles of whisky (which sells at £2.70 per 25ml measure), 6 bottles of sherry (at £2.50 per 50ml measure) and 5 kegs (9 gallons each, selling at £2.50 per pint):

Whisky:	12 × 30 measures × £2.70	=	£972.00
Sherry:	6 × 15 measures × £2.50	=	£225.00
Kegs:	5 × 72 pints × £2.50	=	£900.00

(Note: Keg = 9 gallons × 8 pints = 72 pints)

Estimated takings	=	£2097.00
Actual cash takings	=	£2184.26
Surplus	=	£ 87.26

£87.27 is 4.16% of estimated takings

Variations in beverage gross profit

The relative proportion of wines, beers and spirits that have been sold will often help to explain why a certain month's gross profit is low (a lot of beer sold) or high (more spirits have been sold). There are, however, other reasons for a high or low gross profit:

- Under-ringing and keeping the difference, for example, by ringing perhaps £0.50 instead of £1.50, whereby the bar loses a £1. The cash register should be sited so that both the customer and the management are able to check visually the amount being keyed or rung up.

- Too many 'No sales' on the till roll may give a clue to shortages. It is not always possible to prohibit the use of the No sale key altogether. Therefore, the till roll should be examined each time it is removed so that excessive use of the No sale key may be queried at the time.

- The till roll itself can be very revealing. It is sometimes found that there are a lot of very small sales recorded or that the average sale is lower than usual or lower with one operator than with another. Such indications can be taken as evidence that there are potential problems.

- Working with the till drawer open. If the till is not set on closed drawer then it is possible to give change without keying in, or ringing the amount up.

- Failing to ensure that all off-sales are kept apart from the bar where measures are sold, and a separate stock used. All off-sales should be entered into a separate book. The difference between the bar measure prices and the off-sales prices will be needed by the stock taker.

- Letting bar staff cash up could lead to the balance of the receipts being made to fit the expected sales recorded.

- Lounge sales or sales at a table away from the bar may also be vulnerable. The till ticket provides one simple method of control. If each waiter is provided with a float and has to pay for drinks at the time of collecting, then they will have a ticket to present to the customer. The customer then knows that the money has gone into the till and this gives the customer confidence in the establishment. The other advantage is that, unless there is collusion, the bar staff will not overcharge the waiter or under-ring the transaction. Even though this is a simple method of control it is still open to abuse. Staff have been known to use the same chit twice, but only if they are able to get drinks without paying for them.

The efficient manager will ensure that the receipts are counted first and then the till is read rather than reading the till first and then checking the receipts. In busy bars it is good practice to collect most of the receipts before the end of a session, leaving a temporary receipt in the drawer.

The use of electronic equipment may help to reveal that losses have taken place, but it will not in itself prevent them. Most electronic equipment is designed primarily to facilitate the analysis and recording of sales. Such equipment may, for example, provide automatic pricing for up to 1,000 items, including for instance a half-pint and pint of beer, whisky, gin, gin and tonic, and thereby greatly reduce the likelihood of miscalculation and make under-keying/under-ringing easier to detect.

10.4 PERFORMANCE MEASURES

Table 1.5 on page 8 identifies a variety of performance measures or operating statistics. This section provides information on these various performance measures (see also Level of demand, page 425).

Sales mix

Sales mix figures may be taken from a sales summary sheet (see page 410) and shown in a simple report, as in Table 10.3 and 10.4.

Food and drink sales may be broken down further to provide sales mix data. This not only reconciles sales of items with differing gross profits but also provides information on:

- popular/unpopular items on the menu/drinks lists
- records for stock control, for example, to help predict future demand
- changes in customers' interests
- where profits/losses are being made.

Table 10.3 Simple sales report

Service	Total £	Food £	Liquor £
Lunches	90	60	30
Dinners	80	50	30
Snacks	15	15	–
Daily total	185	125	60

Table 10.4 Application of percentages

Service	Total £	%	Food £	%	Liquor £	%
Lunches	90	49	60	67	30	33
Dinners	80	43	50	62	30	38
Snacks	15	8	15	100	–	–
Daily total	185	100	125	68	60	32

Elements of cost

In foodservice operations there are three elements of cost:

■ *Food or beverage costs*: often called cost of sales.

■ *Labour*: wages, salaries, staff feeding, uniforms.

■ *Overheads*: rent, rates, advertising, fuel.

Sales in foodservice operations are always equal to 100%. The relationship between costs and profits in foodservice operations may be seen in Figure 10.9.

Note: In kitchen operations gross profit is sometimes called kitchen percentage or kitchen profit.

Fig 10.9 Elements of cost

Food and Beverage costs	Cost of sales
Labour costs	
Overhead costs	Gross profit
Net profit	
Total sales £	**Revenue 100%**

Table 10.5 Labour cost percentages

Sales		Direct labour costs	% of total labour costs	% of department sales
Food	£125	£35	78%	28%
Liquor	£60	£10	22%	17%
Total	£185	£45	100%	24%

Thus:

■ Total sales *less* food and beverage costs *less* labour costs *less* overhead costs *equals* net profit.

■ Revenue *less* cost of sales *equals* gross profit.

Costs such as labour may be classified in relation to sales. Thus:

$$\text{Labour costs as a percentage of total wages cost} = \frac{\text{Department labour cost}}{\text{Total wage cost}} \times 100$$

$$\text{Labour costs as a percentage of sales} = \frac{\text{Labour cost}}{\text{Revenue}} \times 100$$

These calculations are summarised in Table 10.5.

By using the same approach, all costs (food, drink, labour or overheads) can be attributed to a return in revenue.

Index of productivity (alternative method of showing labour costs)

The index of productivity is calculated by dividing the total sales figure by the total labour costs (including any staff benefit costs).

The index of productivity will vary according to the type of operation. For example, a popular catering operation should have a high index of productivity, as the labour costs should be relatively low, whereas a restaurant with a high ratio of staff to customers should have a relatively low index of productivity. As payroll costs can be controlled, and should be related to the forecasted volume of business, a standard index of productivity can be established over time to measure how accurately the two elements are related.

Seat turnover

Seat turnover is a pointer to efficiency. It shows how many times a seat is being used during a service period. It is calculated by dividing the number of covers served by the actual number of seats available per service period. Therefore:

■ in a snack bar the seat turnover might be four to five times per service period

■ in an expensive restaurant the seat turnover might be once per service period.

Table 10.6 Example of seat turnover calculation

Service period	No. of covers served	No. of seats available	Seat turnover
Lunch	60	80	0.75 times
Dinner	85	80	1.06 times

In operations where customers do not occupy specific seats (such as in cafeterias or take away operations), customer throughput may be calculated by the number of till transactions per service period or time period (e.g. per hour).

Average spend per head/average check

The average spend per head is a calculation of the average amount spent per person during a service period. It is calculated by dividing the total sales by the number of people or covers served. This performance measure is useful in restaurants where the total number of customers (covers) is known.

The average check is a calculation of the average spend per order taken, during a service period. It is calculated by dividing the total sales by the number of orders taken. This performance measure is useful in bars or take away operations where the actual number of customers is not known.

An example of both of these calculations is shown in Table 10.7.

Working out these performance measures assists in the interpretation of sales figures. For example:

■ If revenue goes up from one trading period to the next, is this due to higher selling prices or more customers being served or the same number of customers spending more?

■ If the revenue reduces from one trading period to the next, is this due to fewer customers being served or to the same number of customers spending less?

Table 10.7 Example of average check and average spend per head calculations

	Total revenue £	No. of orders taken	Average check	No. of covers served	Average spend per head £
Food	490	16	30.62	48	8.54
Beverages	280	13	21.54	39	7.18
Overall	770	29	26.55	87	8.85

The data can also be used to calculate the average number of persons in a group. This is calculated by dividing the number of covers served by the number of orders taken. Using the data in Figure 10.7 for food sales, this would be:

48 covers served, divided by 16 orders taken = an average of 3 persons in each group.

Sales per seat available

Sales per seat available shows the sales value that can be earned by each seat in a restaurant, coffee shop etc. It is used for comparison of different types of operation as well as a record of earnings per seat over a period of time. It is calculated by dividing the sales figures by the number of seats available in the dining area for specific service periods.

Sales per square metre

An alternative method of comparison between establishments is to calculate the sales per square metre or per square foot. This is particularly useful in bars or take away operations where earnings per seat cannot be calculated. It is calculated by dividing the total sales by the square meterage of the service area, for a specific service period.

Stock turnover

The rate of stock turnover gives the number of times that the average level of stock has turned over in a given period. It is calculated as follows:

$$\text{Rate of stock turnover} = \frac{\text{Cost of food or beverage consumed in specific period}}{\text{Average stock holding (food or beverage) at cost}}$$

The average stock holding is calculated by taking the opening stock value, adding the closing stock value and dividing by two. High stock turnover should be expected in a restaurant using predominantly fresh foods. Low stock turnover indicates usage of convenience food. Too high a turnover indicates potential problems through panic buying and lack of forecasting. Too low a turnover indicates that capital is being tied up in unused stocks.

10.5 CUSTOMER RELATIONS

Section 5.2 (page 180) highlighted interpersonal skills for staff. Chapter 5 also identified the various interpersonal skills associated with different tasks and duties in food and beverage service.

Customer relations is concerned with the conditions staff work under which may assist or prevent good standards of interpersonal skills being maintained. There are two aspects to this: firstly, the physical staff conditions and, secondly, the satisfaction or otherwise customers receive from the food and beverage service experience.

In order to develop and maintain good customer relations, the supervisor must have the ability to:

- recognise the symptoms of a deterioration in customer relations
- minimise the causes of customer relations problems.

The following list indicates some of the symptoms of customer relations problems:

- increasing complaints about products/staff
- increasing accidents
- mistakes by staff in orders etc.
- customers arriving without prior bookings being noted
- arguments between staff
- poor staff morale
- breakages or shortages of equipment
- high turnover of staff.

Minimising customer relations problems

Below is a series of questions that the supervisor should consider in order to minimise customer relations problems.

- *Why is that member of staff not smiling or being courteous to customers?*
  - If a waiter is not smiling their feet might be hurting and no amount of telling them to smile will change this. Their shoes might be the problem.
  - In the society in which we live, we are trained from an early age to be polite. We all know how to say 'please' and 'thank you'. In foodservice operations the use of 'sir', 'madam', 'please', 'excuse me' and 'thank you' is expected. If it is not being done, the supervisor needs to ask: Is the member of staff in the wrong job? If they are in the right job, then what is the problem?
- *What are the problems of each department in working with other departments?*
- *How does each department's problems affect the others?*
- *What are the difficulties that a customer could experience?*

  For example, lack of information or direction signs.
- *Is the emphasis in the work areas put on the customer?*

  For example, a barman eating behind the bar takes the emphasis away from the customer.
- *What problems can be solved by physical changes?*

  For example, staff congregating round a central sideboard will face inwards and not outwards to observe customers.
- *What problems exist because information to customers is insufficient other than that which can be obtained from staff?*
- *Are members of staff given enough information about the establishment and locality before they meet customers?*
- *Are foreseen problems minimised?*

  For example, are large parties organised in advance?
- *Are members of staff informed of set procedures for foreseen problems?*

  For example, running out of food items.
- *Are complaints used as an opportunity to show care for customers?*

- *Are there set procedures for dealing with complaints?*
- *Are there set procedures for dealing with difficult customers?*

  For example, customers who are quarrelsome, drunk or non-compliant with establishment requirements such as smoking, dress codes or the use of mobile phones.
- *How can staff be encouraged to identify and propose solutions for their problems?*

Handling complaints

Should a problem arise and the customer makes a complaint the following steps should be taken.

1 Do not interrupt the customer – let them have their say and make their point.
2 Apologise – but only for the specific problem or complaint.
3 Restate the complaint briefly back to the customer to show you have listened and understood.
4 Agree by thanking the customer for bringing the matter to your attention. This shows you are looking at the problem from the customer's perspective.
5 Act quickly, quietly and professionally.

Never:

- lose your temper
- take it personally
- argue
- blame another member of staff or another department.

Valid complaints provide important feedback for a foodservice operation and should be used to improve service.

Customer satisfaction

In Section 1.5 (page 11) the factors contributing to the meal experience were summarised. The factors that might affect the customer's enjoyment of a specific meal experience in a particular operation include the following:

- welcome, décor and ambience of the establishment
- level of efficiency shown, for example, has the booking been taken properly, using the customer's name?
- location of the table
- presentation and cleanliness of the menu and drinks list
- order being taken – recognition of the host
- availability of dishes/items
- speed and efficiency of service
- quality of food and drink

- courteousness of staff
- obtrusiveness/attentiveness of staff
- ability to attract the attention of staff
- other customers' behaviour
- method in which complaints are handled
- method of presenting the bill and receiving payment
- departure attentiveness.

The supervisor is responsible for minimising potential customer relations problems. He/she should be as much concerned with the physical aspects of the service as with the way in which the service is operated and with the interpersonal interaction between customers and staff.

In food and beverage service operations interaction also takes place with people outside the service areas, such as kitchen staff, bill office staff, dispense bar staff and still room staff. It is important that the provision of food and beverages within an establishment is seen as a joint effort between all departments, with each department understanding the needs of the others in order to meet the customers' demands.

10.6 STAFF ORGANISATION AND TRAINING

Staff organisation in food and beverage service centres on having sufficient trained and competent staff on duty to match the expected level of customer demand.

Level of demand and customer throughput

The first step in staff organisation is to determine the expected level of customer demand. This can be done from sales records. As most operations have limitations in the number of customers that can be served at any particular time, it is also necessary to calculate the potential customer throughput.

There is a relationship between the volume of customers to be served and the length of time they stay on the premises. The time customers take in different types of operation varies. An indication of these times is given in Table 10.8.

There is also a relationship between the volume of customers and the opening times of the operation. For example, in a full service restaurant the seating time of customers might average one and a half hours. If the restaurant is open for four hours, then it might be possible to fill the operation twice. If, however, the opening hours were only two and a half hours, then this would not be possible.

Opening times are determined by the consideration of:

- local competition
- local attractions, such as a theatre
- location of the premises, e.g. city centre/country/suburb
- transport systems
- staffing availability
- volume of business anticipated
- local tradition.

Table 10.8 Seating/consumption times in various types of operation

Operation	Consumption time (minutes)
Restaurant	60–120
Carvery	45–90
Popular catering	30–60
Cafeteria	15–40
Wine bar	30–60
Pub (food)	30–60
Take away with seating	20–40
Fast food with seating	10–20

Customer throughput in table and assisted service operations

Customer throughput can be determined since all customers are usually seated for both table and assisted service methods. For new operations the throughput must be estimated as it is limited by the length of seating time and the opening hours of the operation. For existing operations sales records will provide a guide to potential throughput.

Staffing for each service period can then be estimated and allocated to specific jobs. Staffing will also need to be estimated for mise-en-place duties prior to the service period and for clearing following the service period. Thus, a restaurant that is open for two and a half hours at lunchtime may require staff to be on duty for up to five hours.

To calculate the total staffing required:

1 Estimate the number of staff required per service period in one week.

2 Multiply the number of staff per service period by the number of hours to be worked in each period.

3 Divide total staff hours by full-time working week hours. This will give the full-time equivalent of number of staff required.

4 Mix part-time and full-time staff hours to cover all service periods.

5 Draw up staff rota, which may need to be on a two- or three-week cycle to allow for days off etc.

For example: A restaurant opens six days per week for luncheon and dinner; maximum of 80 covers.

Volume of customers

	M	T	W	T	F	S
Luncheon	65	75	85	80	85	54
Dinner	85	90	120	140	135	160

Opening times

Luncheon	12.30 p.m. to 2.30 p.m.	Last order 2.00 p.m.
Dinner	6.30 p.m. to Midnight	Last order 11.30 p.m.

Staff time
11.00 a.m. to 3.00 p.m. (4 hours)
6.00 p.m. to 1.00 a.m. (7 hours)

The number of staff to each service period can now be calculated.

For this example the staffing and staff calculations might be estimated as:

Service staffing	M	T	W	T	F	S	S	Total staffing	Total number of working hours
Lunch	3	4	4	4	4	3	-	22	88 (22 staff × 4 hours)
Dinner	4	5	6	7	7	8	-	37	259 (37 staff × 7 hours)
Total number of staff hours for the week									347 (88 + 259)
Number of full-time equivalent staff (at 35 hours per week)									10 (347 hours ÷ 35 hours)

As the numbers of staff for each service period have been calculated, a working time rota can be drawn up. In this example the full time equivalent staffing is 10. Mixing full and part-time staffing could mean that this operation might employ, for example, five full-time staff working 175 hours (5 staff × 35 hours) with the rest of the required 172 working hours (347 hours – 175 hours) being covered by overtime and/or part-time staffing.

Similar approaches for estimating staffing requirements exist for the other service method groups although the calculation of throughput differs, as indicated below.

Customer throughput in cafeteria operations

There are five factors that influence potential throughput in cafeterias:

- *Service time*: the time it takes each customer to pass along or by the counter and reach the till point.
- *Service period*: the time the cafeteria is actually serving.
- *Till speed*: the time it takes for a customer to be billed and payment taken.
- *Eating/seating time*.
- *Seating capacity*.

The main criterion is seating capacity. The speed required in the queue is determined by the seating capacity and the average seating time.

For example, if there are 186 seats and the till speed is nine customers per minute, it will take 20.66 minutes to fill the cafeteria. If the customers' seating time is 20 minutes, then the cafeteria will be filled just after the first customers are leaving. A faster till speed will mean that the last customer through the till will have nowhere to sit. Too slow a till speed will mean the cafeteria is not being fully utilised. For one till, four to six people per minute is a maximum.

Assuming the service period is to be one hour, this cafeteria will be able to provide service as follows:

- 55 minutes (60 minutes less 5 minutes service time) × 9 (people per minute till speed) = 495 people.
- The cafeteria would need to be open for 1 hour 20 minutes (1 hour service period and 20 minutes for the last person to finish eating).

To calculate the seating capacity of a cafeteria required to serve 200 people in one hour, with a service time of 5 minutes and an average seating time of 20 minutes:

Example 1:

- All customers will need to be served in:

60 minutes		(opening time)
less	20 minutes	(seating time)
less	5 minutes	(service time)
=	35 minutes	(service period)

- The number of seats required will be:

$$\frac{200 \text{ (people)} \times 20 \text{ (minutes seating time)}}{35 \text{ (minutes service period)}} = 114.25 \text{ seats}$$

- There will need to be 115 seats in the cafeteria.
- The till speed will need to be:

$$\frac{115 \text{ (seats)}}{20 \text{ (minute seating time)}} = 5.75 \text{ people per minute}$$

Example 2:

- If the seating time is reduced to 15 minutes then all customers will need to be served in:

60 minutes		(opening time)
less	15 minutes	(seating time)
less	5 minutes	(service time)
=	40 minutes	(service period)

- The number of seats required would then be:

$$\frac{200 \text{ (people)} \times 15 \text{ (minutes seating time)}}{40 \text{ (minutes service period)}} = 75 \text{ seats}$$

This is 40 fewer seats than required in Example 1, which represents a considerable saving in seating provision.

- Till speed will reduce to:

$$\frac{75 \text{ (seats)}}{15 \text{ (minutes seating time)}} = 5 \text{ people per minute}$$

Hence the service speed will also reduce which may mean a saving in staffing.

Generally, if the seating time is greater than the service period then the actual number of seats will need to equal the total number of customers. If the eating time is less than the time it takes to serve all the customers then the number of seats may be less than the actual number of people to be served. However, the queue may need to be staggered to avoid excessive waiting before service.

Customer throughput in single point service operations

Customer throughput in single point service operations may be determined by looking at the records of till transactions. The increase or decrease in the service that is required is provided for by increasing or decreasing the number of till points available at different times (or in the case of vending, additional machines). If seating areas are provided then similar calculations as for cafeterias above can be carried out. The percentage of the customers using the seating facilities will also need to be known.

Customer demand in specialised service

For hospital and airline tray methods there is a limitation on the number of customers that can be accommodated in beds or in aircraft seats. For other forms of specialised service methods there are records or estimates of potential take-up of services in specific locations, such as hotel rooms, lounges and home delivery.

Daily duty rota

The object of a duty rota is to ensure that all the necessary duties are covered in order that efficient service may be carried out. The exact nature of the duty rota will vary according to the type of establishment, the duties to be performed, the number of staff, time off and whether a split/straight shift is worked. Figure 10.10 gives an example of a daily duty rota for pre-service duties for a table service operation and shows how they may be allocated.

A duty rota also provides the basis for staff training. Detailed lists are drawn up for all the tasks and duties that must be covered. These task and duty lists will also identify the standards that are to be achieved for the operation. (See also Planning training, page 434.)

Staff training

'Training' is the 'systematic development of people'. The general objectives of training are to:

■ increase the quantity and quality of output by improving employee skills

■ reduce accidents

■ increase the return to the employee in personal rewards, such as increased pay, recognition and other benefits which the employee wants from the job

■ make the operation more profitable by reducing the amount of equipment and material required to produce or sell in a given unit

Waiter	1.6.06	2.6.06	3	4	5	6	7	8	9	10	11	12	13	14.6.06	Task No.
A	1	11	10	9	8	7		6	5	4	3	2	1		1. Menus
B	2	1	11	10	9	8		7	6	5	4	3	2		2. Restaurant cleaning
C	3	2	1	11	10	9		8	7	6	5	4	3		3. Linen
D	4	3	2	1	11	10	C	9	8	7	6	5	4	C	4. Hot plate
E	5	4	3	2	1	11	L	10	9	8	7	6	5	L	5. Silver
F	6	5	4	3	2	1	O	11	10	9	8	7	6	O	6. Accompaniments
G	7	6	5	4	3	2	S	1	11	10	9	8	7	S	7. Sideboard
H	8	7	6	5	4	3	E	2	1	11	10	9	8	E	8. Dispense bar
I	9	8	7	6	5	4	D	3	2	1	11	10	9	D	9. Still room
J	10	9	8	7	6	5		4	3	2	1	11	10		10. Miscellaneous
K	11	10	9	8	7	6		5	4	3	2	1	11		11. Day off

Fig 10.10. Example of a daily rota

- make it possible for the supervisor to spend less time correcting mistakes and more time in planning
- minimise turnover of staff because of inadequate skills
- improve morale and achieve a more satisfactory working environment
- enable new employees to meet their job requirements and enable experienced employees to accept transfers, adapt to new methods, increase efficiency and adjust to changing needs
- encourage willingness, loyalty, interest and the desire to excel.

Terms used in staff training

Job

All the tasks carried out by a particular employee in the completion of prescribed duties, within the setting of a particular working environment.

Job analysis

The process of examining a job to identify its component parts and the circumstances in which it is performed. This would normally require an examination of:

- the *purpose* of the job – what it exists for and what key results are expected from it
- the *setting* of the job – the physical, organisational and social conditions of the job

- the main *tasks* that have to be performed in order to achieve the results – what the employee does
- the *resources* or facilities available to the employee – what people, equipment, services etc., he/she can call upon.

Job description

A broad statement of the purpose, scope, duties and responsibilities of a particular job. This would normally include the following:

- job title
- purpose and scope of job
- to whom responsible
- place of work
- for whom responsible
- main duties
- main characteristics and working conditions
- key performance measures.

Task

An identifiable element of a job, by means of which a specific result is achieved.

Task identification

The process of identifying, listing and grouping the tasks that make up a job.

Task analysis

The detailed and systematic examination of the skills used by an experienced worker in performing a task to the required standard.

Job specification

A detailed statement of the tasks involved in a job, the standards required and the corresponding knowledge and skills involved.

Syllabus

A statement of what a trainee needs to learn, based on the comparison between the job specification and his/her present knowledge and competence.

Training programme

A broad outline of training that indicates the stages or sequence of the training and the time allowed for each part.

Training manual

This is a guide for the training staff and trainees that specifies the points to be covered in training, standards to be achieved, methods of instruction to be used, equipment and materials required, forms and records to be kept and any tests or targets which have to be achieved. These manuals are sometimes called 'Standards of Performance Manuals'.

Training programmes and the role of the supervisor

The advantages of clear and thorough training programmes include:

- identification of standards of performance required
- improved ability of staff
- a means of measuring ability
- more efficient working
- clearer responsibilities for staff.

The role of the supervisor in training is to:

- ensure that staff are competent to carry out the duties required of them
- ensure that legal and company requirements are met (for example, no staff under 18 to work with dangerous machinery)
- develop and train staff as required
- develop existing staff to train others
- identify training needs of staff, now and in the future
- develop the necessary skills to achieve the list of advantages of well-produced training programmes described above.

What is a training need?

A training need is present when there is a gap between:

- the knowledge, skills and attitudes displayed by people in their jobs, and
- the knowledge, skills and attitudes needed for them to achieve the results the job requires, both now and in the future

Identifying training needs

In order to systematically determine what the training needs of the operation are, it is necessary to find specific answers to the questions listed below.

Present needs

The first action is to examine the current staffing position and determine where the immediate training needs are. This includes consideration of:

Staffing

- What staffing does the establishment currently have?
- Where do they fit in?
- How long do they stay and why?
- Where do they come from?
- How are they chosen?
- How many new people are recruited and how often?

Agreed job descriptions

- What do the members of staff do in theory and in practice?
- Do they know clearly what they have to do?

Standards and performance

- What results and standards are expected from the staff?
- Are the staff aware of these?
- How well do they meet the requirements?
- What prevents these requirements from being met?

Present training

- How do members of staff currently learn their jobs and from whom?
- How well do they learn?
- How quickly do they learn?

Key problems

- Are there any special difficulties:
    - in the skills people have to learn?
    - in the circumstances under which they work?
    - in organising training?

Resources

- What training facilities exist within or outside the organisation that can be used or developed?

Future needs

Any change brings a training need with it. It is therefore necessary to ask questions in order to find out what future training will be needed, for instance:

Normal staff changes and development

- What is the age range of the staff?
- What posts are likely to have to be filled due to:
    - retirement?
    - normal replacements?
    - transfers?
- Is anyone earmarked for promotion?
- What potential for promotion is there?
- What plans are there for craft or other trainees?

Other changes

- What plans, if any, are there for:
  - expansion?
  - new equipment?
  - new working methods?
- How will existing jobs have to be altered to meet these changes?
- What further training will existing staff need?
- Will new staff be required?

Induction training

Induction training must be given to all new members of staff and should cover such things as:

- health, safety and security policies and procedures
- company employment policies and procedures (related to grievance, disciplinary, sickness, holidays, periods of notice etc.)
- organisation of working department including duties of colleagues
- other departments – their role and responsibilities
- where things/people are
- duty rota.

Planning training

The contents of this book have been based upon an operations hierarchy, which was used to identify tasks and duties in food and beverage service operations. These tasks and duties are summarised in the Master Reference Chart shown on pages xii and xiii. This identification of tasks and duties forms the basis of the content of this book.

For individual operations a similar list of tasks and duties can be drawn up that are specific to that particular operation. The set of tasks and duties, when compiled, are then analysed to identify specific knowledge, skills and attitudes required for each task. In other words, each task and duty is defined and standards of performance identified. Existing members of staff are then assessed against these criteria. The gaps are the training needs and plans should then be drawn up to carry out the training that is required.

10.7 SALES PROMOTION

Chapter 1 considered the range of foodservice operations within the hospitality industry. Sectors were identified, based on the nature of demand being met rather than the type of operation. In addition, the factors that affect the customer's enjoyment of a meal were identified. This section considers various aspects of sales promotion relevant to foodservice operations.

Sales promotion involves activities designed to promote regular sales. It is also concerned with promoting temporary sales to encourage increased business at slack periods such as Mondays, early evenings and during January/February. Examples of such activities include:

- offering meal (deal) packages, for example, free wine (or a 'buy one get a second free' deal), or offering a free soup or starter as part of the meal package.
- developing customer loyalty schemes.

Special product sales may also be used to increase sales by promoting particular products such as:

- festival promotions or links with local, regional or national celebrations
- wine and spirit promotions (possibly in association with suppliers)
- children's menus
- diabetic menus
- 'Taste of England' menus etc.
- products to complement specific calendar dates etc.

Three types of sales promotion are particularly useful for foodservice operations:

- *Sales promotion through advertising*: concerned with contacting and informing the existing, or potential market of a business, providing information on the products available and encouraging buying.
- *Sales promotion through merchandising*: related mainly to point-of-sale promotion. Its main role is to improve the average spend per head of the customer. However, it is also used to promote particular services or goods.
- *Sales promotion through personal selling*: refers to the ability of the staff in a food and beverage operation to actively contribute to the promotion of sales.

Advertising

Advertising media includes:

- *Broadcast*: radio, television.
- *Print*: newspapers, national daily, regional daily, national Sunday, regional Sunday, weekly regional and free distribution.
- *Consumer publications*: directories (Yellow Pages, Thompson's), guides, business publications, executive travel publications, technical and professional publications, journals and other magazines (including local free ones).
- *Other media*: commercial transport, terminals and stations, posters, cinema.
- *Postal advertising*: direct mail, hand drops.

In addition to the above, it is always worth considering the use of mailing lists to advise existing customers of special events etc. Retaining existing customers is always less costly than finding new ones.

Merchandising

Merchandising is related mainly to point-of-sale promotion. Its main role is to improve the average spend per head of the customer. However, it is also used to promote particular services or goods.

Examples of food and beverage merchandising tend to be mainly visual, but may also be audio or audio-visual. Food and beverage merchandising stimuli can include:

- aromas
- bulletins/black boards/floor stands
- directional signs
- display cards/brochures
- displays of food and drinks
- trolleys (sweet, liqueurs etc.)
- buffets/salad bars, self-service counters, bar displays, flambé work etc.
- drink coasters and placemats
- facia boards and illuminated panels
- menus, drinks and wine lists
- posters
- tent cards
- other customers' food/drink.

Written/printed merchandising materials should be effective. As well as considering using images, make sure the words used are descriptive and attractive, as shown in the examples below.

- *Describing the freshness of the product*: freshly prepared, pure, natural, real, freshly squeezed, hand picked each day, fresh
- *Describing the environment*: free range, corn fed, naming a specific location, source or a heard name, stating that foods are from a local market, home grown, or referring to 'happy animals'
- *Describing the overall product*: local flavour, traditional, warming, inventive use of ingredients, house speciality, signature dish.

Note: Care should be taken in using terms such as 'healthy' – what may be part of a healthy diet for one person is not necessarily part of a healthy diet for another (see Section 3.4, page 77, for health influences on menus).

Personal selling

Most merchandising stimuli must also be supported by good personal selling techniques. Personal selling refers specifically to the ability of the staff in a food and beverage operation to contribute to the promotion of sales. This is especially important where there are specific promotions being undertaken. The promise of a particular type of menu or drink, a special deal or the availability of a particular service can often be devalued by the inability of the staff to fulfil the requirements as promised. It is therefore important to involve service staff in the formulation of particular offers and to ensure that briefing and training are given so that the customer can actually experience what has been promised.

Members of staff will feel more confident about selling if they have information about the products on offer. If staff can tell well they can sell well. Examples of the type of information staff will need to know include:

- a description of the item (food, wine or other drink) and an explanation of how it is served
- where the produce comes from.
- what the local animals are fed on
- where the fish are caught
- where the local fruit and vegetables are grown
- how the produce is delivered
- where and how the local drinks are made
- what the specialities of the establishment are and their origin.

There are various ways of enhancing the product knowledge of staff, such as:

- arranging for staff visits to suppliers
- arranging visits to other establishments using local produce
- seeking out supplier information
- allowing staff to taste products
- arranging for staff to visit local trade fairs
- organising training and briefing sessions for staff.

Within the context of personal selling, the service staff should be able to:

- describe the food, wines and drinks on offer in an informative and appealing way, that makes the product sound interesting and desirable
- use the opportunity to promote specific items or deals when seeking orders from the customer
- seek information from the customer in a way that promotes sales, for example, rather than asking *if* a sweet is required, ask *which* sweet is required
- use opportunities for the sales of additional items such as extra garnishes, special sauces or accompanying drinks, such as a dessert wine with a sweet course
- provide a competent service of the items for sale and seek customers' views on the acceptability of the food, drinks and the service.

Ability in personal selling is necessary for all aspects of successful food and beverage service. The contribution of service staff to the meal experience is vital. The service staff contribute to the customers' perception of value for money, hygiene and cleanliness, the level of service and the perception of atmosphere that the customer experiences.

Good food and beverage service staff therefore must have a detailed knowledge of the food and beverages on offer, be technically competent, have well developed interpersonal skills and be able to work as part of a team.

ANNEX A: FOODS IN SEASON

Buying on a world rather than a local basis has meant that most foods are available all year round, although there is often a price premium. However, foods tend to be more plentiful and cheaper when they are available locally in season. In some cases, though, the dates and seasons have traditional associations that are often related to calendar dates in animal breeding, for example, the game seasons, and therefore changes in these dates are limited.

Key advantages of using foods in season

- Quality is at its best.
- Taste is at its peak.
- Often nutritionally at its peak.
- Usually cheaper.

Environmental benefits of using foods in season

- Reduction in convenience packaging and waste problems.
- Reduced food miles and transportation costs.
- Reduction in pollution from food transportation.

Potential business benefits of using foods in season from local suppliers

- Often there is an improvement in quality and particularly in freshness.
- Improved menu planning, as suppliers can give information in advance on what they are able to provide.
- Seasonality of product ensures good prices at optimum quality.
- More reliable products.
- More reliable service.
- Greater flexibility to respond to customer needs.
- Increased marketing opportunities.
- Support for training of staff.
- Potential support for special promotions.
- Customising of products (establishment branding).

Using local ingredients in menus

- Traditional local dishes made with local produce.
- Well known dishes but which are made using local ingredients.
- House specialities (or chef signature dishes) made using local produce.

Notes on the foods in season chart

The chart that follows contains information on the seasonality of foods, but this should only be seen as a guide. The seasons indicated for fish and game mainly apply to wild rather than farmed foods. Variations in annual weather conditions may mean that food seasons can be earlier or later (or shorter or longer) than indicated. The dates given in the chart are to indicate the start and end dates for the season of specific foods.

FOODS IN SEASON

Food item	French menu term	Spring			Summer			Autumn			Winter		
		M	A	M	J	J	A	S	O	N	D	J	F
Shellfish (Crustaces et mollusques)													
Crab	Crabe				●	●	●						
Crayfish	Ecrevisse	●							●	●	●	●	●
Crawfish	Langouste	●	●	●	●	●						●	●
Lobster	Homard				●	●	●						
Mussel	Moule	●	●	●				●	●	●	●	●	●
Oyster	Huître	●	●					●	●	●	●	●	●
Prawn	Crevette rose	●	●	●				●	●	●	●	●	●
Shrimp	Crevette grise	●	●	●	●	●	●	●	●	●	●	●	●
Scallop	Coquille St Jacques	●	●					●	●	●	●	●	●
Fish (Poisson)													
Barbel	Barbeau	●				●	●	●	●	●	●	●	●
Bream (sea)	Bréme					●	●	●	●	●	●	●	●
Brill	Barbue	●					●	●	●	●	●	●	●
Cod	Cabillaud			●	●	●	●	●	●	●	●	●	●
Dab	Limande					●	●	●	●	●	●		
Dover sole	Sole de Douvres			●	●	●	●	●	●	●	●		
Eel	Anguille	●	●	●	●	●	●				●	●	●
Flounder	Flet	●	●	●							●	●	●
Haddock	Aiglefin	●	●	●	●	●	●	●	●	●	●	●	●
Hake	Merluche							●	●	●	●	●	●
Halibut	Flétan	●	●	●	●		●	●	●	●	●	●	●
Herring	Hareng	●	●					●	●	●	●	●	●
Lemon sole	Limande	●							●	●	●	●	●
Mackerel (red)	Rouget	●	●	●							●		●
Plaice	Plie/carrelet			●	●	●	●	●	●	●			
Salmon	Saumon	●	●	●	●	●	●	●					●
Salmon trout	Truite saumonée	●	●	●	●	●	●						
Smelt	Eperlan	●	●	●					●	●	●	●	●
Skate	Raie	●	●	●					●	●	●	●	●
Sole	Sole	●	●	●	●		●	●	●	●	●	●	●
Sturgeon	Esturgeon		●	●							●	●	●
Trout (river)	Truite de rivière	●	●	●	●		●	●	●				●
Turbot	Turbot	●	●	●	●	●	●				●	●	●
Whitebait	Blanchaille	●	●	●	●	●	●	●					
Whiting	Merlan					●	●	●	●	●	●	●	●

Food item	French menu term	Spring			Summer			Autumn			Winter		
		M	A	M	J	J	A	S	O	N	D	J	F
Butcher's meat (Viande)													
Beef	Boeuf	●	●	●	●	●	●	●	●	●	●	●	●
Lamb (British)	Agneau		●	●	●	●	●	●	●	●	●	●	●
Mutton	Mouton	●	●	●				●	●	●	●	●	●
Pork	Porc	●	●					●	●	●	●	●	●
Veal	Veau	●	●	●	●	●	●	●	●	●	●	●	●
Poultry (Volaille)													
Chicken	Poulet	●	●	●	●		●	●	●	●	●	●	●
Duck	Canard	●	●	●	●	●	●				●	●	●
Duckling	Caneton		●	●	●								
Goose	Oie								●	●	●	●	●
Gosling	Oison								●				
Guinea fowl	Pintade	●	●	●	●		●		●	●	●	●	●
Spring chicken	Poussin	●	●	●									
Turkey	Dinde	●	●	●	●		●		●	●	●	●	●
Game (feathered)													
Wood grouse	Coq de bruyère						12th	●	●	●	12th		
Partridge	Perdreau							1st	●	●	●	●	1st
Pheasant	Faisan								1st	●	●	●	1st
Ptarmigan	Ptarmigan						●		●	●	●	●	●
Quail	Caille	●	●	●	●	●	●	●			●	●	●
Snipe	Bécassine	1st					●	●	●	●	●	●	●
Woodcock	Bécasse	1st					●	●	●	●	●	●	●
Teal	Sarcelle	●	●	●							●	●	●
Wild duck	Canard sauvage	●							●	●	●	●	●
Wood pigeon	Pigeon des bois	15th					1st	●	●	●	●	●	●
Game (furred)													
Hare	Lièvre						●	●	●	●	●	●	●
Rabbit	Lapin	●	●	●					●	●	●	●	●
Venison	Venaison				●	●	●	●	●	●			
Potatoes (Pommes de terre)													
Jersey Royal new potatoes	Pommes de primeurs royales du Jersey		●	●	●	●							
New potatoes	Pommes de terre de primeurs			●	●	●							
Potatoes (main crop)	Pommes de terre	●	●				●	●	●	●	●	●	●

FOODS IN SEASON (continued)

Food item	French menu term	Spring			Summer			Autumn			Winter		
		M	A	M	J	J	A	S	O	N	D	J	F
Vegetables (Légumes)													
Artichoke Globe	Artichaut				●	●	●	●	●	●			
Artichoke Jerusalem	Topinambour	●							●	●	●	●	●
Asparagus	Asperge			●	●								
Aubergine	Aubergine				●	●	●	●	●	●			
Beetroot	Betterave	●	●	●	●	●	●	●	●	●	●	●	●
Broad bean	Fève					●	●						
Broccoli	Brocolis	●	●						●	●	●	●	●
Brussels sprout	Chou de Bruxelles	●							●	●	●	●	●
Cabbage	Chou	●	●	●	●	●	●	●	●	●	●	●	●
Capsicum/ Pimento	Piment							●	●	●	●		
Chilli	Chili								●	●			●
Cardoon	Cardon	●							●	●		●	●
Cauliflower	Chou-fleur	●	●	●	●	●	●	●	●	●	●	●	●
Carrot	Carotte	●	●	●	●	●	●	●	●	●	●	●	●
Celery	Céleri	●						●	●	●	●	●	●
Celeriac	Céleri-rave									●	●		●
Cep	Cepe					●	●	●					
Cucumber	Concombre				●	●	●						
Chicory (Belgian)	Endive belge										●	●	●
Endive (frizzled)	Endive	●								●	●	●	●
Flageolet	Flageolet					●	●	●					
French bean	Haricot vert					●	●	●					
Leek	Poireau	●							●	●	●	●	●
Lettuce	Laitue				●	●	●						
Mushroom	Champignon	●	●	●	●	●	●	●	●	●	●	●	●
Onion	Oignon	●	●	●	●	●	●	●	●	●	●	●	●
Pea	Petit pois				●	●	●	●					
Parsnip	Panais	●							●	●	●	●	●
Pumpkin	Citrouille							●	●				
Radish	Radis				●	●	●						
Runner bean	Haricot d'espagne						●	●	●	●			
Salsify	Salsifis								●	●	●		●
Sea kale	Chou de mer	●										●	●
Shallot	Echalotte								●	●	●	●	●
Spinach	Epinards	●	●	●	●		●	●	●	●	●	●	●
Swede	Rutabaga	●							●	●	●	●	●
Sweetcorn	Maïs							●	●				
Tomato	Tomate	●	●	●	●	●	●	●	●	●	●	●	●
Turnip	Navet	●							●	●	●	●	●
Vegetable Marrow	Courgette					●	●	●					

FOODS IN SEASON (continued)

Food item	French menu term	Spring			Summer			Autumn			Winter		
		M	A	M	J	J	A	S	O	N	D	J	F
Fruit (Fruits)													
Apple	Pomme	●	●	●	●	●	●	●	●	●	●	●	●
Apricot	Abricot			●	●	●	●	●					
Blackberry	Mûre							●	●	●			
Blackcurrant	Gosseille noir				●	●	●						
Cherry	Cerise			●	●	●							
Cranberry	Airelle rouge								●	●	●		
Damson	Prune de Damas							●	●				
Gooseberry	Groseille à maquereau				●	●	●						
Greengage	Reine-Claude							●					
Grapes	Raisin	●		●	●	●	●	●	●	●	●	●	●
Melon (Cantaloup)	Melon			●	●	●	●	●	●				
Nectarine	Brugnon				●	●	●						
Peach	Pêche				●	●	●						
Pear	Poire							●	●	●	●	●	●
Plum	Prune				●	●	●	●	●	●			
Pineapple	Ananas	●	●	●	●	●	●	●	●	●	●	●	●
Raspberry	Framboise				●	●	●						
Redcurrant	Groseille rouge				●	●	●						
Rhubarb	Rhubarbe	●		●	●	●						●	●
Strawberry (English)	Fraise				●	●	●	●					
Herbs (Fines herbes)													
Bay leaf	Laurier							●					
Borage	Bourrache	●											
Chervil	Cerfeuille	●	●	●	●	●	●						
Fennel	Fenouil	●											
Garlic	Ail	●	●	●	●	●	●	●	●	●	●	●	●
Garlic (clove)	Une gousse d'ail	●	●	●	●	●	●	●	●	●	●	●	●
Marjoram	Marjolaine	●											
Mint	Menthe	●	●	●	●	●	●						
Parsley	Persil	●	●	●	●		●	●	●	●	●	●	●
Rosemary	Romarin							●					
Sage	Sauge		●	●									
Thyme	Thym							●	●	●			
Tarragon	Estragon											●	●

ANNEX B: GLOSSARY OF CUISINE AND SERVICE TERMS

This annex gives a selection of classic and other cuisine and service terms and their definitions. Many cuisine terms are derived from the classic European cuisine. French terms are mostly used because it was in France that cuisine terms were codified through, for instance, the development and publication of the Le Répertoire de la Cuisine. This is much the same as the use of Italian terms for music (musical terms being codified in Italy), French terms in ballet (dance terms being codified in France) and English being the international language for aviation traffic control.

A

à la in the style of, for example: à l'Anglaise (English style); à la Française (French style); à la Maison (style of the house)

à la broche cooked on a spit

abats offal, the internal organs of meat and poultry, e.g. heart, kidneys, liver

accompaniment condiment or seasoning offered to a customer to add to and improve the flavour of a dish

aceto vinegar (Italian), e.g. Balsamico

achar Indian pickle

acidity indicates tartness in foods and beverages

Advocaat liqueur made up of brandy, egg yolks, caster sugar and vanilla flavouring; Dutch in origin

agneau denotes lamb on the menu

agrodolce sweet and sour

aiguillettes long, thin, vertically cut strips of meat or poultry

ail garlic

aïoli garlic mayonnaise from Provence

ajo blanco purée sauce of garlic and almonds (Spanish)

al dente cooked until firm and crunchy (pasta/vegetables)

ale general term covering all forms of brewed beer

allumette cut into matchstick shapes

amaretti macaroons (Italian), almond flavoured

amontillado medium dry sherry, classified as a fortified (or liqueur) wine

amuse-bouche small savoury snacks served pre-hors d'oeuvres

anchoide Provençal paste-sauce of garlic, anchovy and olive oil

Angostura Bitters proprietary brand of aromatic bitters used as a flavouring in drinks, e.g. pink gin

anguille eel

antipasti starters other than pasta and rice dishes (Italian)

apéritif drink served prior to a meal in order to stimulate the appetite

arborio rice short, fat-grained Italian rice used for risotto

Armagnac quality brandy made in the Armagnac district of France

aroma indicating smell, scent or fragrance and often alluding to wine

arroser to baste

arrosto roast (Italian)

arugula salad leaf similar to rocket with a sharp peppery flavour (Italian)

aspic clear savoury jelly used in the decorating of joints of cold meat

assiette platter or dish

assiette anglaise plate of cooked meats

au bleu a method of cooking trout. When applied to grilled steaks it indicates 'very underdone'

au four baked in the oven

au gratin topped with breadcrumbs and grated cheese and browned under the grill

au jus with cooking liquors or gravy

au naturel uncooked or in its natural state

au sec until dry

auslese German wine label term indicating specially selected bunches of late picked grapes, high in sugar content, that make a sweet dessert wine

B

baba yeast sponge or bun that may be soaked in flavoured syrup to moisten, e.g. Baba au rhum

babaganoush aubergine purée (Middle Eastern meze dish)

Bacardi proprietary brand of white rum originating from Cuba

back of house work areas not seen or used by customers, e.g. stillroom, linen room, floor pantry

bagel ring-shaped roll with a tough, chewy texture

baguette long, stick shaped loaf of French bread

bain-marie hot water bath or well in which smaller containers may be set in order to cook food items slowly or to keep them warm/hot in readiness for service

baklava Turkish and Greek sweet made from filo pastry, chopped nuts and honey

ballotine meat, fish or poultry, boned, stuffed and rolled

balsamic vinegar the finest is made in Modena in Northern Italy; Italian sweet wine vinegar used to make dressings for salads

or a sauce for fish such as poached sea bass

balthazar equivalent of 16 standard size 75cl bottles of sparkling wine

bard (barder) to cover or wrap poultry, game or meat with a thin slice of fat bacon so that it does not dry out during roasting

baron double sirloin of beef or the saddle of lamb/mutton with the legs attached, e.g. baron de boeuf rôti

barquette boat-shaped tartlette case

basil flavouring herb; goes well with tomatoes

basmati rice aromatic, long-grained rice used in Indian cuisine, e.g. Biryani

baste to spoon over liquid during cooking, e.g. hot fat over a joint

baton stick-shape cut of root vegetables

bavarois Bavarian cream – a sweet custard made with eggs, cream and gelatine and served cold

bayleaf used fresh or dried to flavour various dishes such as casseroles; also found in a 'bouquet garni'

beard (ébarber) to remove the beard from oysters, mussels etc.

béarnaise hot sauce offered with fish and grilled meats, made from beaten egg yolks and reduced wine vinegar and flavoured with tarragon

Beaujolais fruity and light French red wine from the Beaujolais region of France

beaum measure used for sugar boiling

béchamel basic white sauce that is made from a white roux and seasoned hot milk. May be used as a thickening agent in cream soups or extended into other derivative sauces, e.g. mornay, moutarde, persil and anchois

beer term broadly covering lagers, ales and stouts. An alcoholic beverage made from fermented malted barley or other cereals and flavoured with hops

beignets deep-fried fritters (assorted fruits cooked in batter) or doughnuts

belacan south-east Asian fermented shrimp paste

bercy a white wine-based sauce for fish

bergamot orange scented herb, native to America, giving a distinctive flavour to Earl Grey tea and also used in sweet and savoury dishes and in tisanes

beurre blanc light emulsion sauce of white wine, vinegar, shallots and butter

beurre fondu melted butter with lemon juice added and heated until golden brown before use

beurre maître d'hôtel butter with lemon juice and chopped parsley added; used to garnish some fish and grilled meat dishes

beurre manié butter and flour kneaded together and used to thicken soups and sauces

beurre noisette golden brown butter that may have a little lemon juice added to take away the greasiness and add bite

bhaji vegetable deep fried in gram flour batter (Indian)

bianco medium sweet type of white/golden vermouth

bien cuit degree of cooking of a grilled steak – well done

billfold style of wallet used for presenting the bill to the host and returning the receipted bill and any change

bind (lier) to thicken soups and sauces with eggs, cream etc. To mix pasta, chopped meat, vegetables, with sauce

biryani long grained rice, spiced and coloured yellow with saffron. An oven baked rice to accompany meats (Indian)

bisque thickened shellfish-based purée soup, usually with tomato and cognac, e.g. Bisque d'homard (lobster)

bistro small informal restaurant, bar or nightclub

bitters alcoholic spirits, flavoured and of different strengths, e.g. Angostura Bitters, Campari, Fernet Branca and Underberg

blanc water to which flour has been added and used to keep vegetables white when cooking, e.g. celery

blanch (blanchir) placing briefly in boiling water or hot fat/oil and then draining. Also allows part cooking without colouring

blanquette thickened white stew of lamb, veal, rabbit or white fish thickened with egg yolks and cream

blini small, thick, buckwheat flour savoury pancake. Accompaniment to caviar (Russian)

boeuf French menu term for beef

boeuf Strogonoff thin strips of beef in a thick creamy sauce with mushrooms, tomato, onion, seasonings and flavoured with dry white wine, lemon juice and tarragon

boeuf bourguignonne braised, marinaded beef casserole made from braising steak, flavoured with red wine and garnished with button onions and mushrooms, lardons of bacon and heart-shaped croûtons

bollito misto mixture of boiled meats

Bolognaise savoury meat sauce made from lean minced beef, demi-glace (a half glaze basic brown sauce), red wine, onion, tomato and seasonings including garlic and described generally as a meat and tomato sauce

bombe an ice cream dessert made by using two different types of ice cream mixtures

bonito flaked dried tuna used to make Japanese broths and essential for 'dashi', a Japanese soup stock

bonne femme mushroom garnish for fish, with onions and bacon for chicken

bonne-bouche small savoury bite, often in a vol-au-vent case

bordelaise rich brown sauce flavoured with red wine

borlotti dry speckled haricot bean used in dips and salads

Bortsch rich duck flavoured consommé of East European origin

bouchées small sweet or savoury puff pastry bites, being a minature version of a vol-au-vent

boudin French version of the British black or white pudding with the black containing pigs' blood while the white may have chicken, veal or pork

bouillabaise Mediterranean fish soup made by the stewing method with the most popular version coming from Marseilles. Fennel, garlic and saffron are among the many seasonings used

bouillon unclarified meat or vegetable stock

bouillon, court made up liquor for cooking (poaching) fish. Seasonings may include sliced root vegetables, peppercorns, bayleaf, rosemary and condiments

bouquet aroma or smell, e.g. of an improving wine

bouquet garni parcel of herbs such as parsley, thyme, bay leaf and peppercorns used to flavour stews, casseroles, stocks and sauces

bourbon American whiskey made from a fermented cereal (maize) base

bourride garlic flavoured fish stew from the Provence region of France

braisé French menu/cookery term denoting 'braising' of a joint or portion of meat

braising pan (bisière) covered cooking dish

brandy spirit distilled from wine using the 'pot still' method

brasserie small restaurant and bar where food and drinks are served. French in origin

breadcrumb (paner) to cover a piece of fish, meat, poultry etc. with breadcrumbs after first dipping it in seasoned flour, then in beaten egg or melted butter

breathe to allow a wine to come into contact with the air upon removal of the cork, which then enhances the bouquet

brioche soft, light textured roll or bun made from eggs, butter, flour and yeast

brochette, en indicates grilling on a skewer, e.g. Kebab, which is Turkish in origin and often served on a bed of braised rice

brodo Italian term for stock, a base ingredient in soups, sauces and casseroles

broyer to crush or grind finely

brunch late morning meal that often replaces both breakfast and lunch

brunoise a name used to describe vegetables, ham or chicken cut into tiny dice

bruschetta toasted or baked slices of bread, oiled and sprinkled with herbs and served as an appetiser

brut Champagne/sparkling wine label term indicating very dry

bulgur part-cooked cracked wheat

Burgundy wine producing region of France, also a smooth, soft, dry red wine from that same region

busboy/girl American term indicating a person who carries out clearing duties in a food and beverage service area and also used as a general term meaning waiter or server

butter (beurrer) to coat or brush the inside of a mould or dish with butter

C

caffeine bitter white alkaloid found in tea, cocoa and coffee and used as a stimulant

Cajun French/American cuisine where the key ingredients used are capsicum, onion, celery and peppers

calamari French menu term for squid and classified as a mollusc

canapés small pieces of bread, usually

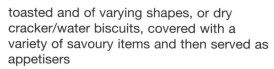

toasted and of varying shapes, or dry cracker/water biscuits, covered with a variety of savoury items and then served as appetisers

cane spirit clear spirit distilled from sugar cane, e.g. rum

cannellini beans creamy white kidney beans, having a slightly fluffy texture and mainly used in Italian cooking

cannelloni type of pasta shaped in large rolls, normally stuffed with cheese, meat and minced vegetables, covered with a cheese sauce and then baked in the oven (Italian)

cannoli Sicilian pastry tubes filled with ricotta cheese, chocolate and candied peel

canteen style of restaurant found in a school, hospital or industrial catering where the style of service is usually self-service. This term may also indicate a temporary or mobile eating place set up in an emergency

Cantonese form of cuisine usually found in westernised restaurants and is one of the five main styles of Chinese cuisine

capsicum Peppers, either sweet or hot, available in many colours and sizes

carafe form of glass bottle or jug used for the service of wine or water at the table. May also be defined as a decanter

caramel burnt sugar, also known as 'Black Jack'

caramelise (carameliser) to line a mould thinly with caramel sugar, or to coat fruit with, or dip it in, cracked sugar. Also to slowly brown sugar or foods such as onions and carrots over heat

carbonara spaghetti sauce of egg, bacon and parmesan

carbonnade beef braised in beer and brown stock and seasoned with garlic

carciofo globe artichoke

carpaccio originally thin slices of raw red meat, now also applied to fish

carpet bag steak fillet steak, filled with oysters, then sealed and grilled

carré French menu term indicating the 'best end' of lamb which is made up of all the lamb cutlets

carte du jour card/menu of the day. Lists the various dishes available on a particular day and the styles of menu available in the eating area

carte, à la menu where all dishes are individually priced and often cooked or finished to order

cassata ice cream dessert made up of layers of different flavoured ice creams, usually three, and mixed with glace fruits flavoured with liqueur

casserole, a style of stew cooked in a casserole dish

casserole, dish fireproof earthenware dish, round or oval in shape, with a lid

Cava term used to indicate Spanish sparkling wines made by the traditional method

caviar roe of the female sturgeon and named after the species of sturgeon that provides it, e.g. Sevruga or Beluga

célestine strips of savoury pancake and is a garnish found in consommé

centilitres hundredths of a litre of liquid

chafing dish style of frying pan used on a flare lamp for cooking at the table or to maintain the warmth of food

champignons French menu term for mushrooms

chantilly whipped cream with sugar and vanilla

chapatti thin flat cake of coarse unleavened bread, Indian in origin. Accompanies various curries

char grill cooking food on a grill which has coke or coals over an artificial electric or gas heat source

charcuterie cold, cooked and cured meat

products, especially pork, such as pâtés, hams, sausages and bacon

chard spinach-like leaves with thick, white edible ribs

charlotte moulded dessert of pastry cream, custard, mousse or puréed fruit

charsiu Chinese glazed pork fillet

chartreuse herb-flavoured, brandy-based liqueur

chartreuse, en feathered game served with cabbage

Chateaubriand double fillet steak cut from the head of the fillet of beef

chaudfroid sauce for cold buffet work, a jellied brown or white sauce used as an aspic to decorate and garnish cold meats and fish

chemiser to line a mould

chermoula Moroccan fish marinade

chervil green leafed herb used in seasoning, especially in French cuisine, with a flavour similar to anise (aniseed)

chèvre goat's milk cheese

chiffonade salad leaves (lettuce) or vegetables, cut in fine shreds, used in prawn cocktail or as a vegetable dish, e.g. chou (cabbage)

chilli con carne stew of minced meat, normally beef, chillies and purple kidney beans. Mexican in origin

Chinese green teas most familiar as the teas served in Chinese restaurants. These teas are all mild with a fruity flavour. The tea leaves are unfermented and produce a very pale drink with a light flavour

chine backbone of beef, lamb, pork or venison with meat attached

Chingkiang dark rice wine vinegar of Chinese origin and similar to Balsamic

chinois conical strainer

chioca yams

choisum Chinese greens with yellow flowers

chop suey Chinese-style dish consisting of small pieces of chicken or meat cooked with bean sprouts and other vegetables and served with a savoury rice

chorizo spicy pork meat and fat sausage, flavoured with garlic, paprika and pimento and of Spanish origin

choucroûte see sauerkraut – pickled cabbage

choux pastry for sweet fillings, e.g. as used for éclairs and profiteroles

chow mein Chinese dish made up of varying combinations of stewed meat and vegetables and served with fried noodles

chowder creamy thick soup or stew made from shellfish, especially clams, and vegetables, e.g. Clam Chowder

cilantro see coriander

citron French menu term for lemon

civet game stew, usually related to hare

clafouti baked batter tart usually filled with cherries

claret traditionally a red wine from Bordeaux, the wine producing region in France

clarified impurities removed from butter, stock, soup or jelly

cloche dish cover (usually bell-shaped) with a handle at the top, used to cover food and keep it hot until served at the table

cloud ears form of dried Chinese mushroom with uses in soups, fish and chicken dishes

coat (napper) to cover a dish or sweet entirely with a sauce, a jelly or a cream. To mask, to dip

cocotte small, round, fireproof, earthenware dish for cooking an egg, e.g. oeuf en cocotte. Also used to describe a larger oval casserole with a lid for slow cooking chicken, ragoût (brown stew) etc.

Cognac quality brandy from the Cognac region of south west France

compôte fruit poached in a sugar/fruit syrup and recognised as stewed fruit

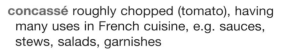

concassé roughly chopped (tomato), having many uses in French cuisine, e.g. sauces, stews, salads, garnishes

condé cold sweet made up of poached fruit (pears) on a creamed rice base

condiment seasoning offered to a customer to give added flavour/contrast to a dish served, e.g. salt and pepper, apple sauce, horseradish sauce

confit virtually boneless meat (game, duck, goose or pork) cooked slowly in their own juices and fat

confiture French menu term for jam

consommé clear soup made from beef or chicken stock and may be served hot or cold, with various garnishes added

coque, à la soft boiled in its shell, e.g. eggs

coquilles Saint-Jacques scallops

coral roe or eggs of some shellfish

corbeille denotes a 'basket', usually of fresh fruit and nuts and offered as an alternative to the sweet course

cordial fruit-based, sweet, non-alcoholic drink. Also term for concentrated fruit squash, such as lime cordial

coriander sometimes known as Chinese parsley, this herb has a fresh taste, similar to orange and is an important ingredient in curry

corkage charge made for opening and serving bottles of wine brought into a restaurant by customers

corked spoilt wine due to a faulty or mouldy cork, or because of bad storage

cos sometimes called Romaine lettuce, this has long, slender, crisp but coarse leaves and is mainly used in salads and for garnishing

cotechino Italian origin, this is a sausage made with lean and fat pork, white wine and spices and is often served hot with beans

coulis purée of fruit or vegetable, used to garnish and decorate

courgette British term for a 'baby' or miniature marrow. Called 'zucchini' in America and often termed 'Italian squash' in Italy

court bouillon seasoned poaching liquid, usually for fish

couscous cereal processed from semolina into tiny pellets and originating in North Africa

couvert a cover. Number of guests at a function. A place setting for a guest for a set meal. A place setting for a specific dish ordered

couverture confectioner's chocolate which may be sweet or semi sweet and used in baking, coating, ornamental work and sauce making

cover charge an additional charge added to the customer's bill

crème Anglaise rich custard sauce, of pouring consistency, to accompany a sweet

crème brûlée thick, smooth and rich custard with a covering of caramelised sugar

crème fraîche thick cream that has had a 'culture' added to it. Available either plain or in varying fruit flavours

crème pâtissière custard or pastry cream, thickened with flour or other starch

crêpe thin pancake with sweet or savoury filling

crevettes French menu term for shrimp

croissant crescent-shaped roll, made from a yeast-based Danish pastry dough

croquettes minced fowl, game, meat, fish or vegetables bound with a sauce, seasoned and shaped like a cork, then flour, egg and bread crumbed and deep fried

cross-contamination transfer of bacteria to food from another food, equipment or work surface

crostini bread canapés, see 'canapés'

croustades deep, scalloped, tartlet cases with either sweet or savoury fillings

croûte bread or pastry crust

croûtons fried bread used as a garnish, cut into small cubes for soups and other dishes in a variety of fancy shapes, e.g. heart-shaped croûtons

crudités served as an appetiser and made up of small pieces (batons) of vegetable, such as carrot and courgette, with an accompanying savoury dip

crumb down to brush debris (crumbs) from the tablecloth between courses

crustacean shellfish having a segmented body and limbs, e.g. lobsters, crabs, shrimps, crayfish, Dublin Bay prawn

cuisine minceur cooking method where low calorie ingredients are used to replace traditional rich foods of the French cuisine

D

dacquoise layers of meringue with whipped cream or butter cream and fresh berries

daikon large, white radish, sometimes called the Japanese pickled radish and often eaten with fish. May be grated and used as a garnish

dariole small, tin lined, copper or aluminium, cylindrical-shaped mould, having sweet or savoury items baked in it, e.g. crème caramel

darne thick slice from a round fish, including the central bone

dashi Japanese soup stock made from bonito flakes and konbu seaweed and combined with 'miso' to produce miso soup

daube, en method of cooking meat (stews of beef or mutton) very slowly in the oven, in a hermetically sealed dish (daubière) to preserve its full flavour

dauphinoise sliced potatoes baked in cream (or milk and cheese), seasoned with nutmeg and garlic

decant to pour a wine or other liquor, slowly, off the sediment in its container with the aid of muslin or filter papers

deglaze dissolve caramelised sediment in a roasting pan by adding wine or stock

dégorger to soak fish or sometimes vegetables to remove impurities

délice French menu term denoting a trimmed and folded fillet of fish, e.g. Délice de sole

demi-glace refined Espagnole (basic brown sauce). Smooth glossy sauce of pouring consistency used as base for other sauces, soups and stews

demi-tasse half-cup (espresso coffee cup)

dépouiller to remove skin or scum formed on top of liquid

dessert fresh fruit and nuts served from the fruit basket, but nowadays it also means the choice of sweets available from the menu

dessert wine style of sweet wine, e.g. Sauternes, Muscat, Auslese, often offered with the dessert (sweet) course

devilled – à la diable applied to fried or grilled fish or meat prepared with the addition of very hot condiments (cayenne pepper) and sometimes a highly seasoned and spiced sauce

dhal thick purée of lentils offered as an accompanying dish with curry

digestif any alcoholic liquor served as an after dinner drink, e.g. liqueurs, brandy, port

dim sum Chinese meal consisting of a variety of hot snacks

donburi Japanese dish of a bowl of rice topped with leftovers

dorer egg wash pastry or bread goods with yolk of egg beaten with water. Some bread goods may be brushed with milk

du jour A French menu term literally translated as meaning 'of the day', e.g. carte du jour, which lists an establishment's daily menus

Dubarry garnished with or containing cauliflower

dum Indian method of steaming, especially for pilau rice

dumb waiter indicates either the sideboard found in a food service area or the small lift that sends food from the kitchen to the dining room or to hotel floors

duxelles finely chopped mushrooms and shallots, sweated in butter and used as a stuffing or flavouring in sauces or as a garnish

E

earthenware type of strengthened china much used in the hospitality industry

elver young eel

embrocher to place on a spit for spit roasting or on skewers for grilling or frying

en cocotte cooked in a round, earthenware dish. May be egg (oeuf en cocotte) or meat (pot-roasted)

en papillote French menu term indicating fish or meat baked in a greaseproof bag in the oven

endive vegetable with a slightly sharp taste used in salads or braised, known in Britain as chicory and endive in France and America

entrecôte steak of beef coming from the boned out sirloin (contrefilet de boeuf)

entrée meat dish served with a sauce and made up of small cuts of butcher's meat or poultry, frequently served as a main course, e.g. garnished cutlets, sweetbreads

entremets sweet course on the every day menu and includes a selection of mainly cold sweets and a limited number of hot dishes

escalopes thin slices of flattened and boneless veal, beef or pork. Veal escalopes come from the fillet or cushion of veal, pork from the fillet or boned out pork loin and beef from the boned out sirloin

étuver method of simmering food very slowly in butter, or very little liquid, in a closed casserole, e.g. Chou étuvée

Evian brand of spring water from France

F

falafel rissoles made from dried broad beans, shallow fried and served with a piquant sauce

faraona Italian term for guinea fowl with a slight tanginess of game, reminiscent of pheasant. May be roasted, braised or casseroled

farce cuisine term for a savoury stuffing

fennel bulbous leafstalk which can be used raw with salads or braised whole and served as a vegetable, sometimes with a cheese sauce. The fresh or dried, aniseed tasting leaves are traditionally used with fish dishes whilst the aromatic dried seeds of the fennel plant are used with fish dishes, curries and apple pie

fenugreek seeds of this plant are ground and used as a spice in curries and chutneys. Associated mainly with Indian cuisine

fettuccine thin ribbons of pasta similar to tagliatelle, available in a green and white version, the green being mixed with a spinach purée

feuillantine puff pastry strips brushed with egg, sprinkled with sugar and baked

feuilletage puff pastry used to produce savoury and sweet dishes, e.g. vol-au-vent, bouchées, tranche, cream horns and many others

feuilleté triangle-shaped puff pastry case

fèves broad beans, often served bound in a cream sauce

filet mignon comes from the fillet of lamb and is also used to indicate a small round fillet steak cut from the whole beef fillet

filo pastry thin and crisp paper-like pastry, used in the making of sweet dishes, mince pies, fruit filled filo pastry cases etc.

fine champagne one of the best styles of Cognac and indicative of quality

fines herbes mixed herbs. The traditional French blend being: chives, tarragon, parsley and chervil finely chopped together

flageolet small, pale-green kidney bean

flambé to cook or finish cooking a dish at the table and then 'flaming' it by pouring a spirit or liqueur over, e.g. brandy, rum

fleûrons crescents and other fancy shapes of baked puff pastry used to garnish a variety of dishes such as entrées, poached fish and shellfish dishes

float sum of money of varying denominations placed in a till prior to service commencing

flûte stemmed glass with a tall but narrow bowl and used in the service of sparkling wines. The shape assists in retaining the sparkle (effervescence) of the wine

focaccia flat, round, flavoured Italian bread

foie de veau French menu term denoting calves liver and may be served with onions (Lyonnaise) or with bacon (au lard)

foie gras liver of specially fattened geese either served as a piece or used to make a pâté

forestière garnished with mushrooms

fortified wine wine whose alcoholic strength is increased by the addition of alcohol, usually brandy, e.g. sherry and port. Called liqueur wine in the EU

four, au baked in an oven

frappé Chilled, e.g. melon frappé, or over crushed ice, e.g. crème de menthe frappé

friandises another name for petits fours and offered at the end of the meal with coffee. See also petits fours and sweetmeats

fricassée white stew in which poultry, pork, veal or rabbit is cooked in a thickened sauce throughout the cooking period

frittata flat, unfolded omelette

froid cold. Applies to any item of food or liquor served cold or chilled

fromages, assortis French menu term meaning assortment of cheeses

frost to decorate a glass by dipping its rim in lemon juice and then caster sugar that may be coloured. Applicable to certain cocktails

fruits de mer fruits of the sea. French menu term indicating an assortment of sea foods

fumé denotes smoked when used on the menu, e.g. Truite fumé

fumet stock from fish, meat, game or poultry and the basis for sauces, stews, soups etc.

funghi Italian term for wild mushrooms, the cep being the most well known and is a quality tasting mushroom eaten widely in Europe

fusil sharpening steel

G

gailan Chinese spring greens

galangal root spice related to the ginger family, used in Thai cuisine and has a faint flavour of camphor. Available in root or powder form and is used in the Far East in curries and in Malay dishes

galantine cold dish of poultry or meat, boned, stuffed, braised in concentrated stock and then coated with aspic and garnished

galette flat, round, sweet or savoury cake or biscuit

ganache cake filling or topping made from couverture and whipping cream and may also be used for warm piping or cold modelling

garnish any ingredient which decorates, accompanies or completes a dish. Many dishes are identified by the name of their garnish, e.g. chicken Maryland (corn fritters, sautée banana, grilled bacon rolls and tomatoes), horseradish sauce would be offered separately

gastrique caramelised sugar and vinegar mixture used to flavour sauces

gâteau usually a rich sponge cake that may be decorated and flavoured in a wide variety of ways, e.g. Gâteau Moka (coffee gâteau) or Gâteau Foret Noir (Black Forest gâteau (chocolate)). Certain gâteaux do not have sponge bases, e.g. Gâteau MacMahon (shortbread base) or Gâteau St Honoré (puff pastry and choux pastry base)

gazpacho cold soup of puréed tomato, cucumber, onion, red pepper and garlic. Sometimes garnished with croûtons

gelato soft whipped ice cream (Italian), available in a variety of flavours

genoise very rich and light sponge cake made from equal quantities of egg, caster sugar and soft white flour, plus a small quantity of melted butter

Gentlemen's Relish proprietary brand of anchovy paste, butter, herbs and spices. Used mainly as a spread, often on canapés

ghee Indian term denoting clarified butter and is the yellow liquid left when the sediment has been removed

gibier game, e.g. pheasant, partridge, grouse

glacé French menu term for ice cream

glaze (glacer) to dust a cake or sweet with icing sugar and brown under a grill; to simmer vegetables, cut into fancy shapes, in butter until they have a glossy coating; to give meat a glossy appearance by frequent basting; to give cold dishes, cakes and sweets a shiny appearance by coating with aspic or jelly that is on the point of setting

gluhwein spicy mulled wine served hot, the main ingredients being red wine, caster sugar, lemon, orange, nutmeg, cinnamon and vanilla sticks

gluten protein substance found in cereal grains, mainly wheat, and used as a flour substitute

gnocchi farinaceous (pasta) type dish, made from a starch base that may be flour, semolina, potatoes or maize flour. Italian in origin

gomme syrup white sugar syrup used as a flavouring ingredient in certain cocktails, e.g. whisky sour, and in fruit cups

gosht Indian term indicating meat

gougère ring of choux pastry with savoury filling, often cheese

goujons French menu term denoting thin strips of fillet of fish, e.g. goujons de sole, prepared by dipping in seasoned flour, beaten egg and bread crumbs (pané), then deep fried

goulache casserole of stewing meat, either beef, veal, lamb, pork or mutton and onions, flavoured with paprika and tomato

grana grating cheese

gratin, au a dish that has been sprinkled with grated cheese, possibly mixed with breadcrumbs and a little butter, and then browned under a grill or in a hot oven. May also simply mean a sweet or savoury dish that is browned under a grill

gravadlax/ gravlax raw salmon cured in sugar, salt, pepper and dill

gremolata combination of lemon zest, parsley, garlic, tomato concassé and seasoning used to garnish osso buco (knuckle of veal casserole)

griottines Morello cherries, usually preserved in alcohol

grissini long, thin and crisp bread sticks offered as alternatives to rolls (Italian)

gros sel coarse or rock salt, this is a less refined salt than table salt

guacamole spicy avocado sauce with tomato, onion, hot green chilli, cilantro (the fresh leaves of the coriander plant), lemon juice and cream added to the mashed flesh of the avocado

guéridon trolley or service side table on

which food is served or prepared and cooked at the customer's table

gumbo spicy casserole of seafood and vegetables, including okra (thickening agent). In the USA this term applies to any dish incorporating okra as one of its ingredients

gurnard small round salt water fish known as the 'sea robin', e.g. Red gurnard and Ray gurnard, and may be braised or baked

H

HACCP Hazard Analysis Critical Control Point, a food safety self-inspection system

hacher French term meaning to mince or finely chop meat such as stewing beef, e.g. hachis de boeuf (savoury beef mince)

haggis traditional Scottish dish made of oatmeal, chopped offal of either a sheep or calf and seasonings and boiled in the stomach lining of the animal

halal meat killed and prepared according to Muslim law

Haldi Indian term for turmeric. See turmeric

halloumi goats milk cheese

hang to keep freshly killed meat or game in a cool place and exposed to the air, for a period of time, until it becomes more tender and improves in flavour

harissa red chilli paste of medium strength that has been seasoned with cloves of garlic, coriander, cumin, caraway seeds and dried mint, used in the North African dish of couscous and also in Moroccan cuisine

harusame transparent, rice-flour noodles

hash browns dish of American origin made up of puréed potato and onion, bound with egg, shaped and fried

haute cuisine originally a French term meaning highest standard of cooking and service

Hawthorn strainer essential piece of

equipment in the cocktail bar and used in conjunction with the Boston shaker and bar mixing glass when making cocktails

hock English name for German wines produced in the vineyards along the banks of the river Rhine

hoisin sauce made from soy, flour, vinegar, garlic, sesame, salt and pepper

Hollandaise egg yolk and butter-based sauce. This or one of its derivatives may be offered with grilled steaks e.g. sauce béarnaise

Hollands A Dutch style of gin made from malted barley and rye and double distilled in a pot still. Often sold in stone bottles

homard lobster

homardine white wine sauce finished with lobster butter and garnished with diced lobster

hors d'oeuvre an appetizer or starter, may be hot or cold

house wine red, white or rosé wine recommended by the establishment as being acceptable to the average palate and sold at a modest price. May be served by the glass, half bottle or bottle and sometimes by the carafe

I

infuse to soak ingredients, e.g. herbs, tea leaves, in liquid to impart flavour

insalata indicates salad, either served as a dish in its own right or used as a garnish to decorate a particular dish (Italian)

Irish coffee liqueur coffee made using Irish whiskey, sugar and floating double cream over the surface

J

jaggery unrefined sugar

jalousie baked pastry tart topped with latticed pastry strips

jambonette ham and pork sausage-like dish

jambonneau small leg – applied to poultry

jardinière matchstick-shape cut of spring vegetables, used as a garnish or as a vegetable dish

Jasmine tea Chinese green tea scented with jasmine flowers

Jeroboam large bottle holding the equivalent of four standard size (75 cl) bottles

joue beef or pork cheek

jugged hare traditional hare dish made with red wine marinated hare cooked in a casserole with its own blood being added at intervals to flavour and thicken the cooking sauce. A little red wine, vegetables and seasoning are also added to this sauce

julienne foods, especially vegetables, cut into fine, even strips

jus juice, e.g. fruit juice or juice extracted from roasted meats

jus lié thickened gravy

K

kebab Turkish term equivalent to the French 'en brochette' meaning grilling on skewers. Requires small, evenly cut pieces of meat, such as chicken livers, lamb or veal kidneys and liver and bacon or fish, with vegetables and seasonings. Marinaded prior to use

kedgeree savoury dish of cooked rice mixed with hard boiled egg, smoked fish (usually haddock) and may be flavoured with either turmeric or saffron

ketjap manis thick and sweetened derivative of soy sauce and the main condiment in the Far East and China, used in place of salt

khao niao glutinous rice from Thailand which, when boiled, becomes sweet and sticky and is used mainly in confectionery and baking

khoresh meat stew with fruit and nuts

khoshaf macerated dried fruit salad containing apricots, raisins and almonds

kilojoule (kj) the metric measure of the 'energy' contained in food

knead (fraiser) to work dough on a pastry board or marble slab with the ball of the hand

kohlrabi turnip/cabbage style vegetable that is either purple or green in colour and has a swollen, edible stem with a delicate turnip flavour. Boiled or grated and used in salads

konafa Turkish pastry which resembles shredded wheat

korma mild, spicy, meat casserole that is cooked in a rich coconut sauce and originates from northern India

Kosher meat killed, and food prepared and served according to Jewish dietary laws

kulebyaka Russian salmon and rice pie

kulfi Indian ice cream made from reduced milk

kway teow Malaysian flat noodles

L

lady's fingers originating from Africa and indicates Okra or Gumbo. Used to thicken soups and stews and also eaten as a vegetable

lager bottom fermented beer

laifen type of Chinese tubular noodles

lait, au denotes 'with milk' as in café au lait

laksa noodle and seafood soup from Malaysia

langouste denotes a crawfish and is almost the size of a lobster but clawless. Prepared and cooked like lobster and classified as a crustacean

langoustine scampi, classified as a crustacean. See 'scampi'

lard (larder – piquer) to draw strips of

larding bacon through the middle of a piece of meat by means of a larding tube (larder). To lard the surface by means of a larding needle (piquer)

lardon strip of bacon or pork fat that may be used to enhance the flavour of raw meat during its cooking process and also used as a garnish in both salads and with vegetables

lasagne large flat pieces of ribbon pasta made with whole wheat dough or with the addition of puréed spinach (lasagne verdi)

légume vegetable with seeds in a pod, such as peas, broad beans, mange tout and lentils

lentil type of bean, rich in protein and the basic ingredient of dhal which is a side dish to curry. Also produces a thick soup

levin starter dough made from live yeast and flour

linguini pasta cut into long and very thin, flat strands

liqueur sweetened and flavoured spirit, sometimes termed a digestif

loin joint of meat, either lamb, pork or veal, that may be boned, seasoned, rolled and tied and stuffed if required. All regarded as first class roasting joints

lumpfish roe eggs of the lumpfish and often referred to (incorrectly) as caviar, available in both orange and black. Usually from Iceland

lyonnaise sauce sauce of chopped onions sautéed in butter with wine vinegar and demi glace

lyonnaise, à la denotes a garnish or sauce of onions, e.g. pommes lyonnaise or foie de veau sauté, sauce lyonnaise

M

macaroon chewy almond flavoured biscuits made with caster sugar, egg whites and ground almonds and sometimes coconut

macchiato extra strong espresso coffee served with a dash of cold milk

mace outer covering of nutmeg

macédoine small, evenly cut dice of vegetables or fruit, e.g. macédoine de lègumes

macerate to pickle briefly, to steep, to soak or to souse. A term that is generally applied to fruit, usually diced, and then sprinkled with caster sugar and liqueurs in order to improve the flavour and soften the fruit

magret boneless breast of the mallard duck

maître d'hôtel butter herb butter containing parsley and lemon juice and served with grilled meats.

malt cereal grain, the best is barley, soaked in water to germinate and then dried by hot air. The duration and intensity of this drying process (kilning) produces different coloured malts, from pale malt to black malt. The degree of kilning determines the type of beer to be produced, e.g. pale malt makes pale ale

mancha powdered green tea

mandolin manual vegetable slicer

mange tout thin, flat, green pea that is eaten whole after topping, tailing and cooking

mantecato the action of beating butter and Parmesan into risotto (Italian)

marbling fat deposited within muscle tissue

marinade seasoned liquid used for flavouring and tenderising raw fish, meat, poultry and game

marinate to soak fish, meat, poultry and game for a short while to improve flavour and make more tender, in a marinade

marjoram perennial, seasoning herb with a very delicate flavour and very similar to oregano. Appears in many French and Italian dishes, especially tomato-based sauces

marmite, petite beef and chicken flavoured clear soup (consommé) and also the name given to the container in which the soup is served

marron chestnuts that may be eaten raw, roasted, boiled or preserved in sugar and then glazed in syrup, e.g. Marron glacé

Marsala fortified (or liqueur) wine from Sicily, classified as a dessert wine and used mainly in cooking

Martini brand of Vermouth, which is an aromatised wine that has been fortified. May be red, white or rosé and dry or sweet (Bianco)

masalas aromatic spice blend originating from India and known as masalas, it may be mild or strong. Ingredients of the blend may include pepper, ginger, turmeric, coriander, cumin, clove and chillies, e.g. garam masala

matelote French freshwater fish stew made with red or white wine

meat glaze (glace de viande) boiled down bone broth of marrow bones etc., and reduced to the thickness of jelly. Used for glazing cooked meats and improving their appearance and flavour

médaillon small round cut of meat that may also be termed a 'rosette' and is cut from the boned out, rolled and tied loin of lamb. Often sautéed

melba toast very thin, curled toast, made either by splitting toasted bread, after removing the crusts and toasting the untoasted sides or from toasting very thin sliced bread

membrillo quince paste

mesquite tree from America, the wood of which is used for barbecuing

méthode Champenoise process by which French Champagne is made

meunière menu term that denotes shallow fried, e.g. filet de plie meunière

mignonette coarsely crushed peppercorns

mille-feuille gâteau puff pastry cake filled with jam and whipped cream and decorated on the surface with fondant

millet a grain native to Africa and Asia

mineral water water containing various minerals and said to promote health. May be still or sparkling, e.g. Perrier, Evian, Buxton, Vichy

minestrone soup containing a wide variety of assorted vegetables, vermicelli and herbs in a meat or vegetable broth (Italian)

minute steak thin, tender steak, often cut from the sirloin and sometimes termed an entrecôte minute. May be fried or grilled, but very quickly (for a minute) to seal the outsides without overcooking the interior

mirepoix garnish of diced, browned onions, carrots, celery and bacon, with various herbs and used to flavour stocks, soups, sauces and stews

mirin sweet Japanese rice wine, used in sukiyaki and Japanese sauces

mise-en-place French term meaning 'to put in place'. Refers to preparation beforehand, this includes all the tasks that have to be completed to get a food service area or kitchen ready for service

miso salted and fermented soy bean paste available in red or yellow, enhances the taste of many dishes.

mitsuba Japanese green leaf used as a herb

mizuna salad leaf with a peppery flavour

mocha Arabica type of coffee bean. Produces a very strongly flavoured coffee. Originally from the old port of Mocha in Yemen

moelle beef marrow

monté to enrich by incorporating butter, egg yolks, cream

morilles edible fungus with a delicate flavour and sometimes termed the sponge mushroom, picked fresh during spring and early summer

mornay cheese sauce, normally made with milk and with dried mustard added to improve flavouring, e.g. Choufleur mornay

mortadella large Italian sausage that has

been lightly smoked. The ingredients may consist of pork, garlic and seasonings

Moselle lively and crisp-tasting white wine produced in the vineyards lying along the banks of the river Mosel in Germany

moule French menu term denoting a mussel that may be steamed open and served in the half shell. Classified as a mollusc. Best known for its use in the classic dish moules marinière

moussaka dish of Greek origin, made of minced lamb or mutton, aubergine, tomato, onion, garlic and seasonings with a topping of cheese sauce and baked

mousse light and fluffy mixture, which is usually sweet to the palate, and served cold, e.g. mousse aux frais (strawberry mousse)

mousseline light fish or meat purée strained extra fine and mixed with cream. Sauce mousseline is a derivative of sauce Hollandaise, having whipped cream added to the basic sauce, and is served with poached fish or vegetables

muddle cocktail-making term that indicates a number of ingredients being crushed together in the bottom of the bar mixing glass using the flat end (muddler) of the bar mixing spoon, e.g. mint and caster sugar

mulled wine red wine slowly heated, with sugar, citrus fruits and spices added to the liquor. Served hot

murgh Indian term for chicken

muselet wire muzzle used to clamp the cork of a bottle of sparkling wine securely in place

mushimono Japanese cuisine term for steaming a food item

N

naan flat, but puffy and light leavened bread that may accompany curry

nage, à la cooked in a court bouillon

nam pla Thai fish sauce

nam prik Thai chilli sauce

nantua crayfish sauce

nappé to mask or coat evenly with a sauce or jelly, e.g. aspic used in cold buffet work

naturel, au in its natural state, e.g. plain boiled without additional flavouring, ingredients or garnish

navarin brown lamb or mutton stew with vegetables and potatoes

neat term relating to liquor and meaning undiluted, e.g. neat rum

niçoise French salad dish that traditionally includes green beans, tomatoes, potato, tuna, anchovies, olives and garlic

nimono Japanese cuisine term indicating a simmering technique

nip small measure, legally recognised, and usually of spirits, e.g. nip of whisky (25 ml or 50 ml)

noisette small cut of meat from the rib, usually lamb

nori thin, black seaweed sheets used in wrapping sushi, a Japanese sweetened vinegar rice

nose combination of the aroma and the bouquet of a wine when wine tasting

nouvelle cuisine form of French cooking that promotes lighter alternatives to replace the very rich dishes of the traditional classic French cuisine

oeuf en cocotte egg baked in its own dish (cocotte) in a bain marie in the oven

oeuf mollet soft boiled and shelled egg, the boiling time being five minutes

offal the organs of animals, e.g. heart, liver, brains, kidneys, tongue, tail, tripe and sweetbreads

on-the-rocks poured over a quantity of cubed ice, e.g. scotch on-the-rocks

oregano perennial seasoning herb similar to marjoram that blends well with oil and vinegar salad dressings, French, Italian and Greek dishes and tomato-based sauces

osso buco knuckle of veal casserole stewed in a dry white wine, tomato and vegetable sauce flavoured with garlic, chopped parsley, basil and thyme and traditionally served with rice

ouzo aniseed-flavoured spirit of Greek origin and similar to Pernod, coming under the heading of pastis (aniseed or liquorice flavoured spirits)

oyster shellfish usually eaten raw, the best coming from Colchester and Whitstable, and may be served either hot or cold. Classified as a mollusc

oyster cruet group of accompaniments offered with oysters and comprises of cayenne pepper, peppermill, Tabasco sauce and chilli vinegar

oyster sauce brown sauce used in Chinese cuisine for flavouring various dishes

P

paella rice dish flavoured and coloured with saffron, containing chicken, shellfish, various vegetables including peas, pimento, garlic sausage, chopped garlic and seasonings. Cooked in chicken stock

pak choi Chinese white cabbage – classified as a brassica, this plant does not form a 'heart' and appears very similar to leaf spinach. Eaten raw in salads, but may also be stir-fried with rice and is used mainly in Chinese cuisine

pakora Indian term indicating a deep fried vegetable fritter

panada dough used to bind forcemeat that is made from flour, milk or water, eggs and butter

pancetta streaky bacon (Italian)

panée food item dipped in seasoned flour, egg and breadcrumbs, then either shallow or deep fried

paneer fresh milk curds used in Indian cookery

panna cotta cooked, rich, cream Italian dessert, similar to bavarois, the consistency of which is similar to a sauce sabayon

papillote paper wrapping to contain aroma and flavour when cooking meat or fish

pappardelle long, flat egg noodles with a crimped edge

paprika powdered red spice produced from dried and ground sweet peppers, giving an appealing flavour to food as well as a deep red colour, e.g. Hungarian goulash

parboil to partially cook in boiling liquid

parfait enriched ice cream made from a caster sugar, egg yolk and double cream base

Parma ham delicate tasting, cured Italian ham, served with salads or as a starter dish, e.g. melon and Parma ham

Parmesan very hard dry cheese of Italian origin, eaten as a cheese and used in Italian cooking and as an accompaniment

passato puréed and sieved or strained

pasta pastes made from Durum wheat semolina flour, in a variety of shapes and dried, e.g. macaroni, spaghetti, vermicelli, noodles, lasagne and ravioli

pastilla traditional Moroccan dish of pigeon pie in egg, lemon and onion sauce sweetened with almonds in pastry layers covered with cinnamon and sugar

pastis aniseed or liquorice-flavoured alcoholic beverage such as ouzo and Pernod

pâté de foie gras made by blending together a fine paste of fattened goose livers and decorating/garnishing with truffles. See foie gras

pâté maison pâté particular to the establishment (house) and made according to the chef's recipe

paupiettes thin slices of meat or fish filled with forcemeat (sausage meat stuffing) then rolled up, tied and braised in the oven. Usually of beef, veal or sole, e.g. paupiettes de boeuf braisés

pave a special cut of rump steak that is leaner and less sinewy than a traditional rump cut

Pavlova meringue cake filled with whipped cream and topped with fruit and may be served with a fruit coulis, e.g. raspberry

paysanne vegetables cut into small, very thin slices the size of a 1p piece and used as a garnish, e.g. Consommé paysanne

peach Melba sweet dish of peaches, vanilla ice cream and a raspberry sauce (coulis). Decorated with whipped cream

pecorino ewes' milk cheese

peperonata pepper and vegetable stew (Italian)

pepperoni dry Italian sausage that is made up of coarsely chopped pork and beef and strongly seasoned with ground red pepper and other spices. Commonly used on pizzas

persillade chopped parsley spiked with crushed garlic

petits fours wide variety of tiny, fancy, oven-cooked cakes or biscuits, but now used to also mean fruits dipped in chocolate or sugar syrups or other sweetmeats made up of such things as marzipan, ice cream, stuffed dates and fruits, shortbreads etc. Offered with coffee and sometimes termed friandises

piatto plate or dish (Italian)

piccata Italian term denoting an escalope

pieds de mouton sheeps' trotters

pilaff dish of spiced rice braised in the oven and garnished with prawns, chicken livers, ham, mushroom or chicken. Literally translated pilaff means braised savoury rice

pilau Indian version of pilaff and usually includes chicken, mutton or goats meat or a mixture of these and is well seasoned

pimento large, sweet red pepper

pimentón Spanish spice similar to paprika and made from the Spanish pepper which, in its fresh form, is more well known as the red stuffing inside green Spanish cocktail olives

pipe to force a soft mixture or dough through a forcing bag containing a plain or fancy nozzle. In liquor terms it also relates to a cask holding 523 litres (115 gallons) of port

piquant denotes spicy, sharp, appetising, a sharp flavour, a bite to the sauce or dish, e.g. sauce piquante (a combination of shallots, capers, gherkins, wine vinegar and fines herbes added to demi-glace)

piquer food items studded with fat, garlic, truffle, cloves, etc

pirozhki small savoury pastries

pitta bread of Greek origin, sometimes called 'pocket bread' as it can be split open and filled. It is a double-layered bread that is flat and round or oval in shape

plancha, à la grilled on a griddle

poach (pocher) to simmer dishes in a mould in a bain marie until done or to cook food in water that is kept just on boiling point (simmering), without actually letting it boil, e.g. Oeuf poché

poêler to casserole in butter, in a covered dish, with the absolute minimum of liquid added together with diced root vegetables and is sometimes known as a pot roast. Used only for the better cuts of meat and poultry

point, à denotes medium degree of cooking of a grilled steak

polenta maize flour which is ground from Indian corn and can be eaten either as a type of porridge or used to garnish fish and meat dishes

pomme de terre potato

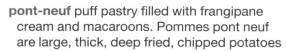

pont-neuf puff pastry filled with frangipane cream and macaroons. Pommes pont neuf are large, thick, deep fried, chipped potatoes

poppadum very fine, thin and crisp wafer-like pancake, made from lentil flour, deep fried or grilled and served with curry

pot roast joint of meat baked in the oven with stock and vegetables, in a covered pan or casserole dish. See poêler

pot still traditional still used to distil cognacs, armagnacs, dark rums, tequila, calvados and malt whisky. Here the spirit is distilled in batches

pot-au-feu French dish of meat and vegetables cooked in stock – the broth is eaten first followed by the meat and vegetables as a main course

poulet French menu term for chicken, e.g. poulet rôti à l'Anglaise

poussin baby or young (spring) chicken weighing from 450 – 900 g (1 – 2 lb), that may be roasted, grilled, sautéed or baked. It is usual to serve one to a portion

praline almonds, sometimes with hazelnuts added, caramelised in sugar, then crushed and added to a variety of sweet dishes

preserves assorted jams that may be offered at either breakfast or afternoon tea, e.g. strawberry, raspberry, cherry, plum, marmalades

profiterole cold sweet dish of small choux pastry buns filled with whipped cream and coated with chocolate, either fondant or couverture

prosciutto Parma ham originating from Italy. A raw, delicate tasting, cured ham that is sliced very thinly. See also Parma ham

Prosecco term now used to indicate Italian sparkling wines

provençal sauce of tomatoes, onions and garlic sautéed in olive oil

Provençale, à la provincial or regional way or style and generally accepted as meaning cooked with garlic, onions and tomatoes

pumpernickel dark brown or black rye bread that may be used as a base for canapés

punch alcoholic beverage made from a wine base with spirits, liqueurs, fruit juices, lemonade, tisanes and fruit syrups added to enhance the taste. Can also be flavoured with spices, such as cloves, cinnamon and nutmeg and citrus fruits. Sometimes served hot

punt hollow found in the base of some wine bottles which strengthens the bottle, especially if a secondary fermentation takes place in the bottle itself, e.g. Champagne

purée to finely mash or pass food through a sieve or a thickened variety of soup, namely a purée

Q

quail small game bird that may be roasted, grilled or sautéed. Often serve two birds per portion

quenelles Oval shaped. Also indicates light oval-shaped dumplings, made from various types of fine forcemeat, such as veal, chicken, game and fish, that are poached.

quiche flan case filled with a savoury egg custard plus other added ingredients, such as vegetables, mushrooms and bacon

quince hard, yellow and acid tasting Asiatic fruit, with a delicate scent, which when cooked turns pink and is mainly used in preserves

R

râble French menu term indicating the saddle, and usually of hare

rack (of lamb) menu term indicating a joint made up of the lamb cutlets – a best end (the ribs) – usually roasted, e.g. carré d'agneau rôti

ragoût thick and rich brown stew/casserole

of meat, usually beef or lamb and cooked with root vegetables, e.g. ragoût de boeuf

ragu basic meat sauce for pasta

raita yoghurt-based side dish of Indian origin

ramekin small earthenware, individual, circular baking dish holding one portion

rang French term indicating the team or brigade of food service staff and their level of authority within that team, e.g. commis de rang

rapini member of the broccoli family with a bitter, assertive flavour

rare degree of cooking of a grilled steak meaning underdone

Ras-el-hanout Moroccan spice mix used to flavour rice, couscous, and 'tajines', the slowly cooked stews common to Morocco

ratatouille Provençal vegetable stew of diced aubergine, tomato, courgettes, red and green peppers, onions and garlic, cooked in olive oil

ravioli small meat or vegetable filled pasta squares (Italian)

réchaud spirit lamp used for cooking at the table and to keep food warm

réchauffé reheated dish made with previously cooked ingredients

reduce to add wine or other liquid to the pan residue and simmer down to a desired consistency to concentrate flavours

rémoulade cold mayonnaise-based sauce containing capers, gherkins, anchovy essence, parsley and fines herb for flavouring

rillettes shredded belly of pork cooked in its own fat, mixed until smooth and potted. Sometimes has goose or rabbit added. French in origin

ripieno Italian stuffing

ris de veau calves sweetbreads that are pale in appearance and delicate in taste, coming from the thymus glands found in the neck

and heart of young animals and are braised, fried or sautéed

risotto savoury rice containing vegetables, such as finely chopped onions, and a bouquet garni for flavouring, cooked in chicken stock

roast (rôtir) roast meat, poultry or game and vegetables, e.g. potato, parsnips

roe fish eggs, the soft herring roe having a creamy, smooth texture and is served as a savoury dish or garnish. Smoked cod's roe is used for taramasalata which is of Greek origin

romesco Catalonian sauce of tomato, almond, sherry, garlic and paprika

rösti grated and fried potatoes

roti of Indian origin and denoting bread. Usually a circular, flat unleavened bread similar to chapati

rôti French menu term indicating a roasted item, e.g. côte de porc rôti

roulade stuffed roll of food that may be sweet or savoury, e.g. thin slice of meat stuffed and rolled – paupiette de boeuf, or a thin, flat sponge spread with jam and whipped cream and rolled swiss roll style

roux mix of flour and butter cooked together slowly until white, blonde or brown in colour and used to thicken soups and sauces

royale, à la French menu term denoting a garnish for a soup, e.g. consommé royale (diced savoury egg custard)

rye cereal used in the making of bread and also used in its fermented form in the making of American whiskey

S

sabayon French term meaning a dessert sauce and used to thicken, enrich and improve the appearance of various dishes. Together with Marsala and caster sugar produces the Italian sweet Zabaglione

sablé French shortbread

sachertorte rich chocolate cake, coated in ganache with apricot jam

saffron spice used for flavouring, produced from the stigmas of the crocus. Colours food bright yellow and is a key ingredient in paella, bouillabaisse and the liqueur Chartreuse

saké originating from Japan, this is a slightly sweet, colourless rice beer, usually served warm but may also be served chilled

salamander grill with top heat and used for browning and cooking

salami strongly seasoned sausage of Italian origin and served cold. Made from beef, pork and pork fat and seasoned with garlic and pepper, often used for antipasto and in hors d'oeuvre

salmis game birds and ducks, skinned and boned after roasting, placed in a rich, brown, red wine flavoured sauce and served as a game stew

salpicon mixture of foods cut into a small dice, bound with a sauce and used as a filling, e.g. Salpicon de volaille (Salpicon of chicken)

salsa Mexican in origin but nowadays means an uncooked tomato-based relish flavoured in varying degrees by onion, cilantro and chillies

salsify white root vegetable with oyster-like flavour

sambal sharp, spicy and vinegary sauce or chutney of raw vegetables or fruit, used as a relish or in cookery. Comparable to chutneys in Indian cuisine

samosa small, pastry coated food item with a spicy meat or vegetable filling and deep fried

sansho prickly ash powder sprinkled on grilled meat

sashimi Japanese origin, this term indicates sliced fish eaten raw

satay cubes of fish or meat on a skewer and grilled over a charcoal grill, served with a thick peanut flavoured sauce

sauce gribiche cold sauce, mayonnaise based and mixed with capers, gherkins, hard boiled egg whites and seasonings

sauerkraut (choucroûte) pickled, finely shredded white cabbage served hot with bacon and sausages. National dish of Germany and Alsace in France

sauté shallow fry in butter, with a little oil added, to a golden brown colour

sauter quick cooking process, to brown quickly in a sauté or frying pan, or toss in fat anything that requires quick cooking at considerable heat

sauteuse shallow pan with sloping sides and a lid, in which food may first be fried and then braised

savarin circular yeast sponge cake, often soaked in a rum-flavoured syrup and filled with fresh fruit salad, e.g. savarin au fruits

scampi recognised in Britain as the Dublin bay prawn, in America as the saltwater crayfish and occasionally known as langoustine

schnitzel thin slice of veal or chicken. A breaded veal cutlet, e.g. wiener schnitzel

score parallel cuts made on the surface of food items

sec degree of sweetness of Champagnes and sparkling wines or the amount of sugar they contain; here it means medium sweet

sekt quality German sparkling wine produced by the Charmat method (secondary fermentation in a sealed tank)

sepi a cuttlefish, prepared like calamari (squid), either sautéed whole in oil or stuffed and poached while the legs are blanched and stewed

service cloth cloth approximately the size of a table napkin, used by food service staff as a protection against heat and to assist in handling equipment and in the service of food

shaoxing an amber-coloured rice wine

Sherry Fortified (or liqueur) wine, having a grape spirit (brandy) added to improve the alcoholic content, and is made from white grapes

shiitake dark brown Japanese mushroom that has a distinctive earthy flavour and is used for garnishing and flavouring

shish kebab term of Turkish origin indicating small pieces of meat, usually fillet of lamb, interspersed with button mushrooms and grilled on a skewer. May be accompanied by a Madeira sauce

shooter layered cocktail consisting of alcoholic liquors of varying densities, the heaviest lying at the base of the glass and the lightest on the top. Also known as the rainbow cocktail or pousse café and served in an Elgin shape liqueur glass

short (of pastry) having a high fat content

shred (émincer) to cut meat or vegetables into thin slices or strips

sichuan peppercorns fragrant Chinese seasoning from a plant unrelated to pepper

skim to remove impurities and fat from the top of soups and broths by using a skimming ladle

skorthalia garlic sauce of Greek origin

smorgasbord term of Scandinavian origin which indicates a self-service buffet. In Scandinavia this may take the form of quite a substantial meal of several courses, offering a varied number of dishes such as salads, cheeses, pâtés, cold meats and almost always includes dishes of herrings

smorrebrod open or Scandinavian sandwich. Various breads, wholemeal, rye, pumpernickel, bread rolls and white and brown sandwich bread, are used for these sandwiches, onto which selected food items (meats, soused fish, meat and fish pastes, salami and salad) are placed

soba noodles, Japanese in origin, made of white wheat or golden buckwheat and accompanied by nori (Seaweed) and horseradish

soffritto a sauce/stew base of fried diced vegetables and sometimes pancetta (streaky bacon)

sorbet soft fruit-flavoured water ice, sometimes flavoured with liqueur or wine and served as a sweet dish or between courses to cleanse the palate

soubise smooth onion pulp served with a variety of meat entrées

soufflé sweet or savoury baked pudding made with whipped egg whites

soy bean round bean, rich in protein and used to make tofu (unfermented bean paste), it can be cooked fresh or dried in stews

soy sauce key ingredient of east Asian cuisine, and in particular Chinese and Japanese cuisine, enhancing many dishes, e.g. soups, stews and sauces. Made from the soy beans, the Japanese equivalent is shoyu

spaetzele (spaetzeli) Swiss and Austrian paste speciality made by pressing an egg noodle dough through a colander and simmering it in salt water

spare ribs rib bones of beef or pork, marinated and then baked or grilled

spatchcock young game bird or chicken that is split open down the backbone and flattened and then fried or grilled (English style). The French style is termed crapaudine (the shape being toadlike), e.g. Poulet en Spatchcock or Poulet en Crapaudine

spirits overall term for all distilled alcoholic liquors, the most common of which are whisky, brandy, gin, vodka and rum

spring roll pancake-type roll of Chinese origin, filled with minced meat and vegetables and deep fried

spumante Italian wine label term denoting sparkling

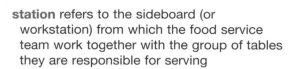

station refers to the sideboard (or workstation) from which the food service team work together with the group of tables they are responsible for serving

still equipment used to produce spirits, either the pot still or the continuous still, e.g. brandy distilled from wine in copper pot stills

stillroom area in the back of house that provides those items, both food and beverages, not provided by the key sections of the kitchen or bars

stillset traditional commercial installation consisting of a water boiler and bulk storage containers for coffee and hot milk. The latter is steam heated and a steam injector will also be attached

stir fry the East Asian process of preparing food by cooking over a very fast and high heat

stockfish dried salt cod, braised, stewed, fried and eaten raw in salads. Also pounded to make a savoury paste or butter used in pâtés

stout strong dark beer with a smooth, malty flavour and creamy consistency and brewed from a very dark roasted malt

strudel fruit dessert made of either a puff pastry or filo pastry case filled with various mixtures of fruit and served hot or cold

sugar syrup sweet liquor of sugar and water boiled together and when used as an ingredient for cocktails it is termed Gomme syrup

sumac middle eastern spice, the berries being deep, brick red when dried. Used whole or ground and may be sprinkled on fish, added to salads and used to season kebabs

suprême denotes cuts from the wing or breast of poultry and feathered game. Also indicates a cut of fish on the slant and free from bone

sushi Japanese sweetened vinegar rice and toasted nori sheets (a tissue-thin Japanese seaweed used as a wrapping) are key ingredients in sushi. Other fillings may be spinach, mushrooms or pickled ginger

sweetmeat sugar-coated confection, e.g. small fancy cake, and may also take the form of crystallised fruits. Also see petits fours

syllabub rich dessert dish of sweetened cream and lemon juice, flavoured with sweet white wine and brandy, served well chilled in a glass

T

Tabasco pungent Indian pepper sauce, two key ingredients of which are vinegar and red peppers. Used largely in Creole cooking. Also a very hot sauce

tabbouleh salad of bulgur wheat mixed with tomatoes, onion, lemon juice, mint and parsley

tagliolini thin noodles. Italian in origin

tahina crushed sesame seed paste, widely used as a flavouring in Middle Eastern and Latin American cuisine

tamarind fruit pods of an African tree that may also be found in India. Pods contain a very sour juice used in some Indian curries. Fruit of the tamarind tree is dried and ground and used in flavouring curries

tandoor open topped clay oven originating in Northern India

tandoori food that has been cooked in a charcoal fired tandoor, e.g. tandoori chicken

tannin obtained from the pips and stalks of grapes during the wine making process and acts as a preservative, especially in red wines. Is also the brown colouring of tea

tapenade paste of capers, black olives, anchovies, garlic and often tuna

taramasalata Greek in origin, a dish made from dried, salted and pressed roe of mullet or cod, seasoned with garlic, lemon juice and olive oil to form a pink, creamy paste

tarka Indian method of tempering spices in hot oil

tarragon flavouring herb with long, narrow, green leaves and found in fines herbes, sauce béarnaise, poached fish and chicken dishes. Used either fresh or dried

tartare cold mayonnaise-based sauce with finely chopped capers, gherkins and fines herbes added. Served with deep fried fish

tartare, steak minced raw fillet of beef mixed with parsley, capers, gherkins, finely chopped onion, raw egg yolk and seasonings and served cold

tarte tatin French apple tart baked upside-down

tartufo Italian term for truffle, an edible fungus, see truffle

T-bone steak (porterhouse) steak on a T-shaped bone that is cut from the fillet end of a sirloin of beef. Includes both the fillet and the sirloin of beef

tempura seafood and vegetables dipped in batter and deep-fried

tequila Mexican spirit distilled from the fermented juice (pulque) of the agave plant

teriyaki fish or meat marinated in teriyaki which is a mixture of mirin (sweet Japanese rice wine), Japanese soy sauce and chicken stock

terrine mixture of meat, fish or vegetables and seasonings in a lined dish that is cooked, cooled and served cold in a terrine – an oblong, straight-sided cooking utensil with a close fitting lid

tian shallow gratin of chopped, layered vegetables

tikka marinated pieces of fish, meat or poultry. Indian in origin, e.g. tikka masala (aromatic spice blend). Also see masalas

timbale half conical tin mould. The dish is cooked and served in this single portion

mould. Usually fish, meat, rice or vegetables in a sauce, or fruit with Chantilly

tisane all forms of herbal teas containing no caffeine or tannin and consumed either cold or hot, e.g. mint, rosehip and lemon

tofu a highly nutritious unfermented bean paste made from soy beans, Japanese in origin

tokay Hungarian sweet white wine, available in three styles, the most well known of which is probably tokay aszú

torte German for a round, rich, layer cake or flan, decorated and divided into portions. Contains nuts, cream and fruit or jam

tortilla Mexican round, flat, unleavened pancake made from cornmeal, filled with beans or meat and a sauce. Served hot

tostada Spanish for toast

tournedos fillet steak cut in round, neatly trimmed portions from the heart of the fillet of beef

toxin poisonous substance, secreted by certain organisms

tranche length of puff pastry, with a puff pastry wall either side and often with a fruit filling. Served hot or cold, e.g. tranche aux pommes (apple)

trenette long, flat pasta; another name for linguini

trifolato method for sautéing vegetables in oil, garlic and parsley

tripe lining from the first and second stomach of oxen. The classic dish is stewed tripe and onions

tronc collection of tips received by food service staff

tronçon portion of flat fish cut across the body, on the bone, e.g. tronçon de turbot

truffle edible fungus found underground near the roots of oak or beech trees. The Périgord black from France and the Piedmontese white from Italy are noted for their taste and scent. The black truffle is used as a decorative garnish in pâté and

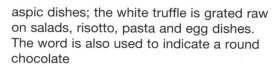

aspic dishes; the white truffle is grated raw on salads, risotto, pasta and egg dishes. The word is also used to indicate a round chocolate

truss to bind or truss poultry or game birds for cooking, giving them a better shape

tuile crisp biscuit, traditionally flavoured with almond

tureen deep, covered dish from which soup is served when working from the guéridon. The tureen may be large enough for one portion only or for a number of portions

Turkish coffee Traditionally made in a long handled container called an ibrik. A dark, very strong but sweet coffee served in small cups

turmeric mild peppery spice, bright yellow in colour and used in many curry mixtures. Called haldi in India and obtained from the root stems of a plant belonging to the ginger family. The stems are dried and then ground producing the powder called turmeric

tutti frutti confection, especially ice cream, mixed with a variety of diced candied fruits and Italian in origin

U

udon very narrow, ribbon-like, Japanese white wheat noodles served in hot soups and mixed meat and vegetable dishes

Underberg proprietary brand of German herb-flavoured bitter with a brandy base

underliner an underplate. Plate or flat with a napkin, doily or dish paper on it placed underneath another dish or accompaniment

univalve mollusc with a shell consisting of one valve, e.g. snails, clams

V

vacherin sweet dish made up of meringue, fresh soft fruit such as raspberries or strawberries, whipped cream and a fruit coulis

veal meat of a calf, the French menu term being veau, e.g. escalope de veau. Also see escalopes

vegan strict vegetarian and one who consumes no animal products at all

vegetarian person who does not eat either fish or meat, but may eat eggs and dairy products

velouté rich, smooth, white sauce made from white stock, a white (blond) roux and seasonings. The style of velouté relates to the variety of stock used: fish, veal, mutton or chicken, e.g. Velouté de volaille. Also used to indicate a soup made in the same way

verjuice sour grape or crab apple juice used in place of vinegar

vermicelli very thin pasta style noodles, Italian in origin and often used to garnish soups. Capellini is the finest ribbon pasta

vermouth fortified and flavoured wine. Three main types are bianco, rosso (Italian) and white dry (French)

vichyssoise thick potato and leek soup, garnished with chives and usually served cold

viennoiserie yeast dough bakery products

vierge whipped butter or olive oil, seasoned with salt, pepper and lemon juice and served with vegetables

vindaloo very hot, sour curry sauce from southern India and spiced and flavoured with vinegar, e.g. chicken vindaloo

voiture term for a trolley used in the food service area, for the purpose of hors d'oeuvre, sweets, cheeses, liqueurs, carving and the like

vol-au-vent round or oval, open baked, puff pastry case being a large edition of a bouchée and filled with savoury items such as chicken, mushroom or asparagus, each bound with a thick, creamy sauce

W

waiter's friend corkscrew, bottle opener and small penknife blade combined and safely carried in the pocket so that it is available at all times. Also called a wine knife

wakame Japanese seaweed with a mild flavour and a pleasant green colour, popular in salads, added to pickles and sprinkled over rice dishes

wasabi Japanese horseradish, green paste or powder used as a condiment

whitebait very small young fish of the herring family, deep fried, eaten whole and best in the spring and summer

wok large basin-shaped frying pan that concentrates the heat in a small area. Used in East Asian cuisine, especially for stir fry dishes

won ton wrappers of Chinese noodle paste similar to ravioli

Y

yakimono Japanese method of grilling and pan frying

yellow bean sauce made from fermented and puréed yellow soy beans that are highly nutritious

yum neau Yum is a form of cooking unique to Thailand, involving searing the sirloin steak in a steak and spice combination to produce a hot and sour flavour and then tossed with a salad of cucumber, tomato, onion, coriander and fresh chillies

yuzu Japanese citrus fruit

Z

zabaglione light and creamy sweet dish made by whipping together egg yolk, caster sugar and Marsala (a dark, sweet, fortified wine from Sicily). Accompanied by sponge finger biscuits

zahtar Lebanese seasoning of thyme, salt and sometimes sumac

zest outer skin of citrus peel, without the oils it produces and the pith and obtained by rubbing on a fine grater. Used as a flavouring in a variety of desserts, confectionery and in salads

zucchini American term, known in Britain as courgette. A baby or miniature marrow. May be sliced and eaten raw with dips, steamed, baked, used in soups and stews, or battered and deep fried

ANNEX C: COCKTAILS AND MIXED DRINKS LISTING AND RECIPES

Whisk(e)y cocktails	Ingredients	Methods
Highball	1 part whiskey Dry ginger ale	Place ice in the Highball glass. Add the whiskey and stir to chill well. Add the dry ginger ale to taste. Decorate with a twist of lemon peel.
Highland Cooler	2 parts Scotch whisky 1 teaspoon caster sugar 1 part lemon juice Dashes of Angostura bitters to taste Ginger ale	Shake whisky, lemon juice, sugar and Angostura with ice. Serve in a Rocks glass with ice and top up with ginger ale.
Manhattan	2 parts American rye whiskey 1 part sweet vermouth 1 dash of Angostura bitters	Pour ingredients into mixing glass and stir until well chilled. Strain into a cocktail glass. Garnish with a Maraschino cherry.
Dry Manhattan	Substitute dry vermouth for the sweet	Garnish with a thin twist of lemon or an olive.
Mint Julep	2 parts Bourbon whiskey Soda water to moisten Caster sugar Mint leaves Crushed ice	Place mint leaves and sugar into a Highball glass. Moisten with soda water and muddle the mixture to dissolve the caster sugar. Add the Bourbon whiskey and fill the Highball glass with the crushed ice. Stir and decorate with mint. Serve with straws,
Old Fashioned	2 parts rye whiskey Dash Angostura bitters to taste Caster sugar	In an Old Fashioned glass saturate either one lump of sugar or one heaped teaspoon of caster sugar with Angostura and add a dash of water. Muddle to dissolve caster sugar and then add whiskey. Fill glass with ice, stir and garnish with a slice of orange and a cherry.

Whisk(e)y cocktails	Ingredients	Methods
Rusty Nail (or Kilt Lifter)	1 part Scotch whisky 1 part Drambuie	Stir on ice in the bar mixing glass. Always serve on the rocks, with ice partially crushed, in an Old Fashioned glass.
Scotch Mist(Also Bourbon Mist, Rye Mist etc.)	1 part Scotch whisky Crushed ice Lemon twist Short straws	Fill an Old Fashioned glass with crushed ice and pour whisky over ice. Decorate with lemon and add straws.
Thistle	1 part Scotch whisky 1 part sweet vermouth Dash of Angostura bitters to taste	Put ingredients in a mixing glass with ice. Stir until well chilled and strain into a cocktail glass.
Whiskey Collins	1 part American rye whiskey 2 teaspoons caster sugar 1 part lemon juice Soda water	Collins is a Fizz served on the rocks in a Collins (or Highball) glass and topped with soda water. Garnish with lemon and add straws.
Whiskey Fizz	1 part American rye whiskey 1 part fresh lemon juice 2 teaspoons caster sugar Soda syphon	Place the rye whiskey, fresh lemon juice and caster sugar on ice in the cocktail shaker. Shake well together. Strain into an Old Fashioned glass and top up with soda water. Garnish with lemon and add straws.
Whiskey Sour	1 part American rye whiskey 2 teaspoons caster sugar ½ part lemon juice 1 dash of egg white 1 dash of Angostura bitters	Shake all ingredients well with ice until the caster sugar is dissolved. Strain into a Sour (or Rocks) glass. Garnish with a slice of lemon.
	Variations are: *Gin Sour, Bourbon Sour, Rum Sour* (dark rum) *Scotch Sour, Daquiri Sour* (light rum).	

Gin cocktails	Ingredients	Methods
After One	1 part gin 1 part Galliano 1 part sweet vermouth 1 part Campari	Stir on ice in the bar glass and serve with crushed ice in Highball glasses. Garnish with a cherry and orange slice.
Claridge	2 parts gin 2 parts dry vermouth 1 part Cointreau 1 part Apricot Brandy	Place all the ingredients on ice into a cocktail shaker. Shake vigorously. Strain into a large size cocktail glass. Decorate with a cocktail cherry and a twist of lemon.
Clover Club	2 parts gin Half part grenadine 1 part fresh lemon juice 1 part white of egg	Place all ingredients on ice into a cocktail shaker. Shake vigorously. Strain into a large size cocktail glass. Decorate with a cocktail cherry and a twist of lemon.
Dry Martini (Gin and French)	2 parts gin ½ part of dry vermouth	Pour the gin and dry vermouth into the bar mixing glass. Stir on ice until well chilled. Strain into a cocktail glass and garnish with either a stoned or stuffed olive on a cocktail stick or a twist of lemon.
Fallen Angel	1 part gin Dash of lime juice 2 dashes crème de menthe Dash of Angostura bitters to taste	Shake all ingredients on ice and serve into a cocktail glass with crushed ice.
Gibson	2 parts gin 1 part dry vermouth Dash of Angostura Bitters to taste Dash of orange Bitters to taste	Place all of the ingredients on ice into a cocktail shaker. Shake vigorously. Strain into a cocktail glass. Decorate with a cocktail onion and a twist of lemon.
Gin Fizz	1 part gin 1 part fresh lemon juice 2 teaspoons caster sugar Soda syphon	Place the gin, fresh lemon juice and caster sugar on ice into the cocktail shaker. Shake well together. Strain into an Old Fashioned glass and top up with soda from the syphon. Garnish with lemon and add straws.

Variations are: *Golden Fizz*, same as Gin Fizz plus egg yolk; *Royal Fizz*, same as Gin Fizz plus whole egg and *Silver Fizz*, same as Gin Fizz plus egg white only.
Note: A *Royal Fizz* topped up with a largish amount of soda is an excellent hang-over remedy.

Gin cocktails	Ingredients	Methods
Orange Blossom	1 part gin 1 part fresh orange juice	Shake well with ice and strain into a cocktail glass.
Pink Gin	1 part gin 2 or 3 drops of Angostura bitters to taste Iced water	Place the Angostura bitters into a spirit glass (Paris goblet or Rocks glass), swill around and then tip out the excess. Fill the glass with crushed ice and pour over the gin. Serve with iced water according to taste.
Pink Lady	2 parts gin Dash grenadine 2 parts white of egg	Shake all ingredients vigorously on ice and strain into a cocktail glass.
Satan's Whiskers	1 part gin 1 part Grand Marnier 1 part dry vermouth 1 part sweet vermouth 2 parts orange juice Dash of orange bitters to taste	Shake all ingredients well on ice and serve in a Collins (Highball) glass with crushed ice.
Singapore Sling	1 part gin ½ part cherry brandy ½ part lemon juice Soda water	Shake the gin, cherry brandy and lemon juice with ice in a cocktail shaker. Serve in a Highball glass. Top up with soda water and garnish with an orange slice and a cherry.
Snake In The Grass	1 part gin 1 part Cointreau 1 part dry vermouth ½ part fresh lemon juice	Shake all ingredients well with ice and strain into a cocktail glass partially filled with crushed ice.
Sweet Martini (Gin And Italian)	2 parts gin ½ part of sweet vermouth	Method as for dry martini. Garnish with a red maraschino cherry.
Tom Collins	1 part Old Tom gin (sweeter) 2 teaspoons caster sugar 1 part fresh lemon juice. Soda water 1 dash of Angostura bitters	Shake all ingredients (with the exception of the soda water) vigorously with ice, and strain into a cocktail glass. Stir in soda water if it is to be added. Serve in a Collins or Highball glass. Garnish with a lemon slice.
White Lady	2 parts gin 1 part Cointreau 1 part fresh lemon juice Dash of egg white	Place all ingredients on ice into a cocktail shaker. Shake well and strain into a cocktail glass. Decorate with a twist of lemon.

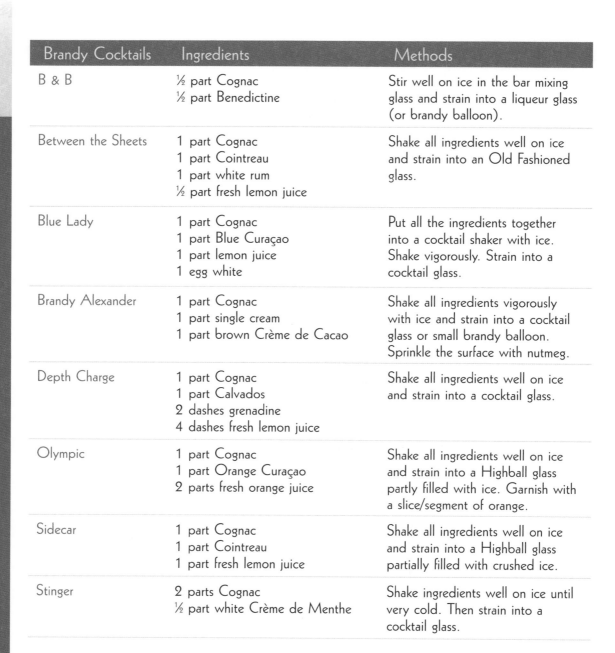

Brandy Cocktails	Ingredients	Methods
B & B	½ part Cognac ½ part Benedictine	Stir well on ice in the bar mixing glass and strain into a liqueur glass (or brandy balloon).
Between the Sheets	1 part Cognac 1 part Cointreau 1 part white rum ½ part fresh lemon juice	Shake all ingredients well on ice and strain into an Old Fashioned glass.
Blue Lady	1 part Cognac 1 part Blue Curaçao 1 part lemon juice 1 egg white	Put all the ingredients together into a cocktail shaker with ice. Shake vigorously. Strain into a cocktail glass.
Brandy Alexander	1 part Cognac 1 part single cream 1 part brown Crème de Cacao	Shake all ingredients vigorously with ice and strain into a cocktail glass or small brandy balloon. Sprinkle the surface with nutmeg.
Depth Charge	1 part Cognac 1 part Calvados 2 dashes grenadine 4 dashes fresh lemon juice	Shake all ingredients well on ice and strain into a cocktail glass.
Olympic	1 part Cognac 1 part Orange Curaçao 2 parts fresh orange juice	Shake all ingredients well on ice and strain into a Highball glass partly filled with ice. Garnish with a slice/segment of orange.
Sidecar	1 part Cognac 1 part Cointreau 1 part fresh lemon juice	Shake all ingredients well on ice and strain into a Highball glass partially filled with crushed ice.
Stinger	2 parts Cognac ½ part white Crème de Menthe	Shake ingredients well on ice until very cold. Then strain into a cocktail glass.

Rum Cocktails	Ingredients	Methods
Bacardi	1 part Bacardi 1 part fresh lime juice or to taste 1 level teaspoon of caster sugar	Place all ingredients on ice into a cocktail shaker. Shake well. Strain into a cocktail glass. Decorate with a twist of lime peel. May also be made with Grenadine instead of the caster sugar.
Cuba Libre	1 part white rum 1 part lemon/lime juice Cola to taste	Pour the white rum and lemon/lime juice into a Collins glass with ice. Add a slice of fresh lemon/lime. Top up with Cola to taste.
Daiquiri	2 parts Daiquiri white rum 1 part fresh lime juice 1 level teaspoon of caster sugar	Place all ingredients on ice into a cocktail shaker. Shake well. Strain into a cocktail glass and decorate with a slice/twist of lemon or lime peel.
Jump Up and Kiss Me	1 part white rum 1 part Galliano 1 part pineapple juice Dash of Apricot brandy Dash of fresh lemon juice 1 egg white	Shake all ingredients vigorously on crushed ice and strain into a Highball glass.
Pina Colada	1 part white rum ½ part coconut cream 3 parts pineapple juice 1 dash Angostura Bitters	Shake all ingredients vigorously on ice and strain into a Collins glass (or Paris goblet). Garnish with fresh pineapple. Add straws.
Shanghai	1 part white rum 1 dash Pernod 1 part fresh lemon juice 2 dashes Grenadine	Shake all ingredients well on ice and strain into an Old Fashioned glass partially filled with crushed ice.

Vodka Cocktails	Ingredients	Methods
Black Russian	1 part vodka 1 part Kahlúa	Stir on ice in the bar mixing glass. Serve on the rocks in a cocktail glass.
Bloody Mary	1 part vodka 5 parts tomato juice (or as required)	Place ingredients in the cocktail shaker and shake well on ice. Season and serve in an Old Fashioned glass if 'off the rocks'. Serve in a Collins or Highball glass if served 'on the rocks'.
	To make tomato juice spicier, add salt, pepper and Worcestershire sauce to taste. Any of the following may also be added to enhance flavour: dash of Tabasco, fresh lemon juice, pepper from the peppermill or cayenne pepper. Garnish may also be varied by the use of a stick of celery, carrot stick or a wedge of lemon.	
Blue Lagoon	2 parts vodka 1 part Blue Curaçao 2 parts lemonade 1 part double cream	Place the vodka and the Blue Curaçao on ice into the cocktail shaker. Shake well and strain onto crushed ice in a Collins glass. Add lemonade and float the double cream on the surface by pouring over the back of a teaspoon.
Harvey Wallbanger	1 part vodka 4 parts or more orange juice ½ part of Galliano	Shake the vodka and orange juice well, on ice, in the cocktail shaker. Strain into a Collins glass filled with crushed ice. Float the Galliano on top by pouring over the back of a teaspoon.
Moscow Mule	1½ parts vodka 1 part fresh lemon juice Ginger beer to taste	Fill a Highball glass with ice. Add the vodka and fresh lemon juice. Stir well to blend and chill. Top with ginger beer to taste. Decorate with a twist of lemon/lime.
Piano Player	1 part vodka 1 part Crème de Cacao 1 part fresh single cream	Place all the ingredients in the cocktail shaker and shake vigorously on ice. Strain into a cocktail glass.

Vodka Cocktails	Ingredients	Methods
Quiet Sunday	1 part vodka ½ part of Amaretto 4 or more parts orange juice to taste Dash of Grenadine	Place all ingredients into the cocktail shaker and shake well on ice. Strain into a Collins glass partially filled with crushed ice. Garnish with a twist/segment of orange.
Screwdriver	1 part vodka 4 parts fresh orange juice	Place all ingredients on ice into a cocktail shaker. Shake thoroughly. Strain onto partially crushed ice in a Highball glass. Decorate with a slice/twist of fresh orange.
Vodka Martini (Dry or Sweet)	2 parts vodka ½ part dry/sweet vermouth	Method as for dry martini. Garnish with an olive, twist of lemon peel or a Maraschino cherry. Name according to the vermouth used.

Tequila Cocktails	Ingredients	Methods
Brave Bull	1 part tequila 1 part Kahlúa	Place ingredients into cocktail shaker. Shake well over ice and strain into an Old Fashioned glass filled with partly crushed ice.
Margarita	1 part tequila 1 part fresh lemon juice ½ part Cointreau or Triple sec	Place all ingredients on ice into a cocktail shaker. Shake well. Strain into a cocktail glass rimmed with salt.
Mockingbird	1 part tequila 3 parts grapefruit juice ½ part fresh lime juice	Place all ingredients into a cocktail shaker. Shake well over ice. Strain into an Old Fashioned glass partially filled with crushed ice. Garnish with a cocktail cherry.
Tequila Sunrise	1 part tequila 2 dashes grenadine 4 parts orange juice	Place the tequila and fresh orange juice on ice in a Collins glass. Stir well to chill and blend. Add grenadine. Decorate with orange segment or twist of orange peel. Add straws and serve.

Wine based Cocktails	Ingredients	Methods
Kir	1 glass white wine (Dry white Burgundy) 10 to 15 ml crème de cassis	Place the crème de cassis in a chilled wine glass. Add the well-chilled white wine. Stir thoroughly.
Mulled Wine (Serves 20)	2 bottles of Burgundy or Rhône red wine ¼ bottle dark rum ½ bottle Dubonnet ½ bottle drinking water Whole orange studded with cloves 2 cinnamon sticks 25 g (1 oz) sultanas 2 lemon halves 5 g (¼ oz) mixed spice 1 × 400 g (1 lb) jar of clear honey	Heat the clouted orange for 10 minutes in the oven to bring out the flavour. Tie the mixed spices in a muslin bag to prevent clouding the wine. Place all of the ingredients with the exception of the rum into a large pot. Hold some of the honey back so as to be able to adjust the flavour later. Place the pot on a low heat and stir occasionally. Bring the mixture to boiling point but do not allow it to boil. When ready to serve add the rest of the honey to taste. Finish with the rum just before serving into small Paris goblets. Sprinkle a little grated nutmeg onto the top of each drink.

Champagne Cocktails	Ingredients	Methods
Bellini	2 parts well chilled Champagne 1 part fresh peach juice	Prepare in a flûte-shaped Champagne glass by pouring in the fresh peach juice first and topping up with the well-chilled Champagne. Garnish with fresh peach. Peaches can be minced to make a smoother juice.
Black Velvet	Guinness Chilled dry Champagne	Top up the Guinness with the chilled dry Champagne. Sometimes served in silver tankards.
Bucks Fizz	2 parts well chilled Champagne 1 part fresh orange juice	Prepare in a flûte-shaped Champagne glass by pouring in the fresh orange juice first and topping up with the well-chilled Champagne. Decorate with a curl/twist of orange peel.

Champagne Cocktails	Ingredients	Methods
Champagne Cocktail **Note:** This cocktail may be made with any sparkling wine but should then be called by the name of the wine used and not a Champagne cocktail.	1 sugar cube Angostura Bitters Champagne (well chilled) 1 teaspoon of brandy **Note:** The use of the tulip/flute-shaped Champagne glass assists in retaining the sparkle (effervescence) much longer in the glass.	Place the sugar cube soaked in Angostura into a flûte- (or tulip-) shaped Champagne glass. Pour over the well-chilled Champagne and float the brandy on the surface by pouring over the back of a teaspoon. Garnish with a slice of orange and a Maraschino cherry.
Kir Royale	1 tulip glass of dry Champagne 10 to 15 ml crème de cassis	Place the crème de cassis in a chilled tulip-shaped glass. Add the well-chilled Champagne. Do not stir.

Other Cocktails	Ingredients	Methods
Americano	1 part Campari ½ part sweet vermouth Soda water	Place the Campari and sweet vermouth over ice in the bar mixing glass. Stir well to chill and blend and strain into an Old Fashioned glass generously loaded with ice. Top up with the soda water to taste. Garnish with a slice of orange.
Cobblers	Sherry or port or brandy or Champagne etc. Fresh fruit pieces	Fill a Highball/Cobbler glass with crushed ice. Place the fresh fruit pieces into the glass and top up with the alcohol. Serve with a straw and spoon. Named according to the alcohol used.
Coolers	Whisky, gin, rum, Cognac or Arrack etc. Ginger ale Caster sugar	Place ice, two or three teaspoons of caster sugar and the alcohol into a cocktail shaker and shake vigorously. Strain into a Highball glass. Top up with the ginger ale. Serve with a straw. Named according to the alcohol used.

Other Cocktails	Ingredients	Methods
Daisies	Whisky, gin, rum, Cognac, Peach Brandy or Cherry Brandy etc. Grenadine to taste Soda water Juice of half lemon Cherries	Place the ice, lemon juice, Grenadine and the alcohol into a cocktail shaker and shake vigorously. Strain into a Champagne glass. Add three to four cherries. Top up with soda water. Serve with a straw and a spoon. Named according to the alcohol used.
Egg-Nogs	Cognac or other brandy or whisky or gin etc. Whole egg Caster sugar to taste Nutmeg	Place the ice, whole egg, two teaspoons of caster sugar and the alcohol into a cocktail shaker and shake vigorously. Strain into a cocktail glass and sprinkle with the grated nutmeg. Named according to the alcohol used.
Flips	Cognac or port or sherry or Kirsch or Cherry Brandy Egg yolk One to two teaspoons of caster sugar to taste Nutmeg	Place the ice cubes, fresh egg yolk and caster sugar with 50 cl of the alcohol to be used into a cocktail shaker and shake vigorously. Strain into a cocktail glass and sprinkle the surface with the grated nutmeg. Named according to the alcohol used.
Golden Dream	1 part Galliano 1 part Cointreau 1 part fresh orange juice 1 part single cream	Shake all ingredients vigorously over ice in the cocktail shaker. Strain into a cocktail glass.
Grasshopper	1 part single cream 1 part Crème de Menthe 1 part white Crème de Cacao	Place all ingredients over ice in the cocktail shaker. Shake thoroughly. Strain into a cocktail glass.
Grogs	Rum, Arrack, Cognac, whisky or gin etc. Half a lemon Two to three teaspoons of caster sugar according to taste Boiling water	Place two to three teaspoons of caster sugar into a Collins/Rocks glass. Add the alcohol to be used, juice of half a lemon and top up with the boiling water. Stir well. Garnish with a slice of lemon. Serve with a teaspoon. Named according to the alcohol used.

Other Cocktails	Ingredients	Methods
Negroni	1 part gin 1 part sweet vermouth 1 part Campari Dash of soda water	Stir all ingredients over ice in the bar mixing glass. Strain into a Collins glass filled with crushed ice. Add the soda water to taste. Garnish with a slice of lemon.
Pimms	2 parts Pimms No 1 cup 5 parts or more of lemonade/tonic water/Seven-up	Pour Pimms into a Worthington or Highball glass. Add ice and top up with lemonade or alternatives. Decorate with slice of apple, orange, lemon, lime and a twist of cucumber peel. Alternatively just use mint leaves. Stirrer and straws are optional.
Round The World	1 part banana liqueur 1 part Scotch whisky Dash Cointreau Dash orange cordial Orange slice	Put the banana liqueur and whisky into a shaker with plenty of ice. Add Cointreau and undiluted orange cordial. Shake and strain into a cocktail glass. Add orange to garnish and serve.
Sherry Cup	1 part dry sherry 4 parts Medium cider Fresh sliced unpeeled cucumber	Use very chilled ingredients. Put one part of sherry into a Highball or Worthington glass and top up with cider. Garnish with freshly cut cucumber slices.

Non-alcoholic Cocktails	Ingredients	Methods
Fruit Cup	1 part orange juice 1 part grapefruit juice 1 part apple juice Lemonade/soda water	Pour all ingredients, with the exception of the lemonade/soda, onto ice in a glass jug. Stir well to blend and chill. Add sliced fruit garnish. Top up with lemonade or soda water. Serve well chilled in Highball or Worthington glasses.
Pussyfoot	2 parts orange juice 1 part fresh lemon juice 1 part lime cordial Half part grenadine 1 egg yolk Soda water	Place all ingredients with the exception of the soda water on ice into a cocktail shaker. Shake vigorously to blend well together. Strain over crushed ice into a Collins glass. Top up with the soda water. Add straws.

Non-alcoholic Cocktails	Ingredients	Methods
Saint Clements	1 part orange juice 1 part bitter lemon	Mix equal quantities of the orange juice and bitter lemon on ice in a Worthington glass. Stir well to blend. Garnish with a slice of orange and lemon.
Shirley Temple/ Roy Rogers	Ginger ale Dash of grenadine	Place ice in a Highball glass and add a dash of grenadine. Pour over the chilled ginger ale. Decorate with full fruit garnish and add straws.
	Variations: Ginger ale and fresh lime juice or Ginger ale and lime cordial to taste.	
Tropicana	1 part pineapple juice 1 part orange juice	Mix the well chilled ingredients on crushed ice in a Slim Jim glass and serve with straws.

INDEX